Fontanka 16
The Tsars' Secret Police

Fontanka 16 takes a fresh look at the feared Russian tsarist secret police, the Okhranka, during the period of the imperial regime leading up to the Revolution of 1917. It is a fascinating account of the development of a secret police organization that was deeply rooted in tsarist Russia but provided a model for Soviet police organizations.

From police headquarters at Fontanka 16 to the secret offices in major Russian post offices where specialists opened and read correspondence, the Okhranka blanketed the huge Russian empire with a network of secret agents and informers. In many cases they were involved in a desperate effort to track down terrorists before they could assassinate government officials and members of the imperial family. Charles Ruud and Sergei Stepanov have mined police archives, including Moscow's State Archive of the Russian Federation and the archives of the Hoover Institution, to produce this first post-Soviet look at the Okhranka's covert operations, which spread as far as Western Europe.

In many ways *Fontanka 16* reveals as much about the enemies of the tsars as the police who fought them. Although each side saw its cause as a struggle for good over evil, the authors show that the two sides strongly resembled one another in method, psychology, and morality. In this strange nether world of intrigue and deception, police agents often assisted revolutionaries and a number of former revolutionaries rose through the ranks of the secret police. The authors shed new light on the supposed anti-Semitism of the imperial government, as well as the origins of the Protocols of the Elders of Zion.

CHARLES A. RUUD is professor of history, University of Western Ontario. SERGEI A. STEPANOV is doctor of history, Russian Independent Institute of Social and Nationality Problems, Moscow.

FONTANKA 16

The Tsars'
Secret Police

CHARLES A. RUUD
and
SERGEI A. STEPANOV

McGill-Queen's University Press
Montreal & Kingston · London · Ithaca

© McGill-Queen's University Press 1999
ISBN 0-7735-1787-1

Legal deposit second quarter 1999
Bibliothèque nationale du Québec

Printed in Canada on acid-free paper

Published simultaneously in the UK, Eire, and Europe by
Sutton Publishing Ltd.

Publication of this book has been assisted by a grant from
the J.B. Smallman and Spencer Memorial Fund,
University of Western Ontario.

McGill-Queen's University Press acknowledges the
financial support of the Government of Canada through
the Book Publishing Industry Development program for
its activities. We also acknowledge the support of the
Canada Council for the Arts for our publishing program.

Canadian Cataloguing in Publication Data

Ruud, Charles A., 1933–
    Fontanka 16: the tsars' secret police
    Includes bibliographical references and index.
    ISBN 0-7735-1787-1
    1. Russia. Okhrannyia otdielen iia – History. 2. Police –
    Russia – History. 3. Secret service – Russia – History.
    1. Stepanov, S. A. 11. Title.
    HV8227.2.A2R88 1999   363.28'3'0947   C98-901352-9

Typeset in Sabon 10/12 with American Typewriter display
by Caractéra inc., Quebec City

Contents

Preface

The address, number 16, on the Fontanka embankment in St Petersburg is as well known to Russians as Number 10 Downing Street is to the English, but it is not known at all in the world outside of Russia. Russians know about Fontanka 16 because it was the headquarters of the tsarist secret political police from sometime in the 1830s until the Revolution of February 1917.

Before Nicholas I claimed the throne in late 1825, imperial political police had been variously housed. Centralizer that he was, Nicholas had at once founded his own contingent, the Third Section, and, to have them near at hand, seated them for a short while in an office facing the Moika Canal and then in building Number 16 on the Fontanka. Also quartered there was the next and final tsarist security force, the Okhranka. Because many easily learned what went on within its walls, Fontanka 16 came to mean secret police in and beyond the capital at least by the 1880s.

Anyone who walks along the Fontanka Embankment to find Number 16 will confront gardens, trees, and a series of elegant structures in early eighteenth-century classical design; for Trezzini, as architect and city planner for Peter the Great, designated lots on the banks of the Fontanka for some of the great gentry palaces built in Peter's new capital, including those of the Yusupov, Sheremetev, and Vorontsov families. During the reign of Catherine II, then-chief planner A.V. Krasov enhanced the canal itself by lining with granite this channel for the Fontanka river, a tributary of the Neva. A number of graceful spans across the waterway were added next, including the Tsepnoi bridge that can be seen as one reaches the address that titles this book.

N.V. Veselago, an officer in the Department of Police from 1911 to 1913, left a diagram of the layout of Fontanka 16. On it he shows that the Special Section occupied an entire floor of the main building and that a separate taller building at the rear housed four of the special secretariats that served the far-flung political police organization known as the Okhranka.

This study concentrates on the Okhranka and its allied organization, the Gendarmes, over the last forty years or so of the Imperial regime.[1] To describe the two forces only in organizational terms would present an incomplete picture, for their members regularly interacted to conduct political investigations on an ad hoc basis. This study therefore describes how the officers and agents of the Okhranka and Gendarmes worked and behaved in particular cases.

With respect to nomenclature, the general term "police" rightly applies to the Okhranka, as the Okhranka was a part of the Department of Police. It was a unique branch, however, in that its mandate was to detect and counteract subversives at home and abroad, preferably before they took steps to undermine the state. Thus the Okhranka, precisely defined, were the "political" police.

Archival and printed materials constitute the foundation of this book. Its main sources came from the collection of documents on the Okhranka at the State Archive of the Russian Federation in Moscow, and, for the Foreign Okhranka, from the Hoover Institution in Stanford, California. One or other of the authors also worked in archives in Kiev, St Petersburg, at the New York Public Library, and at Yale University.

From among the vast published materials on political investigation in Russia, several books by former Okhranka officials have provided valuable insights for this study. They include the works of Gerasimov, Men'shchikov, Spiridovich, Zavarzin, Novitsky, Vassilyev – to cite the main ones. Other rich sources for this work are books and documents published by S.G. Svatikov and P.E. Shchegolev, investigators of the Okhranka for the Provisional Government; Vladimir Burtsev's *Byloe* (*The Past*); and *Padenie tsarskogo rezhima* (*The Fall of the Tsarist Regime*), edited by Shchegolev, which is a verbatim record of the interrogations of former police and other high officials by the investigators of the Provisional Government.

The authors wish to express their thanks to all those who so greatly assisted in the preparation of this book. They include the librarians, archivists, and historians who work at the libraries and archives

---

1. This work is a revised version of *Fontanka, 16: Politicheskii ssysk pri tsariakh*, published by Mysl' Press in Moscow in 1994.

mentioned in the introduction. We wish to give special thanks to Diane Mew of Toronto and Marjorie Ruud of London for their outstanding editorial work. We wish to acknowledge permission granted by Charles Schlacks, Jr., to use sections of Charles Ruud's "A.A. Lopukhin, Police Insubordination and the Rule of Law," published in *Russian History* 20, nos. 1–4 (1993).

The Library of Congress system of transliteration has been followed, except that the "ii" ending of Russian surnames has been rendered as "y." All Russian dates are according to the Julian calendar, in effect in Russia until March 1918.

Count Peter Tolstoy, the head of Peter the Great's Secret Chancellery, a secret political police organization during the reign of the reforming tsar. Tolstoy persuaded the tsar's son, Alexis, to return to Russia from abroad, causing Alexis's conviction for treason and condemnation to death.

Prince-Caesar Fedor Romodanovsky was honoured by Peter the Great with the special title of "Prince-Caesar" because of his valued work in the late seventeenth century to deal with the tsar's enemies. As head of the new secret police organization, Romodanovsky personally investigated, judged, condemned, and beheaded several rebels.

Count A.Kh. Benckendorff, a trusted high official of Nicholas 1, advised the tsar of the need for a new secret political police following the Decembrist rebellion in 1825. The Third Section was formed, which became intrusive and arbitrary in its treatment of the tsar's subjects.

The Chancellery of the Third Section during the reign of Nicholas I by an unknown artist who has depicted the secret police as a benign organization. In this watercolour of the Third Section's headquarters in St Petersburg, two officials have nothing better to do than to play chess. In reality, the Third Section encouraged informers and became a centralized and ubiquitous spying agency.

A Gendarme officer reports to the chief of staff of the Corps of Gendarmes during the reign of Nicholas I. By this time the Gendarmes, although a military unit, had become a chief component of the Third Section's information-gathering apparatus. General L.V. Dubel't, a major Third Section official, is shown at the right in this nineteenth-century watercolour by an unknown artist.

Prince V.A. Dolgorukov, head of the Third Section for the first decade of the reign of Alexander II. Desperate to destroy burgeoning criticism in Russia, he failed, however, to prevent a disturbed young man from firing at Alexander II and he was removed as head of the political police.

Count Peter A. Shuvalov was Alexander II's second Third Section head and he became known as Peter IV because of his extensive authority. Shuvalov streamlined the organization of the secret political police, raised requirements for officers, and improved their educational qualifications.

General N.V. Mezentsov, head of the Third Section and commander of the Corps of Gendarmes in the late 1870s when a spate of terrorist attacks commenced against high public officials. Mezentsov scoffed at the idea that his own life was in danger. But the general fell to an assassin's knife in broad daylight not far from his own headquarters.

General M.T. Loris-Melikov, a hero of the Russo-Turkish war of 1877-8, was summoned by Tsar Alexander II to head the Supreme Investigating Commission in 1880 to deal with the revolutionary movement. As minister of the interior, he later acquired dictatorial powers in order to fight terrorism. His recommendations produced the new security divisions, to become known collectively as the Okhranka.

The leg chains in this photo from Russian secret police files are authentic, although the formally posed male who wears them is more likely a model Gendarme than a convicted revolutionary. Such chains prevented the escape of political prisoners while they were being marched to camps and exile.

So-called outside agents who worked for the Okhranka conducted operations under elaborate instructions designed to make them inconspicuous while gathering information. These three detectives appeared in what is probably a police photo to be used for instructional purposes. Their garb would enable them to blend into any Russian crowd.

Count N.P. Ignatiev, a conservative nationalist, was the first minister of the interior appointed by Tsar Alexander III. He assumed administrative authority over the newly created Department of Police and introduced legislation to control the revolutionary movement following the assassination of Alexander II in March 1881.

Count D.A. Tolstoy, the second minister of the interior for Alexander III, continued the shaping of a centralized secret security system by recruiting more inside agents to penetrate revolutionary groups. Tolstoy could not tolerate the interference of amateurs in police work and persuaded the tsar to shut down the so-called Holy Bodyguard, staffed by aristocrats who had volunteered their services to protect the tsar.

V.K. von Plehve was the first major director of the new Department of Police in the 1880s. Under his supervision the tsarist government launched a corps of secret agents whose major assignment was to penetrate the organizations of the revolutionaries. When minister of the interior, Plehve was killed on the streets of St Petersburg by a terrorist bomb in 1904.

I.N. Durnovo, a minister of the interior for both Alexander III and Nicholas II. Durnovo regarded perlustration, or the secret opening and recording of correspondence, an essential source of information.

A.I. Spiridovich, an experienced Gendarme colonel. He is credited with breaking up a number of revolutionary circles as a result of extensive study of their modes of operation. Spiridovich was one of the Gendarme officers whose mistakes during the security operations in the fall of 1911 proved fatal for the prime minister, P.A. Stolypin.

A.A. Lopukhin, director of the Department of Police from 1902 to 1904. He discovered that high officials were condoning illegal acts by police subordinates. After stepping down, Lopukhin provided information to the revolutionaries about the secret agent Evno Azeff. As he intended, Lopukhin ended Azeff's career and exposed the secret police and the tsarist regime to widespread criticism.

Evno Azeff, the Okhranka's most successful internal agent, penetrated to the highest levels of the Socialist Revolutionary party before he was exposed. He played a principal role in planning the assassination of V.K. von Plehve, the minister of the interior. Azeff showed no strong ideological attachment to either side; he appeared to favour first the police and later the revolutionaries. He had a passion for playing a dramatic role and living on the edge of danger.

S.V. Zubatov, head of the Moscow Okhranka. His policies profoundly alarmed conservative officials who forced his dismissal. Zubatov believed that the Russian police could take the offensive against socialists and persuade workers and students to accept Russian monarchism and reject socialism.

Father George Gapon believed that the Russian Orthodox Church should confront social problems, especially those created by Russia's rapid industrialization. As a part of this attempt, he helped build "police unions" sponsored by the Okhranka. Radical workers from St Petersburg murdered him when his link to the secret police became known.

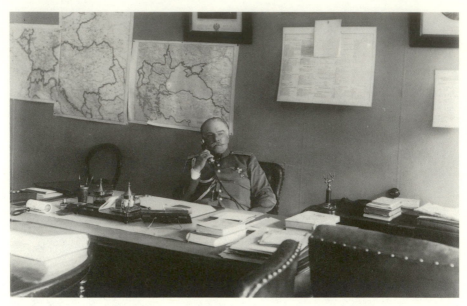

The commander of the Corps of Gendarmes, shown here in his office, exercised authority over a unit that had police functions but also remained part of the regular army. Many Gendarmes climbed high in the ranks of the Okhranka.

Gendarme officers at work at headquarters. The Gendarmes carried out numerous functions for the government, including policing and gathering information on radical and revolutionaries. Their institutional connection with the political police was always ambiguous. The Gendarmes successfully resisted all attempts to subordinate them completely to the police.

Fontanka 16 as it appeared about the turn of the twentieth century. The façade facing the Fontanka river embankment in the Russian capital of St Petersburg fits nicely with the elegance of other buildings and palaces along the Fontanka. The Special Section, which served as the heart and brains of the Okhranka, was in an area sealed off under tight security. Agents were warned never to appear at Fontanka 16 with their reports.

P.A. Stolypin, chairman of the Council of Ministers of Imperial Russia, tried to fight the enemies of the tsar by both cultivating public opinion and striking hard against revolutionaries and terrorists. His elaborate security system failed to shield him from a lone gunman who shot him at point-blank range in the Kiev opera house in 1911.

The Kiev opera house, where Dmitry Bogrov assassinated P.A. Stolypin on the evening of 1 September 1911. Bogrov was a trusted tsarist secret agent at the time and gained entrance to the opera house through his controlling officer. Suspicions quickly arose that the secret police had engineered the assassination, perhaps at the bidding of higher officials.

Dmitry Bogrov, as assassin of Stolypin, removed the last effective statesman from the high councils of the government. Bogrov is sometimes described as a Jew who avenged blatant anti-Semitism in ruling circles, but a better explanation of his motives can be found in his own sense of meaningless in his personal life. Bogrov was the most striking example of the terrible toll an untrustworthy but trusted agent could exact.

Boris Savinkov, a leading Russian terrorist who worked with Azeff, the police agent. The two collaborated on several assassinations of tsarist officials, including von Plehve, the minister of the interior. Savinkov led the group that assassinated the tsar's uncle, the Grand Duke Sergei, in 1905.

M.E. Bakai, the kind of secret operative most feared by the Okhranka – the police insider who revealed information to the other side without the knowledge of the Okhranka. Bakai told what he knew to Vladimir Burtsev, who eventually pieced together a case against Evno Azeff. He was able to show that Azeff was a police agent who had penetrated into the most secret leadership circles of the Social Revolutionary Party.

V.L. Burtsev, a populist and former sympathizer with terrorism who turned his energies to exposing what he saw as illegal activities by the Russian Okhranka. He published his findings in his journal, *The Past* (*Byloe*).

L.P. Men'shchikov, under arrest as a young man, was pressed into informing for the Okhranka. As he rose to high position, he systematically collected documents that he handed over to revolutionaries in 1910. The Okhranka never fully recovered from Men'shchikov's revelations.

Gendarmes in Kiev acting as guards at a prison. The Gendarmes were selected from among officers and soldiers serving in the regular military who applied for the more prestigious and better-paid unit. They comprised a security force within the Department of Police but were subject to recall to regular military duty.

I.F. Manasevich-Manuilov was a shadowy figure on the Russian political scene who made himself useful to a number of high officials and then used personal information about them to his own advantage. In 1916 he insinuated himself into the circle around Rasputin.

Black Hundreds marching in Kazan' in 1905. Their ominous name embraced nationalistic, monarchist, and anti-Semitic activist groups, and included gangs of urban toughs. Invoking the name of the tsar, they attacked Jews and others they labelled enemies of Russia. Some Russian police, especially at the local level, collaborated with Black Hundreds groups.

The Jew Mendel Beilis following his acquittal in his trial in Kiev in 1913 on the false charge of having ritually murdered a young Christian boy. The episode is sometimes seen as Russia's Dreyfus case and widely discredited the Imperial government.

V.F. Dzhunkovsky, a Gendarme officer and assistant minister of the interior in charge of the Department of Police, provided accurate information on Rasputin to Nicholas II in an attempt to encourage the tsar to repudiate the self-styled holy man from Siberia. Dzhunkovsky failed and Rasputin's influence on the imperial family went unchecked.

A.D. Protopopov became the last minister of the interior of imperial Russia in December 1916 at the behest of a group around Rasputin. Protopopov upon joining the government became an ardent nationalist and his actions to please the Rasputin group only increased tensions between the tsar's government and the Duma.

S.P. Beletsky, director of the Department of Police, was dismissed by Dzhunkovsky in 1912 because of illegal police operations that he personally supervised. Beletsky later became assistant minister of the interior to replace Dzhunkovsky, in large part through the influence of Rasputin.

Armed militia men in Petrograd in 1917 escort apprehended policemen who had doffed their uniforms and donned civilian dress. All branches of the police became special targets of revolutionaries in 1917.

PART ONE

History, Tradition, Precedents

CHAPTER ONE

Political Investigation to 1825

Political investigation in what became Russia began as small principalities were absorbed into an increasingly unified state during the fifteenth and sixteenth centuries. From then on into the nineteenth century, as edicts and laws variously defined subversion and its penalties, every tsar used special agents to search out dangers to him and his rule.

Princes who commanded small areas in the Russian north in early medieval times intermittently met together in the fourteenth century to share information about known plots and conspiracies.[1] Because outside lands constituted enemy territory, to leave Muscovy even briefly was to join or consort with the enemy and thereby to commit treason. Among the rights the princes gave up during the next two centuries to join Muscovy was just such free movement.

For the first crowned tsar of Russia, Ivan IV (1533–84),[2] disagreement with his policy was treason, a case in point being the opposition of members of his aristocratic class, the boyars, to his conduct of the Livonian wars in 1564. Countenancing no limits on his rule, Ivan abandoned Moscow late that year and from a nearby town issued two letters: one to the Council of Boyars and another to his subjects.

Both vilified the boyars as traitors, and the aroused population forced those nobles, through their Council, to grant Ivan IV his demand to rule absolutely over "set-apart" lands, the *oprichnina*, which comprised about one third of Russia. Ivan in turn began to expel boyars from his new country and to give their lands to his own agents. To command Russia as a whole, he formed a terrorist band of pseudo-monks, the *oprichniki*, and sent them out to frighten resistors into subservience.

Bearing symbolic brooms and the severed heads of dogs on the saddles of their black horses, the black-robed oprichniki made clear their mandate to sniff out and sweep away opponents of Ivan. Two foreigners among them, J. Taube and Elbert Kruze, identified the tsar as their monastic head: "Himself [Ivan IV] was the Father Superior, Prince Afanasy Viazemsky was the Cellarer, Maliuta Skuratov was the Sexton and along with the others they managed the various activities of monastery life. Himself, both of his sons, and the Sexton would ring the bell." Members not in church each morning at four "were sentenced to eight days penance."[3]

As the infamy of the oprichniki spread, one visiting Englishman, the trader and diplomat Jerome Horsey, wrote of their acts: "This crueltie bread such a generall hatred, distreccion, fear, and discontentement thorow his kyngdom, that there wear many practices and devises how to distroy this tirant; but he still did discover their plotts and treasons, by inoiblinge and countenancinge all the rascalest and desperatt souldiers he could peek owt, to affront the chieff nobillitie."[4]

Showing signs of deepening derangement, Ivan IV insisted that plotters lurked everywhere. To identify them, he put select oprichniki to work as political investigators under M.L. Skuratov-Bel'sky and V.G. Griaznoi, who solicited denunciations as their prime source of evidence. That many came forward caused a German then in Russia, A. Schlichting, to write: "Muscovites seem to possess a kind of innate malevolence that makes them accuse and slander one another in front of the tyrant and fume with hatred for one another so that they kill themselves by mutual slander."[5]

Sometimes the oprichniki concocted charges, as Skuratov and Griaznoi did to rid the tsar of a cousin, Prince Vladimir Staritsky, whose rule over a separate territory made him suspect. Soon after his arrival for a visit, the two confronted Staritsky with the charge that his cook had confessed to a plot to poison Ivan. Thus justified, they forced the prince to down a lethal drink.

Likewise targeted was the Metropolitan Philip, the head of the Russian Orthodox Church, who came into disfavour for interceding on behalf of innocent persons denounced as traitors. The bribe for Philip's accuser was a bishop's mitre. When, during a visit from Skuratov, Philip died in the monastery where he was imprisoned, the chief of the oprichniki blamed the airlessness of Philip's cell.

Whole families, clans, and even townships fell victim, but most brutal was the 1571 purge of Novgorod, a formerly independent city-state that Ivan distrusted. As told in the "Chronicle" of Novgorod, a tramp directed the oprichniki – very likely the instigators – to a forged document conveying that Novgorodians wanted to serve the king of Poland, then at war with Ivan.[6] A three-week probe followed, during which the oprichniki tortured and killed thousands. Some reports set the toll at sixty thousand, but historians estimate from two thousand to fifteen thousand fatalities.[7]

Ironically, denunciations cost nearly every oprichnik leader his life, an exception being Maliuta Skuratov, who was early killed in combat. Death by beating was the fate for Ivan's trusted dispenser of medicine, A.I. Viazemsky, after a fellow oprichnik charged him with forewarning Novgorodians. In the case of one of the founders of the oprichniki, A.D. Basmanov, his son Fedor served as his father's executioner in Ivan's presence to prove his fealty, only to be exiled to the wild where he perished.

When he abruptly abolished the oprichnina in 1572, one year after the Novgorod massacre, Ivan ordered punishment for any who so much as mentioned that special unit. Although he briefly revived it in 1575, no subsequent tsar ever replicated this disruptive mix of political investigation and manifest terror.

During his remaining years, Ivan used temporary commissions for political investigations, as happened under his son, Tsar Fedor (1584–98). Midway through Fedor's reign, an important commission probed the sudden death of the sole dynastic heir, Tsarevich Dmitry. Its 1591 finding that Dmitry had accidentally stabbed hiwmself did not, however, lift suspicion from Tsar Boris Godunov, whose accession had become possible because of Dmitry's death. For that reason, suspicions always surrounded Godunov and he was never able to suppress the doubts his enemies raised.

As another claimant to the throne, the so-called False Dmitry, marched on Moscow with a Polish army to seize the throne, Godunov died and the city's defences crumbled. Once False Dmitry wore the crown, the head of the 1591 probe, Vasily Shuisky, sided with the imposter by claiming that the commission lied to hide that assassins sent by Godunov had killed another boy than the Tsarevich. Eleven months later Shuisky reversed himself to justify unseating False Dmitry.

When King Sigismund III of Poland at this point sent enough troops to put Moscow under the rule of his son, that incursion galvanized Russians to expel their conquerors. It remained for an Assembly of the Land to select a "born tsar," and their choice was Michael Romanov, a sixteen-year-old member of a family connected to the previous dynasty.

Tsar Michael (1613–45) relied heavily on his father Filaret, who, assuming the title of Great Sovereign, made political investigations a centrepiece of policy. An edict from Michael consequently required all subjects to inform a boyar should they discern any threat to the tsar or his rule; a sharp increase in denunciations from 1621 to 1623 coincided with a concerted drive to silence dissent.[8]

Provincial administrators, or *voevodas*, emerged as the primary investigators of alleged political crimes, however trivial. Through their interrogations, they also sampled "public opinion" and generalized its tendencies for their superiors – as would political investigators in every successive reign.

First reference to a "tsar's word" crime appeared in a 1622 document with respect to a Cossack who had imprudently vowed to cut the tsar's throat.[9] Whereas the Cossack's verbal threat could rightly have been termed lese-majesty, the document uses the colloquial Russian equivalent: *Slovo Gosudarevo [Tsar's Word].*

Just as everyone by then understood the gravity of a "tsar's word," they likewise knew "tsar's deeds." Most under Michael would thus have used "tsar's deed" to describe the conspiracy of two cousins to prevent the tsar's marriage (for which crime the pair were exiled).[10] They would have said the same of a 1639 case in which one Dashka Lomanov was executed for complicity in the death of Tsarevich Ivan because she allegedly strewed ashes in the tsarina's footprints.[11]

Denunciations that mattered to political investigators had to fit into the broad sense of "tsar's word and deed" crimes. To report drunkenness on the part of a peasant or storekeeper carried no relevance unless that besotted individual had maligned the sovereign. Most offences reported, moreover, stemmed from intoxication, and a full 64 percent of all denunciations in the first half of the seventeenth century coincided with celebrations rife with alcohol.[12] (Just over 30 percent of all denunciations in that same period came from prisoners in custody, some having informed under duress, others in hope of reprieve.)[13]

Incentive to rush from a revel to denounce was strong given the severe penalties in place for not reporting tsar's words and deeds. An added incentive was the shared sense of "collective responsibility" that required everyone to report crimes to preserve social order. Few felt bound, however, to report family, friends, neighbours or other close acquaintances.[14]

According to investigative procedures laid down by the government, once a denouncer had declared that he knew of a word or deed crime, the voevoda had to distil the facts from that person's accusation in the presence of a scribe. The scribe then sent his written report to Moscow for a verdict by the Service Chancellery, which returned it in the form of an edict. Accusor and accused alike could be held in prison pending the verdict. In a minority of cases, officials in Moscow ordered the voevoda to press the principals for more testimony by coercive means that ranged from public hearings to threats of torture, mild torture, and severe torture.[15] Three bouts of torture in which the accused consistently answered questions authenticated his words.

Of great significance to political investigations was the Law Code adopted in 1649 under Tsar Alexis (1645–76) because the twenty-two articles in Chapter 2 concern "The Sovereign's Honour, and How to Safeguard his Royal Well-Being."[16] Most of these articles on crimes against the tsar focus wholly on acts of treason, whether merely planned or fully perpetrated.

Two articles, both on denunciations, couple treasonous acts with crimes of another sort as legitimate accusatory grounds. According to Article 13, denunciations can concern "the matter of the sovereign's well-being, or any treason case." Article 16 differentiates the two as "an important case involving the sovereign, or treason." Both these paired wrongs are equivalent to "tsar's words and deeds."

When this new code took effect, political investigations not handled at the local level by voevodas were still being conducted by temporary commissions and also, as circumstances dictated, by clerks in the some eighty prikazy, or government departments. Thus the Kazan' Palace Prikaz investigated political cases in its administrative bailiwick, the territories along the Volga River, unless, say, the involvement of a strelets, or musketeer, put the probe under the Strelets Prikaz.

Placing himself at its head, Tsar Alexis created a department in 1664 to handle highly important political cases, his Prikaz of Secret Affairs. Within a few years it took over the decision-making role of the Service Chancellery with respect to local "word and deed" cases. As well, clerks belonging to the Secret Affairs Office began acting as secret police by filling posts in provincial departments and Russian embassies to spy on their operations for the tsar.[17]

Given the immensity of the peasant insurrection put down in 1671, Tsar Alexis sent to the scene a special investigative commission under Prince Iu.A. Dolgorukov to decide what penalties an accompanying punitive expedition would effect. The result was "Hell's threshold," wrote an English traveller, who claimed to have seen some forty corpses dangling from each of the gallows and, beyond them, "headless bodies lying in pools of blood" and "impaled rebels ... many of them still alive." He estimated eleven thousand executions over three months.[18]

Cossack Stepan Razin, leader of the revolt, went to the block with his brother Frol, who there stayed his own death by shouting the phrase that forced a halt to any official proceeding: "Word and Deed." What followed was his denouncement of the already-doomed Stepan for seditious letters allegedly hidden on an island of the Don River.

Only after a vain search for them was given up after six years did the
government execute Frol.[19]

Peter I (1682–1725) did not assume actual rule until 1689, when he
was seventeen years old, and by then there had been established, in
1686, a department that would become one of his two main agencies
for political investigations. Named for Peter's childhood village, it was
the Preobrazhenskii Prikaz, which initially kept order on Moscow
streets and issued uniforms to the guards' regiments. Political investigation came under its purview in 1696, but it dealt that year with only
five "word and deed" crimes.[20]

Other departments proceeded to send their political cases to the
Prikaz, and Peter in 1702 required that centralized handling. By then
the number of "word and deed" crimes was sharply on the rise as
displeasure mounted about Peter's severe rule and constant warfare.
Dissenters from the official church known as Old Believers, for example,
condemned Peter I as the anti-Christ and committed the "tsar's deed"
of demonizing him in broadsheets.[21]

Treason was the ultimate "tsar's deed," of course, but laying that
charge against someone well trusted could backfire, as happened in
1707 to the monk Nikander. He sought only to deliver a warning to
the Preobrazhenskii Prikaz that the Ukrainian Cossack hetman Ivan
Mazepa had traitorous designs. Because a lowly Prikaz official
diverted Nikander to the Monastery Prikaz, where no one took interest, the monk returned to the Prikaz and demanded to see the chief.
Instead he was shackled and, once questioned, disbelieved. His ultimate fate was to be handed over to Hetman Mazepa, who ordered
him beheaded in July 1708. That October, Mazepa allied with a king
then at war with Peter, Charles XII of Sweden.[22]

So important were denunciations to fight opposition, however, that
Peter purposefully fostered them through well-publicized commenda-
tions and rewards. Public praise and freedom from bondage were his
favours to serf Akim Ivanov in 1721 for reporting his drunken master's defence that the tsar himself was fond of the bottle.[23] To a
freeman who denounced a landlord for a lesser offence went just "a
cow with a heifer and some hay to feed them as well as geese and
Indian hens, a nest of each."[24]

Most informers settled for cash, usually in amounts from 5 to 30
rubles but more for serious revelations. In 1722, for example, a
tradesman in Penza won 300 rubles plus the right of free trade and
official protection for denouncing the marketplace shouts of a retired
captain that Tsar Peter was the anti-Christ. Again the reward came
with a well publicized commendation from Peter.[25]

Tishin, a clerk from Tobolsk, got yet more by denouncing a general, Prince I.A. Dolgorukov, who suffered exile. Along with a transfer from Siberia to Moscow, Tishin won 600 rubles – paid bit by bit because of his "excessive drinking and wastefulness."[26]

Whereas the Code of 1649 inferentially made "tsar's words" a crime punishable by death, Peter clearly classed lese-majesty as a capital offence through his universally-applied Naval Regulations of 1720. Article 20 read: "Anyone who commits the sin of abuse in reference to His Majesty's personage, expresses contempt towards His actions or intentions, and discusses them in an unseemly way, shall be deprived of life by execution through beheading."[27]

Through the Church Regulations of 1721, Peter required clergy to report any parishioner who at confession admitted "an intention to commit treason or start a revolt and not repent."[28] This stricture violated the sanctity of confession but applied only to words that put the tsar at mortal risk.

To his credit, Peter no longer allowed officials to base investigations on unsigned denunciations. He continued, however, their obligation to act on denunciations from condemned prisoners – a practice finally stopped in 1730, by Empress Anna, because it was so often abused.

Massive rebellion by the streltsy (essentially infantrymen used to maintain public order) in 1698 pushed the Preobrazhenskii Prikaz, headed by the tsar's trusted viceroy, Prince Fedor I. Romodanovsky, into political investigation on a large scale. Showing no mercy, Romodanovsky himself interrogated and executed rebels, reportedly beheading four at once with a single blade. His bent for cruelty would later cause Peter to chide him from abroad: "Beast! How long are you going to keep on burning people? Even here I meet those who have been injured by you."[29] Never did this Prince-Caesar lose Peter's full confidence, however. (Peter invented for Romodanovsky the title of Prince-Caesar and subordinates addressed him as Your Majesty.)

When Romodanovsky died in 1717, headship of the Preobrazhenskii Prikaz passed to his son Iury. Peter found the younger Romodanovsky less effective, however, and so diverted important security cases to temporary investigative commissions under officers of the guards. Needing an effective organization to report to him on his restless subjects, Peter soon merged his commissions into a permanent agency, the Secret Investigative Chancellery. Its assignment was to help set aside Tsarevich Alexis as a contender for the throne.

The likelihood that Alexis would not further his father's reforms had convinced Peter and his allies to compel the tsarevich to renounce worldly affairs by taking holy orders, but Alexis foiled them by going abroad. Acting as secret police, agents of the new Chancellery were dispersed to find Alexis – which they did on an island near Naples where Austrian authorities had given him secret refuge.

The tsar sent the head of the Secret Chancellery, Peter A. Tolstoy, to persuade Alexis to return by promising complete forgiveness. The trusting tsarevich complied, only to be forced to renounce succession and to be handed over to the Secret Chancellery. Tolstoy set about linking Alexis to anti-Petrine elements and, in the process, proved the pre-eminence of the Chancellery in security matters.[30]

Among those subjected to torture to wrest a conspiracy confession from them was Dosiphei, the bishop of Rostov. As he was broken on the wheel, he reportedly cried out: "You have caught just me in this case ... But look, what do all others have on their minds? Open your ears to what people are saying."[31]

From 19 to 24 June 1718, the tsarevich endured six sessions of torture. During one he uttered these words that Tolstoy construed as admitting a conspiracy with the Austrian emperor: "And if it had come to it and the Caesar had started action, as he had promised me, to obtain the Russian Crown for me, even then I would have spared nothing to get hold of the inheritance ..."[32]

Voltaire, in his book about Alexis, roundly rejected that such testimony could ground a criminal charge. "How," he asked, "can an idea, a hypothesis, an assumption of an incident that never did take place be tried in court?"[33] Voltaire did not, of course, take into account that admitted intent to defy the tsar constituted treason under Russian law. On just such evidence assembled by Tolstoy, Alexis was sentenced to die for treason. Officials described his death in the Fortress of Saints Peter and Paul as a natural one caused by a stroke, but rumours predictably implicated Peter.

In the wake of Alexis's death, the Chancellery came under the direction of four ministers, later called judges and, occasionally, inquisitors. As one of them, Tolstoy remained the key figure, even as all officially held equal authority. From an office served by a secretary and six clerks, each used subordinate agents to process political cases from the investigative stage through sentencing and on to the imposition of penalties.

Peter in 1722 clarified, through a decree, that the responsibility for political investigation rested on both the Secret Chancellery in St Petersburg, Peter's capital since 1712, and the Preobrazhenskii Prikaz in Moscow. Because the Chancellery mainly investigated high political crimes and the Prikaz mainly processed "word and deed" denunciations, caseloads for the two institutions from 1719 to 1724 were very uneven. Records show that the Chancellery handled 280 cases; the Prikaz, 1,363.[34]

When Tolstoy chose to retire at Peter i's death in 1725, Empress Catherine i (1725–27) dissolved the Secret Chancellery and assigned all political investigations to the Prikaz, still headed by the younger Romodanovsky. Emperor Peter ii (1727–30) abolished the Prikaz in 1729.

Needing to secure her shaky rule, successor Anna Ioannovna (1730–40) two years later restored the Secret Chancellery and placed at its helm a former assistant to Tolstoy, Alexander i. Ushakov, who had helped her fend off efforts by the Supreme Privy Council to restrict her powers. To guard against further incursions, Ushakov added more agents and opened a Moscow bureau in Lubianka prison under S.A. Saltykov, a kinsman of Anna. Within the next four years, Saltykov considered 1,055 cases and arrested 4,046 people.[35]

Ushakov kept his post under regency for the infant emperor Ivan Antonovich (1740–1) but got caught up in investigating a false charge laid by the first regent, I.E. Biron, to eliminate a personal enemy, A.P. Volynsky. As security chief, Ushakov himself used the rack to extort false testimony from Volynsky and others that Volynsky meant to usurp the throne. Then followed conviction of the accused, the cutting out of his tongue in Ushakov's presence, and peremptory execution.[36]

Continuing well into the reign of the Empress Elizabeth (1741–61), the methodic Ushakov stepped down from heading the Chancellery only because of old age. As for Elizabeth's attentiveness to political investigations, for all her laxness as ruler, this daughter of Peter regularly heard reports from Ushakov and his successor A.I. Shuvalov. Only late in her reign did Elizabeth begin to restrict the Secret Chancellery as too arbitrary.

Elizabeth's successor, Peter iii (1761–2) did away with the Secret Chancellery altogether, explaining in his decree that need for such an agency dated to earlier times of exceptionally low moral standards. By specifying that the "hateful phrase 'word and deed' shall henceforth mean nothing," he also discarded a pointless and costly legacy from Peter: the mandatory processing of "word and deed" denunciations.[37]

In addition, because the tsar was a fervent admirer of the Prussian king Frederick ii, the Secret Chancellery may have helped provoke its own demise by investigating alleged German espionage in the Russian army. Perhaps, as well, the tsar acted under the influence of the reformist statesman, M.I. Vorontsov.[38] In the view of one contemporary, the memoirist A.T. Bolotov, abolition was simply a response to what the people wanted.[39]

Even before he published his decree eliminating the Secret Chancellery, however, Peter iii took steps to start an agency under the Senate that he called the Secret Expedition.[40] He signed the edict that effected it in June 1762, just before his wife Catherine and her supporters dethroned him.

Going forward as though Peter's institutional changes were her own, Empress Catherine (1762–96) immediately issued two decrees that repeated her husband's almost word for word. The first eliminated the Secret Chancellery; the second created the Secret Expedition.

Catherine controlled the Expedition from the outset and personally chose its head, Stepan I. Sheshkovsky, previously a key player in the Secret Chancellery as secretary to Shuvalov. All the officers of the former Secret Chancellery received appointments under Sheshkovsky and took up their duties in familiar space: the old Chancellery offices in the Fortress of Saints Peter and Paul or the old Chancellery quarters in Moscow's Lubianka prison.

But despite its no longer having to handle "word and deed" denunciations, the new imperial security agency replicated the old one. It still had to deal with accusations of political wrongdoing laid by citizens because subjects were, of course, still required to inform officials of substantive crimes of any sort. Meanwhile punishment was put in place for anyone who, in public or before an official, tried to prompt an investigation by saying "word and deed."

Some accounts insist that Catherine made frivolous use of this security agency to settle small scores. One anecdote on record had her ordering no less than Sheshkovsky to remove M.D. Kozhina, a general's wife and inveterate scandal-monger, from a masquerade ball. To teach her that she had misbehaved, he was to "apply slight corporal punishment" and then return her to the festivities "with due decency."[41]

Special commissions to investigate very important political crimes were appointed, as required, by Catherine. One probed an attempt by Lieutenant V.Ia. Mirovich to free the deposed emperor Ivan Antonovich from Schlusselberg Fortress, where he had spent twenty-three years in solitary confinement not knowing his heritage or his name. Complying with secret instructions, officers of the guard had killed Ivan Antonovich when Mirovich undertook his venture. For that rebel act, Mirovich was convicted and executed.

Count G.G. Orlov, then the empress's favourite, investigated the Plague Mutiny of 1771 in Moscow. In turn, two special commissions headed by General P.S. Potemkin conducted an inquiry into the uprising led by Emelian Pugachev from 1771 to 1773. Experts from the Secret Expedition helped out, and Catherine sent Sheshkovsky to Potemkin with the endorsement that he had a "special gift for dealing with common people and has always succeeded in the most intricate examinations."[42] Catherine especially wanted to learn why Pugachev had styled himself as her late husband, Peter III. Sheskovsky duly interrogated Pugachev day and night and, at his execution, accompanied him to the scaffold with a priest.

To show herself enlightened, Catherine solemnly renounced torture but could not stamp it out. Too many opposed that reform, even churchmen, as was shown when the procurator of the Holy Synod, without a hint of censure, advised Catherine about the Mirovich investigation that some high clergy favoured "torturing the villain."[43]

Almost certainly the Secret Expedition exempted itself from the empress's prohibition. Sheshkovsky is said to have boasted that he could make anyone talk and described such tactics as striking with his stick the chin of a suspect to make his teeth crackle. One account insists that the walls of Sheshkovsky's torture chamber were covered with icons and that the chief chanted acathistus to Jesus while victims moaned; another relates that Prince G.A. Potemkin once asked Sheshkovsky in public how his knouting was going.[44] But none of this anecdotal evidence is conclusive.

Past practice, rather, makes it highly unlikely that security agents under Catherine wholly abandoned torture. The obvious truth that fear of torture in itself induces suspects to cooperate and reveal information about enemies of the tsar would have been sufficient justification in the late 1700s for keeping the torture chamber in place.

At his arrest in 1790 for a political crime, writer A.N. Radishchev is known to have fainted upon learning that Sheshkovsky would be his interrogator, quite plausibly out of fear of torture. Catherine had ordered the arrest in response to *Journey from St. Petersburg to Moscow*, a lengthy book that Radishchev had printed anonymously on his own press and circulated in only thirty-two copies. By its "spreading of the French madness, aversion for authorities," stormed the empress, the volume undermined her rule.[45]

To guide the investigation, Catherine forwarded her notes on *Journey* to Sheshkovsky and ranked the author for him as a "rebel worse than Pugachev." Then followed lengthy questioning, during which Radishchev regretted being audacious but insisted that he had not sought to foment a rebellion, only to stimulate debate.[46] In his official summation of that testimony, Sheshkovsky dismissed Radischev's defence as having "nothing to it."[47]

Four judges of the St Petersburg Criminal Court convicted Radishchev of lese-majesty, incitement to rebellion, and treason, for which they sentenced him to penal labour in exile followed by beheading. The Senate upheld that penalty, but the empress reduced it to ten years' exile. It seems likely that Catherine intended all along that the court inflict severe punishment to emphasize the heinousness of Radishchev's crime, whereupon she would show mercy.

N.I. Novikov, a leading Freemason in Moscow whose publications had earlier irritated Catherine, was arrested and subjected to political investigation in the spring of 1792. Sheshkovsky by then had expressed suspicions to the empress that the Moscow Masons were plotting to unseat her on behalf of her son Paul, his grounds being that they had discussed the question of the succession, hoped to initiate Paul into their order, and had contacts with officials of Frederick II and his successor Frederick William II.

Because no solid evidence of such conspiracy could be found, Novikov was taken into custody on a different but still dubious charge: that he was profiting unduly from his publishing activities.[48] The seventy-two-year-old Sheshkovsky again headed the investigation, but would die before the year ended. As one part of the probe, Catherine provided questions that Novikov answered in writing from his cell in the Schlusselberg Fortress; as another, Novikov had to explain documents, some of which he was not allowed to see.[49]

One new charge levelled at Novikov was that he and the Moscow Masons had enticed the secretary of the Moscow bureau of the Secret Expedition to join their lodge. Novikov explained that they had reasonably believed that the secretary wanted to join in order to report their activities to the Expedition, with whom they wished to cooperate fully.

The Secret Expedition also arrested several colleagues of Novikov who belonged to the Order of the Rosicrucians, accusing them of favouring the French Revolution. The bafflement of one of them, M. I. Nevzorov, is clear from this exchange recalled by a fellow arrestee: "'Do you know where you are'? Sheshkovsky asked. Nevzorov: 'No, I don't.' Sh: 'Why, don't you know that you are in the Secret Expedition'? N: 'I don't even know what this Expedition is; they may as well capture me and take me to some place in the forest ... and start questioning me.'"[50]

Neither Sheshkovsky nor his successor, A.S. Makarov, found sufficient grounds to charge anyone – a seemingly clear indication that neither used torture. Release of all suspects in custody except Novikov came in 1793, and he remained in his cell in the fortress until Catherine's death in 1796.

Finally attaining the throne at the age of forty-five, Paul I (1796–1801) at once differentiated himself from his mother Catherine by not only releasing both Radishchev and Novikov but also by making a strange attempt to assess the political climate. His means was a box, with a lock to which he held the key, that he had fixed to an exterior wall of the Winter Palace so that it was accessible to all. Removal followed shortly because the box attracted letters denouncing the new ruler.

Despite his early efforts to sample public opinion, Paul failed to grasp the smouldering discontent developing against him among the nobility and high officials; and although he had continued the Secret Expedition, still headed by Makarov, he failed to control it closely enough to ensure that it kept him fully informed of threats to his security. Some of the highest officials of the realm consequently moved with relative ease in organizing a plot to depose him. Among them were the military governor of the capital, Peter Pahlen, and, peripherally, Paul's son, Tsarevich Alexander.

In the dead of night on 12 March 1801 the main conspirators assassinated Paul I in his own bedroom. Alexander seemingly agreed only to the removal of his father, not his death, and found himself on the throne obligated to ruthless men who demanded change.

Immediately promising to rule "in accordance with the laws and thinking of our grandmother Catherine the Great," Alexander I (1801–25) one month later abolished the Secret Expedition because of its shortcomings – a seeming allusion to its use of torture, for at the same time he ordered an absolute end to that long-banned practice. Nothing replaced it until 1805, when, before joining his army's campaign in Europe against Napoleon, Alexander formed an interdepartmental Committee of Superior Police to ensure domestic political stability during his absence.

Two years later he established the Committee of General Security and, on the advice of his close friend Nicholas Novosiltsev, confined its work to intelligence analysis. Governing regulations required that the Interior Ministry supply it with "information received through governors or discovered by the Post Office Directorate from suspicious correspondence."[51]

Investigations of political crimes, as of all crimes, came under the new Ministry of Police when it opened in 1810, while its subordinate Special Chancellery initially dealt with foreigners in Russia and Russian subjects abroad and with censorship problems. Named minister was a former chief of police in both capitals, A.D. Balashov, and heading the Chancellery was Ia.I. de Sanglen, who had before directed the registration of foreigners.

Both men had central roles in the conservatives' plot against the tsar's liberal advisor and secretary of state, M.M. Speransky, whom they accused of treason for his alleged secret contacts with Napoleon and with the Poles. Alexander I knew these charges to be false but ordered Balashov and de Sanglan to arrest Speransky in March 1812 and to arrange his exile to Siberia.

Balashov continued as minister of police, but Alexander removed de Sanglen from the Special Chancellery, by then a fledgling security agency. In 1819 the tsar merged the Ministry of Police with the Ministry of the Interior, to which the Special Chancellery transferred intact.

By then the Secret Chancellery was a full-fledged security agency, and it would move intact to the Ministry of the Interior when Alexander merged the Police Ministry with Interior in 1819. Separate from it were the secret agents of General A.A. Arakcheev, the tsar's chief lieutenant during the 1812 war who had become virtual prime minister without office, and the Expedition of Secret Police under the St Petersburg governor-general.[52] In 1821 the Guards Corps, as well, added a secret police unit approved by the tsar.[53]

Agents of these police detachments were meanwhile finding signs that gentry were debating how to transform the autocracy into a constitutional monarchy – a change strongly favoured by members of the elite regiments who returned from Paris imbued with Western thinking. (Most gentry in this camp tended to agree that, for greatest effect, they must not assert themselves until the accession of Constantine, whom they thought liberally inclined.)

Alexander read the reports on gentry restiveness but indifferently dismissed them, for his overriding preoccupation with the destiny of his soul was causing him to let all aspects of government drift. He did, as the insistence of his close mentor A.N. Golitsyn, sign an 1823 decree naming Nicholas heir to the throne because Constantine had taken a morganatic wife; but, from bad judgment or inattentiveness, he kept that politically important change secret. Alexander's death in November 1825 would set off immediate confusion and security repercussions.

CHAPTER TWO

Imperial Security Centres at Fontanka 16, 1826 to the 1870s

Soon after assuming the throne, Nicholas I (1825–55) established both the headquarters and the modus operandi of imperial political investigations for all the tsars that followed him. That is, in 1826 he made Fontanka 16 in St Petersburg the centre for state security by seating there the new Higher Police, or Third Section, of His Majesty's Own Chancellery; and by ordering sent there, for analysis, all the intelligence that he had newly mandated from the Gendarmes of the Ministry of War.

This combining of forces, with the Third Section chief in charge, gave Russia its first comprehensive secret police. Neither part would markedly grow, nor confront strong threats, during the thirty-year reign of absolutist Nicholas I. During the next two decades under Alexander II (1855–81), in contrast, reforms would loose agitation that justified adding many more agents overall.

When news of Alexander I's unexpected death one thousand kilometres to the south in Taganrog reached the capital on 27 November 1825, officials, troops, and Nicholas swore allegiance to presumed heir Constantine, then viceroy of Poland. Constantine's formal renunciation arrived several days later from Warsaw, but a wary Nicholas refused to accede without fuller assurances from his older brother. In another week he bowed to signs of unrest by agreeing to receive loyalty oaths as tsar on 14 December.

Watching closely were Guard officers tied to the secret Northern Society, a gentry league committed to forwarding constitutional monarchy at Alexander's death. In a hasty conspiracy, they set about convincing troops to reject Nicholas on oath day by massing on Senate Square to shout "Constantine and Constitution." That rally was the Decembrist uprising: an armed protest by a mere three thousand men that fell apart within hours under cannon fire. (Nicholas ordered the fusilade after the assemblage refused his order to disband and one among them killed his emissary.) By the next day, all the leaders had been arrested and the soldiers disarmed and confined.

Nicholas had suffered an alarming affront, and, with that challenge as added incentive, he moved at once to create a top-level security agency. In his subjects' best interest, it would uphold and safeguard autocracy, the one form of government he held to be intrinsically right for Russians.

To recentralize power after Alexander's loose reign, Nicholas formed His Majesty's Own Chancellery, a tripartite administrative body immediately at his command. He assigned to its First Section his cabinet of ministers, ending the near-governing role it had played in his brother's final years; to its Second, his commission to codify the laws; and to its Third, his new security agency, officially named the Higher Police. Of those three, the last alone would become widely known by its Chancellery designation.

Nicholas's choice to head the Third Section was Lieutenant-General Alexander K. Benckendorff, who bid for the job at the beginning of the reign. In a brief proposal, he called for an elite strategy centre in St Petersburg served by a network of agents that would "embrace all the Empire, would subject itself to strict subordination, would be feared and respected, and would be inspired by the moral authority of its chief."[1]

Benckendorff claimed such authority. Born of Baltic Germans in 1783, he had joined the army at fifteen and fought in the Napoleonic wars. In 1821, having learned through Masonic circles of the constitutional agenda of the Decembrist-spawning Union of Welfare, he had vainly urged Alexander to examine these "hot-heads," at the same time rightly predicting that they "deceive themselves, if they hope for general support."[2]

Benckendorff began looking into some of those same men for Nicholas three days after the Decembrist revolt as a member of the Special Commission named to investigate everyone involved. Under the war minister A.I. Tatishchev, he and seven others examined over five hundred suspects in St Petersburg Fortress in mostly nighttime sessions over the next four months, releasing about half of them as innocent.[3] Their 30 May report ordered all in custody to trial.

A Supreme Court named from the State Council, Senate, Ministry, and Synod decided the relative guilt of each accused with respect to their "design of assaulting the sacred person of the Sovereign Emperor."[4] On 6 July, its judges ordered death for five and penal servitude and exile for the rest of the 121 held most responsible and, for the 134 found guilty of minor offences, various terms of miltary servitude. Nicholas granted no stays, and the executions took place immediately.[5]

To thwart any more challenges, Nicholas had, three months before, ordered Benckendorff to establish the new Higher Police in offices on the Moika Canal but soon after at Number 16 on the Fontanka Embankment. In keeping with the small size of the other two sections of His Majesty's Own Chancellery, Benckendorff and just sixteen others – most from the Secret Chancellery of the previous reign – comprised the Third Section at its founding. At least one hundred times larger was its main investigative force: the army's sixty or so Gendarme units.

By the late eighteenth century, "gendarmes" (the French word meaning "armed police who maintain public order") had entered Russian military usage. In 1792 Tsar Paul so termed the martial guard at one of his estates; and, in 1815, the Russian supreme commander in Europe, Barclay de Tolly, ordered each cavalry regiment to form a six-man "gendarme" unit to "maintain order during bivouacs ... apprehend pillagers, and the like."[6] (At war's end, these cavalry police became "dragoons.")

Gendarmes became a Russian proper noun in 1817 when the army officially gave that title to a contingent formed seven years before to train recruits. Because the original group, called the Corps of Internal Guards, had gradually taken on the policing of both civilians and soldiers, civil officials had intruded into its chain of command. By renaming the Guards, army officials regained sole authority over this special force of civil/military police in regular army uniforms. Their versatility justified subsequent postings in both army camps and urban centres and an increase in units that raised their total to roughly sixty in 1825.[7]

Although as security chief Benckendorff had wanted to take full command of the Gendarmes, the tsar opted to continue army control to keep these special units battle-ready for any insurgency (an arrangement still in place in 1917). Nicholas did, however, give Benckendorff a ready means to dictate Gendarme policies by empowering his Higher Police chief to commandeer generals and ministers alike in all affairs that affected state security.

Further adding to Benckendorff's authority, Nicholas seated his head of the Third Section in the realm's highest chamber, the State Council, and conferred on him the honorific title of Chief of Gendarmes – a ceremonial rank that would accrue to all successive heads of the Third Section, even civilian ones.[8] The tsar also made Benckendorff his frequent companion and guard and bestowed on him estates, serfs, and, in 1832, the title of Count.

Thus empowered, Benckendorff easily caused the army, under the Ministry of War, to raise Gendarme standards. As before, any imperial soldier or sailor in good standing aged twenty-five years or older could apply, but consideration would now go only to those strongly recommended by persons of importance. Benckendorff also induced the army to raise Gendarme pay to well above that of regular soldiers and, in 1827, to add "Corps of" to the Gendarme name and to uniform its members in blue, not the army's green.

As for their code of conduct, Benckendorff insisted that the Gendarmes command both respect and fear by fairly but rigorously performing their civil/military duties. Their prime duty for him, however, was to find and report political intelligence; and, from the start, Benckendorff secretly ordered the Gendarmes to spy so covertly that the public remained unaware. Given the charter mandate of the Third Section to inform the tsar on "all events," moreover, Benckendorff demanded broad reports from the heads of Gendarme units. He required, for example, information on immoral behaviour in young people (which, he believed, could destabilize society) and on miserly state salaries (which could turn otherwise loyal civil servants against the tsar).[9]

As early as the mid-July coronation of Nicholas in 1826, however, Benckendorff received a call for moderation from his own executive director, M.Ia. Von Vock, the former head of Interior's Special Chancellery. Arguing that the government should not be "sticking its nose into trivia," Von Vock objected that it was becoming "impossible to sneeze in one's home … without the Sovereign's finding out about it within the hour." Before long, he warned, public outrage over unwarranted surveillance could ripen into rebellion.[10]

Von Vock likewise urged the smoothing of another abrasive policy: censorship. Because its conservative overseer, the minister of public education A.S. Shishkov, was using his May 1826 press statute to allow only "useful" printed content, writers resented what they saw as an arbitrary effort to "close their mouths."[11] On this issue, at least, appearances mattered to Benckendorff and the tsar, and Nicholas turned to a committee separate from Shishkov for a redrafting of censorship rules.

As the liberal-seeming new law neared completion in early 1828, the first annual report of the Third Section – written by Von Vock and signed by Benckendorff – called for liberal changes to win back the disaffected younger generation. Not spelled out was the other side of Benckendorff's overall strategy: continued enforcement, in secret, of unpopular authoritarian controls.

What followed were the censorship "reforms" of 22 April 1828 (which incidentally assigned the censorship of theatricals to the Third

Section); the resignation of Shishkov two days later; and, on 25 April, the tsar's confidential order to the Third Section to muzzle anyone who published, or tried to publish, words or images that hurt the realm. That is, the tsar issued with fanfare a statute that barred censors from inferring hidden meanings only to require them, in secret, to refer to Benckendorff all texts that could possibly be construed as subversive.

Through this arrangement, Benckendorff acquired a new set of political investigators: imperial censors. As had happened with the Gendarmes, censors suddenly had no choice but to answer to the Third Section should security concerns arise. They too remained in service to the official sector that paid them (in their case, the censorship administration of the Ministry of Education) while secretly indentured to the Third Section as security agents.

At Benckendorff's insistence, postmasters likewise worked for the Third Section – to assist with "perlustration," or the perusal and copying of suspicious letters in transit. "Opening letters is one of the methods of the secret police," Benckendorff would write in a confidential memoir in the 1840s (in a line equally notable for its candid admission that he headed a secret police). Rating it the "very best" strategy, he bragged that perlustration was by then "constant and carried out everywhere in the Empire" by postmasters "known for their meticulousness and zealousness."[12]

Agents of another sort were the relatively few citizens who reported political wrongdoing to the Third Section on a casual basis. They came from all walks of life, and their amateur reporting necessarily came under close scrutiny at Fontanka 16. (Staff there likewise evaluated some twenty-five hundred to five thousand "denunciations" that the public yet volunteered yearly.) On two occasions, for example, the Third Section would reject charges received from informer F.V. Bulgarin against rival journalists. In the first, its analysts would compare handwriting samples to disprove Bulgarin's claim that N.A. Nekrasov and V.G. Belinsky had penned an anonymous letter condemning the tyranny of Nicholas 1. In the second, they would examine texts by A.A. Kraevsky to rule that Bulgarin had falsely cited particular lines as subversive by taking them out of context.[13]

Always, of course, the staff at Fontanka 16 remained on alert for the most prodigious informer of them all: the turncoat confidant of revolutionaries in hiding. But, as the records now stand, neither such spies nor such revolutionaries came to light under Nicholas 1.

Because political investigators from 1826 to 1855 mainly tracked public opinion, the bulk of imperial intelligence concerned ordinary exchanges of ideas. Analysts at Fontanka 16 paid especial attention to published discourse, both because it reflected and shaped opinion and because, by reviewing most of it, they could gauge the competence of censors. Nicholas consequently required in 1829 that the Third Section receive one copy of every periodical published. In summing them up for that year's annual report, Benckendorff deplored that so few strongly supported the autocracy; and, as his remedy, he urged expending secret funds to bribe malleable but ostensibly independent journalists to back the regime,, a strategy of European rulers that Nicholas did adopt.[14]

To deal with legally published commentary that seemed to him to violate censorship limits, Benckendorff acted on his own; and, in November 1830, he summoned editor A.A. Delvig of the *Literary Gazette* to Fontanka 16 to explain his journal's unacceptable political tone. When Delvig protested that the censorship statute placed all responsibility for published content on the censor who approved it, Benckendorff made clear his own authority to override that law when he, as security chief, saw fit. Within days he had caused Shishkov's successor, K.A. Lieven, to end Delvig's editorial role (the education minister decided who could or could not edit a periodical).[15] Four months later a secret order placed responsibility for published words that undermined either the autocracy or the Orthodox Church on whoever wrote, edited, translated, published, and/or censored them, as warranted. Moreover, it gave overriding authority to the Third Section to identify such words and to allot blame, leaving understood that those charged had no avenue of appeal.[16]

Among the many times that the Third Section invoked that secret rider, one infamous case resulted from *Moscow Telescope*'s publication in October 1836 of Peter Chaadaev's "Philosophical Letter," a negative assessment of Russia's past and future that had privately circulated in French since 1830. On 20 October the then-minister of education, S.S. Uvarov, asked the tsar's approval to dismiss the errant censor, A.V. Boldyrev, and to close *Telescope* at year's end, when subscriptions expired. He took no stand against the editor and author, having no such authority.

Not so Benckendorff, who ordered officials in Moscow to confine Chaadaev to his home as mentally impaired and to forward all of his personal papers to the Third Section; and, in St Petersburg, he directed Uvarov to put an end to lax censorship.[17] He also sent Third Section staff to Moscow to interrogate Chaadaev and ordered *Telescope* editor N.I. Nadezhdin and censor Boldyrev to report for questioning at Fontanka 16, where he confined them both.

After reviewing all the evidence, a four-man special commission that included Benckendorff and Uvarov gave orders, on 28 November, for

Nadezhdin's exile and Boldyrev's dismissal both as censor and as rector at Moscow University. (By then the tsar had closed *Telescope*.) As for the author, the commission found Chaadaev not responsible by reason of insanity. Never again, however, would the autocracy use this expedient ploy to silence a writer.[18]

On both occasions that he filled the headship of the Third Section, Nicholas I turned to the army, but he chose civilians as its first two executive directors: Von Vock, until his death from cholera in 1831, and A.N. Mordvinov, from 1831 to 1839. Then a new factor entered the selection process: the decision that the executive director coterminously serve as Gendarme chief-of-staff. Because no civilian could fill an army post, it followed that the person who filled these paired offices had to hold a military rank.

Chosen in 1839 by Benckendorff and the tsar was a Gendarme general, Leonty Vasil'evich Dubel't, another career soldier who had enlisted at fifteen, pursued Napoleon into Europe, and stood firm against the Decembrists.[19] As the health of Benckendorff declined over the next five years, Dubel't became de facto security chief; and he would be cited by one of the writers he called in to lecture – the future emigré-editor of *The Bell*, Alexander Herzen – as the most intelligent official within His Majesty's Own Chancellery.[20]

When Benckendorff died in 1844, Dubel't stayed in place under the new chief, Count Alexander Fedorovich Orlov, another stalwart against Decembrism. Since that uprising, Orlov had twice commanded troops to quell rebels and twice helped to negotiate peace with Turkey; and, because he preferred diplomacy, he largely left the direction of the Third Section to Dubel't.

During February 1848, just as the tide of Europe-wide revolutions began in France, the minister of the interior, L.A. Perovsky, launched a political investigation on his own after a January tract by M.V. Petrashevsky, a minor official in the Foreign Affairs ministry, raised doubts about the author's loyalty. By mid-April Perovsky felt that he had enough grounds to prove that Petrashevsky and thirty-three others comprised a subversive secret society. Only then did he pass his findings, backed by forty surveillance reports, to security chief Orlov.[21]

Made especially wary by Europe's turmoil, Orlov at once issued orders, signed by Nicholas, for Gendarmes to round up all the suspects just before dawn on 23 April. That same day Nicholas named Dubel't and three others as a special commission to probe the alleged conspiracy and decide who should be tried. As a first step, all in custody were required to reply in writing to questions, and Fyodor

Dostoevsky, one of the detainees, flatly denied in his response that "the Petrashevsky group has some hidden, clandestine purpose, bearing in mind all the confusion of ideas and personalities." No single goal could emerge, he insisted, "in all that chaos."[22]

By September the commission had questioned 252 persons and compiled a list of ninety-four participants in a so-called "plot of ideas."[23] Although other officials added twenty-eight names, the commission found grounds to proceed against just twenty-three men, including Dostoevsky, for intending to subvert autocracy (which was treason under the 1649 law code still in effect). That same month a high military court convened to judge the accused.

When its judges sentenced just fourteen defendants to death and the rest to exile, Nicholas raised the number of capital penalties to twenty-one by ordering a retrial on security grounds. He also had the second set of verdicts immediately made public in the government's *Russian Veteran* to intimidate would-be critics and rebels. As for how those convicted felt, a Third Section agent expressed surprise that none showed the "reverential emotion and fear that one ought to expect."[24]

In a perverse ceremony on 22 December, all the condemned were blindfolded and marched to what they thought was their place of execution. Once assembled, however, they heard no command to the firing squad but, rather, a decree from Nicholas I commuting their sentences to various forms of exile. (To Petrashevsky alone went the harshest exile: lifetime penal servitude in the mines.) Behind this show of stern retribution tempered by mercy lay not just the 1848 revolutions but also the Decembrists, whose armed defiance might have been prevented had Alexander I acted when warned of the Union of Welfare. Given that lesson, Nicholas had moved at once to make an example of the Petrashevsky group.

However the Petrashevsky episode factored in, political calm continued in Russia all through 1848 to the outbreak of the Crimean War in 1853 and on through the two remaining years of the reign. No grounds exist to establish how much credit belonged to Nicholas's secret police, just as there is no way to rate public feelings in this period regarding the Third Section.

Given the too-frequent use of torture to compel political conformity in previous reigns, along with the existence of interrogation rooms and detention cells at Fontanka 16 and the secrecy that shrouded the Third Section, rumours of "secret police" excesses surely became accepted truths among the unsophisticated. One contemporary claimed that even members of the intelligentsia believed the rumour that the security chief could, "in the course of a pleasant conversation" in his office at Fontanka 16, activate a specially-rigged chair to drop his summoned victim through a trap door to a torture chamber below.[25]

Objective evidence presents a different picture. With respect to secret surveillance over the general population, for example, the few casual informers who served the Third Section comprised a very limited watch; and the Gendarmes, except while on sporadic assignments from Fontanka 16, gathered political intelligence only randomly. As for the staff at Fontanka 16, that Higher Police contingent had increased to only thirty by reign's end. Finally, with respect to political repression, a mere handful of Nicholas's subjects were punished – none by death and only one, late in the reign, by life-long punitive exile – for undermining the autocracy.

When Alexander II succeeded Nicholas I in 1855, he moved at once to sue for peace in the Crimean War, and the official he sent to Paris as chief negotiator was his Third Section head, Orlov. When Russia won relatively easy terms in the treaty of February 1856, the grateful tsar made Orlov chairman of both the State Council and the Council of Ministers. Named as security chief was Vasily Andreevich Dolgorukov, a Winter Palace guard and Decembrist foe whom Nicholas had made an aide to Tsarevich Alexander and, in 1852, minister of war.[26] Alexander II had kept him in that office through the signing of the peace treaty.

When Dolgorukov took command of the Third Section in April 1856, Alexander had just made clear that security considerations required an end to the "ownership of souls" in Russia. "It is better to begin to abolish serfdom from above," he told the Moscow gentry marshalls in March, "than to wait that time when it will begin to abolish itself from below." Neither Dolgorukov nor Orlov favoured immediate emancipaton; for, as diarist A.V. Nikitenko put it, both belonged to a "party" of officials who were "unwilling to grant freedom to the enserfed peasants, or to develop education, or publicity in government affairs – in a word, no improvements along the lines favoured by public opinion after the death of Nicholas."[27] Thus would the tsar force their involvement, in January 1857, by making them both charter members of his Secret Committee on the peasant question.

Meanwhile Dolgorukov ordered and got back an assessment of the Third Section from an in-house commission, which recommended clear regulations, strict lines of command, and no assignments from outside "departments or institutions." Their report also urged a precise definition of the security role of Gendarmes – a task that Dolgorukov put off to a "better time."[28]

Dealing with emancipation took precedence, especially once Dolgorukov and ten fellow members of the Secret Committee set about deriving confidential "principles" for freeing the serfs. The plan they completed in August 1857 was too gradual for Alexander II, who turned to the gentry for better terms. By December the Secret Committee, whose majority favoured liberation without land, agreed to make public three of its dispatches to the gentry that implied that serfs might buy their freedom.

Dolgorukov at this same time began drafting his annual report on security for the tsar. Predictably, he focused his twelve-month review, duly submitted in April 1858, on public reaction to rumours of an imminent emancipation.[29] Educated persons who owned no "souls," he wrote, commonly opposed serfdom as unChristian. Among educated owners, some favoured liberation but all believed Russia unready, while uneducated owners stood wholly opposed. Peasants had reacted to possible freedom with calm, so that unrest was unlikely, barring "unexpected external instigations"; but when liberation did take place, Alexander must grant the gentry some authority over freed serfs – or lose both gentry support and the "hierarchy essential for the continuation of the autocracy." This security chief opposed full freedom with land, the very terms that the tsar sought and would ultimately win.

Dolgorukov made no mention of another liberal change that he opposed but that Alexander II had effected in January 1858: lifting of the long-standing ban on published commentary on the peasant question. During February, as one result, N.G. Chernyshevsky had published in his journal *Contemporary*, with censorship approval, his criticism of the field rents serfs would have to pay if freed without land.[30] When part two of Chernyshevsky's article appeared in April to oppose the gentry's retaining authority over the peasants, a strong protest from Dolgorukov helped to effect a late April ruling that the press could no longer discuss "future arrangements for the peasants." At Fontanka 16 Dolgorukov made certain that the January and April articles were entered as evidence into a Chernyshevsky file that would greatly expand in the next four years.

In his annual report on 1858, the year when committees began drafting liberation terms, Dolgorukov noted a rash of disturbing presumptions. Too many peasants, he said, were refusing to work for their owners and, at the same time, claiming their dwelling and a plot of land as already their own; but rural disorders had been "incomparably fewer than expected."[31] In the cities, not only were students disrupting classes and journalists inflating public expectations with their demands, but so were the smuggled-in publications of such emigrés as Alexander Herzen pushing for "reforms in all areas right away." Worst among those inside Russia who insisted on "public courts, no more bureaucratic abuses, freedom of thought, and unlimited publishing" was Chernyshevsky.

To discover what emigré agitators were planning, Dolgorukov had increased the number of agents abroad, especially in London. Such external agents were still too few to constitute a separate corps, but a typical example was Genrikh Mikhailovsky, who had worked in the London bookstore of a Russian emigré allied with Herzen until discovered and exposed as an imperial agent in 1857.[32]

In his review of publishing for his report on 1858, Dolgorukov deplored that Russian journalists were flooding periodicals with "exposure"-style articles on "bureaucratic evils and social inadequacies." Some had even brazenly succeeded in pillorying specific officials through word plays on their names and allusions to familiar details about their lives.[33] A year later, in his report on 1860, Dolgorukov labelled as very dangerous those journalists who were urging Russian reforms along Western constitutional lines.[34] Because their advocacy was "fermenting" minds with revolutionary ideas, such writers threatened the "existing order and the Monarchy itself."

In assessing 1861, the Emancipation year that he termed a "crisis," Dolgorukov again criticized journalists, this time for fanning anger among the gentry, "disorders ... in our universities," and an "almost universal ... lack of confidence in our government." Charging that some had formed a radical "party of opposition" disguised as a chess club, he named Chernyshevsky as a founder and placed him first on his list of the fifty most dangerous enemies of the state.[35]

About this time Dolgorukov also requested the tsar's approval to add a covert arm to His Majesty's Third Section. In secret offices within the municipal police of both capitals, veteran officers of the Third Section were already training a new phalanx of security detectives (later termed outside agents) to conduct surveillance during Third Section political investigations.

Primary justification for the new agents was the Chernyshevsky case. Surveillance teams organized by the Third Section had begun a constant watch of the outspoken journalist on 2 October 1861, with the goal of finding grounds to charge him with political crimes. This former divinity student was addressing liberal arguments to some six thousand subscribers – then a substantial number – while staying strictly within the law, and Dolgorukov was intent on permanently silencing him.

A rash of illegal, radical pamphlets earlier in 1861 had alerted Dolgorukov to the possibility of linking them to Chernyshevsky. *Young Russia* had appeared in May to urge an armed rebellion; by October, three issues of *The Great Russian* had called for sweeping reforms. In what was an unprecedented operation, Dolgorukov ordered his plain-clothes agents to record all visitors to Cherny-shevsky's apartment and to follow the writer wherever he went.[36] Further to identify Chernyshevsky's every contact, special agents in the post office read his mail, and in time his doorman and personal cook became paid informers.

In February 1862, while Dolgorukov was still formulating his 1861 report, the gentry of Tver province had petitioned for a national convention elected by all the people. Under orders from the tsar to frame a response, Dolgorukov and the ministers of justice and the interior had decided on a dramatic censure: the arrest of thirteen leading gentry from Tver and their confinement in a fortress.[37] During that same month, Chernyshevsky had given his censor an article entitled "Letters without an Address," which boldly summoned the gentry class to demand a popularly elected legislative assembly.[38] His censor had had no doubts about banning the piece and had passed it at once to his superiors, who forwarded a copy to the Third Section.

On 15 May, Dolgorukov advised Alexander II to launch an aggressive investigation of subversive publicists through a special commission, and, to head it, the tsar named a member of the nobility, Prince A.F. Golitsyn.[39] Completing the task force with representatives from the Third Section and his main ministries, he empowered the group to use any extraordinary measures necessary.

Dolgorukov was already closely monitoring serial publications as they legally circulated through his Fifth Secretariat within his enlarged Third Section. By 1862, its fourteen members were reviewing every issue of some one hundred select periodicals; and what they sought, on Dolgorukov's orders, ranged from anti-government sentiment to useful ideas on social needs.[40] Their findings went to the Third Section's executive director, who forwarded on to the education minister, as a rebuke, any singled-out wording that his censors should have excised.

Just a month after the Golitsyn commission set to work, the ministers of education and the interior jointly ordered eight-month suspensions for *Contemporary* and another radical journal, *Russian Word*, for "dangerous orientation." The detainment of Chernyshevsky by the Third Section followed on 8 July, the pretence being an intercepted letter to a friend of Chernyshevsky in which Herzen offered to publish *Contemporary* abroad.[41] Frustrated that neither the Herzen letter nor surveillance findings justified a judicial arrest, Dolgorukov used his own powers of administrative detention to remove Chernyshevsky from society. But this expedient allowed for only a temporary or indefinite incarceration. A definite sentence required proof of criminality.

In another eight months, Dolgorukov would have that proof: sworn testimony from a confessed accomplice that Chernyshevsky had authored a revolutionary tract. The witness was V.D. Kostomarov, whom police arrested in August 1862 for operating an illegal press and attempting to publish the tract in question, "To the Landlords' Peasants." In deciding his fate, judges gave Kostomarov a lighter sentence because he named a cohort of Chernyshevsky, Alexander Mikhailov, as the author. By early 1863, Kostomarov had instead identified Chernyshevsky as responsible and, records show, later received substantial state benefits.

As of November 1862, Dolgorukov had not gone beyond trying to establish that Chernyshevsky had criminal links with Herzen; for all questions put to the hapless editor during his initial interrogation by the Golitsyn Commission on 30 October and 1 November 1862 centred on that charge. By then, moreover, the security chief was facing indignant outcries from the press and the public that, after four months of detention, Chernyshevsky must be charged or released. Within another three months, Dolgorukov was able to provide the commission with the Kostomarov testimony that incriminated Chernyshevsky; and in March 1863, during his second and last questioning by the commission, Chernyshevsky first become aware that the Senate, as Russia's highest court, would try him for high treason on the authorship charge.[42]

A dossier of findings to support that charge went in May to the Senate, which ultimately found Chernyshevsky guilty of writing and attempting to circulate a seditious appeal to the landlords' peasants. Its offical decision on 5 April 1864 set a punishment of fourteen years hard labour (the tsar would halve that term), followed by life-long exile in Siberia.[43]

Nikitenko tells how Dolgorukov, during the final review of the case by the State Council on 7 April, prevailed over the misgivings of some officials. To counter expressed doubts that evidence was sufficient, wrote the diarist, Dolgorukov waved papers that he said contained absolute proof but which, regrettably, he could not disclose without jeopardizing security.[44]

In retrospect, the treatment of Chernyshevsky, whom Dolgorukov had pronounced guilty in advance, strongly supports the view of many both at the time and since that the writer was the victim of a rigged political investigation. Without question, he paid dearly, having to serve seven years hard labour and then a difficult exile in Siberia until 1883, six years before his death.

The case also shows a Third Section head having for the first time to factor in public and press attention – including expressed criticism

– as he went about silencing a writer deemed a political threat. Because that scrutiny made it politically unwise for Dolgorukov or Alexander II to act unilaterally, the security chief had to work within limits imposed by the trial system in place, whether honestly or not.

Dolgorukov's manoeuvring against the editor of *Contemporary* in the cause of security had its correlatives at lower levels, and one petty version in the provinces in this same decade clarifies the role of Gendarmes as agents for the Third Section. The case concerned the *Voronezh Newssheet*, which appeared twice weekly in a city of the same name about five hundred kilometres south of Moscow. Its publisher, Vladimir Gol'dshtein, had received the necessary security clearance from the Gendarme district head to start his tabloid in 1861, but a year later a local Gendarme officer detected a political threat in its contents, despite a censor's approval.[45] In his next security report, the Gendarme district head specified that editor Malykhin, also the holder of a politically sensitive job teaching cadets of the Mikhailovsky Corps, had denigrated "highly placed officials."[46]

By early 1864, repeated complaints against *Newssheet* from the district head had caused the minister of the interior, as new overseer of censorship, to suspend that paper for eight months. When Gol'dshtein sought approval for a new editor before reopening, the Gendarme district head rejected the candidate, one Gradovsky, as politically unreliable. His reasons are instructive: Gradovsky had purportedly lost an earlier job as editor of the provincial government bulletin for giving it a "nasty orientation," had once offered to lecture at Khar'kov University on the structure of English government, and had an "irritable temperament."[47]

Thus Malykhin stayed in place, but only until early 1866, when the Gendarme district chief had him ousted for *Newssheet*'s thinly disguised report of a local school ball. Presented as a fictional diary entry from the 1840s, the piece by Malykhin's brother-in-law ridiculed the event's sponsors, claimed the district chief, to avenge the author's near-expulsion from the ball for smoking. By causing "general indignation" in Voronezh, he continued, the article was "dangerous for society." Particularly unseemly was the author's having alluded to a woman admitted to the ball as a "saucy coquette" whose mere presence could have stirred in the students "passions not appropriate to their age group."[48]

In a subsequent report, the Gendarme district chief described the next editor, G.M. Veselovsky, as "somewhat liberal" but still acceptable. He also verified that the preliminary censorship of *Newssheet* would henceforth take place in the office of the provincial governor.[49] Taken as a whole, his treatment of the paper confirms that Gendarmes, as security agents for the Third Section, still looked not just for political subversion but also social impropriety because both undermined the existing order. Their treatment of *Voronezh Newssheet* from 1861 to early 1866 was clearly highhanded, but Dolgorukov himself set that standard.

In early 1866, moreover, Dolgorukov felt well satisfied with security and was framing an optimistic annual report. Rating popular support strong, he credited several factors: the tsar's stern suppression of rebel Poles in 1863; his expansion of local self-government through the 1864 *zemstvo* edict and of press freedom through the 1865 censorship "reform," while keeping control of both; his institution of *glasnost'*, or openness, through public trials under the 1864 judicial reform. Because of these moves, Dolgorukov held, most journalists had foresworn revolutionary propagandizing.[50]

Then intruded the disquieting incident of 4 April 1866, when a one-time student, Dmitry Karakozov, came close to killing the tsar. Within six days Dolgorukov had been transferred to a new honorific post, at his own request. His tearful farewell – during which he regretted that he could not remain in place, "engulfed in kindness," for another decade – caused one highly placed witness tellingly to cast him as an old school bureaucrat.[51]

Named successor was a decided modernist: thirty-nine-year-old Count P.A. Shuvalov (1827–89), a well-born and confident rationalist bent on reforming security operations. Not only did he immediately advise Alexander II that Slavophil Iury Samarin could not expect the modern Russian state to promote the program of the Russian Orthodox Church, but just the next month he demanded conciliatory gestures, not censorship warnings, for editor M.N. Katkov to keep him strongly pro-government.[52]

Prior service by Shuvalov included posts as chief of the St Petersburg police (1857–59), as head of Interior's Department of General Affairs (1860), and as executive director, or chief of staff, of the Third Section (1861–63). Most recently, he had governed Livland, Estland, and Kovno provinces and commanded the Riga military district.

To Shuvalov, as his best hope against terrorism, Alexander allowed power second only to his own; for so narrow a miss by a bullet had convinced the tsar that his security chief must have unlimited scope to effect new countermeasures. Thus would Shuvalov command not just his own security operations but ministers as well – and come to be called "Peter IV."

Alexander II himself initiated the investigation of his near-assassination and placed his special commission under Count M.N. Muraviev, a hard-line general who had fiercely crushed demonstrations in

Lithuania as governor in 1863. On 13 May, less than six weeks after the failed attempt, the commission announced its finding that Karakozov had acted alone and unaided. What set him off, members held, was the collective harangue of journalists against the autocracy.

Given that others resembling Karakozov most likely were at large, Shuvalov methodically set about improving the scope and efficiency of his Russia-wide monitoring. His strategy was to press for changes in the numbers, placement, calibre, and command chain of the Gendarmes, whose just over seven thousand men then served in eight provincial districts (under the respective governors), in the administrative regions of Poland and the Caucasus (under the respective administrators), and on six railway lines (under the Ministry of Communications).[53] As a start, he personally called on the Gendarmes, through a communiqué, to fulfil their security role "with the same zeal and diligence" they had always shown.[54]

By the end of his first month in office, Shuvalov had taken command of the Gendarmes who guarded the railway and trains from St Petersburg to Tsarskoe Selo and Peterhof because the imperial family and many officials used this line to reach palaces on the Gulf of Finland. By November, he likewise controlled all Gendarmes in volatile Warsaw; and he had caused the army to abolish fifty-seven mounted Gendarme units, surely to help finance its wider placement of regular Gendarme units.

To improve Gendarmes qualitatively, he brought about higher standards for rank assignments and a review of existing personnel to ensure that each man fit his standing. In a secret memorandum of 1 January 1867 to his Gendarmes in Poland, Shuvalov barred from service there all converts to Russian Orthodoxy since the 1863 rebellion and all husbands of Catholics. (Like his predecessors, Shuvalov kept secret any order that might discredit the government or otherwise hurt security.)

One day earlier he had divided into two documents, one public and one secret, directives of 31 December 1866 to these same Polish Gendarmes. In the first, he required strict obedience to the laws and court system effected by the judicial reform. No Gendarme, he specified, could pursue a case "under judicial investigation" by a procurator. In his secret instructions, which overrode the first, Shuvalov ordered Gendarme officers to ignore any "inconvenient" judicial investigation should they see "urgent" need for a security probe. Then he detailed work of a kind not mentioned in the public orders: surveillance of all persons and activities district-wide. To safeguard the state, wrote Shuvalov, Gendarmes must discern the "moral orientation and spirit" of clergy, schools, periodicals, even army units. In turn they must report anyone who "incited minds by means of dangerous words or oral advocacy" and any military officer who held "literary evenings" for his men.[55]

Word of these secret instructions leaked to some. On 6 April 1867, Baron A.P. Nikolai complained to A.V. Golovnin, a former minister of public education, that Shuvalov had given his Gendarmes inordinate power as "judges of everything, administrators of everything, with the right of interference in everything."[56] What struck Slavophil Ivan Aksakov, on the other hand, was the sheer "fantasy" of Shuvalov's assumption that Gendarmes could carry out the instructions.[57] Nikitenko had even earlier objected, in his diary, to Shuvalov's acting "outside the law and all the established government institutions." By having direct access to Alexander II, he wrote, Shuvalov could win imperial approval for every move he wanted "though others completely disagree with him."[58]

On Shuvalov alone rested changes at Fontanka 16, where, again to improve efficiency and scope, he greatly increased the size and duties of the Fifth Secretariat. Besides having it continue to review what the public was reading and to analyse all reports received in writing, he ordered its members to initiate and direct political investigations on their own when findings so justified; for this sector weighed the findings of the plain-clothes detectives, or outside agents, who now served Shuvalov in the two capitals – the very ones that Dolgorukov had organized and hidden within the police departments of Moscow and St Petersburg.

Not only did paperwork proliferate, but so did file-keeping, cross-referencing, and other such tasks that required the First Secretariat, in charge of personnel, to add more workers, all of whom the Second Secretariat, which conducted security checks and otherwise maintained staff quality, had to approve. The Third Secretariat still dealt with casual and regular informers, while the Fourth handled a greatly increased budget (expenditures in 1867 of 1,712,000 rubles would total nearly twice the 871,990 rubles that Dolgorukov spent in 1861).

Seventeen months after taking office, Shuvalov got the Gendarme changes he wanted through the tsar's edict of 9 September 1867. Logistically, it increased jurisdictional units to fifty-six (most were provincial districts, which before numbered eight) and required the Gendarme head of each to send security reports directly to Fontanka 16. It also stipulated that Gendarme schools must upgrade their teaching staffs.

Of great importance to Shuvalov, the statute narrowly defined the Gendarmerie as an "observation corps," thus to give the corps a benign image more suited to this decade of reforms.[59] To underscore that its members were primarily to watch society, not police it, the new law barred Gendarmes from handling ordinary crimes, with two exceptions: should local police be absent or should they ask for help. But nothing had actually changed. Gendarmes still served as agents for the Third Section and reserve soldiers for the army that paid them.

Another provision in the statute authorized that select Gendarmes staff "observation posts" soon to be set up in urban centres. Their presence was meant to show the state's commitment to public well-being and openness to public counsel (informants being particularly welcome). What resulted was thirty-one street-level offices, five of them in Moscow and four in St Petersburg, each manned by seven Gendarme officers who regularly sent their findings to their jurisdiction head.[60]

Training institutions for Gendarme commissioned officers also came into being, along with separate ones for non-commissioned officers. On 1 January 1870 Shuvalov opened the elite Corps Preparatory School, where one hundred select Gendarmes annually enrolled in a one-year program. Adding to its prestige was its nearness to the Imperial Lyceum and to the tsar's palace at Tsarskoe Selo.

First-time partnership between the Third Section and the judiciary in an important political case had begun just the year before, when the municipal police of Moscow had summoned the Third Section after discovering the political nature of a local murder. Because a prosecutor of the Moscow Court of Appeals had already begun a *doznanie*, or preliminary inquiry, Shuvalov and select Gendarmes entered into proceedings already tied to the judiciary.

Behind the murder was a young radical, Sergei Nechaev, who, like many, expected a broad revolt by disenchanted peasants in February 1870 on the ninth anniversary of the Emancipation. To organize secret support, he posed as the agent of a non-existent World Revolutionary Alliance to win eighty members for his People's Vengeance in September 1869. Within weeks he had convinced four of them to help kill a purported traitor in their ranks; but once they had done so, on 21 November, Nechaev had fled abroad.[61]

By using leads provided by the Third Section, Gendarmes involved in the doznanie helped the local police of both capitals to find evidence, round up suspects, and detain three hundred. At the end of that initial probe, the prosecutor found grounds to arrest 152 detainees, or just over half. But it was wholly unacceptable to Shuvalov that the rest should go free. He covertly redetained and exiled most or all of them. His means was an addendum to the judicial reform that allowed administrative processing of suspects on security grounds should legal or security impediments rule out judicial processing; for, again to safeguard security, all administrative processing took place in secret.[62]

By not defining applicable charges and standards of proof, the addendum gave full discretion to the administrative judge – meaning that Shuvalov could have exiled detainees for, say, subversive tendencies. Without question, administrative processing was subject to abuse and counter to the spirit of the judicial reform, but security arguments for its inclusion had prevailed in 1864.

Meanwhile under way for the suspects held under judicial arrest was the *sledstvie* (judicial investigation). During this second phase, examining magistrates vetted, organized, and explicated the evidence (which investigators could continue to gather) to enable the presiding prosecutor to decide whom to indict for what crimes. Here brought in, as chief prosecutor, was the justice minister himself, K.I. Pahlen; for these were unprecedented arraignments of great import: the first in the reformed courts on political charges, and against not just one person but many.

After initial deliberation, Pahlen informed Shuvalov and other high officials that he had to that time found grounds for seventy-nine indictments; and he blamed that low number on the irrelevance or inadmissibility of much of the evidence gathered by Gendarmes and police.[63] It was pointless, he instructed, that a suspect had, among other examples, written non-incriminating letters to a conspirator. Likewise of no use was evidence collected through illegal searches, seizures, or interrogations. In even stronger words, he condemned what he said he had only chanced to discover: the administrative detainment and exile of the Nechaevist suspects who had been released from judicial processing for lack of evidence. Pahlen deplored this imposition of double jeopardy in violation of the criminal code.

To solve the problems raised by Pahlen, Shuvalov proposed that they should collaborate on new rules for handling political investigations. A joint drafting commission resulted, and, on 19 May the tsar issued a new law that fused judicial and administrative proceedings during the doznanie of security-related cases. In deference to Shuvalov, it required that Gendarmes take part in all security-related doznanie and, in deference to Pahlen, that each be directed by a prosecutor at the Appeals Court level.[64] At the close of every doznanie, the justice minister and Third Section chief jointly had to decide which detained suspects to process and, case by case, whether to proceed judicially or administratively. The tsar decided when they disagreed or he opposed their ruling.

By getting the tsar on his side, either Shuvalov or Pahlen could prevail; but Shuvalov seems to have had more influence with Alexander II. Shuvalov also had the upper hand in cases where he could claim to hold crucial evidence that could not be entered into judicial processings for reasons of security. Also possible, but less likely, he could bar judicial routing by having a Gendarme mishandle crucial evidence to make it inadmissable in court.[65]

Another provision in the new statute gave Gendarmes the discretionary right to detain suspects on their own, whether the alleged wrongs were political or not. In judicial inquiries about non-political crimes, not just political ones, moreover, the prosecutor in charge could "entrust responsibility" to the Gendarmes, if he saw fit. Finally, those Gendarmes assigned to railroad lines effectively gained all the powers of local police. If some had doubted the 1869 depiction of Gendarmes as mere observers, the 19 May 1871 statute wholly confuted that image.

In close proximity to the May statute, Pahlen issued eighty-five indictments for the Nechaevist trials scheduled in St Petersburg. In each he charged some degree of participation in a specific crime – whether murder, failure to report a conspiracy, membership in an illegal society, or possession of illegal literature – so that the counsel for the accused could prepare a defence (a right in judicial but not administrative hearings).

Confident that his procurators' arguments would convince most hearers, Pahlen admitted the press and public to the trials to effect glasnost'. He had another reason, as well, to expect resounding wins for the state: judges decided cases at the Court of Appeals level, not quixotic juries. That July the well-publicized trials began before sixty-four judges on twelve panels (one for each of twelve categories of defendants).[66] As portrayed by the procurators, the accused were skilled subversives bent on destroying the established order; as defended by their lawyers, they were naive recruits for a secret society incapable of conspiracy.

To Pahlen's chagrin, the judges handed down thirty-four convictions of various terms of imprisonment, hard labour, or exile, and fifty-one acquittals. Although many hailed the results as a credit to the government, Shuvalov had at once obtained special approval from Alexander to detain and exile nearly all of those acquitted. When persons close to the exiles spread word of their unnanounced fate, some newspapers objected in print to the arbitrary use of administrative punishments.

In his post-trial comments to peers, Pahlen confined himself to condemning the preponderant number of acquittals and faulting the judges for verdicts based more on feelings than judgment. The best guarantee of judicial strictness, he had to concede, was to try all security-related cases at the Senate level.[67] He so stated in a formal proposal; on 7 June 1872, Alexander II issued a decree that limited glasnost' in political trials and required that a Special Bench of the Senate try all political crimes but one.[68] (The exception, that of "possessing illegal literature not yet distributed," remained at the Court of Appeals level.)

In the previous two years, Shuvalov had summarily sentenced about two hundred Nechaevists in near-secret. Court of Appeals judges, in full view of the world, had sentenced just thirty-four. The difference was administrative versus judicial proceedings under the 1864 reform; for, through the former, Shuvalov had covertly, swiftly, and independently dispatched persons he deemed dangerous to the state. That he also stirred criticism from the press did not seem to trouble him.

He kept his focus, rather, on shaping up the Gendarmes as security police, especially by implementing in Gendarme schools new curricula on the procedures and standards set by the 1864 statute, the new laws of 19 May, and the criminal code with respect to investigations and law enforcement. He also opened an elite Corps Preparatory School in Warsaw in 1873.[69]

That same year, Shuvalov used the seeming quiet to assess Gendarme education levels. Surveys of 486 commissioned officers showed that 3.5 percent had some higher education, 57 percent had a secondary education, 2.2 percent had some secondary education, 11.4 percent had some elementary education, and 25.9 per cent were schooled at home. Lower-rank literacy tests showed that 90 percent could read and write, 5 percent could read but not write, and 5 percent were illiterate.[70]

In reporting these good results, Shuvalov took full credit; for he never wavered in his cockiness and drive, traits much remarked upon by colleagues. Near-dictatorial ways were making him increasingly intolerable, however, to fellow officials and the tsar alike. Reasons for change were mounting, and they would reach their peak when, in 1874, Shuvalov would prove himself unwittingly remiss as security chief.

CHAPTER THREE

From the
Third Section to the
Department of Police

Within several years of the Nechaevist trials, security police would face the first violent revolutionaries, who, despite their small numbers and youth, sought to destroy the autocracy through terrorism. Calling themselves *narodniki*, or populists, they plotted and acted in secret, sometimes martyring themselves for their cause. The toll they took through repeated assassinations would force a reorganization of security operations in 1880; but, just as the popularist agitators were being fully contained, one of them would strike down their ultimate target, Alexander II.

Youth first took on a populist cause by joining the To-the-People Movement, a non-violent effort to radicalize the peasantry that caught the Third Section by surprise. In the spring of 1874, just as universities ended their school year, thousands of these youthful agents of change set out on their mission, well aware that they were breaking the law. Humbly garbed and armed with illegal tracts and false passports, they spread through thirty-seven provinces. Somehow these propagandists escaped government notice until the end of May, when a few were discovered in a Gendarme raid on a cobbler's shop in Saratov, along with boxes of revolutionary pamphlets marked "lemonade." Shuvalov at once placed the Gendarmes and all municipal police on alert, with many consequent detainments and the discovery of the illegal printing plant in Moscow that was providing tracts.

The tsar believed that the police should have had advance knowledge of the mass exodus from the university cities to the countryside, and he wanted counter measures. On 4 June 1874 he himself issued a new law raising the penalties for persons found guilty of participating in "illegal societies," a crime newly and broadly defined. His decree also empowered Gendarmes and police to arrest, not merely detain, suspected members of illegal societies because arrestees, unlike detainees, could be held in separate confinement – a means to prevent discussions among those in custody that might enable them jointly to "hide traces of their crimes."[1]

But because immediate arrest eliminated the preliminary inquiry, Gendarmes who arrested suspects automatically became part of the judicial investigation, a position which they believed put debilitating restrictions on their investigative work. Very likely Third Section objections to that shortcoming had, until the crisis of mid-1874, deferred adoption of the new law, which had been drafted earlier in response to the Nechaevist trials.

A month later, Shuvalov ended his eight-year tenure as security chief, having compounded his problems with the tsar by opposing the efforts to secure a railway concession by friends of Princess Catherine Dolgorukaia, the tsar's mistress.[2] (Shuvalov all along had been hostile to that well-known liaison because it shamed the tsarina and presented special problems for the security police.) Shuvalov accepted a respectable but lesser role as the tsar's ambassador to England, and insiders recognized at once that he had lost his place in the inner circle of power.

By the beginning of 1875, the number of orders for the arrest of suspected populist agitators totalled 750 (612 men and 158 women), but there were only 717 actual arrests. Because the alleged crimes were related to security provisions of the criminal code, the task of deciding which arrestees would go free, which would be punished administratively, and which would receive judicial indictments fell to the minister of justice, K.I. Pahlen, and the new head of the Third Section, Adjutant General A.L. Potapov. Wary caution by them, by the Gendarmes serving as investigators, and by the examining magistrates slowed the process to a crawl.

For the 267 youth who were ultimately indicted, confinement pending trial would last for a full three years, at least part of that time spent in the jail governed by the chief of the St Petersburg municipal police. So many would suffer derangement, death, or administrative exile in that waiting period that only 193 would finally stand trial – in what became known as the "Trial of the 193" – and three of them would die during the court's deliberations. That high human toll was widely publicized by foes in order to discredit the government.

How best to conduct the trials had faced the authorities from the first arrests, and, already in March of 1875, the Committee of Ministers met to ponder strategy. They decided in favour of glasnost' because publicizing the procurators' arguments and evidence would expose "the perniciousness of the [defendants'] expressed ideas and the degree of danger that flows from them."[3]

During this same year, Pahlen assessed the security implications of the populist agitators in an official report.[4] The Third Section should, he wrote, spread agents throughout society to detect and stifle subversives before they acted against the state. Gendarmes and security agents should, for example, monitor all self-education circles because radicals used such groups to inflame well-meaning persons into committing crimes.

Even more important, Pahlen urged that security agents infiltrate the secret cells of revolutionaries to enable the Third Section to foil their plots and arrest their members, a course that would, in a few years, become a major thrust of the tsarist security force. He left unexamined how such arrestees would be investigated and processed, just as he said nothing about his ongoing concern that Gendarmes, as Third Section agents, too often put security objectives above judicial standards during preliminary inquiries and, since 4 June 1874, judicial investigations.

Gendarmes agreed with Pahlen on their priorities and, in January of 1877, a twenty-year veteran of the corps named Bachmanov directly made that point in a report to the new head of the Third Section, General N.V. Mezentsov.[5] Having been asked to sum up the historic role of the Gendarmes, Bachmanov began with the days of true tsarist paternalism under Nicholas I when the corps had dealt on its own with wrongdoing as circumstances demanded. Then its role had been to serve as mediator between the government and the governed. Under Alexander II, he said, the Third Section had assigned to the Gendarmes two inappropriate tasks: spying and, even more onerous, conducting criminal investigations under procurators. The latter imposed upon the Gendarmes, complained Bachmanov, the niggling demands of a westernized judicial system that did not always punish wrongdoers.

During February and March 1877, open court proceedings that became known as the "Trial of the 50" took place before the Special Bench of the Senate to decide if fifty Moscow labour agitators had ties with an "illegal society" that was plotting to overthrow the government. So auspicious seemed its beginning sessions to Dmitry Miliutin, the minister of war, that on 24 February he applauded Pahlen for his strategy of glasnost' to combat the "anti-social doctrines that have attracted many superficially-minded people."[6] To Pahlen's satisfaction, only three of the defendants were acquitted. Of the rest, fifteen were convicted to one- to three-year terms of hard labour (a sentence commuted for the women), twenty-one to live in Siberia as exiles, and eleven to serve one- to four-year prison terms. Given these encouraging results, the Council of Ministers approved that the rules of procedure used in the Trial of the 50 govern the pending Trial of the 193.

At least one council member – the minister of foreign affairs, Prince A.M. Gorchakov – dissented, and he pointed to a flaw in the proceedings. As he explained to Pahlen, the speeches of the "self-possessed" defendants in the Trial of the 50 had struck him, and surely many other observers, as the product of "mature minds." Whereas Pahlen thought that the deliberations had convinced "our society and Europe that this was an affair of a little group of dreamers with a smattering of learning, and, with them, a few drunken peasants," Gorchakov regretted that "now Europe knows that the enemies of the government are not nullities, as you wanted to show."[7] His argument against fighting subversives in open trials before the court of public opinion was gaining supporters within the government.

By the time that the Trial of the 193 began in October 1877, also before the Special Bench, the Gendarmes had helped to interrogate over four thousand witnesses and suspects. Never had there been so lengthy a judicial preparation, and never had the courts been called upon to judge so many co-defendants in a single trial. Aware that the world was watching, officials recognized the critical need to convey through the proceedings that an aggrieved government was acting responsibly and justly.

Because the control of publicity – so far as officials could control it – was important, Pahlen chose a small courtroom for the court sessions and refused the defence attorneys' request for a larger one that would seat more observers from the public and the press. A few reporters did attend, but no private paper could print trial details beyond those already published in the official *Government Messenger*.

In its final verdicts of 23 January 1878, the Special Bench acquitted ninety of the 190 defendants still alive. For the four found guilty of organizing an illegal society, the judges handed down sentences of hard labour for as much as ten years. Varying terms of labour, prison, and exile (ranging from days to years) went to the rest for such crimes as belonging to an illegal society, knowing about but failing to report an illegal society, disseminating literature aimed at inciting rebellion, knowing about but failing to report this dissemination, and possessing illegal literature.

Third Section officials termed the trial results "lamentable" and laid blame on the examining magistrates who vetted evidence during the judicial investigation.[8] Whereas the Gendarmes had gathered sufficient grounds for convictions, they contended the magistrates had not only rejected too many of those findings but had also distorted or misstated the portion that they did present to the prosecutor. They therefore recommended that no political suspects undergo judicial investigation – meaning that they wanted all of them subjected to swift, covert processing by administrative panels that could base decisions on all the evidence that Gendarmes could gather.

What infuriated the Third Section were the negative effects for the government from the long-delayed public Trial of the 193. One, in particular, was the cause-effect connection between the public announcement of the verdicts on 23 January and, on the very next day, the attempt by a radical young woman, Vera Zasulich, to kill the military governor of St Petersburg, General F.F. Trepov.

Links between the two are certain, for radicals like Zasulich assumed that public knowledge of the deaths and sufferings of the students while held for trial had generated dislike for the government and, in particular, for the general in charge of their incarceration. Thus she targeted Trepov for his "brutality" to yet another student in St Petersburg jail.

Zasulich had fired the gun that wounded Trepov before witnesses in the reception room of his office, and guards had seized her immediately. When time came for laying a specific charge against her, however, officials had to choose between indicting her for the common crime of attempting to murder Trepov or for the political crime of attempting to assassinate him. In their determination to exclude politics entirely, given the furor set off by the Trial of the 193, they decided on the murder charge.

That choice meant proceeding at the normal juridical level, the Circuit Court, where a jury of citizens would decide the verdict. Having no doubts that that panel would readily convict Zasulich, officials welcomed the unlimited glasnost' of Circuit Court hearings because the publicizing of so despicable a crime would, they believed, discredit the entire radical movement. The government was sticking with the Pahlen strategy.

Never was there an imperial trial more sensational or widely covered by the press. Citizens, many of them from the upper classes, crowded the courtroom galleries each day, while some fifteen hundred students gathered outside to express their solidarity with Zasulich. Then, when his time came to address the court on his client's behalf, Zasulich's lawyer outmanoeuvred the state prosecutor by introducing politics. To argue Zasulich's innocence, he effectively counter-charged Trepov with unconscionable provocation. The military governor, stated the counsel, had ordered the cruel flogging of a radical named

Bogoliubov in the St Petersburg jail; and that inhumane act had caused in Zasulich a revulsion so extreme that it had overcome her reason and provoked her to attempt to kill Trepov. The tsar's official was guilty, not she.

The jury of minor officials and lay professionals fell in behind the defence on 31 March 1878 to pronounce Zasulich innocent, and observers in the galleries expressed their approval with loud applause. Because the Gendarmes could not rearrest her that day without written orders from the tsar (the autocrat alone could immediately overrule the verdict of a court), Zasulich was able to leave the courtroom and surround herself with supporters. When, with orders in hand, the Gendarmes did approach her outside the prison, where she had gone to collect belongings, friends staged a fracas that enabled Zasulich to slip away. She shortly fled to Switzerland.

Three days after the jury decision had so publicly discredited the government, Alexander II convened his Council of Ministers to ponder the handling of volatile political crimes. Minister of Justice Pahlen, who would step down the next month, had surprisingly advised the government to put such cases in the hands of those who would "do the bidding of authority."[9] In other words, his courts should not try security cases precisely because judicial panels made independent and, consequently, unpredictable decisions.

Still in search of a winning strategy against his political enemies, the tsar in late July 1878 called a Special Conference comprised of the new justice minister, D.N. Nabokov; an assistant minister of the interior; and the head of the Third Section, General Mezentsov. Arguing that the best offence against the revolutionaries was to penetrate their secret groups, especially in Khar'kov, Odessa, and Kiev, Mezentsov called for many more secret agents.[10] Infiltrators could discover not only the identity of revolutionaries but also their plans; agents who won the absolute trust of subversives could even prod them into acts that would outrage society against them. Finally, because local administrations lacked funds and local police lacked undercover skills, the Third Section alone should select, train, pay, and oversee all such double agents and provocateurs.

In its report to the tsar, the Special Conference called for more Gendarmes and secret agents, as well as for an end to certain restrictions on Gendarme investigations (one being the ban on impromptu searches of printing establishments), for tighter surveillance over persons sent into exile for political offences, and for stronger means to counter rampant anti-police propaganda.[11] In the midst of these deliberations, the tsar approved 400,000 rubles for the recommended increases in personnel.

Another government response was a special study commission under Senator E.V. Frish, which would meet in late 1878 and again in 1881. The commission endorsed increasing powers of the Gendarmes during the initial inquiry of a political investigation and the involvement of the courts only if a case were airtight. It also gathered figures to establish that administrative processing of cases required on average from two to three years, whereas almost exactly the same amount of time was necessary to bring in a judicial indictment, which then would be followed by a trial.[12]

When, in May 1878, Staff Captain G.E. Geking, the adjutant to the head of the Kiev Gendarme command, had been killed by an assassin who managed to elude his pursuers, Colonel V.D. Novitsky, the head of the Kiev command, warned Mezentsov that he could expect an attack on his person in the near future. Mezentsov had brusquely replied that his own authority and that of the Third Section "is so extensive that any such suggestion is in the realm of fantasy and country women's babble and not in the realm of reality."[13] Such hubris was to prove fatal. On 4 August Stepan Kravchinsky stabbed Mezentsov to death at midday on a street not far from Fontanka 16. Before fleeing abroad, Kravchinsky described the motives for the attack in a pamphlet that others distributed through the mails. His justification was the Zasulich defence: the brutality of Mezentsov, as overseer when the last of the populist students died awaiting trial, had provoked the retaliation.[14]

Again, the weaknesses in the security system were shown to a wide audience, for the regular and security police got nowhere in producing suspects. When Mezentsov's temporary replacement as head of the Third Section, General N.D. Seliverstov, reported to Alexander II that "everything is calm in the city, the investigation is proceeding energetically, but so far has not been as successful as one would hope," the tsar wrote in the margin, "So far I see not a single result." Seliverstov was more candid in assessing the security police for his colleague, Miliutin; he confessed that the police system was "in a pitiful condition" for lack of able persons and funding.[15]

Four days after the death of Mezentsov, the Council of Ministers and the tsar approved the recommendations of the Special Conference but left their implementation "for the future."[16] Meeting one day later, the Committee of Ministers decreed that military courts try all persons who physically attacked officials in any way or who used armed resistance against them. Suspects would there be subject to quick, closed trials, with no possibility of appeals.[17]

Through imperial legislation of 1 September 1878, the Gendarmes, who before could arrest persons suspected of belonging to an illegal society, won the added right to arrest anyone whom they thought linked to political offences of any kind or to "assemblies and demonstrations of a political nature."[18] In turn, justified by what they saw as "sufficient evidence," the head of the Third Section and the minister of the interior could together exile persons so arrested, having merely to inform the minister of justice of what they had done.

Although the law directed the two high officials and the Gendarmes to use their new discretionary powers solely against political suspects, abuses could easily occur. But that possibility seemed insignificant to harried and even panicked officials who might next confront an assassin. To them, these times of extraordinary threats justified extraordinary political investigations. These necessary expedients minister of war Miliutin approved, recording in his memoirs his own view, shared by many, that the Mezentsov assassination was part of a "satanic plan ... to terrorize the entire government; and this plan is beginning to succeed."[19]

General Selivestrov, still temporary head of the Third Section, on 25 September issued secret instructions to his Gendarmes to explain the law of 1 September and to underscore that they must use their additional arrest powers with care.[20] Any "superficial" arrests that wrongly deprived citizens of their freedom, he warned, would "arouse public opinion against the government." As for the post-arrest processing of political suspects, the state would continue to use administrative means only when evidence was inadmissible in a judicial court – that is, when it had been obtained by secret means or could not be exactly confirmed. In all cases based on evidence admissible in court, the law of 19 May 1871 remained in effect.

Given the growing number of secret operatives – whether outside agents (detectives who did surveillance) or inside agents (infiltrators or double agents) – and the growing quantity of their intelligence, Selivestrov went on to explain that evidence obtained by secret means would have major importance in the fight against political crimes. Whenever there was the slightest possibility that secret evidence might surface to prove a suspect's guilt, the state justifiably had to use administrative, not judicial, processing.[21]

By means of these several changes in the fall of 1878, the government expanded its system for dealing with political offenders outside the judicial system. From one perspective, these measures were an attack on the reforms of 1864; but from another, they protected a judicial system on the verge of arousing enormous opposition within the government. Sharing that second view, justice minister Pahlen had initiated several revisions of the statute of 1864 and had gone outside the bounds of his ministry to advocate changes in the security police.

In October 1878, General Alexander Romanovich Drentel'n became head of the Third Section, and one of his first acts was to advise against any further efforts to convince Swiss authorities to extradite Vera Zasulich to Russia. The government of Switzerland had already refused to do so on the grounds that Zasulich had been duly exonerated of the charges against her by an imperial court of law. Any further attempt to return her for a new trial was counterproductive, Drentel'n successfully argued, because highly disruptive protest demonstrations would certainly follow and would cost the government public support.[22]

In mid-November, following up on the recommendations of the Council of Ministers, the Committee of Ministers sought to remedy two other problems, but only with respect to the local police.[23] It provided funds to increase the local police in nine "centres of agitation" and the plain-clothes detectives within the local police in all but a few remote provinces. In addition, it ruled that political exiles be sent to Irkutsk, in Siberia, because persons exiled to closer cities too often illegally returned to the capital cities to rejoin their radical comrades.

As 1878 drew to a close, Drentel'n understood that attempts to strengthen the police over the previous several months had been uncoordinated; he now joined with other officials to discuss the centralization of police forces to improve the effectiveness of the fight against revolutionaries. Seen as necessary was an entirely new administration, perhaps a Ministry of Police, to absorb the "Separate Corps of Gendarmes" but to supplant the Third Section. So far, all the special conferences had only produced recommendations to extend, stiffen, and tighten the existing system of political police, while the revolutionaries, or self-proclaimed narodniki, had seemed to grow in numbers and audacity.

One of them tried to kill Drentel'n himself in March 1879. Less than a month later, on 2 April, Alexander Soloviev, another narodnik, fired three shots at Alexander II as he left the Winter Palace, and only bad aim saved the tsar's life. The government responded on 5 April by naming temporary governors-general in St Petersburg, Khar'kov, and Odessa. To them and to governors-general in Moscow, Warsaw, and Kiev went special powers of arrest and censorship.[24]

Within months, in the summer of 1879, the underground revolutionary party, People's Will, combined a number of radical cells into a single terrorist organization. As conspirators, these narodniki sharply differed from the naive radicals whom police had so easily rounded up when they went to the people in 1874. To move freely and anonymously, for example, the narodniki forged internal passports for themselves that bore false names. They used the proper forms, an archive of official signatures, and appropriate stamps and seals.

People's Will also placed an agent of its own within the Third Section. The idea belonged to Alexander Mikhailov, a leader of People's Will and a revolutionary of iron will and absolute convictions. Back in 1878, he had met Nicholas Kletochnikov, a sickly, leftist provincial, adrift in his mid-thirties, and had sensed his longing for a noble commitment. Mikhailov had therefore convinced Kletochnikov that he could be enormously useful if he would join the Third Section and inform on its activities. On Mikhailov's advice, Kletochnikov had taken rooms adjacent to those of a Third Section officer's widow and then cultivated her. Through her ministrations and influence, he had become a valued specialist in the Third Section in 1879 and had gravitated into its political department, the Third Secretariat, later that same year.

As a trusted insider, Kletochnikov was able to copy the most secret documents and pass them on to People's Will, and he used his extraordinary ability for memorization to the same end. Lev Tikhomirov, the terrorist, personally dealt with Kletochnikov and credited him with an impressive capacity for detail. "He studied with strong interest and devotion, and his notes about the matters that passed before him had the quality of those of a talented novelist. He passed on not only names and pseudonyms of agents, but even striking portraits of each of them, wonderfully capsulized in a few words. He described their physical features, character, and habits."[25]

Kletochnikov would move to the Third Section's successor agency in 1880 and avoid detection as a radical spy until January of 1881. In his subsequent statements to interrogators and the judges who would convict him of treason, he would claim not to have known that he was dealing with terrorists. Although his death sentence would be commuted to life imprisonment, he would die behind bars in 1883.

Meanwhile, in August 1879 Alexander II had again nearly fallen victim to an assassin. In a widely publicized follow-up, People's Will made the chilling announcement that it had condemned the tyrant tsar to death. The group gained yet more notoriety in November when several of its terrorists used dynamite, the recent invention of Alfred Nobel, to blow up the train that they mistakenly thought was carrying the tsar.

A still greater impact would result three months later from the assassination attempt by Stepan Khalturin, who, by securing a position as a mechanic at the Winter Palace, had managed to smuggle several pounds of dynamite into the basement of the palace, two floors below the imperial dining room. While Khalturin was making his preparations, Third Section agents arrested a leader of People's Will, A.A. Kviatkovsky, and found among his papers a plan for the Winter Palace with the imperial dining room marked by an X. Police at once conducted a surprise nighttime search in the mechanics' quarters but missed the dynamite that Khalturin was concealing under his pillow. On 4 February 1880, he lit a fuse and walked out of the palace. The huge explosion destroyed the guard room immediately below the dining room, killed eleven persons, and injured fifty-six more, but the blast entirely missed the tsar and his circle. They had not yet entered the dining room, which, in any case, suffered little damage.

Intended to kill the tsar, the dynamite put an end to the Third Section by forcing Alexander to reorganize his security forces. Named to impose central control over all security personnel was his new Supreme Executive Committee for the Preservation of State Order and Public Tranquillity. Given dictatorial powers as its head was Count Mikhail T. Loris-Melikov, a distinguished general in the Russo-Turkish War of 1877–8. Although he soon became known as "vice-Emperor," Loris-Melikov would show a commitment to reform that would prompt many to term his time in office a "dictatorship of the heart."

Loris-Melikov asserted his authority by ordering Drentel'n on 26 February to hand over to the Supreme Commission all political cases and supporting materials.[26] In addition, he gave the commission command over all security forces and mandated pushing agents hard to get results.[27] With quick dispatch, the commission itself set an example by reviewing and deciding five hundred political cases between 18 March and 21 July 1880.[28] Meanwhile Loris-Melikov imposed sharper limits on the outside agents whom Dolgorukov had hidden within the St Petersburg police two decades before to track and report every move and contact of suspected subversives. Loris-Melikov believed that Imperial Russia faced an historic turning point and that institutional reform, especially with respect to police work, was essential.[29]

In ceremonial gestures, Alexander II had assigned authority over the Third Section to Loris-Melikov on 3 March 1880 and over the Corps of Gendarmes the following day. The general confessed that, prior to his audience with the tsar at which these important questions were to be decided, he was more agitated than he was just before the storming of the strong Turkish fortress at Kars in the Caucasus mountains.

To commission member I.I. Shamshin went the task of inspecting the Third Section and identifying its weaknesses. He found that investigative reports were badly compiled, sometimes carried home, and often scattered around headquarters. Despite its lack of data on underground organizations, moreover, the Third Section was remarkably well informed about the personal lives of ministers and other high officials.[30]

Concerned that ambiguous terms in the emergency statute of 1 September 1878 would continue to plague anti-subversion efforts, state secretary M.S. Kakhanov in March advised Loris-Melikov that justice minister Nabokov should spell out precisely those special circumstances that freed the Gendarmes from strictly judicial methods of inquiry.[31] Nabokov had been in office when the problematic law was drafted and declined now to clarify it. Rather, he took a stand against allowing "the rank and file of the Gendarmes to conduct investigations of arrested persons" – a reference to the Gendarmes' emergency authority to arrest, rather than merely detain, political suspects. Each time they resorted to that authority, objected Nabokov, the Gendarmes effectively commandeered what should be the judicial investigation – an implicit complaint that they thereby made a judicial trial impossible. But, he admitted, even before the Statute of 1 September 1878, the procuracy had never effectively controlled the Gendarmes' political investigations.[32]

For the chairman of the Supreme Administrative Commission, here was one more example of the failure of individual institutions to work for the good of the whole, for solidarity and a single governing idea. Loris-Melikov therefore deemed it an "urgent necessity" that all police agents, state and local, overt and covert, come together as one department within the Ministry of the Interior.[33] (That ministry already governed the local police through the provincial governors.) He also proposed to the tsar that he abolish the Supreme Commission and its emergency rule and appoint him minister of the interior. In other words, Loris-Melikov voluntarily gave up dictatorial powers for authority over a huge bureaucratic apparatus, although with his reformist objectives in mind.

Alexander II complied on 6 August 1880, naming no less than state secretary Kakhanov as an assistant minister to Loris-Melikov. At the same time the tsar created the Department of State Police and transferred to it all needed functions and able personnel of the defunct Third Section. For several months that department coexisted with a Department of Administrative Police, but in November the two merged at Fontanka 16 as a single Department of State Police. Named as director was Baron I.O. Velio, a civil servant without experience in police work who had for many years headed the Department of Post and Telegraph. Of the seventy-one officials of the old Third Section, twenty-one joined the new organization, including Kletochnikov, the spy for the narodniki.

As had been their role since 1825, the Gendarmes remained a Ministry of War contingent whose members dually served as militiamen and political police. Henceforth the intelligence they gathered was to go directly to the Department of State Police and also, as the tsar had ordered on 10 March, to the governors of the province where they served. A typical warning would again soon be voiced that the Gendarmes must be "fully subordinated to [Department of State Police] supervision in everything that touches police service."[34] But, again, no such change would take place.

To focus the Police Department strictly on fighting crimes, both ordinary and political, the government transferred elsewhere inspection duties and other peripheral responsibilities of the former Third Section. In further trimming, the reformers established only three secretariats (their number would rise to five by 1883 and to nine by 1910). The first managed the department's budgets and personnel; the second monitored non-government establishments (ranging from monasteries to taverns) and passports; and the third handled political investigations that were significant enough to "attract the attention of the government." Organizers also set up a Judicial Section equivalent to the Third Section's Legal Advisory Office, but it would disappear within a year. While it lasted, this office decided which cases should be forwarded to the judiciary.

As this year ended and the next began, People's Will suffered a series of setbacks. In November, eleven months after their failed palace explosion, the plotters floated dynamite in place under a St Petersburg bridge only to have the detonator fail at the crucial moment when Alexander II passed above. That same month, imperial security agents captured Mikhailov, a People's Will leader, thanks largely to the help of a captured narodnik, Grigory Gol'denberg, the assassin of the governor-general of Khar'kov. Loris-Melikov had helped win him over as an informer.

Taken into custody in January 1881 was a dedicated terrorist in the People's Will, Ivan Okladsky, who, when threatened with a long sentence of hard labour, agreed to switch his allegiance to the tsar. Soon after he revealed the locations of two apartments, one printing plant, and one dynamite factory belonging to his former comrades. He would enter imperial service as a secret agent and play that role for the next thirty-seven years.[35] In January, as well, the revolutionaries lost their eyes and ears at Fontanka 16 because their spy Kletochnikov was exposed.

At the end of February came the arrest of the top strategist for People's Will, Andrey Zheliabov. The police had been able to take him into custody once he entered an apartment that was already under surveillance as a known meeting place for conspirators.

Political investigations that enabled the state to incarcerate such foes as Mikhailov, Kletochnikov, Okladsky, and Zheliabov had proved highly worthwhile. Far less significant – even counter-productive, an assistant to Loris-Melikov argued – were time-consuming investigations of the political crime of slandering the tsar, the charge that lay behind half of the 1,020 trials for crimes of all kinds between 1875 and 1880.[36] Most offenders of article 246 of the criminal code, this assistant further pointed out, were simple folk made rash by strong drink. But his appeal for downgrading the offence from criminal status, made in a report dated 4 November 1880, would go nowhere.

With the arrest of Zheliabov, almost none of the experienced leadership of People's Will remained at large. Nonetheless, on 1 March 1881, narodniki struck down Alexander II near the Catherine Canal in St Petersburg. Although the first bomb thrown had stopped his carriage but not harmed the tsar, several members of the royal convoy were wounded. As Alexander approached the injured guards, a second bomb exploded at his feet, inflicting fatal wounds. He died the same day.

Blaming the security forces for failing to provide adequate protection, well-placed residents of St Petersburg formed a "Temporary Committee" in March under the municipal governor, Major-General N.M. Baranov, to bolster safeguards for the new tsar, Alexander III. (They expected to "control the police," a former minister of the interior surmised.[37]) A leader from the outset was Count I.I. Vorontsov-Dashkov, the head of the *Okhrana*, or palace guard. In deference to the committee, he established a new unit of bodyguards to accompany the new tsar wherever he went.

Trial proceedings against six narodniki charged with the assassination began on 26 March before the Special Bench, which had been inactive since 1878. Three days later, that court sentenced all six to death for regicide, one of them a woman. She alone escaped hanging on 3 April because she was pregnant, her sentence later being commuted to life imprisonment.

Alexander II's death proved an especial catastrophe for Loris-Melikov. Several hours before the bombs went off, the tsar had approved naming from gentry and commercial circles two commissions to work out legislative proposals. Put forward by Loris-Melikov, he had considered it a logical completion of the reforms of the 1860s.

Opponents in the government, led by K.P. Pobedonostsev, condemned this modest proposal as a first step towards parliamentary government. They also insisted to Alexander III that the reforms of the 1860s had led to his father's death and convinced him to reject the interior minister's project. On 29 April Loris-Melikov resigned and was replaced by Nikolai P. Ignat'ev, a former ambassador to Constantinople who had negotiated the Peace of San Stefano with Turkey in 1878.

To reserve to his ministry all Gendarme intelligence, Ignat'ev abolished the 1880 order of Alexander III that Gendarmes also report their findings to their respective governors. In turn he wrote the Statute on Measures for the Protection of State Security and Public Tranquillity. A special commission under Kakhanov worked out the details of the project, finally promulgated by Alexander III on 14 August 1881. This legislation, introduced for a three-year period, provided measures for two kinds of emergencies that will shortly be discussed and was repeatedly renewed until 1917.[38]

Scholars often cite the 1881 law as a prime example of the desperate and excessive use of administrative power by the imperial regime in its twilight years. Historian P.A. Zaionchkovsky, for example, writes: "The publication of this statute was not only symptomatic of the crisis of the autocracy, but also of the instability of the political system in general."[39] Marc Szeftel calls the statute an over-reaction to the assassination and argues that the government repeatedly renewed it because of its "reluctance to give up repressive power" and its "basic distrust of the Russian population, especially of the educated class."[40] Such arguments, however, fail to credit the pragmatic character of the statute on emergencies. The government, having been caught off guard by terrorism in the 1870s, required some means of anticipating more such politically coercive violence and forestalling its harmful effect on public opinion. Both had been the main purposes of Loris-Melikov's reforms in the security system.

In the aftermath of the assassination, moreover, the government had to quell not just the revolutionary movement but also the unpredictable flashes of violence known as pogroms. In May 1881 such assaults on Jews and their property broke out in several cities and erupted elsewhere in the summer and fall. The new law was as useful against these threats to security as it was against terrorism.

Under the 1881 statute, the interior minister could employ "intensified security" during emergencies of two kinds: first, when attacks actually occurred against the state, persons or property and ordinary laws were inadequate for the circumstances; and secondly, when he deemed such attacks imminent – as he could choose to do at any time for cause. To determine the extent of special measures in either instance, the minister also had to decide whether the public was "alarmed" or merely "disturbed." He could seek the tsar's approval for his plan of action through the Committee of Ministers, if he thought it necessary.

The minister of the interior, then, had open-ended authorization to take emergency measures appropriate to the public mood. Most important and wholly new, he was, to the best of his ability, to anticipate disruptions and consequent downturns in public opinion and respond accordingly. Among his array of powers, he could close down publications, prohibit meetings, fire officials, set up provisional institutions, close schools, and detain suspects. He could, in other words, make pre-emptive strikes to prevent possible disorder, a right that gave him immense leeway to limit freedoms.

Emergency periods thus expanded his powers, while those of the judiciary contracted. The Gendarmes and police could, for example, detain suspects for up to two weeks without recourse to the judiciary and could extend pre-trial detention to one month on the order of a governor or a mayor. The minister of the interior could require the courts to transfer cases already in their hands to military tribunals.[41] He, or a governor-general, could also organize special "military-police teams to assist the existing police bodies."

Other provisions permitted introducing features of the security system to provinces neighbouring on those under emergency law or even to other places in the Empire if approved by the Committee of Ministers. In instances of crimes against the state, the minister of the interior could seek agreement of the minister of justice to set up military courts elsewhere.

In 1881 military courts would conduct sixty-six trials for crimes that undermined security (including eleven for attacks against the state and fifty for attacks against Jews or their property). In 1882 also, most trials in military courts (thirty-one out of forty) would concern pogroms. By deciding these sensitive cases in closed military hearings, the state avoided publicity of any kind.[42]

The government prosecuted forty-two of the seventy-three trials of persons affiliated with People's Will in the early 1880s in the military tribunals, but thereafter the number of such trials fell off markedly. Between 1885 and 1903 the state prosecuted only seventeen cases involving civilians in the military courts and eleven of those cases concerned espionage. From the record, the imperial government employed the provisions for military courts under the statute of 14 August 1881 mainly to sentence members of People's Will in the 1880's.[43]

To institutionalize administrative "trials," the August legislation created a new body and mode of operations that, once again, vested greater authority in the Ministry of the Interior than in the Ministry of Justice. Henceforth a five-man Special Conference (three members, including the chairman, from Interior; two members from Justice) sentenced suspects on the basis of their "protocol" – that is, a record of the life, health, and conduct of each prepared by the Fourth Secretariat newly set up within the Department of State Police to serve the Special Conference. The Fourth Secretariat also directed the investigations of suspects by police and Gendarmes and incorporated their findings into protocols. (Under the new law, the minister of the interior could detain a suspect beyond the new two-week maximum if more time were needed to prepare that suspect's protocol.)

In the nearly two decades from 1881 to 1900, the Special Conference would decide 7,159 cases involving 11,879 persons. According to police records, most cases involved "depraved behaviour" (46 percent) and "political unreliability" (41 percent), both terms suggesting conduct that was not strictly criminal. The rest fell within the categories of "factory disorders" (5 percent), "agrarian disorders" (5 percent), and "sectarian propaganda" (3 percent).[44] Another set of police records, from July 1881 to January 1888, compares convictions of political offenders by the Special Conference (2,872) with those by the judiciary (224). Among those convicted by the conference, just over half were exiled to European Russia, nearly a quarter to Siberia, and the rest (but for nineteen foreign nationals who were deported) were given lesser penalties. Court sentences for convicted political criminals were harsher: death (9 percent), hard labour (57 percent), Siberian exile (20.5 percent), and lesser penalties (13.5 percent).[45]

By 1881 increasing activities of the security organizations of Imperial Russia had expanded the demands for investigative information on which to make decisions in security cases. The Gendarmes had therefore grown in importance, and the preliminary inquiry and judicial investigation, the first two stages in a case proceeding to judicial trial, had by the end of the reign of Alexander II become separated. The supervising prosecutor of the Senate, N.A. Nekliudov, wrote: "The business of the inquiry and the business of the preliminary investigation are so different from one another that they require different people and different knowledge."[46] He explained that the information produced during the inquiry was simply "inaccessible" and "unfit" for court because it was not properly prepared and documented for judicial purposes.

By August, when the new security statute took effect, the unofficial Temporary Committee of March had spawned a 729-member Holy Bodyguard (*Druzhina*) made up largely of aristocrats. Within a year it would boast a Volunteer Guard of fifteen thousand recruits and four active units of spies, termed the Agentura (agency) – one in each of the capitals, one on the railways, and one abroad.[47] Because many officials belonged, this private and ostensibly secret brotherhood had close links with the government; an approving tsar seems to have given it one million rubles from court funds.

Vorontsov-Dashkov, a long-time friend of the tsar, had emerged as the head of the Druzhina; in the second half of 1881 he joined the top circles in government as minister of the Imperial Court. When a Druzhina colleague, General Cherevin, succeeded him as head of the palace guard, Vorontsov convinced Cherevin to seek imperial permission to combine his previous role with his new one – that is, to oversee both the Department of State Police and the Okhrana. But, sensing a strategic move by the *Druzhina*, Minister of Interior Ignat'ev stepped in to dissuade the tsar from any such fusion. However diplomatically he spoke, Ignat'ev privately agreed with a subordinate's assessment of the meddlesome brotherhood as a "mob under protection."[48]

Believing he enjoyed the full confidence of Alexander III, Ignat'ev at this time proposed summoning a *Zemskii Sobor*, or Assembly from the Land, an institution which had not met since the seventeenth century. (When called by the tsars in the late medieval period, the Zemskii Sobor had provided a forum for discussion of questions of high state policy by delegates who initially were named by the separate estates and later by the government.) Alarmed conservatives accused Ignat'ev of trying to revive the constitutional proposals of the era of the "dictatorship of the heart" and forced him from office. Name as successor on 30 May 1882 was Count Dmitry Andreevich Tolstoy, an education minister during the previous reign who had resisted measures to use education to break down class barriers. Tolstoy believed strongly in preserving the status quo.

Ignat'ev had already set police work on a new course. Political investigations by non-uniformed state agents had grown dramatically since the assassination of Alexander II. Increased surveillance of the public was now being conducted by outside agents,[49] and more inside agents were infiltrating subversive groups. Now both secretly served the newly-named successor of the Third Section, the Division for the Protection of Order and Social Security, over time to be commonly known as the Okhranka.*

---

* Because the division bore the Russian name *Otdelenie po okhraneniiu poriadka i obshchestvennoi bezopasnosti*, common usage would shorten that name to *okhrannoe otdelenie*, or security division, for over subsequent years, other locales came to have such a division. All of these *okhrannoe otdelenie* plus their command post, the Special Section (which would be set up in the Department of Police in the 1890s), came to be known to officials and the public alike as the Okhranka. Many historians use the word Okhrana, which was the formal name of the particular unit that guarded the imperial family. The authors have maintained the distinction between the two words.

When he became minister, Tolstoy made an off-the-record acknowledgment of the nature of the security force that had come under his command by appointing an "Inspector of the Secret Police"[50] – an official never publicly mentioned and one whose salary was never listed in documents within the ministry. Among his duties, moreover, this overseer of secret political investigations was empowered to go anywhere he saw problems of security and to assume complete control over the police and Gendarmes there. At the close of 1882, to show the autocracy once more in firm control, the tsar, at Tolstoy's insistence, shut down the Druzhina as no longer useful to the state. His government now deployed a centralized security agency so secret, well-staffed, and well-funded that it would keep the revolutionary movement in check for the rest of the century.

PART TWO

Structure, Methods, Agents

CHAPTER FOUR

The Okhranka as a Compiler of Information

In its war against revolutionaries after 1881, the collective security force known as the Okhranka combined time-honoured spying with the new police science of data quantification. Through surveillance and infiltration, its agents in the field searched out and reported political suspects of all kinds. That intelligence, in turn, went through systematic processing at headquarters, where analysts compressed it onto standardized forms that clerks could store and retrieve in a hurry. Officers assumed that the bigger their bank of data, the better could the Okhranka detect and thwart those planning crimes against the state. Their primary needs, therefore, were many agents and file cabinets, along with a secret and secure base of operations. The Department of Police provided the latter in its official building on 16 Fontanka in St Petersburg; it also furnished many of the full-time, plain-clothes operatives who formed the core of the Okhranka.

Full-time covert operatives who served across the Empire were mainly of three kinds: loners in the field, officers, and technical specialists, either at central headquarters in St Petersburg or at regional offices. The loners included the large group called outside agents (detectives) and a new elite known as inside agents (the infiltrators). The officers included heads of local offices of the Okhranka and the controllers of agents. The technical specialists included code-breakers, archivists, data analysts, as well as the part-time perlustrators (mail interceptors) in the post office.

Making up the Okhranka's front line were the detectives. These outside sleuths, all men, mingled with the public to spot and then monitor those suspected of being enemies of the tsar. The conscientious worked irregular hours, and often sacrificed both meals and sleep. Ideally they met the rigours of their work with a sound body and calmly retentive mind, and with a fierce loyalty to the tsar. Supervisors, nonetheless, complained that too many mediocrities worked in the corps and hampered its work.

Upheld as the supreme example was E.P. Mednikov, who honed his detecting skills in Moscow and St Petersburg in the 1880s and who was credited with helping to destroy the radical People's Will early in that same decade. Mednikov exemplified the unobtrusive but tenacious gumshoe who never lost sight of his quarry, even if it meant catching a horse-drawn cab or a train at a moment's notice, whatever its destination. On home territory, he never got lost because he committed the names and locations of streets to memory, just as he schooled himself in each area's mix of businesses and habitations. This Old Believer and former police inspector was, in the words of a colleague, a "simple, semi-literate man" driven by "native intelligence, sharpness, cunning, a capacity for work, and persistence." For him, success in detecting boiled down to "systematic work."[1]

Mednikov collared his first criminal in 1882 when he apprehended a deserter from the navy, one Sergei Sosin, who had been living under a forged passport with a woman in Moscow. Within a month, he had found two political radicals, Anatoly and Olga Bulanov, who had falsely registered under the name Vorobiev. Although the pair briefly eluded him by moving to another apartment, Mednikov tracked them down; then, instead of arresting them, Mednikov began a watch that netted three "state criminals." In the next month, he nabbed a "known terrorist" in his "conspiratorial apartment" – Iury Bogdanovich, living illegally as one Prozorovsky. Follow-up surveillance by Mednikov and two agents of the Moscow Okhranka led to the break-up of "an entire passport bureau" and the discovery of an arsenal of weapons.

Following new leads, Mednikov leased rooms next to those of Nadezhda Andreeva and Alexandra Orlova, and spent two months identifying all their callers. Arrests resulted for a number so incriminated, one being Savely Zlatopolsky, whom Mednikov happened to recognize in a chance encounter on the street. Learning that Zlatopolsky had just come from another apartment that housed an escaper from Siberian exile, Mednikov pursued the fugitive that evening and arrested him as he attempted to flee Moscow by train.

So exemplary was his record that, in 1883, Mednikov won a major assignment: to spend five months ridding Moscow of anyone who might disrupt or terrorize the coronation of Alexander III. In 1884, when the first revolutionary brochures of the "Students' Union" appeared, Mednikov commenced watching "unreliable persons" in Moscow and identified the printing source as the legal shop of one

Iankovsky. In April detectives searched the print shop and uncovered a store of illegal literature.

As his next exploit, Mednikov again staked out an apartment, this time because the tenant "drew attention to himself by the cautiousness and circumspection of his behaviour." The suspect turned out to be an illegal, Stanislav Mikhailevich, who, when confronted with arrest, resisted by throwing soda in the eyes of Mednikov and striking out with an umbrella against a second agent. The two detectives nonetheless prevailed before the miscreant could get at the dagger in his belt or the pistol in his pocket.[2]

At the request of his superiors, Mednikov later agreed to set up a school for detectives in Moscow and to organize an elite and ultimately renowned flying squad of detectives for hard-to-crack cases anywhere in the realm. Insisting that his recruits be army veterans because the fight against revolutionaries often turned brutal, he demanded "high levels of self-assertiveness and courage" in his investigators, along with "resourcefulness and ingenuity." Besides being clever and tough, the detective that met Mednikov's highest standard was self-effacing and never conspicuous. He kept his voice, dress, and manner quiet. He shifted his gaze constantly. Because the eyes are the most memorable part of the face, Mednikov taught, the good detective tells his controller at once about any eye contact with the quarry that could be compromising. Mednikov also tabooed strong drink, and he warned against any "excessive tenderness to family or weakness for women."[3]

Detectives-in-training sat through lessons partly on the doctrines and tactics of subversives but mostly on how to perform as outside agents. Drills focused on such problems as staying under cover. If a detective chose to watch a building while parked at the curb as a cab driver, for example, how should he explain his lingering to a curious doorman or his unavailability to would-be passengers? He should plausibly say that he awaited a doctor attending a patient. Repeatedly stressed was one cardinal rule: "The Okhranka wants the truth." It required the detective to mail each day an exact report on where suspects went, whom they met, what they did, with a summary at week's end. Top secrets he was to pass to his controller, usually his lone contact, in a discreet rendezvous well away from headquarters. When one director of the Department of Police discovered that detectives were walking in the front door of the Fontanka building to drop off reports, he quickly reminded agents that such short-cuts were simply impermissible.

Fully instructed, each trainee rehearsed the fine art of detecting in simulated situations on the street, and then proved he could file a report that met the rules. He had to remember, for instance, always to refer to suspects by code names only. If his solo performance satisfied his trainer, he joined the corps and acquired a cover or code name of his own.

Competence among detectives ranged widely, as did standards for their selection and training in the far-flung Okhranka network. According to one first-hand witness, most detectives were analytically "little developed, almost illiterate," and wrote "with difficulty."[4] Those deficiencies plus low pay, difficult conditions, open assignments, and indirect supervision gave plenty of cause for indifferent detecting. Some operatives were sloppy in reporting information; some even invented reports to demonstrate that they were hard at work. Despite the limitations, however, the Okhranka valued detectives enough to increase their numbers year by year.

Elite inside agents, on the other hand, opened a new intelligence front after 1880. Loners in the strictest sense, these hand-picked men and women went behind the lines to penetrate the hidden command posts of the revolutionary enemy. They appeared in the guise of co-conspirators. So often had faceless terrorists killed officials that the imperial government, for the first time, gave high priority to gathering intelligence by means of these double agents. They were so successful that they became the pride of the Okhranka.

Inside agents had to make their way onto the territory of the enemy by winning acceptance as terrorists themselves. They were required to operate under strict rules and could never relax their guard. Only with express permission from their superiors in the Okhranka could they use illegal weaponry and distribute illegal literature. Should they commit a criminal act without prior approval, they were subject to prosecution. (Should they be caught in a group arrest of subversives, on the other hand, the Okhranka eased them into safety in ways that did not make their radical comrades suspicious.) Barred from having a wide circle of friends and owning frivolous possessions, these disciplined, self-restrained agents were not unlike monastics. Each inside agent swore to report nothing but the truth, used code names for himself and others, dealt in secret with a single Okhranka contact – his case officer or controller – and forfeited his job if he lost his cover or credibility. He or she dealt with pressures and risks on a daily basis. The controller therefore constantly tested both the reports and the psychological state of his agents. Given the stresses, the inside agent usually retired within two years, or sooner, if his controller insisted.

Overseers of the infiltration units, says Zhilinsky, were the "intelligentsia of the police."[5] Some of them were educated liberals who favoured gradual reform and felt some respect for the commitment of the radicals, but not for their methods. When it came to psychological warfare, however, these same officials were keen to fight back with covert tactics chosen by the revolutionaries themselves. Infiltration would serve to demoralize conspirators by eroding their trust in their own operations and in one another. Deft interrogation to "convert" captured revolutionaries would accomplish the same end.

In the early 1880s, Colonel G.P. Sudeikin of the St Petersburg Okhranka, who would lose his life in the course of duty, stood out as a dedicated practitioner of psychological warfare. "The struggle against the nihilists was for him something like a passion," testified a contemporary.[6] In confronting persons zealously principled, his tactic was to prick their consciences with disarming reasonableness.[7]

One of Sudeikin's cases involved a hapless radical named Grebencho who suffered expulsion as an auditor at St Petersburg University for demonstrating there in February 1881.[8] Grebencho, a Bessarabian, was "older than the average university student, very dark, but with a completely shaved head, with eyes smouldering like live coals." Most acquaintances shied away from him because he seemed a complete misfit, even among revolutionaries. He was compulsive, impatient with discussions of theory, and "dedicated to the use of the dagger." When Grebencho travelled to the south of Russia to assist in the murder of a government prosecutor, Strelnikov, who was hated by the revolutionaries, he realized on the return trip that at least four government agents were tailing him. On Sudeikin's orders, he was not arrested until the morning after he reached the capital, the delay intended to impress on Grebencho that the all-seeing Okhranka felt free to toy with him.

According to a comrade who recorded what happened, Sudeikin knew that Grebencho had no wish to help the government. Focusing instead on Grebencho's poverty, Sudeikin thrust money into the pocket of his captive and riffled through a stack of rubles to show that more would be forthcoming. Never would he ask Grebencho to reveal the names of his comrades, but Grebencho should understand that high officials, whom Sudeikin named, had long-term reform plans for the imperial autocracy that terrorist attacks were undermining. If only Grebencho would give advance warning of planned terrorist attacks, Sudeikin could head them off and stop needless bloodshed.

Let free to ponder, Grebencho consulted his comrade and returned to Sudeikin with the story that the shattered state of his nerves had caused his revolutionary group to expel him. Next, showing "clear signs of an abnormal condition," he had entered a psychiatric hospital. "It was clear that he could not bear the weight of the matter he had taken on himself [participation in the murder of Strelnikov] and, wishing to relieve himself of it, completely tangled himself up morally and practically. He felt that he had fallen into the hands of Sudeikin, but he also felt the pangs of conscience and, in the depth of his soul, starkly understood that he had not conducted himself in the entire matter in a way prescribed by his conscience."[9] Because Grebencho never returned to terrorism, Sudeikin had effectively subtracted a terrorist from the ranks of the government's opponents.

The episode that cost Sudeikin his life began in 1881 when the police arrested a distributor of anti-government propaganda, Sergei Degaev of the People's Will revolutionary party, and handed him over to Sudeikin for questioning. Coming right to the point in their first meeting, Sudeikin had offered to release him, claims Degaev, in exchange for "real service." When Degaev indignantly refused to become a spy, Sudeikin agreed that he was "too noble for such a role."[10] Rather, because the government planned reforms that would satisfy everyone, even revolutionaries, Degaev must help stop the radical acts that hindered positive change. Again, Sudeikin sought advance notice of terrorist attacks.

In his version of events, Degaev pretended to accept Sudeikin's offer but with the intention of infiltrating security forces on behalf of his revolutionary comrades. Only later, when comrades confronted him with his links to Sudeikin, did Degaev, to justify himself, reveal his secret but failed mission. He claimed to be trying to confirm a plan by Sudeikin to assassinate his superior, Dmitry Tolstoy, through a terrorist group of his own that would make Sudeikin one with the revolutionaries. Cast by Degaev as a megalomaniac, Sudeikin purportedly expected to succeed Tolstoy, and, given the weakness of the tsar, to become the effective ruler of Russia. With this explanation surely incurring some scepticism, Degaev agreed to prove his abiding loyalty to the revolutionaries and erase his transgressing links with the police by assassinating Sudeikin. He carried out this deed on 3 December 1883, with the help of two others. Within another year, however, the Okhranka had effectively broken up the People's Will, in large part because of Sudeikin and his methods of weakening the organization from within.

Among the radicals who became genuine informers during this period was S.K. Belov, a peasant from Pskov province who was arrested in the fall of 1881 and accused of distributing anti-government propaganda. Freed by the police, he agreed to work under the supervision of Colonel A.S. Skandrakov, the head of the Moscow Okhranka at the time and a collaborator of Sudeikin's.[11] Belov's main assignment was to report on the activities of Black Repartition, a spin-off from

People's Will with emphasis on promoting evolution toward socialism. He collected information in Moscow, south Russia, and Vilnius before being compromised in 1884, when Skandrakov sent him home to his village. By then, Belov's information had led the police in Moscow to an apartment where they found the names of forty-six members of the Black Repartition; by tracing them to more than dozen cities, they made numerous arrests. In Moscow, meanwhile, the police destroyed the party's central command.

There were other revolutionaries who, without solicitation from the Okhranka, stepped forward to place their expert knowledge of the revolutionary movement at the disposal of the police. Alert to counter-penetration from the revolutionaries, the Okhranka was naturally suspicious of those who volunteered to work for the police. One of these one-time revolutionaries was P.S. Statkovsky, who eventually headed the Okhranka, first in St Petersburg and then in the St Petersburg region, until he retired in 1912 with honours.[12]

Statkovsky's origins, however, gave no hint of his future career. He was born in 1856 in Kherson province into a family with a tradition of serving the state as town clerks and scribes. In 1873 he took the entrance examination for the *realschule*, the technical high school for young men from the lower social orders, but decided instead, at seventeen, to enter the military in an infantry regiment – a conventional career choice for a young man without patrons or high social status. Statkovsky had joined the service at a time when some democracy was being introduced into the military under the leadership of the war minister, Dmitry Miliutin, who was engaged in a broad program to modernize the Russian military forces. After several months, Statkovsky's superior recommended him for the "junkers' school," the completion of which would qualify a candidate for junior officer rank.

An unexplained event then interrupted Statkovsky's progress. The school expelled him for "actions not in keeping with the junker's rank" with the proviso, however, that he could sit for the exam. (The tsarist government would sometimes inflict such penalties on the mildly radical young for some single expression of protest or dissent. Vladimir Lenin, for instance, was expelled from university, barred from law school, but permitted to take the bar exam, for which he studied on his own and passed brilliantly to become a Russian lawyer.)

In 1877 the Russo-Turkish war offered Statkovsky an opportunity for redemption. He served with distinction, won a St George decoration of the fourth class, and, following the conflict, passed the examination to become a junior ensign in the cavalry. Then, for a second time, suspicion fell on him. In 1884 Statkovsky was serving as the head of the military guard at a prison in Kiev. Someone denounced him, alleging that he had carried letters into the prison and had conversed with a political prisoner. No one produced additional evidence, but Statkovsky's superiors recommended that he apply for retirement to avoid dismissal for "political unreliability." He left in August 1884 and was permitted to remain in the army reserve, but the police put him under surveillance.

For three years Statkovsky's career floundered. Although he had moved to St Petersburg to enrol in the Technical Institute, he could not gain admission because he lacked a certificate of political reliability. Other ambitious young men had also encountered such obstacles to their own careers and, deeply frustrated with the tsarist system, joined the revolutionaries. Others, like Statkovsky, found a way to political rehabilitation by means of service to the Okhranka. He began to accept small assignments from the political police, although he remained under suspicion and surveillance until 1893.

In the meantime, Statkovsky, now about thirty, took a chance that paid off. He appealed directly to Tsar Nicholas II in 1895 to request a certificate of political reliability so he could enrol as a full-time agent of the Okhranka and the Separate Corps of Gendarmes. The Gendarmes rejected him as morally unqualified for their ranks, but the Okhranka accepted him and Statkovsky soon became an able agent. He was credited with the break-up of an important Marxist workers' organization, the Union of Struggle for the Liberation of the Working Class, at the end of the 1890s. Statkovsky also became an expert in the student movement. Later, when the Okhranka was asked to prepare a briefing for the prime minister, Peter Stolypin, on its fight against radicals, Statkovsky received the assignment. Through the Okhranka, Statkovsky had found a way to rehabilitate himself in a promising career and to utilize his personal experiences with radical youth.

A police agent, who remains anonymous to this day, describes a different route to a position in the police in his memoir in 1917.[13] The author tells that he was enrolled at St Petersburg University in 1912 during the crackdown on student unrest by the minister of public education, Leo Kasso. When the Okhranka approached him to report on student behaviour as an insider, he saw no harm in describing legitimate student grievances. He himself led a protest against the firing of several liberal professors only to suffer arrest and imprisonment for two years. Denied readmission to the university after his release, he found his income as a tutor insufficient to support his wife and daughter. Only with a certificate of political reliability could he resume work for a coveted university degree, so he asked the Okhranka to give him one. Statkovsky, now a top officer in St Petersburg, demanded service in return. The student was to use his renewed contact with agitators in the university to evaluate secret denunciations already in the hands of the police. He could, after all, save many innocent persons from unfair punishment. Statkovsky reminded his petitioner: "You suffered and ought to know how important it is to know the truth ... I propose that you correct our work."

At their next meeting in a cafe, Statkovsky brought along a blond man in glasses with a kindly appearance, whom he presented as Ivan Fedorov, the student's contact with the Okhranka. Then Statkovsky excused himself. Fedorov, as the conversation developed, turned out to have "an exceptional mind, familiarity with literature, history, social science; he did not resemble the Gendarmes who had crudely conducted the interrogation into my case; each of his words was redolent of a suborning gentleness. He spoke with a soft smile sincerely and simply." This was Dobrovolsky, then the notorious head of the St Petersburg Okhranka's secret agents.

Restored to the university, the student received regular payments from the Okhranka, but his assignments became more demanding. He was to evaluate the student "mood," although without naming persons. Next came pressure for the names of leaders of the continuing anti-Kasso agitation at the university. Von Kotten, the overall head of the St Petersburg Okhranka, made himself known and underscored the demand for detailed reporting. The student now heard a threat from the Okhranka: "Do not try to operate on two fronts ... If you do, we shall have to part from you. If so, we will deal with you in a political sense and will spread the word about our conversations with you ... I say this by the way. I hope that you will understand that you must pass along information on everything that happens ... We do not demand provocations [incitement of others to illegal acts] from you, but only want to be *au courant* on all events."

Soon the reluctant agent learned that his reports had provided the sole grounds for several arrests. With persons denounced by him suffering in prison, the student felt deepening remorse. His comrades, moreover, began to suspect that he was an informer. The student therefore asked for a court of honour, claiming in his memoir that he hoped, without confessing his guilt, to be expelled and thereby released from his burden. To his dismay, Statkovsky assured him that the court would exonerate him because two members of the panel were Okhranka agents.

At this point, the student claims to have lost faith in "truth and justice" and concluded that the Okhranka's power was without limit. Already totally compromised, he decided to raise his earnings to those of a full-fledged officer of the Okhranka. Suborning was everywhere, but the student blamed neither the Okhranka nor himself. The fault lay with "the system, the environment of the government and society, that life of abnormalities which drives a man from the revolution to the Okhranka and from the Okhranka back to the revolution."

Even as radicals were enlisting in the Okhranka, through a combination of inducements, subtle pressures, and threats, there were Okhranka agents and officers who were passing over to the revolutionaries. The American writer Lincoln Steffens, for years an investigative reporter of corruption in the governments of large cities, observed psychological similarities in many policemen and the criminals they pursued. Numerous corrupt policemen, although remaining overtly law enforcement officers, engaged in criminal activity.[14] In Russia, of course, not only did the police become "criminals," in the sense that they joined the radicals; but the reverse also happened: the "criminals" became able and dedicated policemen. Steffens did not observe this reverse phenomenon in America, but it was characteristic of the Okhranka that some of its best agents and officers had started their careers as dedicated opponents of the imperial regime.

Crossing the line from one side to the other offered no great change in the nature of the work. Both camps operated extensive clandestine organizations and used similar methods. Both camps included many opportunistic persons who transferred their allegiances from one side to the other at will. On the other hand, some of the defectors who had been totally dedicated to a cause became disillusioned, and deserted to work for the enemy. Another factor was that each side was actively trying to recruit or place persons in the other camp because of the enormous intelligence advantages to be gained. The existence of persons extending blandishments naturally led to at least some who were attracted by the bait. Then there were persons who managed to help both sides substantially and it is extremely difficult even today to calculate and compare their contribution to the police as against their contribution to the revolutionaries.

There is another possible motive for those who served one side and then the other. Because there were agents who threw themselves into their work – whether for the police or the revolutionaries – it seems that the work, not the allegiance mattered most. They might have been attracted to the thrill of dangerous life based on deception. There seem to have been persons who relished the hunt, only they were the game and their object was to deceive the hunters from both camps.

Crossing over from the revolutionaries to the Okhranka or the reverse presented the police with a permanent uncertainty about the loyalties of officers and agents and, accordingly, the information they gathered and the analyses they wrote. Was a piece of information coming into the Fontanka office designed to enlighten or to mislead Okhranka planners? To verify observations sent in by agents, analysts required reports from more than one source for cross-comparison.

Because it began its data bank with the files of the old Third Section, from the start the Okhranka held a large collection of single-identity cards. As a former agent explained, "the foundation of any security organization is its files or archives."[15] The Okhranka multiplied entries quickly; well before 1914, their number exceeded one million, each one of them on a colour-coded card. Yellow ones, for example, denoted students; green was for anarchists. Red meant allegiance to the Socialist Revolutionary Party, and blue to the Social Democrats. Persons relegated to white cards had no known links to the revolutionary movement, but were, for the most part, in the main stream of cultural, social, and business affairs.

Anyone privy to the files, says Zhilinsky, could "find the names of all public figures, of any highly-placed individual, a card on almost any intelligent man who at any time in his life thought about politics."[16] There were women, too, as in the listing in the 1890s of some 250 members of the Moscow Committee for Literacy, a group that included scholars (Paul Miliukov and V.O. Kliuchevsky), publishers (V.A. Goltsev and I.D. Sytin), and assorted members of the intelligentsia working together to teach Russians how to read.[17] If not already covertly at odds with the government, officials assumed these activists with democratic leanings might yet openly challenge the old order. Given their resources and influence, they could add formidable strength to the opposition.

Much of the information on the white file cards was already in the public record, but the information on the coloured cards depended on reports from secret agents. From those same reports came the information entered on summary of external observation sheets to record ongoing patterns of contact among persons under surveillance. To process intelligence data, then, analysts at the Fontanka assessed each person for entry on two primary forms: the single-identity card, and the summary of observation sheet. Entered on each identity card was the basic information of name, age, sex, address, and, possibly, a small photograph. Completing these sparse data were reference numbers to cite the location of every other file relevant to this individual, whether a summary sheet, a personal dossier, a record of finger prints, or additional photos.

This same person was next entered as one of a number of circles that formed a diagram on a summary of observation sheet, indicating the contacts that each person under observation had made with others. Each name connected by a line to a circle was a name that matched a single-identity card. The larger and more central the circle, the more important the individual. (Lenin, for example, on the schematic representation of the Social Democrats, was the biggest circle of the diagram.) A line between circles denoted contact, and the heavier the line the more frequent the contact. Diagrams were redrafted when, over time, a summary sheet became too crowded with additions. Sometimes updated intelligence called for new diagrams that combined or split old ones.

As a process, from field to headquarter's archive, here was a labour-intensive method of information storage and retrieval whose basic purpose was to reveal patterns of activity to enable the police to head off revolutionary acts. It seemed a methodical way to find the secret, lethal enemy. A theretofore hidden group of conspirators might leap to the eye when the headquarter's officer assembled the connecting information and entered it on the sheets. The drawback of the system was its omnivorousness and absence of discrimination at the primary level. Because contact with a suspected revolutionary in the eyes of the police was sufficient for entry into the system, many persons who were completely innocent became part of the files of the Okhranka. Many others' names found their way into the archives because of their ideas.

To assist the work in the field, the headquarters staff assembled pocketbooks of photos and biographical summaries to alert detectives to known suspects that they should watch for. The detectives carried these booklets with them for guarded reference while on duty and for off-duty study.

Fontanka also kept abreast of technical inventions that revolutionaries might use. Through their own office on inventions, okhranniki acquired information on new contrivances around the world and maintained an archive of such developments. The first successful flights of airplanes after the turn of the century attracted the attention of the Okhranka because the new conveyance was a plausible instrument for carrying out assassinations and terrorist attacks. In August 1909 an order would go out to the Gendarmes to monitor all airplane flights in their jurisdictions, as well as aviators, persons learning to fly, and members of the "aero-clubs," all of whom had to register with the government.[18] To keep abreast of developments in explosives the police maintained a collection of bombs and used them to instruct officers who would raid the revolutionaries' bomb-making and storage warehouses. The Okhranka also warned its agents against terrorists' use of the so-called Kaiser torpedo which could be fitted to an automobile with a timing mechanism to be fired at passing trains.[19]

As the control centre for a spy network, headquarters also dealt with code names. A few specially trusted staff tended the confidential files that specified the code names that the Okhranka assigned both to its own agents and to important persons under surveillance. Those who assigned these names seemed to take some pleasure in generic consistency. Zhilinsky mentions two apt examples, "Sugar" and "Bun" for suspects in the Union of Bakers. At one time the Okhranka insisted on code names that conveyed some evident external characteristic of the subject under surveillance. A.F. Kerensky, the future prime minister of the Provisional Government, was labelled "The Quick One," in obvious reference to his energetic and hurried manner. The banker P.P. Riabushinsky bore the appellation "Money-bags" and the poet Sergei Esenin, who had worked in a print shop as a youth, "Type-setting."

Secret information about the revolutionaries and their plans was the lifeblood of the Okhranka. The secret political police of Imperial Russia therefore became a huge information-gathering, storage and retrieval system. Although the Okhranka sought information that was true, it had to rely on a system that probably produced too much information about too many people; much of it was unreliable because of the nature of the reporting system. The effort to make certain of sources required the Okhranka to be constantly alert with no time to examine its own shortcomings. Such inherent flaws were one reason for the weakness of the tsarist political police.

Another of the Okhranka's principal means of gathering information was perlustration. The opening of letters intended for others, however, was prohibited under the criminal laws (articles 368 and 1035), and penalties for conviction were terms in prison or exile. The criminal code required prosecution of an alleged offender, although only with the permission of the Circuit Court. However, to prosecute a Gendarme officer for the offence required the special permission of the minister of justice, and the existence of criminal penalties did not inhibit the spread of a series of offices in the post offices of the Russian Empire under the control of the Special Section.

Perlustration had existed in Russia for at least a century before the appearance of the Okhranka. Catherine the Great approved the practice in a secret order to the director of the post office, Count Bezborodko. Paul 1 ordered his postal director to monitor the correspondence of certain persons. Alexander 1, another reforming tsar like his grandmother, continued the practice of opening letters and parcels – especially from abroad – in the Secret Expedition of the St Petersburg post office. Count Benckendorff wrote that secret opening of letters was a necessary tool of investigative work. Not only the Higher

Police but the Ministry of the Interior engaged in perlustration. Nicholas I's minister, Prince A. Golitsyn, sounded almost poetic in praise of the practice: "Secret perlustration belongs exclusively to the reigning sovereign. It illuminates for the Emperor subjects that the forms of the law obscure. Where passions and weaknesses completely obscure the truth. Invisible to all, it sees everything."[20]

Authority to conduct perlustration, according to one account, was granted anew to each minister of the interior. A grizzled functionary would appear in the reception room of the new minister and, when his turn came to see the minister, would present him with a sealed packet. The minister would open the packet to find a document authorizing him to conduct perlustration throughout the Russian Empire. The functionary then would seal up the packet and disappear, only to reappear again upon the naming of a new minister.

Perlustration flourished under Nicholas II, although there is no statement on record that he approved of practice which he clearly knew about it. In a secret report to the tsar from the minister of the interior, I.N. Durnovo, on 5 January 1895, the minister explained that perlustration was the "extraction from private correspondence information about state affairs, statements revealing the state of public opinion about the condition of the Empire, and evaluations of the work of official persons that could never be revealed by means of official sources."[21] Durnovo, of course, was in error on one point; the Okhranka conducted perlustration not only of private correspondence, but official as well.

Letters were opened in what were unofficially termed the "black offices." They existed in St Petersburg, Moscow, Kiev, Warsaw, Khar'kov, Vil'no, and Tiflis. In 1889 an office had been opened in Kazan', and in 1894 in Nizhnii Novgorod, but they were soon closed. In February 1913 the Department of Police decided that it needed more perlustration points. It planned to open them in Siberia, the Volga region, and at all border cities, but financial constraints made it impossible to carry through this plan.

Although the Department of Police was the main user of perlustrated letters, it was established practice in the Russian government that members of the Foreign Censorship Committee did the actual work and that the senior censor assigned to the St Petersburg post office was supervisor of such operations throughout the Russian Empire. This position was filled for more than a quarter of a century by Privy Counsellor A.D. Fomin, who was replaced in 1914 by Privy Counsellor M.G. Mardar'ev.

Only authorized personnel could gain admission to the premises of the black offices. New persons were subject to a kind of rite of initiation to fix firmly in their minds the secrecy of the operation on which they were about to embark. V.M. Iablochkov, the senior censor with the Moscow post office, recalled: "They asked me (and others) to sign a statement to the effect that I promised to keep everything in strict secrecy and to no one, not even relatives or acquaintances, to reveal the kind of work I was engaged in."[22] Perlustrators were paid generously, and received double the salary they were entitled to for official rank. In turn, the government demanded high qualifications, particularly the knowledge of foreign languages. One encountered genuine polyglots at work in the black offices.

In six of the principal cities where perlustration took place, the work was conducted in the main post offices. It was said at one time that the St Petersburg censor of foreign newspapers, in addition to his own regular office, also worked in a secret room, the door to which was masked behind a large yellow bookcase in the office of the senior censor. This turns out to have been one of the myths that grew up around the activity of the Okhranka. A May 1917 report based on an inspection of the St Petersburg post office shows that the foreign censorship had two isolated rooms, and admittance to one of them was barred to outsiders. The bookshelf in the office of the senior censor was only for the purpose of holding books. Nor were there any secret elevators, or entrances, or connections to secret basement rooms. In the Moscow post office there was a primitive elevator with blocks and pulleys for raising the mail to the perlustrators.

In Tiflis, Georgia, there was another kind of arrangement for the perlustration of mail. The work area was in the apartment of one V.K. Karpinsky, who had the overt assignment in the city as a representative of the Ministry of Education in Tiflis to study Eastern languages. He lived under a foreign name with a false passport issued by the Department of Police (which had an office that produced very good false passports). In the case of difficulties with the local authorities, Karpinsky produced a certificate which stated that he was an official on special assignment for the assistant minister of the interior and a search of his apartment was permitted only with permission of the Department of Police in St Petersburg.

In opening letters, the perlustrators were guided by lists of persons who were under observation by the secret police, lists that were constantly revised and supplemented. The workers also frequently opened correspondence of known political figures. The talented and experienced perlustrators were able to detect in thousands of letters those of suspicious persons judged by their handwriting. For example, they could often discern the party affiliation of the correspondent from characteristics revealed on the envelopes. Many of the anarchists, for instance, were poorly educated and often wrote crudely, with crooked letters.

Letters selected for perlustration were often opened with the help of a fine stick, forced under the flap of the envelope. Letters were also steamed open. Even packages sealed with wax offered no problems for the postal workers of the Okhranka. The Russian police maintained a special staff of persons with the ability to produce very quickly any stamp for imprinting sealing wax. This particular skill was long-standing for the Russian police; during the reign of Nicholas I, the Austrian government had asked for the methods used by the Third Section to duplicate such stamps. Nicholas obligingly provided his ally with the secrets and received in return a description of the Austrian perlustration service.

The workers ordinarily returned a letter to its original envelope and carefully resealed it. But slip-ups sometimes happened because of the volume of the work and the weariness of the workers. Once an envelope was resealed, the workers put on it an unobtrusive mark – a "fly" in the jargon of the perlustrators, so that others would not open the envelope a second time at another black cabinet. Workers copied a letter of special interest, using the careful script of the Russian bureaucracy on identical paper so the copied letter was indistinct from the original.

Fontanka 16 received all coded letters where the talents of the Okhranka's chief cryptanalyst, I.A. Zybin, came into play. M.E. Bakai, the defector, recalled him in this way: "For Zybin, it was essential to grasp the system of the code and then he would have no difficulty in deciphering the meaning of letters or figures."[23] Zybin claimed that in the course of many years as the Okhranka's chief cryptanalyst he failed to break only a single letter. Cryptanalysis was for him an all-consuming passion. A head of the Moscow Gendarme command, P.P. Zavarzin, recalled summoning Zybin from the capital to deal with a letter that baffled the local black cabinet. He arrived and grabbed the letter like a madman and plunged into a feverish perusal of it, paying no attention to anyone around him and seemingly unaware of where he was. Invited to break for dinner, he attempted to write figures on the bottom of his plate and, that failing, he began to make notes on his cuff. Zybin came out of his somnambulist state only after he had solved his problem.[24]

A collection of invisible inks was essential to the operation of the Okhranka. Once an invisible ink in a letter had been developed, the perlustrators could not send it on to the addressee. The experts would then re-write both the visible and invisible writing in the letter and send it on. V.N. Zverev was a master forger at work for the Okhranka;

he could match any writing, visible or invisible. This was painstaking work and required the exact quality of paper, including the precise gloss and watermark. From time to time Zverev had to order from another city the exact kind of paper required for the forgery.

Every year the number of letters opened by the Okhranka increased. In 1882 the perlustrators opened 38,000 letters and made 3,600 copies. In 1900 the number was 5,431 copies, in 1904, 8,642, in 1905, 10,182, and in 1907, 14,221. The black cabinets sent all copies to the Department of Police where the officials of the Special Section read them. They then filed them in the "archive of secret information obtained by the censorship." When necessary, the Special Section passed along the information to the Gendarme administration or to the security divisions but without giving the source or using only the identifying formula, "from secret agency data."

Okhranka policy prohibited local security agencies from having access to perlustrated mail, but in practice this rule was frequently broken. In Moscow the senior censor would put copies of perlustrated mail in an envelope, write the code name "To Annenkov" on the outside, and drop it in a drawer of the police chief. In other cities, Gendarme officers bribed postal officials with agency sums and regularly received access to private correspondence. At the Ministry of the Interior there arrived regularly packages from "His Excellency Sokolov" – the name of a deceased censor now used as a code name. The secretary of the minister's office understood that these packages were to go unopened directly to the minister. The packages contained copies of perlustrated mail selected by the senior censor for the eyes of the minister.

Those who examined mail understood that they "were not restricted from any persons no matter how highly placed, even if they were close to His Majesty." There were only two persons in the Empire who could be certain that their mail was not being read by others – the tsar and the minister of the interior. Paradoxically, even the mail of persons who administered the system was not immune from perlustration of their correspondence. The assistant minister of the interior, police chiefs, and directors of the Department of Police could all have their correspondence intercepted. P.G. Kurlov, as assistant commander of the Corps of Gendarmes, wrote to the senior censor Fomin that his chief "has become aware that letters addressed to him have arrived in very badly imprinted envelopes, [and] has ordered me – if his letters are to be subject to perlustration – to request that they not show signs that they have been opened."[25]

Ministers of the interior upon leaving office were careful to eliminate evidence that they had been reading the correspondence of their colleagues and subordinates. But the evidence remained when the minister suddenly died or was assassinated while in office. When Plehve was killed by a terrorist's bomb in 1904, Lopukhin, the director of police, was one of several officials who entered his office in order to claim sensitive documents. Lopukhin discovered a packet of his own letters. The majority of them were copies of letters he had sent, but there were two originals that had never reached the addressees. There Lopukhin reflected that Plehve had retained them "in all probability, because in them I ... demonstrated that there would soon be a revolution and the collapse of the autocracy."[26] After the death of Stolypin from Bogrov's bullet in 1911, his relatives insisted that the deceased prime minister had a drawer full of copies of their letters to friends and relatives and they wished to claim them. Kryzhanovsky, the assistant minister of the interior, with great difficulty persuaded them that only secret government documents lay in the drawer in question and that it was impossible to show them the papers.

Foreign diplomats' correspondence from Russia was a source of useful counter-intelligence information for the Okhranka. Special couriers carried correspondence between embassies and home countries, and the Okhranka ordinarily was unable to gain access to it. But the letters of diplomats sent through the regular post were available to the Okhranka. The leather portfolios used by the couriers to carry secret diplomatic correspondence also from time to time fell into the hands of the Okhranka, which considered them fair game. "Any secret has its value," was the view of the okhranniki.

Usually accurate, the perlustrators could make mistakes. On one occasion they mixed up the envelopes from two embassies and sent on to the Dutch foreign ministry a report written by a Spanish diplomat. Another time, the perlustrator accidentally dropped into a courier's portfolio a gold cuff link. The recipient decided that the gold cuff belonged to the diplomat back at the embassy in St Petersburg and sent it back to him. At the St Petersburg post office, the same perlustrator opened the portfolio on its return trip and to his delight discovered his lost cuff link and reclaimed it. He destroyed the accompanying explanatory note to the diplomat.

During the period of the Russo-Japanese War in 1904–5, Capt. M.S. Komissarov of the Okhranka used another means to penetrate the secrets of foreign embassies in St Petersburg. By doffing his Gendarme uniform and assuming civilian dress and a false name, he was able to recruit servants in many embassies and managed to buy the diplomatic codes of twelve foreign governments. He recalled: "The Chinese codes were in six volumes; the American in such a large volume that you could not copy it all down – the whole book had to be copied by photographic means."[27] Komissarov also was able to photograph diplomatic correspondence and encoded telegrams. He claimed that at the time of the diplomatic negotiations at Portsmouth between the Russians and the Japanese to end their war, the diplomatic instructions to the American diplomats – who were providing their good offices to expedite negotiations – were known on the Fontanka before they were known to the diplomats in Portsmouth.

Much intelligence and counter-intelligence work for the Russian government was conducted by departments of the Russian government other than the Okhranka. Inevitably, rivalries developed. The vice-director of the Department of Police, S.E. Vissarionov, following an inspection of the perlustration offices in 1910, wrote: "The censorship works also for the ministries of war and naval affairs but it does not have a direct connection with them and receives directives from them through Messers. Fomin and Mardar'ev."[28] This overtime work in the jargon of the perlustration was called "the evening pastime" and was compensated by whichever department of the government used the service. Vissarionov also noted that the St Petersburg black cabinet was working for the Ministry of Foreign Affairs and for the Ministry of the Imperial Court. All departments knew that nowhere else could they obtain such up-to-date and accurate information. As one official put it, the work was done well because those who did it were shaking with fear.

The Department of Police tried to defend its prerogatives from encroachments. In this respect the experience of junior censor V.I. Krivosh is instructive. He was an able perlustrator and commanded twenty-four foreign languages. For him, perlustration was not merely a job but the essence of life. He invented several useful devices, including a special electrical apparatus to create steam for opening letters. Stolypin praised him for this invention and for "other useful and practical inventions." Unfortunately for Krivosh, however, many of his inventions ran afoul of bureaucratic obstacles and could not be introduced – for instance, a pneumatic system for moving documents in the black office.

Krivosh at one time promised the naval ministry that he would set up a network of offices for the perlustration of diplomatic and intelligence correspondence. Upon learning of this particular "overtime" project, the Department of Police decided to part ways with Krivosh. After long and acrimonious discussions, he finally submitted his resignation in December 1911. Fomin, the senior censor, advised his superiors that prosecution of his former subordinate would be unwise. He wrote: "Upon retirement, Krivosh received an order of St Vladimir, 4th class; in the report recommending the award, various means of perlustration were mentioned carelessly [in support of the recommendation]. In his own hand, the Emperor had written, 'Agreed' and Krivosh had photographed the document and had kept a copy for himself."[29] Like so many who worked for the Okhranka, Krivosh had learned how to protect himself once he had parted company with his former employer.

Telegrams were also intercepted by agents of the Okhranka. In May 1903 in agreement with the Main Administration of Post and Telegraph, Okhranka chiefs received "open sheets" which gave permission to read telegrams. As a result of the 1905 strike on several major railways, the telegraph system was connected to the Gendarme commands. Nothing is known about the results of the Okhranka's ability to listen to telephone conversations; the means to tap phones already existed at the time and in 1913 the apparatus was installed on the premises of the Fourth State Duma.

CHAPTER FIVE

The Foreign Agency, 1884–1917

Two years after its inception, the Okhranka dispatched the first director of its Foreign Agency to Paris to establish headquarters within the Russian embassy at 79 rue Grinelle. His role was to improvise action against the many Russian radicals who were using Western Europe as a safe haven to plot and publish against the autocracy.

Although the Third Section had for many years hired spies to watch its emigré foes, officials taking charge of state security for Alexander III found need for more than casual surveillance to counter subversives abroad. Rather, they decided, tsarist agents must be militantly organized to detect and infiltrate any group in Western Europe bent on toppling the tsar. It therefore became a priority for the Okhranka to wage as aggressive a campaign in France and its neighbours as foreign officials would allow.

As an Okhranka subdivision within the Police Department of the Ministry of the Interior, the new Foreign Agency set to work in 1883 with funding from the government's long-standing budget for secret expenditures. And although records are sketchy, available figures for that budget from 1877 to 1883 show a great upsurge in spending when the Foreign Agency began.

So long as it existed, the Third Section received all of the budget for secret expenditures, those funds having totalled 186,877 rubles in 1877 and 251,877 rubles in 1878. By 1880, when the Police Department inherited the assets of the disbanded Third Section, that same budget had more than doubled to 558,957 rubles; and itemized dispersals, listed for this year alone, show that nearly 20 percent of the funds went to secret agents within Russia (108,580 rubles). A mere 3.4 percent went to secret agents abroad (19,000 rubles), that being slightly less than the amount spent to influence the foreign press (21,000 rubles).[1]

The next available record for the secret expenditures budget is for 1883, the founding year of the Foreign Agency, and it shows another doubling of the annual total to just over one million rubles. No breakdown of allocations is listed, but the overall rise coincides with the sudden increase in the state's secret agents, both at home and abroad. The million-ruble amount also matches what Alexander III had allegedly granted in 1881 or 1882 to the Druzhina, the unofficial spy and militia corps put together by highly placed persons desperate to stop the terrorism that had felled Alexander II.[2]

Linkage is relevant because the Druzhina, during its twenty months of non-government security work through 1882, had used a good share of its funding to open the precursor of the Okhranka's Foreign Agency. It had started in May 1881 when a secretary within the Russian embassy in Paris, complying with a request sent from St Petersburg by K.P. Pobedonostsev, a close advisor to Alexander III and the procurator of the Holy Synod, had conveyed a bid to a police inspector in a Paris prefecture that convinced him to become a full-time Druzhina spy.

Foreign police made ideal secret agents; Henri Bint, the thirty-year-old French police inspector recruited in 1881, would distinguish himself during his eighteen months with the Druzhina followed by thirty-five more years with the Okhranka's Foreign Agency. Bint says he chose to shift from French to Russian service through his acquaintance with Georges D'Anthès-Gekkeren, the French aristocrat who had killed Pushkin in a duel in 1837. Bint, the son of a city council member in an Alsace town, says he grew up admiring the Russian autocracy because D'Anthès, who sat just above his father as mayor, had so often warmly praised it. When, therefore, he had consulted D'Anthès about the Druzhina offer, D'Anthès had convinced him to accept it.[3]

Another Druzhina agent in Paris who subsequently served the Foreign Agency was P.I. Rachkovsky, best remembered for his flamboyant operations.[4] Rachkovsky, born into the hereditary gentry in Bessarabia in 1853 but educated only at home, had first supported himself as a minor bureaucrat and peripatetic informer for the Third Section. By early 1879, he was editing a Jewish newspaper and contriving radical links to make credible his subsequent "arrest" as a political criminal – all to improve his usefulness as a full-fledged inside agent for the Third Section.[5]

On 20 August 1879, however, exposure by the underground newspaper of the People's Will of his role as a double agent had forced

Rachkovsky to leave Russia. When the tsar's assassination brought him back in 1881 under a false name, Rachkovsky joined the Druzhina and proceeded to Paris as part of the secret brotherhood's foreign spy bureau. In 1882 he returned to Moscow, there to enter the reorganized security force within V.K. Plehve's Police Department.

As an assistant to Colonel S.G. Sudeikin, Rachkovsky had engaged in discussions during 1883 with the detained revolutionary, Sergei Degaev, that had seemingly persuaded Degaev to turn against his terrorist comrades and convert him into an accomplice eager to assist in their capture. Rightly doubting Degaev's sincerity, Rachkovsky had vainly conveyed his scepticism to Plehve, and then persisted, according to some accounts, to the point of angering the police director. The murder of Sudeikin arranged by Degaev on 3 December 1883 proved Rachkovsky correct but, as some would have it, made a shame-faced Plehve permanently hostile.

Meanwhile, in June of 1883, Plehve had appointed a police official named Kovrin-Krukovsky to head the fledgling Foreign Agency in Paris. Already at hand there were the old Druzhina agents, and Kovrin at once added six more French nationals: an experienced private detective named Barlé and his five-man squad of investigators. In January 1884, a month after the killing of Sudeikin, Kovrin acquired Rachkovsky.

Because Degaev was still at large and his wife was known to be residing in the French capital, Plehve had sent Rachkovsky to the Russian embassy in Paris "on special assignment from the Ministry of the Interior" – that is, as an agent of the secret Foreign Agency permanently set apart in a closed-off wing. In essence, Rachkovsky was to arrange and direct constant surveillance over Madame Degaev and her contacts and to pursue any plausible leads about her husband and his accomplices, whatever the source.

Next to make the trek from St Petersburg to Paris was the emissary Semiakin, as Plehve's evaluator of security operations abroad. Whether influenced by Rachkovsky or not, Semiakin returned home to recommend that more French nationals be hired as surveillance agents, that cooperative ties be strengthened with the French police, and that Rachkovsky replace Kovrin. On 20 May 1884 Semiakin returned to Paris to install the thirty-one-year-old Rachkovsky as head of an expanded Foreign Agency, its mandate now including Geneva, where emigrés mobilizing against the tsar had become especially dangerous.[6]

Having discovered the quarters in Paris of Lev Tikhomirov, a comrade of Degaev in the People's Will, Rachkovsky at once used his new authority to rent a nearby apartment as a surveillance facility. Then, further to assert his free-wheeling independence, financial and otherwise, he informed St Petersburg that he needed to pay a large retainer of 1,000 francs a month to a promising agent. When the new police director, P.N. Durnovo, ruled that 300 francs would be quite enough, Rachkovsky insisted that he knew better and requested 650 francs, which he won.

Rachkovsky would remain the lavish spender and flamboyant enterpriser during his next eighteen years as head of the Foreign Agency, with results that mainly pleased his superiors. By 1892 his funding from St Petersburg would exceed 300,000 francs a year, including his own salary of 12,000 francs; and, inclined to luxury, he would personally make enough additional income on the bourse to buy a villa in the Paris suburb of St Cloud and to host frequent dinners for the political and governmental elite.[7] Headwaiters in the best restaurants always found a good table for the man they called "le general russe."

Always self-possessed, Rachkovsky was the consummate security professional, and he stands out for wresting years of loyal service from several very effective agents. Bint, whom Kovrin recruited in 1883, was one. Another was Abram Hekkel'man, who first went to work for the Foreign Agency during 1885 on Rachkovsky's second front in Switzerland. Hekkel'man had earlier, while a student at the St Petersburg School of Mines, served as an informant to the security section in the capital. Once compromised there, he had relocated in Riga, where his reportage led police to a hidden printing plant of the People's Will. Under orders from the Okhranka in January of 1885, he had moved to Zurich with a new identity – that of a liberal-spending young radical Pole named Landezen, whose father was a Warsaw banker – and had enrolled in the local polytechnic institute. From that vantage point, Landezen commenced a three-year quest to identify highly dangerous members of the People's Will who were experimenting with explosives in Switzerland.

Midway through 1886, in the first inspection he underwent as head of the Foreign Agency, Rachkovsky opened his confidential files in Paris and discussed his policies with S.E. Zvoliansky, an emissary from Durnovo's Department of Police. As Rachkovsky fully expected, the report that Zvoliansky gave to Durnovo on 6 October endorsed all the agency's operations and justified their high costs. Among the necessary but expensive outlays that it cited, for example, were the rental of a new surveillance apartment in Raincy, where Tikhomirov had moved, and the retention of the old one to watch yet other dangerous emigrés. Moreover, Zvoliansky went on to explain, the fees demanded by informants had risen in Paris, and any refusal to pay them would cause "a noisy scandal"; the surveillance of a single suspect in Switzerland was costing 1,000 francs a month.[8]

Just over a month later, on the night of 20–21 November, three agents from the Foreign Agency in Paris forcibly entered and then demolished the printing plant in Geneva that published the newspaper of the People's Will. Bint was one of the trio, and Rachkovsky himself had helped to plan their strike against what he described as "the main centre of the revolutionary activities of the foreign section of the People's Will."[9] According to one of the party workers who confronted the ruins, he and his comrades had at once blamed Hekkel'man, then using the name Landezen, as the provocateur.[10] (This claim seems to have been improved by hindsight, for Landezen promptly moved to Paris and was welcomed into revolutionary circles there.) Landezen's work was praised by Zvoliansky but he also cited Rachkovsky's over-riding importance. It was "thanks to the constant and very clever guidance by the head of the Agency" that Landezen was doing so well.[11] Ignoring that their agents had violated Swiss laws, officials in St Petersburg warmly endorsed the "victory" over the revolutionaries, as Durnovo put it, by raising the salaries of all involved. Rachkovsky reaped even more: direct praise from the interior minister, D.A. Tolstoy.

From another quarter, the Gendarme headquarters in Kiev, came a totally opposite appraisal of Rachkovsky and his operations. For in this same year, 1886, the chief officer in Kiev complained to his superior in St Petersburg about a provocation that Rachkovsky had personally staged in the provincial capital before he had been sent abroad to work for the Foreign Agency. Wrote Colonel V.D. Novitsky: "Rachkovsky ruined a great number of young people [whom Novitsky considered innocent of revolutionary intent] by means of his provocateur's activity ... and put the higher government in a false position." As for himself, continued Novitsky, his having been forced by Rachkovsky to arrest these youths had made his own official position "impossible."[12] It would seem that the devious tactics of Rachkovsky mainly served to diminish tsarist authority; that was a charge that would recur.

Back in France, as the year ended, Russian radicals there caught public attention by charging that the Russian secret police had criminally sabotaged the printing plant in Geneva. Rachkovsky, in no position to reply directly, responded with a diversionary counter-attack. Adding yet another Frenchman to his payroll, he paid generous fees to a well-known journalist of Danish background, Jules Hansen, for newspaper articles and propaganda tracts that portrayed the plotters against the tsar as despicable anarchists. Then, in February 1887, Rachkovsky sent his agents to destroy a printing plant that the People's Will had established in Paris.

In his overt role as a tsarist official, Rachkovsky continued his efforts to turn French officials against resident foes of the tsar. In

1887, for example, he insisted to the French police prefect, M. Fragnon, that persons from France inciting revolution against the Russian autocracy falsely claimed to represent and to serve the Russian people. Rather, just as they had coopted their ideas from Western radicals, whom Fragnon surely despised, their lineages and loyalties were mainly Jewish, Ukrainian, or Polish.[13] Taking another tack, Rachkovsky would later urge St Petersburg to decorate police prefect M. Gronin and his top aides in order to lessen their "external constraints" on the Foreign Agency and to encourage their giving assistance through "direct (although, of course, secret) services."[14]

On a much more mundane level, in March 1887 Durnovo had proposed to Rachkovsky a cut in costs. Assuming that Rachkovsky commanded the Foreign Agency's internal agents while Barlé directed the external ones, Durnovo proposed that Rachkovsky also take charge of the surveillance force. Back came a reply from Rachkovsky that, from the start of his tenure three years before, he had withheld prime authority from the French detective Barlé by taking it upon himself. Rather than cause "unpleasantness" at that point by excluding Barlé completely, Rachkovsky announced that he would retire him on a pension of 3,000 francs a year. That done, he would retain the few on Barlé's squad who were competent.[15]

In this same period, Landezen continued to inform Rachkovsky about Russian radicals in Switzerland, with whom he still mingled easily as a seeming confederate. One tightly-knit group of explosive experts that Landezen seems not to have penetrated – the Circle of the People's Will, which was allied with a St Petersburg contingent that included Lenin's older brother Alexander – gave itself away on 9 February 1888 by accidentally detonating the bomb that it was assembling. Swiss police easily apprehended one badly injured member, Isaak Dembo, and learned enough from him before he died to establish grounds for expelling nineteen of his comrades from Switzerland.[16]

Maintaining his pose as a dedicated comrade, Landezen followed the revolutionaries to Paris by transferring his studies to the French agricultural institute. And at this juncture, in close proximity to the headquarters of the Foreign Agency, he gained acceptance within the radical emigré circles that included Tikhomirov. Although one or two cautious revolutionaries pointed to circumstantial evidence that could link Landezen with Rachkovsky, the absence of damning proof caused most of the emigrés, including a key leader, Vladimir Burtsev, to find him trustworthy. To guard against compromising Landezen, only Rachkovsky, Zvoliansky, Durnovo, Alexander III, and one or two other officials knew the identity and accomplishments of the Foreign Agency's most effective spy.

Precisely what transpired between Landezen and Tikhomirov remains unclear, but by the summer of 1888, Rachkovsky seems to have known that Tikhomirov wanted to renounce the revolutionary movement and assert his loyalty to the tsar. In exchange, he wanted an imperial pardon allowing him to return to Russia a free man.[17] Any such bargain, Rachkovsky knew, would yield him ammunition for a tremendous volley of propaganda against the revolutionaries, along with loud applause from his superiors. And even greater would be his credit could he imply, as Rachkovsky took pains to do, that he himself had caused Tikhomirov's conversion.[18] Evidence shows, however, that Tikhomirov independently chose to abandon revolution because he found terrorism repulsive and unproductive. A man of strict principles, Tikhomirov made the break openly and on his own terms, for he would not and did not betray his old comrades to Rachkovsky. Still, Rachkovsky, as he claimed, held meetings with Tikhomirov to shape the final agreement between the revolutionary and the tsar.[19]

In any case, Tikhomirov that September sent off his "Petition to the Tsar" that won him Alexander III's forgiveness, and Rachkovsky used his press connections to publicize widely that a leading strategist for the People's Will had turned against revolution and terrorism. By year's end, Rachkovsky had subsidized and helped to circulate a pamphlet by Tikhomirov entitled, "Why I Ceased to Be a Revolutionary."[20]

Zvoliansky helped bring about the awarding of a medal to Rachkovsky, when a report deplored his lack of decoration despite "fifteen years" of accomplished security work. Rachkovsky received the Order of St Anna, third class. In addition, Zvoliansky urged that Rachkovsky no longer be required to submit periodic reports, given the tremendous demands of his work and his proved excellence in meeting them. The Foreign Agency was "among the best (if not the best)" of Russia's security sections, insisted the inspector, and all credit belonged to Rachkovsky.[21]

For all the successes of the Okhranka and its Foreign Agency against the People's Will, this revolutionary group, and others like it, remained a serious threat as the 1880s ended. Whereas Sudeikin and his methods had destroyed the domestic wing of People's Will, scattered members were remobilizing at home with help from the still-strong foreign wing. As Durnovo summed up the problem, "The emigrants cannot on their own mount anything serious without the collaboration of persons who live in the Empire."[22] He therefore favoured returning Landezen to Russia, in his guise as a member of the Paris circle of People's Will, to discover the names and locations of revolutionaries within the Empire and, if possible, to provoke them into incriminating acts.

That return took place in the fall of 1889, when Landezen presented himself to a small group of St Petersburg radicals already known to him as advocates of terrorism. Introducing himself as Dr Miller and as the emissary of two leading revolutionaries in Paris, Iury Rapoport and Vladimir Burtsev, he proposed to help stage an immediate series of assassinations.[23] Although their leader, one "Blondin," demurred and said that he had first to acquire sufficient members and money for such an enterprise, Landezen met yet other confederates, including a local activist, N.K. Istomina, and an obviously important visitor from outside the capital addressed solely as "the Professor." Through them, Landezen learned particulars about revolutionary circles in Moscow, Kiev, Odessa, and Vilnius, including names and addresses.

In a memorandum dated 29 November, Durnovo noted that he had subjected the so-called Professor to surveillance rather than arrest, because jailing him would close off to the police all those connected with him, including the revolutionaries abroad. Landezen, who had detected no imminent terrorism and no dangers for himself, would next visit Vilnius, Moscow, Nizhnii Novgorod, Khar'kov, Odessa, and Kiev, where he had scheduled a meeting with the Professor.[24]

Although that meeting failed to take place, Landezen did discover during his tour that the Professor, whose name was S.Ia. Foinitsky, had helped the St Petersburg group set up a centre of revolutionary organization. Claiming that his Paris comrades needed to know the intentions of that new group in order to frame an alliance, Landezen asked that Foinitsky present him with a written declaration of purpose at a meeting in Moscow on 17 December. The revolutionary who complied was Istomina, but she brought only a general commitment to terrorism. To Landezen's request for specific plans, she evasively replied that "only systematic terror is needed and nothing more."[25]

By mid-December, Durnovo was crediting Landezen with "satisfactory results." Besides defining the actual importance of plotters already known to the police, he had identified additional recruits and two meeting places. All that remained was for Landezen to set the bait – using information derived through the Okhranka's interception of letters from Paris to the St Petersburg terrorists and further reports in the future from Landezen at the centre of the Burtsev circle – to enable Durnovo, at an appropriate time, to arrest "Foinitsky, Istomina, and their friends."[26]

Landezen was meanwhile continuing to insist to the St Petersburg terrorists that he could do nothing for them in Paris without stronger evidence of their commitment to the revolutionary cause. Early in January, to his dismay, the revolutionaries countered that they had decided to talk directly with Burtsev and Rapoport during a clandestine visit by them to Russia. Landezen was about to return to Paris, and Durnovo had immediately taken steps to ensure that "not one emigrant should leave Paris or Switzerland without our knowledge."[27]

When he later wrote his memoirs, Burtsev would recall that he felt merely surprise, not suspicion, when Landezen had suddenly reappeared in Paris in mid-January, just as he and Rapoport were making plans to set off for Russia.[28] Burtsev had consequently felt no reservations about introducing Landezen to some bomb-making comrades before he and Rapoport began their daring journey. Throughout they were trailed by police agents so that, while still in Europe, they lost considerable time evasively crisscrossing Austria, Serbia, and Bulgaria.[29] Durnovo, who was closely monitoring the two men's movements, felt great satisfaction when word reached him that Rapoport's arrest at a border crossing early in 1890 had caused Burtsev to reverse his course. Having thereby shielded Landezen from exposure, the police director had next decided not to move at once to apprehend Istomina and her followers lest he betray that the Okhranka had linked them with Burtsev and Rapoport.

Those arrests would come in the fall, when Durnovo would also send agents to the Lower Volga region for a counter-revolutionary sweep. This was largely made possible through intelligence from a long-time Okhranka agent and ex-terrorist named Ivan Okladsky, whom Landezen had implanted among the southern conspirators.[30] In November, Durnovo's chief of detectives, Mednikov, would personally arrest M.B. Sabunaev, the nominal leader of the People's Will in the Volga region;[31] during the last month of 1890, Zubatov and detectives on the flying squad would go from city to city seizing Subunaev's confederates.

In the early months of 1890, moreover, Landezen had netted eight of the revolutionaries he had met in Paris through Burtsev, a group especially dangerous because they were working together to perfect an explosive device for use against the tsar. What they sought was a small bomb, stable when handled with care but certain to detonate on sharp impact, but their experimentation clearly violated French law.

Landezen became a confidant of the revolutionaries by giving them generous financial help, ostensibly doing so as the prodigal son of a rich Warsaw banker and as a student bored with life at the agricultural institute in Paris. Those claims also justified his excellent attire, his quarters on the Right Bank, and his intermittent visits. When he did come, one of the conspirators later recalled, the thin, youthful-looking Landezen was always "dressed immaculately in a fresh suit, scented, and in a top hat and gloves" – surely to avoid becoming involved in the bomb-making. Such fopishness cast him among the mediocre, continued detractor E. Stepanov, just as it also came naturally to a man of "inferior class standing."[32]

By May of 1890 Landezen felt he had won sufficient trust to set his trap: an offer to conduct the group to remote country fields provided by a friend where explosive tests would not attract attention. Knowing that he had to act at once lest Burtsev return and recognize his bizarre shift in identity as the tell-tale ploy of a spy, he held careful consultations with the eight revolutionaries. They agreed to rendezvous for the covert mission at a specified place and time on 29 May. But keeping that appointment in Landezen's place was a contingent of French police, sent under orders from the minister of the interior himself. The eight duped emigrés, having incriminated themselves by carrying suitcases filled with illegal explosive materials, faced immediate arrest and confinement in jail pending trial.[33]

To retaliate against their betrayer, the defendants had their lawyers publicly expose Landezen's role both as a direct participant and as a provider of funds and materials, and a newspaper alluding to that fact reached Burtsev just after he had abandoned his plan to cross the Russian border. Assuming that Landezen worked for Rachkovsky and the Foreign Agency and consequently seeing great risk for himself should he return to Paris, Burtsev had gone instead to England to continue his efforts against the tsar by launching a newspaper.[34]

The court issued an arrest order for Landezen, whom the police could not find. His conviction in absentia followed, and he was sentenced to five years in prison, a term Landezen never had to serve. Instead he secretly accepted a reward and honours from Alexander III and took up a new European identity outside France. In 1892 or 1893 he would convert from Judaism to accept baptism into the Russian Orthodox Church under a new name, A.M. Harting, with Rachkovsky as a witness and the secretary of the Russian embassy in Berlin as his sponsor. Sometime during the 1890s he would marry a Belgian Catholic from Liège, who believed him to be a Russian diplomat (althoug he still remained a salaried security agent) because he regularly accompanied imperial delegations, including the tsar, on European trips.[35]

On the diplomatic front, Landezen had helped forge better relations between Russia and France by delivering the bomb-makers to the French police in 1890. The reports of Rachkovsky convinced Alexander III of the excellence of French cooperation with the Foreign Agency, with the end result that a softening of differences between autocratic Russia and republican France occurred in the 1890s.[36]

All these successes provided proof to St Petersburg of the essential services, going well beyond their original mandate, that internal agents and the Foreign Agency provided to the imperial government. Their effectiveness against anti-tsarist groups coalescing in Russia and Western Europe was axiomatic to their masters as they made themselves indispensable in areas well outside of police work. Furthermore, they pushed police work into new areas of criminal and semi-criminal activity, political influence, and "public relations." As Landezen had shown, by far the best method of discovering who belonged to the interdependent network of revolutionaries at home and abroad was to infiltrate the ranks of plotters already known. It was a tricky business requiring strong nerve and a special flair, two qualities that enabled internal agents such as Landezen to do so well for so long. But it also required inducing radicals to participate in breaking the law which, it was argued, they would have done anyway. And it required maintaining good relations with foreign authorities.

By 1890, his fifth year as head of the Foreign Agency, Rachkovsky's high standing with the tsar had translated into authority over imperial security matters in Europe that few, if any, dared challenge. Thus it was Rachkovsky who, each fall, personally headed the imperial bodyguard in Fredensborg during the tsar's annual vacation at the palace of his mother-in-law, the Queen of Denmark. He was there, ready to serve as the intermediary, when his agent Jules Hansen arrived in September 1891, with a secret letter from the French premier, Charles de Freycinet, proposing close military consultations between France and Russia.[37]

Recalling this period, Count S.Iu. Witte, who became minister of finance in 1892, singled out Rachkovsky for being instrumental in bringing France and Russia together in an entente. According to Witte's rather extravagent assessment in his memoirs, Rachkovsky "had more influence on the course of our rapprochement with France [a military convention was agreed to in 1893–94] than did our ambassadors."[38] Witte may have let his gratitude for the entente (which made French banks a ready source of loans) colour his thinking, but he further described Rachkovsky as a "remarkably intelligent man, in fact the most gifted and intelligent police official I have ever met." Witte also recounts that Emile Loubet, the French premier, entrusted his security to Rachkovsky on at least one trip within France and mentioned having provided a room for his use inside the Elysee Palace.

When Nicholas II succeeded his father in 1894, Rachkovsky prudently watched for any moves against him by critics who might attempt to exploit the change in leadership. His opponents in St Petersburg could easily argue that his expenditures and gratuities were excessive, especially during a lull in terrorism; they could question also his ethics, his secret powers, and his high living. Vulnerable though he was, however, Rachkovsky knew that most officials favoured granting him free reign, given the amorality and secrecy of ruthless revolutionaries.

With all this in mind, Rachkovsky took exception to the arrival in Paris in January 1895 of an agent sent by the Ministry of the Interior, one Ivan F. Manasevich-Manuilov, a correspondent of the *St Petersburg News* (*Novosti*). Whereas this journalist's official assignment was to influence the French press, Rachkovsky suspected that enemies in the capital had also commissioned Manuilov to gather "information about my personal life, my financial position abroad, about the staff of the Agentura, and about my relations with the prefecture and with the embassy in Paris."[39]

Once satisfied that certain "Okhranka parasites" were in fact using Manuilov against him, Rachkovsky sent back to Russia the man he labelled "a nimble Jew … quite ready to do anything for a goodly sum."[40] The so-called parasites that Rachkovsky had in mind could have included Prince V.P. Meshchersky, the publisher of the St Petersburg *Citizen* (*Grazhdanin*) and an influential figure at court (Witte scathingly termed Manasevich a "spiritual son" of Meshchersky); or, quite possibly, the vice-minister of the interior, Plehve, then overseer of the Department of the Police.

Whether or not he had felt threatened, the next year Rachkovsky formally expanded his operations into Berlin because, as he made clear to St Petersburg, Russian emigrés had concentrated there to avoid his Paris-based security network. Adroitly preparing for a new centre of Okhranka activity, Rachkovsky first obtained permission from the German police to send six Russian agents into the German capital; then, to win the necessary approval to build that force into an Agentura or secret service, he summoned Landezen, now living in Belgium under his new name of Harting, to take up residence in Berlin as a wealthy Russian merchant with connections in high political circles. Following the example of Rachkovsky, Harting courted local dignitaries with sumptuous dinners at his fine house.

At least by December 1900 the secret imperial Agentura in Berlin was in full operation as an independent entity, and Harting would command it until 1905. Among his agents would be Zinaida Zhuchenko, Lev Beitner, and Dr Jacob Zhitomirsky, a deft infiltrator who became a trusted collaborator of Lenin himself. Thanks to Zhitomirsky, the Okhranka would, in 1907, capture the Bolshevik bank robber Kamo (S.A. Ter-Petrossian) and, through him, expose Lenin's plan to convert several hundred thousand stolen rubles at a number of European banks on a single appointed day (sympathizers were to exchange no more than a few 500-ruble notes in any one transaction).[41]

Harting would also take charge of counter-intelligence in Europe against the enemy during the Russo-Japanese War of 1904–5. Ordered by the tsar to manage security for the Russian Imperial fleet that left the Baltic for the Far East in October 1904, he would manage to escape blame for the enormous diplomatic embarrassment that ensued when Russian gunners, fearing a Japanese attack, in fog-shrouded waters of the North Sea, mistakenly fired on an English fishing boat and killed two fishermen aboard.

With his sphere of operations limited once more to France and Switzerland as the new century began, Rachkovsky found himself mainly confined to the commonplace task of embassies worldwide: building foreign sympathy for his government and its causes. As he had done since 1884, Rachkovsky routinely paid locals for pro-Russian tracts and articles, including, besides Hansen, Calmette from *Figaro* and Maurras from *Petit Parisien*. Giving a code name of Ratmir to a writer named Raymond Recouli suggests that he hired some journalists to gather intelligence as well. Or perhaps that he exaggerated the role of favoured persons to justify raising their pay.

Evidence shows that Rachkovsky contrived publicity for what we now call disinformation, or information fabricated to mislead. One documented use by him of such material dates from 1892, when he arranged the publication of a baseless attack against the emigrés that was falsely attributed to a leading Marxist thinker and publicist, G.V. Plekhanov. That forged statement laid charges of malfeasance against the emigrés who were then soliciting help for the 1892 famine in Russia – a lie framed to cause friction among them and public anger against them.[42] Instead the emigrés easily refuted the fakery. Rachkovsky almost certainly made subsequent use of disinformation in subtler forms, but, again, with mixed results. When Russian police backing for Rachkovsky's "La Ligue pour le salut de la patrie russe" became known, this early attempt at enlisting the French to promote sympathies for Russia backfired to the discredit of the imperial government.

Just as lies and propaganda go together, so do subterfuge and spies, and every self-respecting revolutionary or security agent deals sceptically with former foes who volunteer their services. A case in point is that of N.K. Pauli, to whom Rachkovsky paid 600 francs in late 1900 or early 1901 for two months of service to the Foreign Agency. Pauli had served the revolutionary cause inside Russia during the 1880s and 1980s, when he was twice internally exiled as a political criminal. In the first half of 1900, as an emigré in Paris, he had written to the Department of Police in St Petersburg proposing to become an internal agent. Citing as one reason his dismay over a resurgence of the People's Will, he admitted that his second incentive was mercenary: "my wish to compensate myself for long deprivation."[43] That June the vice-director recorded that the department would not respond to Pauli, but Rachkovsky seems to have done so.

By May of 1901 the head of the Special Section in St Petersburg was informing Rachkovsky about covert visits to Moscow, Kiev, and Kharkov by Pauli and about his return abroad after a police search of his living quarters.[44] His two months of service to the Foreign Agency had apparently preceded that trip, and it seems likely that Rachkovsky had hired Pauli in a peripheral role to watch and test him.

Having learned from an Okhranka agent that Pauli had met with revolutionaries in Moscow to organize terrorist acts, the director of police rushed a warning to Rachkovsky that Pauli planned to murder him and to "expose" the Foreign Agency. The next month, on 19 July, Rachkovsky sent to St Petersburg a cryptic, ominous, and perhaps hyperbolic dispatch: "An extraordinary circumstance has forced me to render Pauli harmless and to pull down an extremely dangerous People's Will circle that has come into being."[45]

In July of 1902 Rachkovsky lost the top foreign security post that he had held for nearly two decades. A.A. Lopukhin, who had just taken charge of the Department of Police, claims that he convinced Plehve, newly installed as the minister of the interior, that Rachkovsky too often used illegal tactics. Although the charge is no doubt correct, Lopukhin's specific example – that one of Rachkovsky's agents had participated in what he called the "anarchists' bombing" of a cathedral in Liège, Belgium, in 1895 – seems to have been hearsay rather than documented fact.[46]

Plehve instead exploited sensitivity about a French charlatan named M. Philippe to win assent from Nicholas II to remove Rachkovsky from the Foreign Agency. Philippe, who had drawn close to the tsarina during her visit to France in the first months of 1902, had misled Alexandra into believng she was pregnant, and an imperial announcement to this effect was issued on her return to Russia. Its necessary retraction had caused unpleasant gossip in St Petersburg. Rachkovsky had seen fit to compile proof that Philippe did not, as he claimed, hold a medical degree and that the French had earlier prosecuted him for practising medicine without a licence – findings that Rachkovsky had been told to forget when he personally conveyed them to minister of the interior Sipiagin. Once Plehve had found Rachkovsky's report in the files of his predecessor, the new interior minister had been able to use this proof of meddling in the imperial family's affairs to win the tsar's approval for dismissing Rachkovsky in July.

One year later, on 13 July 1903, a Department of Police report justified that firing by documenting that Rachkovsky had sorely neglected his security work after 1890. With his foiling of the bomb-makers, it argued, Rachkovsky had begun to exaggerate his own importance and "allowed himself to interfere in international political affairs and credited himself with an important leadership role that did not correspond to his actual position" – a reference to his role in the Franco-Russian entente. During an unauthorized and exaggerated pro-paganda campaign against the revolutionaries early in 1902, moreover, he had inadvertently caused the imperial regime to appear on the verge of collapse. Finally, the department was still investigating the Liège bombing, Rachkovsky's misuse of Agency funds, his excessive private business deals, and his misdirection of power against personal foes.[47]

Still backed by important friends, Rachkovsky retained his place with them in high circles. The Grand Duke Sergei Alexandrovich, then governor-general of Moscow, for example, had placed Rachkovsky at his side in February of 1901 to review the Kremlin parade of 45,000 workers on the fortieth anniversary of the Emancipation of the serfs. In February 1905 terrorists would kill the grand duke. One day later the tsar, acting on the advice of D.F. Trepov, the powerful governor-general of St Petersburg, would fully reinstate Rachkovsky by giving him emergency authority over the Okhranka's Special Section.

Rachkovsky's successor at the Foreign Agency, meanwhile, was L.A. Rataev, who had reluctantly surrendered the Special Section in St Petersburg to undertake the monitoring of anti-tsarist forces in France, Switzerland, and England. Later describing the Foreign Agency as a "hollow shell" and relations with French officials as severely frayed when he arrived, Rataev would repeatedly contend that Rachkovsky had effectively handicapped him.

The most notable of Rataev's accomplishments, in any case, was information provided in October 1902 leading to the capture of a terrorist named E.K. Grigor'ev, which in turn led to the arrest of Michael Mel'nikov and Grigory Gershuni, the latter the head of the Socialist Revolutionary (SR) Battle Organization. Thanks to secret agent Evno Azeff, Rataev also provided full reports on two emigré conventions: the 1903 Socialist Revolutionary Congress in Geneva and the 1904 Congress of Russian revolutionary and oppositional groups in Paris.[48] In January of 1905, at Lopukhin's request, Rataev took charge of all European operations by agreeing to oversee Harting's Berlin agency, perhaps for reasons of economy.

For the fiscal year of 1904, police records show that Lopukhin had set a budget of 132,381 rubles for all European operations, a total roughly comparable to the slightly more than 300,000 francs that Rachkovsky had dispersed in 1894 (when the costly Berlin Agency did not exist) from his office in Paris. In 1904, moreover, the funds that Lopukhin sent to Rataev in Paris (50,535 rubles) and to Harting in Berlin (44,780 rubles) provided solely for their own hiring of agents, with the balance of the budget (37,0666 rubles) paid out from the capital to all others (agents in Vienna, for example, received 5,256 rubles; to those in Galicia, Prussian Poznan, and Silesia went 6,400 rubles).[49] That Lopukhin found himself short of funds as the 1904 calendar year ended is clear from his having used that reason to turn down a request that he increase security for the grand duke in Moscow.

Unfortunately for Lopukhin, a month after Harting's demotion in January came the grand duke's assassination. In the wave of changes that followed, Trepov and others forced Lopukhin to abandon the Police Department, which, in turn, came under the supervision of Trepov, as the new assistant minister of the interior, on 24 May. Three months later, on 1 August, just a week before Rachkovsky became vice-director of the Police Department, Rataev was forced to surrender his command of the Foreign Agency to Harting, who seems to have been agitating against him.[50] Rataev went quietly lest, as Trepov threatened, he lose his pension. Nor would he later join the ranks of Okhranka exposers, even though Burtsev would try to recruit him.[51]

As for Burtsev, this former terrorist had, by 1905, emerged as a crusading opponent of all criminal political acts. Having returned to St Petersburg legally in 1905 as the publisher of a journal about Russian revolutionary history, he began to gather material on police misconduct. In 1906, as the autocracy reasserted its authority, Burtsev came to realize that his contacts with an informer from within the police named Bakai had provoked police surveillance, and he quickly moved to France.

During the next several years, Burtsev established himself as an emigré critic ready – too impulsively his critics would say – to publish the names of alleged police agents provided by defectors. In June 1909 he disclosed that A.M. Harting of the Russian embassy was not only directing the secret security activities of imperial foreign agents within France but that he was also guilty of evading a local warrant for his arrest as one Landezen, a convicted fugitive from French justice since 1890.[52]

Harting, aware of his vulnerability, had deliberately avoided attention and travelled a lot. He did this not only in the course of directing the Foreign Agency but also to counter the surge in illegal arms shipments from Europe into Russia that followed the 1905 revolution. Harting had therefore spent considerable time establishing a network of shipping spies in the major European ports, especially in the north. He had quietly courted assistance in interdiction from local police directors, winning little help in England and Finland but reasonably good cooperation in France, Germany, and Denmark, as long as the public did not learn of it. No one knew better than he that ordinary Europeans did not want the Okhranka in their midst.[53]

At the first airing of Burtsev's revelations, therefore, Harting had immediately abandoned France, knowing how difficult it would be for his colleagues to deal with the public outrage that would certainly follow. On advice telegrammed from St Petersburg, embassy officials had stubbornly feigned ignorance and deflected all queries from the press by citing "the absence of any official data at the disposal of the Ministry of the Interior."[54] Lacking specifics, they said, they could neither confirm nor deny anything.

Immediate outrage from socialist Jean Jaurès and fellow left-wing deputies caused the Chamber of Deputies to banish all foreign secret police agencies from French soil. In response, the Agency official filling in for Harting – V.I. Andreev, a Gendarme officer – informed St Petersburg that it was "absolutely necessary, especially now, to have a cadre, although fewer, and to separate from the permanent detectives the suspect and the weak."[55] By August Andreev could report that the French premier, Aristide Briand, had agreed that "our *Agentura* will continue to work in the future completely freely" so long as it took "every precaution" not to cause public scandal or to infringe the rights of French citizens.[56]

Assuming control of the Foreign Agency in November was A.A. Krasil'nikov, whose bogus assignment to the embassy as a full-fledged diplomat hid his connection with the police-tainted Ministry of the Interior. Krasil'nikov, who had been living in Paris, having retired from service in 1901 in the Horse Guards, was without any police or diplomatic experience. He was, however, a friend and former subordinate of General P.G. Kurlov, formerly a guards' commander and now the assistant minister of the interior, and that link appears to have been the reason for the appointment. Filtered into Paris at the same time, but discreetly kept apart, were a number of experienced agents from Okhranka units within the Empire and from the security division of the imperial court.[57]

Given the effectiveness of Burtsev's anti-imperial publicity on French opinion, Krasil'nikov ventured at once to find the impossible: a Parisian editor both influential and bribeable who would give prominence in his newspaper to convincingly commendatory articles about Russia for a reasonable price. Late in December he reported on his approaches to the higher staff of the two largest newspapers in Paris, *Le Journal* and *Le Matin*.

Krasil'nikov mentioned by name editor M. Lhetellier of *Le Journal*, a daily whose circulation hovered around the million mark, but warned that no single person controlled its orientation. Unfortunately Lhetellier had stressed the inherent risk of "des bombes dans les bureaux" should he offend local radicals and the inability of his paper to cooperate without first receiving "compensation" for an earlier shortfall of 60,000 francs. That is, *Le Journal* had received the miserly rate of 2 francs per line for 15,000 lines of pro-imperial content during Russia's negotiations for a French loan compared to the 6 francs per line paid by the embassy to the rival *Le Matin*. Against such an impossible demand, Krasil'nikov thought it preferable "to acquire a large paper ourselves."[58]

In a dispatch two days later Krasil'nikov reported that he had said nothing about money during two exploratory discussions at *Le Matin* but, because a principal editor had left implicit at their second meeting that someone higher had approved negotiations, a "serious figure" would have to arise. What Krasil'nikov hoped for were factual articles reflecting a French viewpoint that would deglorify the revolutionaries.[59] Seemingly no agreement could be reached, so obviously incompatible were the minimum requirements of both sides. It also seems highly probable that French journalists made sport of the Russian overtures.

Keeping watch on emigré opponents posed an additional challenge to Krasil'nikov, who in mid-1910 ruled out the presence at the embassy of any imperial external agents by hiring a private French detective agency to conduct and report all necessary surveillance.[60] He also forbade anyone in the secret service to receive or send communications through the embassy or to drop in for any reason.

Krasil'nikov felt uneasy about the intelligence provided by detectives not directly under his control. So the new director of the Foreign Agency looked for informers he might personally cultivate among French nationals. One effort, which he described to the Special Section in June of 1912, concerned V. Bely, the publisher of the Russian-language *Paris Newssheet*, a daily which Krasil'nikov chose to describe as "clearly dangerous ... with respect to its [radical] influence on emigré circles."[61]

Presenting himself at the *Newssheet* office as a private person with ties to St Petersburg, Krasil'nikov had broached to Bely, in the most general terms, the possibility of his performing "essential services" for the imperial government. Their ensuing talks, however, disclosed no potential spy but, rather, a businessman who "takes no part at all in revolutionary activity, is not interested in it, and therefore cannot be an informer about it." By his own admission, Bely included radical content in *Newssheet* because the only journalists who worked cheaply were revolutionaries. When Krasil'nikov had turned the conversation to the possibility of *Newssheet*'s providing coverage favourable to the imperial government, Bely had cited related business costs that would require an annual subsidy of 50,000 francs. Met with indifference, Bely had sharply reduced his price to 10,000 francs or even less.[62] What happened next is unrecorded, but the implausible venture seems mainly to have been laughable – a characteristic that Krasil'nikov may have intended to convey to the Security Section.

In contrast, a dispatch from the Foreign Agency head to the Department of Police during this same month was conventionally bureaucratic. Citing the high cost of his detectives, coupled with his large outlays to win over cautious local officials and to provision his still-indispensible internal agents, Krasil'nikov had strongly urged his superiors to bolster his "limited funds," a request they had heard before and would hear again.[63]

Police officials in St Petersburg instead sent him an internal agent whom they wanted out of the way, one A.I. Litvin, who had entered into service to the Okhranka in Warsaw in 1904. This operative had first incurred trouble in 1910 through a complaint to the Ministry of the Interior "from the Jewess Lutskaia that Litvin had placed her husband under arrest with the objective of extorting 1,000 rubles." Investigation proved that Litvin and other officials of the Agentura had been arresting people "in violation of the fundamental rules of the Okhranka."[64] As punishment, Litvin was taken off secret work but not discharged.

Severance for Litvin did result a year later, after he had been found guilty of "unconscionable" behaviour during games of cards with members of the Warsaw Russian Assembly. But he took his leave threatening legal action and the exposure of Okhranka secrets before a court of law. In June 1911 his wife had gone to the Department of Police in St Petersburg with complaints that superiors had "forced" Litvin to cheat at cards. Fearing a scandal, the assistant minister of the interior arranged for the Moscow Okhranka to place Litvin on its payroll but specified that he not be given undercover assignments.

For whatever cause, the Okhranka decided in July 1912 to send Litvin to Paris to work for Krasil'nikov. Once more in secret service, he would join a security operation of growing importance during these prewar years: the countering of German military intelligence. Because he would again disappoint his superiors, this time by compromising his identity, he would retire to England before war broke out with a passport listing his surname as Landen.

Krasil'nikov had meanwhile grown thoroughly dissatisfied with his paltry returns from the private, twenty-eight-man detective agency that had been costing him dearly since 1910. Dismissing them in 1913 on the grounds that emigrés no longer had to be watched, he secretly acquired his own surveillance group of half that size – one ostensibly private to satisfy the French government – headed by two Okhranka veterans and French nationals, Henri Bint and Andrei Samben; as a novel financial arrangement, he included in their signed agreement a clause endowing "their" agency's funds and furniture to the surviving partner, should one of them die. Besides limiting their staff to twelve, he demanded from them very discreet recruitment, lest the dismissed detectives learn of it and inform Burtsev, in order to retaliate for not being rehired.[65]

Very basically, as he had specified to St Petersburg, Krasil'nikov had rid himself of agents who seemingly lacked honesty and efficiency – two essential traits that were hard to confirm, especially in operatives acting wholly on their own. Thus he had also dismissed an agent in England for the same reasons in August of 1913; the letter from that Englishman to the Special Section to protest his loss of a monthly stipend casts light on the niggling minutiae of Foreign Agency operations.

According to this disgruntled agent named Filenas, he had only recently been ineptly interviewed in London by the chief of the Foreign Agency himself. (Because, in keeping with security protocol, no real names were mentioned, Filenas had wrongly assumed that his Okhranka interviewer was Krasil'nikov.) Meeting this evaluator for tea at a Lyons restaurant, wrote Filenas, he had been the one prudent enough to insist that they move their heated conversation to the street because, as only he had noticed, the "revolutionary-populist Rapoport" was seated nearby.[66] As they walked, continued Filenas, his briefcase had "alarmed" his companion into demanding to see its contents; and, once he had complied, the man from Paris had rudely doubted that the Russian-language documents inside had come from the Ministry of the Interior, as Filenas claimed, or that Filenas could read them. When Filenas next offered newspaper clippings that praised his journalistic competence, the emissary from Paris had ended their talk by implying that Filenas had not written the pieces himself.

His dismissal for not fulfilling orders had followed that irrelevant interview, Filenas complained, even though he was doing the one job assigned to him, that of writing pro-Russian articles for English newspapers. What Filenas failed once more to provide, however, were clippings to prove that the articles he claimed to have written had actually appeared in print, the very evidence that Krasil'nikov had long been demanding. For the Security Section, as for the chief of the Foreign Agency, that dereliction ended their monthly stipend to Filenas.

By showing animosity, of course, a dismissed agent could often induce the Foreign Agency to continue payments simply to buy his silence about its operations. In this same period, the "inadequate performance" of an Italian detective named Leoni had cost him his Foreign Agency job, and he had reapplied for work a year later and claimed that he had been wronged. When he had then received neither consideration nor a hint of compensation, he had gone straight to Burtsev with documents he had stolen for just such an eventuality.[67]

Long-term agents sometimes bid for immediate retirement on a comfortable pension, likewise expecting the Foreign Agency to comply to ensure their loyalty. An example dates from two months after Filenas' letter, when an Englishman, Michael Thorpe, who had joined the Foreign Agency twelve years before on the recommendation of Scotland Yard, wrote to inform Krasil'nikov that his "ruined" nervous system and "chronic rheumatism" ruled out further service. With no further investigation, Krasil'nikov had duly recommended a permanent administrative pension for Thorpe.[68]

With considerable élan, the widow of a deceased Foreign Agency official in good standing had used her own inside information in 1915 to win herself the pension that her husband, Colonel Erhardt, had not lived to collect. Having been left without means of support, she argued, she had been reduced to selling what she knew to the enemies of the Russian government. Krasil'nikov had urged St Petersburg to recall the widow Erhardt immediately, and he seems to have been instrumental in awarding a pension of 1,000 francs per month that she would receive until 1917.[69]

Foreign Service operations, like the widow's pension, would routinely continue until 1917. Their primary aims in Europe were clear enough: to monitor and penetrate emigré revolutionary groups, to interdict their shipments of weapons and inflammatory tracts to Russia, and to sway European opinion towards sympathizing with the imperial government. Thanks to recurring evidence that Russian radicals tended to experiment with explosives, the police forces of several European countries found it in their own interests quietly to cooperate with the Foreign Agency in its pursuit of anti-tsarist plotters. So on that counter-revolutionary front the Foreign Agency did win some victories. For all the funds it expended in Europe to shape press commentary, however, only a self-promoting director such as Rachkovsky ever claimed much success for the Foreign Agency on that front. From the first, the Russian Foreign Agency had faced problems quite unlike any other police agency: it was compelled to deal with a large army of native revolutionaries who had declared war on the imperial government from distant and widespread foreign sanctuaries. Here was a new kind of police problem and Rachkovsky and his colleagues attempted to devise new means to deal with it.

CHAPTER SIX

The Challenge of Quelling the Fighting Squads, 1906–1909

To stem the widespread civil disobedience of 1905, Nicholas II promised in his October Manifesto to grant political changes that he had long opposed, including the legalization of independent political parties. The government, seriously disrupted and demoralized in 1905 by a massive revolutionary upheaval, including the general strike of October, was unable to restore stability quickly. In addition, it faced mounting campaigns of terrorism and violence. In 1906 and 1907, when extremists on both the left and right alike organized ever more widely at the grass-roots level to wage political warfare through violence and disinformation, the Okhranka faced new challenges.

As for the security implications of the tsar's decision to permit political parties and a broader franchise for Duma elections, Nicholas expected to divide the opposition. What initially resulted was a split in early 1906 between the liberals and the revolutionaries over accepting a legislative role through the Duma. Then, when the radicals did join in, differences erupted over programs and strategies. The links of far left parties with squads of fighters and assassins – a prime concern for the Okhranka – also angered the liberals, because the monarchists found justification for responding in kind.

Both the illegal squads of the left and the squads of the right engaged in violence, but each posed a different dilemma. The Okhranka was accustomed to throwing its resources into the struggle against the revolutionaries of the left; but never before had it faced a violent right-wing movement, and one which espoused the same principles that Okhranka officers were sworn to defend. Government and Okhranka officials held different opinions on the right-wing squads. Some leaders of political investigation were ready to allow the squads to carry out outrages under the tsarist banner. These officers (Klimovich, Komissarov, and Kurlov are the best examples) believed the court favoured such solidarity with all those who supported monarchist principles. Others, and Prime Minister Stolypin was the first among them, conducted a different policy towards right-wing squads: he hoped to maintain contact with them and, at the same time, work to blunt their worst extremes.

In the last two months of 1905, following the Manifesto, organized gangs of political street fighters posed a new security threat. This was illustrated graphically by the armed uprising of radical workers in Moscow on 7 December, just after the government's decisive arrest of the 233-member executive committee of the St Petersburg Soviet. This had resulted in the quick proliferation of bullying squads, left against right, that attracted many youths and criminals. Through 1907 and into 1908, these urban gangs that openly advocated violence on polit-ical grounds continued to shatter the peace and managed to muddle police efforts to stop them.

This new level of revolutionary activity is distinguishable from the terrorist groups of the Socialist Revolutionary party which specialized in political assassinations. The main group was the party's Battle Organization, but an offshoot of its Northern Organization called Karl's Flying Detachment consisted of young persons attracted by the prospect of terrorist activities who were not even members of the party. These groups assassinated several thousand persons, mainly government officials, in 1906 and 1907 until the government under Stolypin took especially harsh measures to end the wave of killings.

Whereas terrorist squads might range over a wide territory, form themselves into small units, employ elaborate intelligence and conceal-ment capabilities and focus on assassinations, urban fighting squads identified with the left were based in a particular city. They received serious attention from the Okhranka, especially since one of their political reasons for mayhem was to show the ineptness of the tsarist regime. Another was to discredit their enemies by staging crimes to make them appear the work of right-wingers and even to suggest complicity by the tsar's police. Given these tactics, the Okhranka came to see these urban squads as a variant of the secret terrorist cells that had existed for years. Security officials understood that they, like the terrorist cells, had direct links to the illegal revolutionary parties on the far left.

In 1906, however, any group that registered as a legal party could exercise political rights as long as it fully complied with imperial law. Put another way, no party admitted to the Duma could use criminal means – fighting squads, terrorist cells, or whatever – to further its goals. In so far as the self-proclaimed revolutionary parties would meet that requirement in exchange for Duma participation, then, the state would pacify extremist opponents and bolster security. But, since parties with their origins in revolutionary ideologies, such as the Social Democrats and the Socialist Revolutionaries (SR), claimed legal status while substantial numbers of members covertly continued their criminal activities, the Okhranka increased its efforts to manoeuvre inside agents into their midst. Right-wing party members also attempted to infiltrate them.[1]

In early 1906 the revolutionaries had broken ranks with the liberals by boycotting and strongly opposing the first Duma, only to reverse themselves following its dissolution. Thus the Socialist Revolutionary party fielded its own candidates in the 1907 vote for the 516-member second Duma and emerged with thirty-seven seats. When those delegates were added to the sixty-five Social Democrats, 104 Laborites, sixteen People's Socialists, and ninety-eight Kadets, a fractious and disunited "opposition majority" resulted, and all within that bloc came under Okhranka scrutiny.

No less subject to security investigations were right-wingers, within the Duma and without, whose tactics went beyond legal bounds or otherwise effectively undermined the autocracy. Left unchecked, they, too, could make the police appear inept – or involved. Not long after the October Manifesto, after all, centrist politicians had begun to vilify right-wing militants, commonly called Black Hundreds; and as rightist rampages increased in cities, towns, and villages in 1906, public outcries against the Black Hundreds also mounted. Duma members echoed these concerns and pilloried the government and police for complicity in right-wing schemes.

The name "Black Hundred" originated in seventeenth-century Russia and referred to tax-paying merchants who loyally supported the tsar. When the right-wing fighting squads that coalesced in 1905 in the two capitals adopted the name, the twentieth-century Black Hundred movement began. Capturing the popular imagination, those initial squads inspired thousands of namesake groups to spring up during the next three years across Russia. With no central leadership, the acts and intensity of these groups varied greatly, although most tended to share a monarchist/orthodox outlook that made them haters of Jews, radicals, liberals, and all persons derisively categorized as non-Russians.[2] Newspapers that espoused this same thinking consequently earned a Black Hundred label, as did sympathetic clergy and teachers, whether or not they had real ties to organized groups that claimed or appeared to be Black Hundreds.

As criminal violence and the Black Hundreds became intrinsically linked for most Russians, monarchists found it imperative to distance themselves from these right-wing squads. An especial dilemma had faced the main monarchist party, the Union of the Russian People, formed in St Petersburg in November of 1905. It had come into being through the combining of a large group of right-wing militants, the Voluntary People's Guard (founded in Moscow in 1881 to protect travelling members of the imperial family) with a better-educated but smaller and non-combative right-wing group called the Russian Assembly (founded in the capital by professional-class monarchists about 1900).

Leaders of the Assembly, with backing from the palace and the Okhranka,[3] had instigated the merger following the Manifesto, and they had done so because the Assembly could not alone attract the broad membership that an influential political party required. Talks had initially taken place between them and leaders of the People's Guard in late October 1905, just after Nicholas II had honoured the guardsmen with a special audience. Representatives for the Assembly were B.V. Nikolsky, V.M. Purishkevich, and the man who would emerge as head of the Union, A.I. Dubrovin, a sixty-year-old doctor of comfortable means who provided his house for the meeting. One Volunteer Guard representative, Poltoratsky,[4] was actually a secret agent for the Moscow Okhranka; through him, the Moscow Okhranka could claim a direct role in organizing the Union. So, too, the St Petersburg Okhranka, under A.V. Gerasimov, would shortly manoeuvre one of its agents, S.Ia. Iakovlev, into the newly formed Union. Of all the secret agents, only Iakovlev told the group he had penetrated because of his police connection.

Given these Okhranka links and the Volunteer Guardsmen majority in its ranks, it was not surprising that, a little more than a month after its founding, the Union provided seven hundred men to assist the police should violence erupt on 9 January 1906, the first anniversary of Bloody Sunday. But the appearance on the streets of this private force, complete with guns, caused even a right-wing journalist to complain. He was Count V.P. Meshchersky, the editor of the daily *Citizen* (*Grazhdanin*), who wrote: "If we have come to the point where the Russian people must get involved in an alliance which, under the protection of policemen, appropriates for itself a monopoly of devotion to the tsar ... and which arms itself with revolvers to kill anybody who is an enemy according to its judgment, then the only thing left for decent and honest people is to cry for help."[5]

Because no private citizen could legally carry a gun without a licence, Meshchersky must have found it highly significant that, in the very next month, the minister of the interior ordered the automatic issuance of a permit to carry arms to anyone who submitted a certificate from the council of the Union of the Russian People. By expediting the arming of persons approved by the Union, the government appeared to confirm a quasi-alliance both with the pre-eminent monarchist party and with the independent militias that were led and manned largely by members of the Union of the Russian People.

At this same time, N.M. Iuskevich-Kraskovsky, a candidate member of the Union's council who laid claim to an office of his own at party headquarters, was coming to public attention as the leader of the prominent right-wing fighting squad in St Petersburg. He was also reported to be a strong influence over other squads. One piece of evidence, not necessarily trustworthy, is testimony from 1917 by a Black Hundred captain to the effect that the brutal Nevsky district fighting squad led by M.P. Zubkov, known as "the murderer," carried out some of its raids and robberies in the post-1905 period to punish "burghers who had provoked displeasure in Kraskovsky."[6]

Some four or five right-wing groups then existed in the capital. One relatively small unit, for example, called itself the Society of Active Struggle with Revolutionaries and claimed to have a single objective: to annihilate members of the Bolshevik faction of the Social Democratic party. Members of the larger group under Kraskovsky struck at other enemies, including, on Easter of 1906, one of their own believed to have filched from the Union cashbox. This Easter reprisal would be recalled by Kraskovsky in March 1911 as a witness before the judicial investigator Alexandrov in another case.[7] There he spoke of the target as V.M. Snesarev, his assistant, whom a mob of his Black Hundred followers insisted "had gone to the council headquarters of the Union of the Russian People and had taken money to pay for a holiday." Kraskovsky said that he dispersed the complainants after they "threatened to kill [Snesarev] and to burn his house" but that his followers returned the next day and committed the arson.[8]

Although Kraskovsky admitted no misconduct by his subordinate, in the summer of 1906 a journal in the capital painted Snesarev as a common thief. Its report, which followed Snesarev's death in a skirmish with Bolsheviks, claimed that an inventory of the belongings of the deceased included "1,600 rubles of the missing money, eight gold wrist watches, fifteen silver wrist watches, a couple of dozen purses and many Astrakhan hats." According to those who knew Snesarov, continued the report, "prior to his 'political' activity ... he had worn ragged footwear and had led the life of a near pauper."[9]

As part of that political activity, the previous April Snesarov very likely had taken part in the resurgence of right-wing patrols in the capital, this time in connection with the imminent inauguration of the

Duma. That same month, as well, cautionary evidence against such freelance militias reached the Okhranka from the Gendarme chief in the Caucasus city of Tiflis. Condemning the culprits as Black Hundreds, the chief expressed concern that gangs of Tiflis residents had "started conducting various investigations on their own, searching and detaining people at their own discretion without any control by police and Gendarme officials."[10]

Even more troubling were the escalating confrontations in the capital between Black Hundreds and Social Democrat fighting squads based in the Semianikov shipyards. One notorious incident was the bombing by Social Democrats that killed eleven in a tavern frequented by Black Hundreds near the front gate of the yard. Among Black Hundred retaliations was the street assassination on 4 May of a shipyard worker named Mukhin by another of peasant origin, G.S. Larichkin, who would later swear that he had killed his socialist enemy on orders from Kraskovsky.[11]

May 1906 also brought the dissolution of the first Duma by Nicholas II, who, like the Union, found the ambitions of his critics in the Duma presumptuous. In July, I.V. Toropov of the Union placed before the Department of Police and the new prime minister, P.A. Stolypin, a criminal charge against a leftist party that would soon campaign against the Union in elections for the second Duma. Toropov claimed that the Socialist Revolutionary central committee had voted to resume a terrorist campaign against government officials. Here, purportedly, was crucial intelligence, and Toropov would later deride the Okhranka and the government for not acting on it.[12]

But the Okhranka and the government had good cause for caution. Plotting to kill certainly constituted a criminal act, but detaining persons on that charge required legal grounds. Whatever evidence Toropov did offer required substantiation and, as he himself later noted, the Okhranka's secret agent in the Socialist Revolutionary leadership, Evno Azeff, presumably contradicted Toropov. At that time, moreover, the Okhranka was already on constant high alert for terrorist attacks and insisting that top officials use bodyguards and other security precautions.

Security analysts also had to factor in that Toropov might well have volunteered baseless charges just to inflate the importance of the Union and himself or, conversely, to hurt the hated SRs. Toropov, after all, openly belonged to the Society of Active Struggle with the Revolution and played a key role in the Black Hundred newspaper, *Veche*, which was published in his home. Even had Okhranka officers found Toropov's assertions credible, they would have had to weigh the possible consequences of counter moves, and to decide whether a particular response might, for example, expose tsarist agents or otherwise jeopardize crucial investigations under way.

Problems notwithstanding, the government still unreservedly welcomed informants, and police officials consequently had to learn to handle them adroitly. Courtesy coupled with discreet scepticism was the prescription favoured by one head of the Moscow Okhranka, Colonel E.K. Klimovich. "People would come to me," Toropov quotes him as saying, "and report that bombs and arms were hidden in this place or that ... the information practically never turned out to be true. On the other hand, when I refused to organize a search, my informants became highly indignant. I complained of this delicate state of affairs to the Governor, and he gave me a piece of practical advice based on his experience: 'Don't listen to them, but don't push them away either'."[13]

One example of volunteered intelligence that must have been received with grave reservations by the Department of Police dates from 13 August 1906, or one day after terrorists had killed more than fifty people at Stolypin's country home on Aptekarsky Island near St Petersburg with a bomb meant for the prime minister himself. In that deposition, Union spokeswoman V.N. Stepanova-Dezorbi belatedly claimed to have learned, a full four days before, "from a person right in the centre of the Socialist Revolutionary party's militant organization ... that in the near future an attempt was to be made on Stolypin's life, and the attempt would be made at a time when the Minister had not yet left his dacha."[14]

Stepanova claimed to have firm evidence to prove that SR terrorists, already the prime suspects, had bombed the dacha; but her version of the timing and source of this intelligence was highly suspect. If the report of the Union's spy had reached her on 9 August, why had Stepanova failed to inform the police at once?[15] More problematic, however, was her claim that the Union had its own secret agent within the tightly-knit cell that had carried out the bombing, a feat that the Okhranka itself was hard pressed to accomplish.

Questionable reports like Stepanova's led nowhere and merely wasted officials' time. Far worse was the volunteered information that caused the police to hurt their own cause, as happened at the end of August. In this case, the intelligence first surfaced when fifteen members of the Society of Active Struggle were taken into custody, because they were armed, by the head of the railway Gendarmes in the town of Gatchina, near St Petersburg. Protesting that they were carrying guns to counter an imminent attack by revolutionaries, they appealed in vain for police assistance, not interference. Two days later, members of the Society's fighting squad at the Putilov factory burst in upon officers of the St Petersburg police with a more compelling proposition: because SR terrorists were already making their way by road to a rendezvous point on the Baltic railway line where they would attack a train in just two hours time, the police must commandeer a special train to enable the Society's fighters to reach the attack site first. Not only did the police comply but they also sent along a squad of their own, and the ensuing ambush killed two of the terrorists. But, known only to the select few who were privy to the identity of tsarist secret agents, one of those deaths deprived the Okhranka of an inside agent, P. Grigor'ev.[16]

Stirred in part by exploits like this railway ambush, membership in Black Hundred groups mounted rapidly in the remainder of the year, as reflected in Department of Police figures. The total number of Black Hundreds that the police reported in mid-1906 (91,450 members in twenty-two provinces) would more than quadruple (to 253,407 members in seventy-four provinces) in the recount filed early in 1907. Although Stolypin would specifically ban these right-wing paramilitary groups in mid-1907, the membership count compiled by the police in early 1908 would show that by then the total had risen another 63 percent (to 404,500 members Empire-wide).[17]

Instrumental in causing Stolypin to effect the 1907 ban were the Black Hundreds that had sprung up in Odessa during the previous summer under Count A.I. Konovnytsin, a scapegrace aristocrat and fanatic anti-semite. Konovnytsin, a naval officer in his youth, had forfeited respectability when, as a marshall of the district nobility and a leader of the local zemstvo, he had been found guilty by the courts of bribing public officials. Initially reduced to the marginal post of justice of the peace, he had turned next to managing a seamen's laundry. Shortly in touch with urban toughs through his new role, Konovnytsin had won a following of anti-semitic bullies. With them as the nucleus, in mid-1906 he organized what became his own Black Hundred squadron, the Odessa White Guard. It became the largest of all urban squads, attracting some three hundred to five hundred members, most of them secondary school students, claimed one Okhranka agent. Modelling his Guard on the Cossack army and the military commander of its units, the ataman grandly dressed each rank in a distinct uniform.[18]

Konovnytsin at the same time enjoyed high status in the Odessa chapter of the Union of Russian People. Its leaders had to have been well aware of what he was doing, and a number of them clearly approved. For the Okhranka, however, the blatantly criminal acts of the Guard made imperative a political investigation of Konovnytsin.

Accordingly, from an inside agent, security officials learned that Konovnytsin would typically "arrive home in the evening drunk as a lord surrounded by combatants standing in line along the stairwell. The count would shout, 'Come on, men, beat the Jews!' His men would answer, 'Hurrah.'"[19]

Agents' reports on similar groups began to arrive from other places. One intelligence dispatch that reached the Okhranka in August 1906, for example, came from the Gendarme chief responsible for the town of Gomel, where anti-Semites were attacking Jews with whips on the streets and even in their meeting places and pubs.[20] Two months later an Okhranka agent reported from the Third Monarchist Congress in Kiev that extremists there had vowed to kill the presumed author of the October Manifesto, Count Witte, on the grounds that he had made disastrous concessions to leftist forces dominated by Jews. In December came details of a vicious pogrom against Jews in Ekaterinoslav Province, another stronghold of right-wing extremists.[21]

Attempts from St Petersburg to curb Konovnytsin's White Guard had meanwhile begun, with the government's appointment, in the fall of 1906, of a Black Hundred opponent as the new governor of Odessa, A.G. Grigor'ev. Although he had immediately called for the banishment of Konovnytsin from the city, Grigor'ev could not sway the acting governor-general, P.F. Glagolev, and the commander of the military district, Baron A.B. Kaulbars, who contended that the Black Hundreds positively helped to maintain public order.

As 1907 began, yet another unsettling incident conveyed to the public the imminence of political violence by hooligans: the discovery of two unexploded bombs, with failed timers, in the St Petersburg home of Witte, the former prime minister. Although the residence had been under constant watch by Okhranka agents since Witte's return from abroad the previous fall, someone had put bombs into a central stove. Servants found the devices when they were about to light a fire on the evening of 29 January.[22] Newspaper accounts immediately appeared, most of them pondering the motives and identities of the perpetrators, who were assumed to have dropped the devices down the chimney by climbing onto the roof. According to police experts, the construction of the bombs clearly differed from that typical of revolutionaries.[23] The well-known animosity of right-wingers to Witte led many to place blame on Black Hundred militants and their supposed mentors in the Union of Russian People.

Denying involvement, Dr Dubrovin, the head of the Union of the Russian People, had rushed a public statement into print the day after the news first broke to condemn both the agents who planted the bombs – "blood-thirsty madmen … who put infernal machines into stoves" – and, more pointedly, their despicable instigators. "Any hang-man," he contended, "would seem a humanist compared with the people who are pushing hot-blooded youths to murder their opponents."[24] Dubrovin might have given something away: he stated as fact that the bombers were youthful and that they had acted on the instigation of others. However, he had framed his words carefully to convince readers that he had nothing to do with the bizarre incident.

In February, as tensions heightened over political hooliganism, both the Austrian chargé d'affaires and the Italian ambassador protested that their nationals were suffering attacks from Black Hundred gangs. Adding to the international outcry, papers in Europe had joined outspoken editors within the Empire to condemn Russia's political violence.

Worst of all was the plague of killings. A particularly startling assassination – again, the seeming work of right-wingers – took place on 14 March in Moscow just as the second Duma, with its opposition majority, got under way in the capital. The victim was G.B. Iollos, who had served as a liberal deputy in the first Duma and edited *Russian Bulletin (Russkie Vedomosti)*, a long-established paper that routinely took the government to task. The murder site, moreover, was near the building that housed Toropov and the printing press for *Veche*, in whose pages Toropov had earlier published death threats against Iollos and two other liberal editors.

Just three weeks later, on 6 April, with still no break-throughs announced in the Witte and Iollos cases, Prime Minister Stolypin publicly ordered the disbandment of Black Hundred detachments everywhere in the Empire. Because ordinary measures to stop the criminal behaviour of these tsarist loyalists had failed, Stolypin required a concerted government campaign to eliminate them entirely. Officials in each region were to put the ban into effect, and police agents would help keep St Petersburg informed on successes and failures.

Learning in mid-April that uniformed members of the White Guard were still appearing on the streets of Odessa, Stolypin, who also served as interior minister, and his director of police demanded an explanation from Governor-General Glagolev; back came his reply that the violators were merely "poor people who had no other suit to wear." But when, the next day, uniformed White Guardsmen fired on passers-by and wounded several in an Odessa suburb, Stolypin responded to the "obvious unwillingness of [Glagolev] to fulfil my instructions" by directing the military commander "to compel explicitly Major Glago-lev to disarm and disband the fighting squad at once."[25]

With the Okhranka meanwhile continuing to track White Guard hold-outs, a secret agent was present on 7 May when members of the outlawed squad met to plan a pogrom. As a result, the Okhranka forewarned the police that the pogrom would coincide with the pending funeral of a slain Odessa policeman, whose death would be blamed on "Jewish revolutionary parties and organizations who were fraudulently masquerading as Russian."[26]

At this same time, leftist deputies in the Duma learned from insiders of their own that right-wing agents had arrived in the capital to kill Witte, their plan being to bomb his car as it conveyed him to a meeting of the State Council. At once they had passed their intelligence to the Police Department and then, through a long chain of mediators, including A.A. Lopukhin, the former director of police – to Witte. As a result, the State Council cancelled its session on 26 May.

On the day following occurred an obscure murder that would soon be widely known; for the victim, a former blacksmith named A.E. Kazantsev, would be identified that summer by Socialists as the chief of the stalkers of Witte and the murderer of Iollos. Even more sensational would be the Socialists' claim that Kazantsev's commander was none other than the head of Russia's leading monarchist party, Dubrovin of the Union of the Russian People.

All through the March, April, and May sessions of the second Duma, dominated as they were by debates on reforms proposed by the left-of-centre majority, rancour was high among the Union and its allies against the Socialists and liberals, and vice-versa. As security guardians, Okhranka officials had consequently been quick to rush protection to P.N. Miliukov, leader of the Constitutional Democratic party, after he was struck on the street by ruffians. Because he later made light of the "agents ... sent by the government to guard my person," mentioning only that they "sat conscientiously in my kitchen until, finally, I requested that they be released from their thankless task,"[27] Miliukov seems not to have believed himself in mortal danger.

In the political arena, however, Nicholas II found the legislative activities of Miliukov and like-minded deputies intolerable; in early June the tsar peremptorily dissolved the second Duma. In its aftermath, as political charges and counter charges came from all sides, the Socialists began their published barrage of blame against the Union of the Russian People with respect to Witte and Iollos. Not only had Dubrovin ordered the killing of both men, they charged, but he had also proved his ties to fighting squads by drafting his chief agent, Kazantsev, from one of them.

The summation that follows comes from the socialists' late June revelations and from details in later accounts about the alleged machinations of Kazantsev, the murder victim of 28 May. According to his critics, Kazantsev had initially committed himself to the left by joining the Socialist Revolutionary party when he worked as a blacksmith at the Tilmans plant in St Petersburg. But on relocating in Moscow, he had aligned with the extreme right-wing Society of Active Struggle with the Revolution, where he was said to have worked closely with A.A. Buksgeweden, a Society member and purported special investigator for the Moscow governor-general.

Returned to the capital during 1906 in the guise of a revolutionary extremist, Kazantsev had cultivated an old Socialist Revolutionary ally, S.S. Petrov, who would later, in his own defence, claim to have been taken in by two lies: first, that the SR's Maximalist group had sentenced Witte to death for causing the arrests of the executive committee of the St Petersburg Soviet late in 1905 (Witte was still head of the government then); and secondly, that the Maximalists had sent him, Kazantsev, to find assassins. Petrov says that he not only agreed to help but also brought twenty-two-year-old V.D. Fedorov into the plot. At that point, however, Petrov was seized by security agents as a suspected revolutionary and exiled to Siberia.

Fedorov stayed in place, later claiming to have believed that Witte himself was a former secret Maximalist agent who deserved to die for betraying that organization to the police. In contrast, A.S. Stepanov, the accomplice that Fedorov signed on, would testify in 1917 that both he and Fedorov "really did not understand" why Witte was "harmful" but agreed to kill him anyway.[28] These two leftists, then, according to the Socialists' story, unwittingly carried out a right-wing plan when they climbed onto Witte's roof and dropped the two bombs into Witte's chimney.

Further testimony related to that same incident would surface from A.I. Prussakov, who served under Dubrovin in 1906 and 1907 as a candidate member of the central council of the Union of Russian People. Among those who heard Prussakov's evidence in 1907 or a year or two later was Witte, but the documented version is a post-revolution statement in which Prussakov tells that he obtained a plan of Witte's house for Dubrovin, on his orders, in December 1906. Some days later, continues Prussakov, he encountered in Dubrovin's office two young men demanding a promised payoff for their attempt on Witte "or they would tell everything to the Count." The response of Dubrovin remembered by Prussakov was this: "My enemies will not leave me in peace. There are the left-wing forces, the Jews, and now Count Witte has sent these people to extract three thousand rubles from me or they will announce that the attempt on Witte's life was organized by the Union of the Russian People and by me, as its chairman."[29]

Even if these revelations were true, Prussakov's testimony does not confirm that Dubrovin instigated the January bomb incident. True, the request for the house plans circumstantially implicates Dubrovin, and one explanation for the demand of the two young men for rubles could be that they knew Dubrovin to be the instigator who owed them a promised fee or hush-money. But Fedorov, the confessed bomber, claimed to have believed until mid-March that he was acting for the Maximalists. If all Fedorov's claims are true, then the two young men seen by Prussakov – if he did see them – could have been poseurs sent by the left to implicate Dubrovin, as Dubrovin's attributed words would imply.

As in so many cases that confronted the Okhranka, the many contradictory claims that surfaced about this bomb incident served to render the political investigation about it "inconclusive." For his part, Witte would assume, more certainly over time, that the government chose not to uncover the facts. In his memoirs he quoted the words of the procurator of the St Petersburg Court of Appeals, P.K. Kamyshansky, about why the police did not detain persons accused by credible informants: "If we arrest these people and conduct an investigation, we don't know what we'll find. We might have to go further and go higher."[30]

According to Fedorov, whose comments the press would quote in July and whose lengthy statement the Department of Police would receive in September, the January bomb fiasco had sent the three plotters to Moscow, where Kazantsev had proposed another vengeance mission. This time, Kazantsev allegedly promised, Fedorov could win admission to the Maximalist group by shooting a former member who had absconded with 80,000 rubles in robbery receipts. When Kazantsev pointed out the "traitor" on a Moscow street on 14 March, Fedorov fired four fatal shots. Only when he read the next day's papers, says Fedorov, did he learn that he had killed liberal editor Iollos and only then did he begin to distrust Kazantsev.[31]

In a sudden twist, Petrov, who had escaped from Siberian exile, surprised Fedorov in Moscow, and the two men shared their suspicions. They began to watch Kazantsev closely and Fedorov claimed to have discovered evidence that damned him: "In the half-open drawer of [Kazantsev's] writing table ... I saw an 'address list' for secret contacts among the organizations of the Union of the Russian People."[32]

When Kazantsev next proposed returning to the capital to kill Witte as he drove to the State Council, Fedorov says that he and Petrov agreed to the trip solely in order to report the plot to left-wing deputies in the Duma; he insists his forewarning alone caused the State Council to cancel its session on 27 May. One day later, he and the unsuspecting Kazantsev had proceeded with Petrov and two Socialist

Revolutionaries to a hidden explosives cache outside the capital to make bombs for some later mission, and there Fedorov had stabbed Kazantsev to death. Petrov had returned to the capital; Fedorov had fled abroad to pen his contributions to the left-wing version of the Witte and Iollos cases that first appeared in print in June and July.

Kazantsev had been an agent provocateur for Dubrovin and the Union, according to the sensational Socialist statement printed in several leading newspapers on 28 June. That is, in a double-cross instigated at the highest level of the Union hierarchy, Kazantsev had posed as a Maximalist to dupe gullible SRs into assassinating two liberals hated by right-wingers. The statement concluded: "We know in advance that the high-ranking members of the Union will order the whole story hushed up. We know in advance that all these Toropovs, Buksgewedens, etc. – their names are legion – will only be called off by their Tsar."[33]

Within a fortnight another criminal charge would appear in the press against Dubrovin, this one relating to the skirmish that had caused the government to send bodyguards to Miliukov's kitchen. Claiming that Dubrovin had initiated the episode by ordering a subordinate named Belinsky to organize a hit squad, this report described the hooligans as first bracing themselves with strong drink. Only then had they "tracked Miliukov as he was walking along Liteiny avenue and finally struck him" – but ineffectually. According to this account, Belinsky berated the squad leader: "Villain. You are worthless! I said to really hit him in such a way that he would remain alive for a day or two at the most."[34]

Reports like those of the Socialists were credible because no one doubted the virulence of right-wing anger against opposition deputies in the second Duma. Consequently, after the Duma's closure, one Kadet deputy who was also a Jew, Professor M.Iu. Herzenstein, took refuge at a health resort in Terioki, Finland, on the seemingly safe territory of the Grand Duchy. On 18 July, Herzenstein had received a letter, signed by the "Comora for People's Reprisal," that pronounced a sentence of death upon him. Within hours of its delivery, assassins had gunned him down and wounded his daughter during their evening stroll along the shore.

This was treated as just another political killing, presumably by a right-wing fighting squad, so the Okhranka began another desultory investigation. Far more compelling to the security police, after all, were the killings linked with leftist extremists, whose usual victims were ruling officials and the police itself. Better to proceed cautiously and with as little commentary as possible on the Herzenstein case, even as liberal journalists, without proof, loudly implicated the Union of Russian People. Meanwhile a third group, lawyers who belonged to the Kadet (Constitutional Democratic party), began their own investigations. They would discover in Vyborg prison two inmates known to have been expelled from a right-wing fighting squad. Gaining access to them, the Kadet lawyers would begin discussions to bring that pair around to confirming the names of the Herzenstein assassins.

What had happened in Terioki was right-wing criminality at its worst. Within days of that assassination, moreover, a letter intercepted by a perlustration agent provided one more piece of evidence of continuing criminal assaults by right-wing squads in Odessa. Its writer, who signed himself "The Knight," boasted of the success of his ten-man unit in "beating up Jews without challenge, men and women, whom we met on our way" and of the "clamour and whistles and cries" that had caused Jewish shops and cafés to close. Moving on to another street, he continued, "we again began to beat the Jews without mercy and to pull Jewish women by the hair."[35]

That fall, trying a new approach surely favoured by the Okhranka, Stolypin replaced Odessa's well-intentioned governor, Grigor'ev, with a stronger figure: the Gendarme chief who had overseen the city of Kiev. Stolypin directed this new governor, Lieutenant-General V.D. Novitsky, to make a priority of disbanding Odessa's Black Hundreds, but even Novitsky, militant though he was over the next several months, proved unequal to the task. So at the close of 1907, in a tactical turnaround, Stolypin appointed an official politically close to the right wing as Odessa governor in order to woo ultra-nationalists into abandoning their physical abuse of Jews, leftists, and foreigners. More precisely, the new governor was to use friendly persuasion to convince the White Guard and its backers that, because criminal tactics served only to discredit them and their cause, they should instead use the Duma and the press to fight the tsar's enemies with words and resolutions – an option made plausible for even the jingoistic extreme by Purishkevich's new far-right party, the League of the Archangel Michael.

Purishkevich, who had helped to found the Union of Russian People in 1905, had begun to organize his League in 1906. Setting its messianic direction, he had made the archangel, slayer of Satan, his party's patron saint, and at the same time had evoked links with the Orthodox Church, revered as the true repository of Russian values by ordinary conservatives and Black Hundreds alike. Drawing attention to his extremism through scurrilous rhetoric, Purishkevich clearly differentiated himself from Dubrovin and the League from the Union.

Subsidies to Purishkevich from 1906 onward show that the government approved of his efforts to form a party of Jew-haters and xenophobes, and officials seeking to regroup and redirect the Black Hundreds could even have designed the League for that purpose and enlisted Purishkevich to run it. According to Department of Police records, Purishkevich received some 40,500 rubles in government subsidies from 1906 to 1916, with close to 20 percent paid to him in 1906, the year the League began.[36] With respect to Odessa, then, Purishkevich's League was already in place when, in late 1907, Stolypin named a new governor to halt the lawless violence of the White Guard.

That new Odessa governor, I.N. Tolmachev, set about his task by courting local members of the Union of Russian People, and one approving participant at an early meeting quoted him as saying: "First of all, my sincere compliments to you, gentlemen, for your activities! Second, I sympathize with the Black Hundreds with all my heart and soul. Even if I cannot be a Union member officially, everyone in my family who can join has done so."[37] By confessing an affinity for the beliefs of Black Hundreds, Tolmachev established common ground. Next, through moral and pragmatic arguments, he convinced leaders of the Odessa Union to drum their members and friends out of the White Guard and withdraw all support. By summer, as a consequence, the remnant Guard units still active had gravitated to the League of the Archangel Michael, whose local leader made them welcome.

At that point the governor brought in Purishkevich, and in September Tolmachev confidently assured the Department of Police that the full elimination of local right-wing fighting squads was imminent. "Together with V.M. Purishkevich," he explained, "I have worked out a plan for the Odessa League to reorganize by replacing [its leader, V.A.] Pelikan and by disbanding its fighting squads."[38] In a final concession to the Guards' founder, however, the governor would agree in early 1909 to allow Count Konovnytsin to keep a contingent of armed bodyguards for his personal safety.

The campaign by the government to eliminate the illegal right-wing militias in Odessa – a goal made the more imperative by Herzenstein's assassination – thus effectively ended in the first months of 1909. By the summer, the tsar's police finally seized the second of the two suspected Terioki assassins, G.S. Larichkin (V. Polovnev had been picked up the year before), for whom the Ministry of the Interior, through its Department of Police, had issued arrest orders more than a year before.

The basis for those orders were allegations about the assassination that Kadet attorneys had collected from the Vyborg prisoners by

December 1907. The Kadet central committee had conveyed those findings to the Ministry of Justice, and a St Petersburg procurator named Gvozdanevich, as a ministry investigator, had ruled that the Kadets' submission provided sufficient grounds to require the police to take Polovnev and Larichkin into custody, subject to prosecution. Stolypin himself had ordered the minister of the interior to comply with the minister of justice's request that the police apprehend the two suspects and hold them pending a request from Finland for their extradition to Terioki for trial.

Polovnev and Larichkin had spent much of 1908 as fugitives at the Pochaev monastery in the Volyn region, and, following their arrests, accusations arose that the Okhranka had helped to hide them. In 1917 V.L. Burtsev, the career exposer of tsarist wrongdoing, quoted an incriminating statement that he attributed to M.S. Komissarov, the assistant chief of the Okhranka in St Petersburg in 1908, which he claimed to have heard second-hand from an Orthodox priest, Iliodor. According to Burtsev, when Iliodor was about to go to Pochaev monastery in 1908, Komissarov warned him: "Those brave fellows, the murderers of Herzenstein, have been sent to you, to the Pochaev monastery. There is a hunt going on for them, but let them stay there for some time until it is over."[39]

When the police did at last catch up with Polovnev and Larichkin, the right-wing press was subjecting Stolypin to especially strong attacks for his reformist policies, and some say that the prime minister instigated the arrests of right-wing terrorists at that time to fight back. Such an explanation fits in with the charge that at least some Okhranka personnel had earlier contrived to prevent the arrests. The capture of Polovnev in June 1908, and Kraskovsky (a leader of the Union of the Russian People) and then Larichkin a year later did, in any case, take place; it remains altogether possible that the arrests happened when they did because both the police and the Okhranka officials in pursuit of the fugitives genuinely remained in the dark about their whereabouts.

Polovnev, a foreman at the Putilov factory twice convicted for theft, was the man whom some capital papers had immediately accused following the Terioki murder. Polovnev himself would testify in 1917 (when it had become advantageous to discredit the Okhranka and the Union of Russian People) that he had been questioned about his involvement by the St Petersburg Okhranka chief, A.V. Gerasimov, within days of the assassination. Gerasimov said he responded to Polovnev's denial of any role with these words: "Well, good for you. Don't say a word, for you have nothing else to say, so just stay calm."

And, concludes Polovnev with no other evidence, "It was obvious to me that Gerasimov was fully informed of the murder of Herzenstein organized by the Union of the Russian People."[40]

Witnesses who testified in the trial of Polovnev from July to October 1908 said they had seen him in Terioki just before the assassination in the company of both Larichkin and Kraskovsky, a member of the Union of the Russian People's central council. So the Finnish court sent a second extradition request to the Department of Police, this time for Larichkin, Kraskovsky, and Kraskovsky's Union superior, Dubrovin. Finding grounds wholly lacking for the Finnish court to implicate or question Dubrovin, the department arrested Kraskovsky and Larichkin and extradited them to Finland. The Finnish court sentenced Polovnev to six years in prison as an accomplice in the murder. The trial of Krasovsky and Larichkin took place from August to October 1909 and they, too, were convicted and sentenced to six years in prison.

Perhaps the department had already filed and taken no action on the undated police document that names Purishkevich, another easy target, as the top instigator. The informer in this instance was V.P. Roznatovsky, the leader of the Union in Tula; and he named as his source the wife of V.N. Kazarinov, a close associate of Purishkevich. In a discussion about the murder of Herzenstein with both the wife and her husband, claims Roznatovsky, "the Kazarinovs told me that the act had been carried out by two men on the order of Purishkevich ... I said to Kazarinova that I had received an anonymous telegram which made it clear that Dubrovin was the guilty one, but she denied it categorically, saying that Dubrovin had known nothing of it and that the killers had been hired by Purishkevich, but for what sum she did not know."[41]

Whether Kraskovsky acted on higher orders remains unresolvable, as does the question of the degree to which ideology, adventurism, personal gain, or some other motive caused Kraskovsky, Polovnev, and Larichkin to kill Herzenstein. Larichkin would suggest by his own later testimony that the prospect of personal gain was the dominant incentive for him; for he would admit to Russian judges in 1911 the killing of the worker Mukhin five years earlier as an agent and then beneficiary of Kraskovsky.[42]

Because Dubrovin had gone to the Crimea for the summer, assurances to him from the assistant minister of the interior, P.G. Kurlov, were relayed to him by the Union treasurer in a letter in early July 1906. There the treasurer ascribes to Dubrovin the message from Kurlov in these words: "Don't pay any attention to any of [the accusations in the Finnish courts] because the Russian government will never give up either on the Union or on you. I don't care what the left-wing press says."[43]

There were attempts to influence the trial in Finland. One of Kraskovsky's fellow members on the central council of the Union of Russian People had travelled to Terioki on behalf of the Union to observe the trials of Polovnev, Larichkin, and Kraskovsky, and a report in the liberal press said he had pulled a pistol from his pocket on the way out of the courtroom, although this alleged event seems to belong in the realm of press sensationalism. More to the point, V.B. Frederiks, the minister of the imperial court, wired Stolypin that the tsar "urgently demands the end of the Herzenstein case in the next session of the courts."[44] When that message was conveyed to them, the Finnish judges would already have been well aware that whatever they decided was subject to revision in St Petersburg.

As overseer of the Finnish courts, the minister of justice evaluated the proceedings that had led to those decisions and found grounds to reject the verdicts for Polovnev and Kraskovsky. Declaring mistrials for both, he told the tsar on 27 December that the judges in Terioki had based their decisions on those two men on testimony from persons with a "revolutionary cast of mind who would not hesitate to use [the Herzenstein case] to humiliate the enemy."[45] That is, the primary commitment of those witnesses to discrediting the tsar's government rendered them wholly unreliable, by judicial standards, to testify in a trial of persons alleged to have committed a crime on behalf of the tsar.

Damning circumstantial evidence for the prosecution in the proceedings against Polovnev and Larichkin included the testimony of a local policeman who said that he had provided overnight housing for the two men, at their request, prior to the assassination because they showed him what he believed to be Okhranka identification cards (on each, he said, appeared the signature of the chief of the St Petersburg Okhranka and the photograph of the bearer).[46] If the court left unchallenged the existence or validity of those alleged cards, the minister had grounds to cry foul inasmuch as the two accused men were not Okhranka agents. (To be sure, the two suspects might well have acquired and carried fake Okhranka cards as a means to expedite their mission, but they would then seemingly have acted with total disregard about possibly incriminating the Okhranka and the tsar's government, as could have been the case with criminal incompetents.) Other circumstantial evidence was provided by employees of the local hotel, where the two had men stayed, who claimed that the clink of concealed metallic weapons was clearly audible when the accused pair walked about in their overcoats. On 30 December, Nicholas pardoned

Kraskovsky and Polovnev. Larichkin was extradited to be tried in 1911 for the murder of Mukhin.

Following the 1905 revolution, agents of the Department of Police and the Okhranka sympathized with right-wing vendettas against political groups on the left, even as the Department of Police attempted to prevent illegal activities by numerous Black Hundred groups. Many who served the Okhranka believed that engaging in violent actions was justifiable in defending the tsar from his enemies.

Insubordination throughout the Okhranka rank and file consequently undercut official policy regarding political activists who broke the law, and the result was leniency to right-wing political activists in their struggle with groups on the left. The actual extent of that insubordination is impossible to assess because the perpetrators took pains to keep such conduct out of the records. Critics then and now have credibly contended that even high government officials deliberately approved or actively encouraged that bias. The government actually attempted to counter the criminal activities of the Black Hundreds, but tended to send mixed signals about right-wing political violence. The tsar, for instance, was unwilling to let the justice system take its course in the case of the murder of Herzenstein.

There was clear and consistent government support for the right-wing political parties, but these were legal entities obliged to conform with imperial laws and edicts. No trustworthy evidence has come to light to prove that the monarchist parties deliberately sponsored violence by illegal fighting squads. The shaky proof that they did came from participants who came forward with confessions, usually made years after the events in question had taken place.

What must be underscored, then, is that the problem of role distortion complicates a straightforward assessment of right-wing political crimes under Okhranka sponsorship in Russia before 1917. The motives of participants are often unclear. In some instances, criminals took refuge behind the cover of the Black Hundred activities. Violence-prone groups on both the left and the right engaged in atrocities to create the impression that their enemies committed them. Some of those who engaged in violent acts on the right claimed to be agents of the Okhranka; but it is not always clear that they were or, if they were, that they were fulfilling orders. The evidence shows that these variants all appear to have occurred, but who did what and for what purpose often remains elusive.

The contention here is that the top security officials after 1905, as in the pre-revolution period generally, genuinely sought to suppress all political crimes, whether leftist or rightist, because they believed that to be the strategy which would best serve to keep the autocracy in place. They were not, however, entirely successful in controlling their own subordinates. Those who disagreed with that policy – or who believed that their superiors at heart disagreed with it – were the ones guilty of ignoring or even abetting the surge of right-wing violence in the three years that followed the insurrection of 1905. As a result, they compounded problems for the Okhranka and served as a major element in the discrediting of the imperial regime.

PART THREE

Double Agents and Dissidents

CHAPTER SEVEN

Azeff,
the Super Agent

Evno Azeff is the best-known agent of the Department of Police but questions remain about how well he served the government in its struggle against the Socialist Revolutionary party and the terrorist Combat Organization. Without doubt Azeff rose high in the leadership ranks of the SR party, but when he was finally exposed, that revelation visited widespread confusion and demoralization in the ranks of the radical opposition to the government.

Evno Fischelevich Azeff belonged to a group of subjects of the Russian tsar – the Jews – for whom police service seemed the least likely career, unless the individual was a revolutionary posing as a spy. Especially since the 1880s, the autocracy had placed many restraints on the lives of the Jewish inhabitants of the Russian Empire, the vast bulk of whom were concentrated in the western provinces of the country, the so-called Pale of Settlement. Azeff was born in 1869 in one of these regions, in a shtetl in the province of Grodno. His father was a tailor, by itself an indication of the restrictions Jews endured. Almost from the time when these regions of Russia became part of the Empire during the partition of Poland under Catherine II, the government had tried to force Jews from the countryside into the cities. Required to support themselves in the cities rather than as financial middlemen and tavern-owners in the country, many Jews took up needle and thread and became tailors.

The Azeff family somehow managed to break out of the Pale and move to Rostov-on-the-Don in south Russia. The father opened a shop of his own and the son began to attend the local gymnasium. Although Jews often banded together in common defence against the anti-Semitism of the Russian Empire, Azeff never showed any particular interest in any Jews other than members of his family. He showed loving affection for his mother, and he provided shelter for long periods of time for his brothers and sisters when he found an apartment of his own.

Azeff first launched out on his own as a newspaper reporter and later became a small-scale trader or broker, buying others' goods and selling them at a mark-up. He had no obvious attractive personal characteristics to help advance his interests. Those who knew Azeff and left their reminiscences are unanimous: Azeff was never good-looking as a young man and he grew increasingly unattractive as he grew older. He became corpulent, stoop-shouldered, and had a sallow complexion. People he met often found him repulsive.

Azeff's name first appeared in the card file of the Okhranka as a member of what the security officials termed "a Jewish revolutionary study group."[1] In May 1892 the Gendarmes of the Don government recorded that Azeff was engaged in propaganda activities among workers and, travelling as a broker, was in a position to keep in touch with "his accomplices from other towns." When Azeff learned that the police were investigating him, he rushed to apply for a foreign passport and set off for Germany, where at the age of twenty-three, he became a somewhat older student in the Karlsruhe Polytechnical School. During his seven-year stay there, he married, had children, and continued his education. It is likely that his pressing financial obligations compelled him to take the next, important step in his career; other impecunious students had made similar career choices. By March 1893, when he wrote to Fontanka 16 to offer his services, he needed money.

Even through Azeff's letter to the Okhranka was unsigned, the agents easily identified the author from his self-description. A system-wide inquiry was made, and Colonel Strakhov of the Gendarmes in Rostov-on-the-Don replied, "I suspect the man you are looking for is Azeff, an old friend of mine."[2] He described him as clever and pushy as an individual and in serious need of money. Having received the approval of his superiors, G.K. Sediakin, the head of the Okhranka's Third Bureau, enrolled Azeff as a secret agent of the Okhranka. He replied to his correspondent, deliberately choosing to display the prowess of his investigators, "I suppose I will not be mistaken if I address you as Mr. Azeff."[3]

With the name "Azeff" written on the cover, the first of many archival files was now opened; the reports in the file were typically signed, "Always at your disposal, Azeff."[4] The personal identification of the agent should have been considered a gross violation of Okhranka security; Sediakin's first letter to Azeff showed a tendency among some Okhranka officers to display their cleverness, but it, too, was a slip in security. Such breaches in the Okhranka system of compartmentalization and anonymity would later put Azeff on his guard in his dealings with the Okhranka.

Reports from Azeff in Karlsruhe began to arrive at Okhranka headquarters, where he was labelled "the agent from the frying pan" because of the close similarity of the name of the German city and the Russian word for the common kitchen utensil, "kastriulia." Meanwhile Azeff, doubtlessly acting under Okhranka instructions, had joined a Russian Socialist Revolutionary group in Karlsruhe, a first step to finding out the plans of the populist terrorists. His value to the Okhranka had increased. Two years later, in 1899, when L.A. Rataev assumed supervision over Azeff, he conducted correspondence correctly, using a code name. Rataev assigned him the name "Vinogradov," only one of several aliases to be used for Azeff as time went on. (Later on, he would be called Raskin, then Kapustin, and then Philippovsky.) Azeff also signed reports using these code names.

Azeff at first received 50 rubles a month, exactly the figure he had asked for his own services, a very modest retainer compared with what he would soon receive. Initially he reported information of little value and, in the fashion of a novice writer, provided too much. For example, he sent detailed information about every student he met, and reported at length remarks made by speakers at student meetings. However, he was developing a sharp eye for detail and his reports became steadily selective. On one occasion he informed on a comrade who was about to carry illegal literature across the border into Russia. "Usually he carries two large suitcases," reported Azeff. "Perhaps I shall be able to advise you of their size and colour by telegraph."[5] Remaining abroad, Azeff also began to supply reports to Rachkovsky, the head of the Foreign Agency.[6]

When he left the Polytechnic Institute as a graduate engineer, Azeff was summoned back to Russia specifically to penetrate the Northern Union, a terrorist group led by A.A. Argunov, which had been operating in Moscow since the previous year. But he ran into an obstacle in advancing his career. The Russian authorities would not permit him to qualify by taking an examination as an external student at a Russian institution. Without passing the examination, Azeff as a Jew could not under law settle in Moscow. Azeff thought Rataev could fix the matter for him, but he had overestimated the power of his police master: "I did not expect to be treated in such a way. I didn't present an application to you only to get a refusal."[7] The agent had discovered again that he could not always depend on the Okhranka.

As he would numerous times in the future, Azeff exploited other possibilities. He put his request to the director of the Department of

Police, S.E. Zvoliansky, who personally negotiated the matter with the Moscow city authorities. The officials agreed not to stand in the way of an agent now highly valued by the police, and granted him a temporary residence permit.

Settled in Moscow, Azeff was under the orders of S.V. Zubatov, the head of the Moscow Okhranka. He became an observer of frictions between the innovative Zubatov, who was a key figure in Okhranka operations against revolutionaries, and the leadership of the Department of Police in St Petersburg. He wrote his former controller, Rataev, "S.V. [Zubatov] has been expounding to me his outlook and his criticism of the Department which, he says, acts very much in a strictly formal and bureaucratic manner." Azeff added, "And, generally speaking, I almost agree with S.V.'s viewpoint."[8] Like Zubatov, Azeff would feel constrained by police rules and regulations, especially those designed to ensure that secret agents did not themselves engage in criminal behaviour. And as he continued to advance as a secret agent, he found additional reason to doubt the administrative sureness of an agency on which his life had increasingly come to depend.

Azeff found employment at the Universal Electric Lighting Company, where he established a reputation as a competent technician. So far he was making more – 225 rubles per month – as an electrical engineer than he was as an agent. But his profession never attracted the interest that his informing did. Fellow employees noticed that "Azeff was constantly distracted by a string of visitors. Now and again he was summoned to the reception hall. His visitors were students of both sexes, but mostly ladies – ladies of differing ages and attire, rich and poor."[9] But Azeff did not engage in love affairs, only in developing contacts with persons who were sympathetic to the revolutionary movement. He began to use his first conspiratorial aliases as a figure in the revolutionary movement at this time. He called himself "Frenchman," then at one time "the Fat One," and then "Ivan Nikolaevich." Azeff was now known by one series of code names within the Okhranka and another among the revolutionaries.

Azeff's greatest achievement as a police agent during this time was the liquidation of an underground printing office in the city of Tomsk. He had, at the request of Argunov, constructed a shaft for a printing press and then told the Okhranka of the two people who were setting off for Tomsk with the shaft and a load of type. The police sent A.I. Spiridovich to Tomsk to command a squad to liquidate the press. "We had to think of a scheme," recalled Spiridovich, "that would allow the police force to act freely and, at the same time, would keep unexposed our secret sources."[10] By sending Spiridovich from Moscow, the police intended that the revolutionaries think that no local authorities – and hence no local secret agents – were involved. Spiridovich broke up the press and obtained useful statements from the revolutionaries arrested along with the printing equipment. Azeff not only took satisfaction from the destruction of the press, but from his outwitting of the revolutionaries. "Argunov and company await arrest from one moment to the next and they have transferred all their contacts, both in St Petersburg and Saratov, to me. Just imagine who they suspect of being the police spy, Tchepik [one of the members of the Northern Union]. They suspect him because he often goes abroad to wander around without much of anything to do."[11]

Argunov eluded the police but was arrested when he left Azeff in charge of all Union operations. In the fall of 1901 Azeff, with police approval, went abroad with Maria Seliuk, a member of the Northern Union, who was to introduce Azeff to the party leadership abroad. Azeff had picked his time very well. A number of populist groups were about to form themselves into a new party, the Socialist Revolutionaries.

Azeff took part in the meeting as a representative of the Northern Union, whose members back in Russia he had so recently identified for police arrest. By now he was thoroughly involved in playing a double game. He warned Rataev, "I have found it necessary to speak in favour of fusing the Union and the Party. For us, I believe that it is important, especially if we consider the circumstances, that is when everything lies open before us; but, on the other hand, I can accept a certain risk, as I can't just play the Maecenas but have to act, so to speak, as part of the organization."[12] Azeff therefore took part in the organization of the Socialist Revolutionary party and informed his superiors that he had done so. He had stepped into an influential role in a party whose techniques of struggle were to include terrorism. He had also put himself in a position to report planned terrorists attacks.

Azeff remained abroad for eight months and returned to Russia to take a position in the St Petersburg branch of the Electric Company. This time he quarrelled with his employers, quit his job and chose the life of a travelling revolutionary. He would move around Europe, from Paris, to Berlin, to Geneva, with frequent visits to Russia. In St Petersburg, he met with the current director of the Department of Police, A.A. Lopukhin, but he was now back under the control of Rataev, who was in charge of a network of agents sent abroad from Russia. This was a separate network from the foreign agents under the supervision of the Foreign Agency in Paris.

Azeff had achieved extraordinary status within the Okhranka. He was working at a very high level and one of his assignments was to develop a conception of the scope of the revolutionary movement. In

September 1904 he sat at a Paris conference of opposition parties alongside P.N. Miliukov and P.B. Struve of the Russian liberals. The police received from him thorough reports on the conference. Azeff accurately assessed the divisions within the Social Democrats. He singled out influential leaders such as Vladimir Lenin, Leon Trotsky, and George Plekhanov. This information assisted the police in identifying leaders of the Socialist Revolutionary party and they moved to arrest them. He alerted the Okhranka, for example, to Chaim Levin and the route he intended to travel to Russia: "In my view, he must be caught while crossing the border, otherwise he will probably vanish from sight."[13] He sent a telegram informing the police of the alias under which the Socialist Revolutionary S.N. Sletov intended to return to Russia and the secret addresses he intended to visit in St Petersburg. He had also decided that Maria Seliuk was no longer useful to him, and he recommended that she should be arrested upon her return to Russia. The police considered his reports highly authoritative and his recommendations were virtual instructions to action. Especially valuable were his reports of impending terrorist acts. He helped to prevent attempts on the lives of the Irkutsk governor-general, Count Kutaisov, the Baku governor, Prince Nakashidze, and the Nizhnii Novgorod governor, General Baron von Unterberger.

In August 1905 Rataev, who was retiring from police service, transferred Azeff to the supervision of Rachkovsky, the former head of the Foreign Agency, who was serving as chief of the Special Section of the Department of Police. He soon stopped receiving money and instructions from his new chief; Fontanka now had its suspicions about Azeff, thanks in part to questions raised by the former director, Lopukhin. Azeff was used for no police operations throughout the fall of 1905 and into the first months of 1906.

But a change in personnel shifted Azeff's fortunes again. The principal change was the appointment of Alexander Vasilievich Gerasimov as head of the St Petersburg Okhranka. Gerasimov had not begun his career in spectacular fashion. The son of a provincial merchant, he attended a provincial officers' school, but his native acuity was to make him one of the best Gendarme officers. After serving in provincial Gendarme postings for several years, Gerasimov was transferred from Khar'kov to St Petersburg in February 1905, determined to improve on what he saw as "a caricature of a secret police." In little more than a year he was advanced by means of two accelerated promotions to the rank of major-general. Gerasimov had taken to circumventing the police bureaucracy to report on investigations directly to the minister of the interior.

Gerasimov found out about Azeff largely by accident. He had known nothing about the secret agent or his work within the Socialist Revolutionary party. Police detectives in St Petersburg ran to ground a group of suspects, and one of the older agents identified the leader of the group as the Okhranka informer "Philippovsky," who had been pointed out to him some time before by the detective chief, Evstraty Mednikov. Gerasimov, to ascertain the accuracy of this claim, got in touch with Rachkovsky, the head of the Special Section at the time, and was told the Department of Police had no such informer. Gerasimov ordered the suspect arrested; under questioning, Azeff denied that he was a police informer. After a few days in solitary confinement, Azeff requested an interview with Rachkovsky. According to Gerasimov, Rachkovsky again pleaded ignorance "as he often used to do, then grew agitated: who was it exactly, and what was it all about? 'Is he really Philippovsky? I don't remember ... can he be Azeff?'"[14]

This was the first time he heard the mention of Azeff's name, says Gerasimov. A quarter of an hour later Rachkovsky appeared on the scene and "with his customary benign smile on his face" proceeded to address Azeff deferentially, "Oh, dearest Evgeny Philippovich, how nice. I haven't seen you for ages." Azeff upbraided Rachkovsky for not having appeared sooner. Gerasimov concluded that Rachkovsky had, indeed, acted dishonourably and bestowed all his sympathies on Azeff and from that moment decided to provide Azeff with better protection. A relationship of mutual trust, almost of camaraderie, developed between the Okhranka general and the informer. They met regularly in Gerasimov's St Petersburg apartment. Gerasimov valued the information that Azeff provided: "It was none other than Azeff who gave me genuine knowledge of the revolutionary underground, especially of its most prominent figures."[15]

Gerasimov used the services of Azeff in a different fashion. Unlike his previous controllers, he did not demand exhaustive reports from him, but only minimal information to take him to the heart of some revolutionary operation. For some time, for example, the Okhranka had been pursuing the terrorist underground group commanded by L.I. Zilberberg, which had been responsible for assassinating the St Petersburg chief of police, F.V. von der Launitz. On receiving notice from Azeff that the gunmen were hiding in a forest area in Finland, Gerasimov sent two of his agents posing as skiers who had lost their way. They discovered the hiding place of the gunmen and directed the police to it.

Azeff also played a major role in the destruction of the armed group of the Northern Union headed by A.D. Trauberg, a man completely unknown to the police except through his alias, "Karl." Azeff learned from him about his scheme to blow up the Council of State with the help of persons who had access to the press gallery. By providing information about Trauberg's identifying physical marks, the agent made it possible for the police to arrest him in Finland.

When the police learned from another agent that the Northern Union intended to assassinate the Grand Duke Nicholas Nicholaevich and the minister of justice, I.G. Shcheglovitov, they asked Azeff to confirm the report. He reported that one of the plotters was one Anna Rasputina, and the Okhranka investigators discovered that she, unsuspecting, had registered in Moscow under her own name.[16] Okhranka detectives used her contacts with the entire terrorist group to track them down and arrest them all, loaded down with explosives, near the house of the minister of justice. Azeff had provided the key piece of information that enabled the police to head off the assassination.

Azeff stayed in the ranks of informers, and did not move into the hierarchy of police officers. His rewards came rather in the great respect he earned from his superiors and in steadily larger pay cheques. When he worked for Zubatov in Moscow he received 150 rubles a month. Under Rataev's supervision he earned 500 rubles, and, working under Gerasimov in St Petersburg, that sum was doubled.[17] His monthly earnings were greater than those of the director of the Department of Police.

As a employee of the Electric Company, Azeff had rented an inexpensive flat and acquired a very modest dacha in the country. He would travel to the country in a third-class coach, sometimes begging the ticket from his acquaintances. A few years later Azeff was wearing expensive suits tailored by the best clothiers. He appeared in costly boxes at the theatre and at gambling houses on the French Riviera. Not even police wages could support Azeff's style of life, and he found reason from time to time to help himself to funds of the Socialist Revolutionary party.

Azeff's public flamboyance, like Rachkovsky's and Harting's, was a means of diverting attention from his secret activities. As long as he continued to deliver valuable information, the Department of Police tolerated the methods of the man who had become their top agent. Azeff constantly stressed to his employers that his methods might seem roundabout, but they paid off in the form of valuable information. He required his controllers to understand that he had to work as a practising psychologist, that he was dealing with human beings, and that he could not know everything. "With respect to attempts on someone's life," he explained, "one can never learn all of the details that are known only to those who are directly involved, and not even they know everything."[18] Azeff appeared to be instructing his chiefs that they would have to learn to live with his secretive ways; they never did fully know and understand their elusive agent. In 1909, when all his former bosses testified under oath, they gave differing summaries of Azeff's activities. Lopukhin stated that he had become aware of Azeff's theretofore unknown role in the central committee of the Socialist Revolutionary party in 1904. Zubatov said his agent had never had a part in any SR organizations. Rataev conceded that his agent might have been a member of the foreign committee of the party. Rachkovsky said that Azeff worked for the party as a supervisor for smuggling illegal literature. Gerasimov, who believed absolutely in Azeff, declared that in the fall of 1906 Azeff had penetrated to the very centre of revolutionary terrorist activity.[19]

While working under the supervision of these high police officials, Azeff had been rising higher in the Socialist Revolutionary party and had finally become, as his party comrades put it, "the general of the Revolution." Since the summer of 1902 Azeff had been a member of the party central committee. At the first party congress held in December 1905 the membership of the central committee was reduced to the five most prominent party leaders, and Azeff was one of them. In arguing for a vote for Azeff, one of his colleagues told the congress that in electing "Ivan Nicholaevich" they would be electing "the man who has pursued and shall pursue the policy of terror." Not a single person in the party knew that Azeff was at that time an Okhranka secret agent.

Suspicions about Azeff's position in the party were voiced among certain of the police as early as 1904, but no doubts appeared among the SRs. Later, after the exposure of Azeff, members argued in their own defence that Azeff had unusual self-control and resourcefulness in order to make his way into the most sensitive areas of party life.[20] Typically, Azeff promoted extreme stands on the issue of terrorism, but showed reluctance to become a member of the Combat Organization. This patience paid off, and others cleared the way for his advancement. The man who introduced him to the innermost secrets of the party was the noted terrorist Gersh Gershuni. Azeff reported to his police controllers when he became acquainted with Gershuni, but he stressed that their relationship was of a personal nature. In reality, Azeff was deliberately withholding key information. He had become Gershuni's closest assistant, and Gershuni had so much confidence in Azeff that he told the other party leaders that in the event of his arrest, Azeff was to be put in charge of all terrorist projects. In May 1903 the police arrested Gershuni in Kiev and Azeff stepped into his position as chief of the policy of "central terror," that is, attempts on the lives of high-ranking dignitaries.[21]

Azeff was now chief of the Combat Organization, a branch that occupied a special place within the SR party. The central committee gave the terrorist group only general directives, and the Combat Organization worked out its own plans to carry out assassinations. Azeff withdrew from actual direction of the Combat Organization for about a year, from October 1906 to the fall of 1907; for the remainder of the time he was the principal planner and director of terrorist projects. He had under his control not more than fifteen or twenty people, but this small group required much time and effort. The group planned meticulously before it carried out an attack. It consisted of fighters and expert technicians who handled explosives. One of them was Azeff's younger brother, Vladimir, a trained chemical engineer. Final planning was usually done abroad and the actual fighters would arrive at the chosen city only just before the attack was to take place. Inside Russia a number of women were awaiting orders, ready to play roles as ladies of high society or kitchen maids – to carry a bomb in a hatbox or rent and maintain a flat for a safe house.

Azeff imposed a strict discipline on his organization. He would accept new recruits only after a rigorous screening. At a first meeting, Azeff would treat the potential recruit with studied indifference and would tell him that his help was unneeded. Only those who persistently and tenaciously pressed their cause gained admission to the Combat Organization. These methods resulted in high-calibre recruits; Azeff's fighters might lack practical skills and they might lose their nerve at crucial moments, but not one of them, even when arrested while carrying out an operation, betrayed his comrades to the police.[22]

To the unknowing eye, the revolutionaries all resembled one another. "Their manners, dress, even their faces seemed all alike." In bearing, said one detractor, they cultivated "the arrogant Imperial Guard Cavalry spirit."[23] Azeff promoted the idea that his combatants were a revolutionary elite who had his leave to look down on other members of the party who did not risk their lives in terrorist operations. Azeff applied his knowledge of practical psychology in running the Combat Organization as he did in cultivating his police superiors. He would champion the dedication of his people before the central committee of the party while upbraiding the committee members for remaining in their sanctuaries abroad. He would tell them they had no right to criticize those who risked their lives constantly in Russia. Azeff thus built up his own mystique as an exceptional leader who would brook no interference with his running of the terrorist group.

The loyal fighters in turn would accept no authority other than that of their chief.

Azeff was an effective terrorist leader, but he did not by any means plot the never-ending series of political murders, assaults, and robberies that are sometimes attributed to him. He was unable to control or even know about the numerous operations of the local branches of the Socialist Revolutionary party or the independently functioning "flying squads" of Zilberberg and Trauberg. But Azeff's resumé does include perhaps the most successful terrorist operation ever carried out by the Combat Organization, the murder of the minister of the interior, V.K. Plehve. This occurred before Azeff became head of the Combat Organization and it made his reputation among the terrorists, especially with Gershuni. The conspiracy to kill Plehve also served Azeff well in building his support within the Okhranka.

In 1902 and early in 1904 Azeff warned of the danger that threatened Plehve. He gave the police information that led them to a terrorist group headed by Seraphima Klitchoglu, which had been stalking the minister. When the police rounded up this group, they did not suspect that a much more formidable group headed by Boris Savinkov had been tracking Plehve for several months. The Socialist Revolutionary party leader who had sent Savinkov to St Petersburg was Azeff.

He was engaged in a stratagem employing surveillance methods used by the police. Some terrorists, dressed as street peddlers, strolled along the Fontanka embankment near the Department of Police building. Others, disguised as cabmen, followed Plehve on his visits to the tsar. Unknown to his security guards, Plehve was surrounded by a network of terrorists. Azeff then personally brought in a load of dynamite from abroad, perhaps, as some said, in a train compartment he was sharing with Rataev.

Before Azeff's arrival in St Petersburg, the nervous tension among the conspirators was nearly unbearable. Some had abandoned the operation and had left the capital. Azeff summoned them back and they came, so inspired by the presence of their chief that they believed Plehve could be attacked right in front of the police building. Before leaving the city, Azeff warned the terrorists against an attack on the Fontanka, but they assembled anyway on 16 March 1904, but then broke up the operation when they felt they were being closely observed.

With Azeff out of St Petersburg, the plotting bogged down once again. Savinkov left town to participate in another attack in south Russia. Alexei Pokotilov tried to carry on but died in his hotel room when the bomb he was assembling exploded in his hands. Again Azeff rallied his group. Savinkov recalled that Azeff had stormed into a group hideout in Kiev and shamed his followers into acting. "What's got into you?" he shouted. "If there are no people who are worth their salt, they must be found. If there is no dynamite, it must be provided. But there is no way for us to drop this matter. Plehve must and will be killed. If we don't kill him, nobody will."[24]

New strategies were developed. Savinkov, playing a rich Englishman, hired a flat in St Petersburg. Another party member, Dora Brilliant, played his mistress. The rest of the group became their servants. On 15 July 1904 Egor Sazonov threw a bomb at the minister's carriage; the powerful blast smashed the carriage into kindling and killed Plehve.

Several features of the assassination of Plehve show that Azeff carefully guarded his own role. When the bomb-throwers appeared on the streets in this and earlier attempts, their chief always happened to be in another town. Then Azeff obliquely warned the police that the attack on Plehve was coming, in this way demonstrating to his Okhranka chiefs that their agent, in typical fashion, had been able to provide leads to a forthcoming terrorist attack. Early in 1904, several months before the murder, Azeff provided a fantastic story about unnamed terrorists who supposedly had appeared in St Petersburg. In the spring he reported that he had learned that an attempt was being prepared on the life of the director of the Department of Police, Lopukhin, and that the terrorists were planning to strike near the Fontanka headquarters. When he analysed these reports a few years later, Rataev concluded that his agent wanted the police to reinforce security in order to seize the terrorists. But Azeff, seeing that all his hints were being ignored by his bosses, "gave up all efforts and let events take their normal course."[25]

The actual explanation, of course, turns on what Azeff intended and who he was truly working for at the time. If his first loyalties had now passed to the revolutionaries, he was giving his police employers just enough information to be able to say later that he had warned them about the plot, although he had not precisely named Plehve. In addition, the information that Azeff provided was likely meant to say that a high police official was the intended victim, although the official in question was Plehve and not Lopukhin, and thus divert the authorities from the revolutionaries' actual target.[26]

Azeff's reports therefore struck a middle ground between saying nothing about the attack on Plehve and revealing the names of the assassins. It is the intermediate character of his reports that offer the best evidence that he was now playing a double game. Another, less convincing, explanation of Azeff's actions is that Azeff had heard accusations that Plehve had connived in instigating the Kishinev pogrom in April 1903. Rataev himself says that Azeff was infuriated and that he had to take steps to calm him.[27] Azeff may have wanted to take revenge on Plehve for his anti-Semitic policies, but this explanation assumes his readiness to accept rumours and press reports about Plehve and a sudden, unprecedented concern about his Jewish brothers.

The assassination was an important event for Azeff. It cemented his position in the ranks of the SRs, and no subsequent rumours about his police activity could now shake his reputation among his comrades. Azeff was now a true hero to all of the party. The SRs were affected in another way: they believed that they had struck a mighty blow against the tsarist regime and they decided to demonstrate right away that they were winning the war against the government. The triumphant Combat Organization gathered in Paris and decided to deliver a triple strike by assassinating three governors-general. Azeff was in the midst of this planning: he split his group into three squads and sent them into action.[28]

Savinkov, one of the most experienced terrorists, led a group to Moscow. On 4 July 1905 Ivan Kaliaev, disguised as a peddler, threw a bomb in the Kremlin at the coach in which the Grand Duke Sergei Alexandrovich was riding. The explosion blew to pieces the man who was an uncle of the tsar, the commander of the Moscow military district, and a former governor general of Moscow. Parallel attempts planned for St Petersburg and Kiev miscarried. Azeff played a much smaller role in the assassination of the Grand Duke Sergei than in the killing of Plehve. He removed himself from the preliminary planning and, despite insistent appeals by members of the Combat Organization, did not even appear in Russia. A year later, in 1906, when a squad gathered in Moscow again to make an attempt to kill the governor-general, F.V. Dubasov, Azeff could not avoid taking part when Savinkov said his own appearance was now too familiar to Moscow detectives and he had to leave the city. Savinkov insisted that Azeff assume control over the operation. After hesitation and attempts to avoid involvement, Azeff agreed and arrived in Moscow on 23 April 1906.

Under his direction, the terrorists took their places the next day along several streets leading from the Kremlin. But Dubasov's carriage circumvented all of the ambushes. One of the bombers, Boris Vnorovsky, suddenly saw the carriage wheel onto Tverskaia Avenue from a side street. He ran towards the carriage and threw his bomb. It exploded and killed the governor's young aide and Vnorovsky himself, but Dubasov was only lightly wounded.

This failed attempt was the only time Azeff assumed the risk of observing a terrorist attack from only a short distance. He was immediately detained by the police together with other Russians who had come from abroad at the Philippov coffee house on Tverskaia. Later, the police released Azeff because they received word that he was an agent; other srs wondered how he had managed to get free of police custody so quickly. In pondering the failure of the assassination, other party members began to examine critically the planning. Azeff blamed the bombers on the street for overlooking the street used by the governor. In later years, after the exposure of Azeff, some revolutionaries said they had become convinced that Azeff had intentionally posted them on routes that Dubasov had never been known to have travelled.[29]

Even more ticklish encounters lay ahead for Azeff. Some police officials looked sceptically on the role of the top agent in the affair. Another secret agent, Zinaida F. Zhuchenko (Gerngross) reported that Azeff had managed the assassination attempt. He was subject to a dressing-down by Rachkovsky, who shouted in the presence of Gerasimov, "It was his affair in Moscow."[30] Although these suspicions led to no action against Azeff from Fontanka 16, it was several months before he regained the full confidence of his superiors.

Once again Gerasimov came to the rescue, and they staged together a complex operation that restored the agent's credibility. Gerasimov recalled their purpose: "The pivotal idea of our project was that of a series of actions, carried out systematically, aimed at virtually paralysing the operations of the Combat Organization in order to force the Organization and the party to the conclusion that 'central terror' was impossible."[31] Azeff began testing separate elements of the new tactics in the course of preparing an attempt on the life of the minister of the interior, P.N. Durnovo; the major test came, however, when the Socialist Revolutionaries commenced surveillance of the movements of P.A. Stolypin, the prime minister.

Savinkov was assigned a group to probe the weak points in the security system of the Winter Palace in St Petersburg, where Stolypin had been working and living since the explosion at his dacha on Aptekarsky Island in 1906. The terrorists now considered several schemes. They would attack him as he was leaving the palace, or they would mount an assault against his yacht while he was on board, or they would drop a bomb from a bridge over the Neva River when the prime minister's launch was passing underneath. The Savinkov group apparently had no suspicions that they were under careful observation even as they were stalking Stolypin. Finally, the terrorists, as Gerasimov had foreseen, concluded that they would be unable to penetrate the security cover around Stolypin. Azeff and his assistant declared the task impossible at a meeting of the central committee of the party and resigned their posts in the Combat Organization. Central terror came to a temporary end.

After an interlude of about a year, in the fall of 1907, the central committee of the party decided to resume the central terror campaign and appointed Azeff to take command of the Combat Organization once again. He was now in position to advance his and Gerasimov's scheme. Azeff had throughout these events been advising Gerasimov on policy with respect to investigation and surveillance of the revolutionaries. Gerasimov even relied on his agent's judgment with respect to the movements of Nicholas II. When Azeff reported that the terrorists had left the city, the Okhranka agreed to permit Nicholas out of the palace; when Azeff said terrorists were in St Petersburg, the tsar did not leave his residence.

At this moment of maximum trust, Azeff began to plot the terrorist act that was supposed to crown his revolutionary career. This time he planned a regicide. The SRs recruited two sailors who belonged to the crew of a new Russian cruiser under orders at a shipyard in Scotland. Azeff provided the sailors with revolvers and they handed to him farewell letters explaining their involvement in the assassination of the tsar. When the completed vessel arrived at the Kronstadt naval base in October 1908, Nicholas II went on board and the moment had arrived for the assassination. But the sailors did not act, and the tsar left the cruiser a few minutes later.[32]

A few years later Azeff said he regretted that his plan to murder the tsar had been unsuccessful. But it is difficult to say whether he actually intended that the sailors commit the deed. It is highly probable that Azeff, who was an expert recruiter of terrorists, did not really believe that the young sailors would follow through and he had arranged the whole episode to impress his colleagues in the party. On the other hand, he could not have guaranteed the tsar's safety because he had withheld from Gerasimov information on the plot.

For fifteen years Azeff had been a secret agent for the Okhranka, an assignment that the police thought could be successfully performed for about two years. Every day of those years presented a danger to the agent that his connection with the police would be discovered and that he would be killed by the terrorists. But despite his flamboyant and attention-getting life, Azeff maintained strong support both from the Okhranka and the Socialist Revolutionaries. Those who later said he should have been exposed much earlier were thinking retrospectively. Azeff unquestionably was a skilled operative, and he understood how to forestall situations that might have led to his exposure.

Real danger threatened him from another quarter and had nothing to do with his ties to either the Okhranka or the Socialist Revolutionary party; he therefore had no power to forestall it. Several police officials, driven by idealism or vengefulness, were seeking contacts with the revolutionary underground and gave warnings about secret agents operating in the ranks of the revolutionary parties. Azeff's reports show that he was picking up the first feelers coming to the revolutionaries from inside the police. "I feel bound to inform you ... I request that you handle these data tactfully," he wrote with early confidence. As the leaks from within the police became more persistent and alarming, he wrote in a different tenor: "I wonder, indeed, at how it is that your Department is unable to conduct its own affairs in an inconspicuous manner."

Azeff's name first appeared in a warning in 1903. A minor police informer had taken offence at something said by a senior detective and told the student N. Krestianinov that a secret agent was in charge of all SR activities in St Petersburg. Krestianinov's report led to a party investigation, but he had no evidence to back up his allegation, and none could be found.

A more serious threat came in the form of the anonymous "St Petersburg letter" delivered to E.P. Rostovsky, a member of the SR city committee in August 1905.[33] The letter had been written by an officer of the Okhranka, L.P. Men'shchikov; he named two traitors, a certain "T" and "the engineer Aziev." The first party leader to read the letter was Azeff himself. Asked by Rostovsky, who knew him only by his party alias, to identify the two persons, Azeff replied imperturbably, "'T' means Tatarov and I am the engineer 'Aziev'." When Azeff reported the letter to his Okhranka superiors, they ordered an investigation to find the leak. Quite by accident, the official charged with the investigation was Men'shchikov, the author of the letter.

A party investigation quickly ascertained that the charge against N.Iu. Tatarov was correct. As a young radical under arrest, he had endured a three-week hunger strike in the Fortress of Saints Peter and Paul. When threatened with exile to Siberia, he negotiated his liberty in exchange for a commitment to inform the police. Tatarov very quickly did what Azeff would never do: he handed over to the police part of the membership list of the Combat Organization. Tatarov was on his way to a brilliant career as an agent, but Men'shchikov's letter ended his prospects.

From its finding that Tatarov was guilty of the denunciation, the party investigative commission drew a favourable conclusion of Azeff. It believed that the letter was a provocation aimed to destroy Azeff within the party, and that the police had decided to sacrifice a lesser agent to discredit a top party leader. This deduction resulted from the unquestioning trust among SRs in the chief of the Combat Organization. Azeff now demanded that the traitor be put to death and the commission accepted his view. Members of the Combat Organization killed Tatarov at home while his helpless parents looked on.

No less unyielding was Azeff in the case of Father Gapon, whose name was linked to the beginning of the revolution of 1905. Gapon had been serving as chaplain at a prison deportation point when he led the workers' march to the Winter Palace in St Petersburg on 9 January that became known as "Bloody Sunday." When troops shot at the marchers and killed and wounded many of the demonstrators, Gapon launched a fiery appeal and called on the people to resist the tsarist autocracy. He soon fled abroad, where he was greeted by Russian emigrés as an authentic leader of the popular rebellion. Gapon joined the Socialist Revolutionary party and even stayed with Azeff, but he never felt truly at home with the revolutionaries. When a political amnesty was declared, he returned to St Petersburg to work once again with legal workers' organizations.

Gapon had been recruited as an Okhranka agent some years before when, as a young theological student, he had been invited to Fontanka by Zubatov. This innovative police official believed that preaching the Gospel in the poor quarters of St Petersburg was in accord with his ideas of police socialism. When Gapon returned to Russia in November 1905, Zubatov was no longer directing political operations; Rachkovsky was now in charge of them. He promised Gapon that he would support his mission among the workers if Gapon would help to put an end to the bloody terror campaign of the revolutionaries. Gapon agreed and promised to recruit his friend P.M. Rutenberg, a member of the SR, to assist in the venture.

Gapon, as Rutenberg later recalled, decided to introduce him to Rachkovsky and to Gerasimov, whether to persuade them to hand over 25,000 rubles on some pretext to use for other purposes or to take advantage of the meeting to kill two high officials in charge of police investigations.[34] Rutenberg rushed to tell everything to Azeff, who flew into a rage at the prospect of such a meeting; he decided that Gapon planned to cooperate with the police. Azeff declared that Gapon should be finished off like a "viper" by luring him out for a walk at night and "knifing him in the back." Other central committee members opposed this action, arguing that Gapon should not be condemned without a trial. Anything else could well rebound to the discredit of the party because Gapon enjoyed wide influence among the workers. Instead, to prove Gapon's ties with the police, it was decided that should he meet with the police officers he should be killed at the meeting. Azeff, the subordinate of Rachkovsky, liked this plan and proclaimed that he "would be especially pleased if they could administer a double blow, aimed at both Gapon and Rachkovsky, as he had long been thinking to mete out justice to Rachkovsky, but could not find a way of getting him within his grasp."[35]

Azeff was now baiting a trap for his chief, and Rachkovsky's life was in danger. But information from other sources had put this experienced police official on guard and had prompted him to avoid risky encounters. Rutenberg had received precise instructions from the central committee that he was not to carry out the death sentences if he could not manage to assemble Gapon and the police chiefs together. Rutenberg failed to carry out this order, and instead he invited Gapon to a country house in the village of Ozerki on 26 March 1906, while a group of workers belonging to Gapon-led organizations were hiding in the next room. They heard a conversation designed to entrap Gapon into discussing his connection with the police and the funds received for his covert work. The workers rushed in, refused to hear any explanations from their former idol, and hanged him on the spot.

Rutenberg insisted that he had acted with Azeff's approval. The leader of the Combat Organization denied it, and the central committee believed Azeff, not Rutenberg.[36] The committee forced Rutenberg to resign from the party, and he left behind the impression that he had arranged the murder of Gapon for personal reasons. For his part, Azeff had strong reasons to push Rutenberg to carry out the murder, because Gapon, as one who was in a position to deny Azeff's reports, had become both a rival and a threat to him. Taking the offensive a few days later, Azeff snapped at Rachkovsky, "Well, have you finally managed to buy Rutenberg? I guess you have made a fine agent of Gapon! Has he already handed the Combat Organization over to you?" Staring hard at his chief, he added, in a new demonstration of his own prowess as an agent, "Do you know where Gapon is now? He is hanging in a lonely country-house ... and you could easily control his fate – if you were still dealing with him."[37]

Gapon had known Azeff only as a revolutionary and the swift end of his life foreclosed his finding out his police connection. But the SR-Maximalist Solomon Ryss managed to unearth his tie with the Okhranka. He succeeded because, rusticating in prison, he had asserted his wish to cooperate with the investigative services. The director of the police, M.I. Trusevich, was hopeful of gaining a reliable informer among the Maximalists, so he arranged the escape of this dangerous criminal. Trusevich sacrificed two warders to make the matter appear authentic. They were tried for neglect of their duties. After his "escape," Ryss told his revolutionary comrades about the deal he had struck with the police. He said he had provided some information, but had withheld truly important information. Having learned of Azeff's police connection, he passed this charge to the SR central committee in September 1906, but the response from the party was that Ryss "will pay a high price for this slander." Soon after, the police arrested Solomon Ryss and he was hanged.[38] One can only speculate about the role of Azeff in the eliminating of his enemy, but it seems likely that he was the instigator. He was in a position to know Ryss's whereabouts, to pass that information to the Okhranka, and to benefit directly from Ryss's removal from the scene. The removal of Gapon and Ryss points to the hand of Azeff, for the Okhranka's best agent was now engaged in a fight for his life.

In 1906 the SR central committee received notice from Odessa that an aide to an Okhranka bureau chief, in exchange for a substantial reward, was ready to disclose the name of an agent who had penetrated the leadership of the party. The committee entrusted S.R. Tiutchev with conducting negotiations, and he set off for the south; Azeff knew of these events and when Tiutchev reached Odessa he found that the police official he was to contact had disappeared without a trace. He was told that the official had been summoned to St Petersburg to answer charges that he had embezzled government funds.[39] Again the link of Azeff to this affair is not solid, but it is plausible. He would have known about the information coming in to the SR central committee from Odessa, and he was in a position to secure the recall of the police official from the south. Azeff had used the immense trust that he enjoyed in two camps to eliminate a threat to his person.

More closely associated with Azeff was the "Saratov letter," but there are key questions about it and they raise doubts about its authenticity. This document, compiled in the fall of 1907, was a detailed summary of all the information that a certain official of the Saratov Okhranka had revealed to the SRs.[40] The letter's author quoted statements by Evstrady Mednikov, the detective, who was in Saratov in August 1905 to learn about an underground SR party congress. Mednikov allegedly said that a delegate at the conference was actually a top secret agent making 600 rubles per month. Detectives listening to Mednikov supposedly pressed him to reveal the name of the agent – a most unlikely request from experienced policemen. Mednikov reportedly said (and it is even more unlikely that Mednikov would be involved in contravening Okhranka policy by throwing out these tantalizing hints) that he did not know the name of the agent, but he did list several code names by which he was identified and he described him. If this is true, Mednikov seems to have had Azeff in mind, for he did take part in the Saratov conference. But none of the detectives was able to infer who the agent was, nor did the Saratov letter fall into the hands of the central committee of the party.

But Vladimir Burtsev was gathering evidence, including the Saratov letter. Azeff, unbeknown to Burtsev, had been closely following his activities since his student days, and had first mentioned Burtsev's name in a police report in 1897. The journalist, a former populist with sympathies for terrorism against the government, had known of Azeff because of his membership in the SR party. As editor of *The Past* (*Byloe*), Burtsev had begun to wonder about Azeff's actual role in 1906 when he knew that he was head of the Combat Organization. He encountered the terrorist on a street of the capital and reflected, "If I have recognized Azeff so easily from afar, why cannot police detectives, who most certainly know him by sight, recognize him when he appears in St Petersburg in so conspicuous a manner?"[41] He concluded that the police had not picked up Azeff because they had managed to infiltrate an agent into his group and wished that he remain at large. Burtsev personally warned Azeff about a traitor in the ranks of his terrorists. Only much later did a, to him, monstrous idea dawn on Burtsev: that the leader of the Combat Organization himself could be a secret agent.

Burtsev was still disbelieving when one of his voluntary informers, the former Okhranka officer M.E. Bakai, who knew of all the SR leaders through police circulars, said that he had never received any information about Azeff and did not believe that he was the chief of the terrorists. "For me not to have known the head of the Combat Organization would have been like not knowing the name of the Director of the Department of Police."[42] To Bakai, the failure to mention Azeff could only mean that he was being protected against arrest.

As Burtsev widened his investigation of Azeff, he inadvertently alerted the Okhranka. The police noted that Bakai, formerly one of their own, was making repeated visits to Burtsev's editorial offices in St Petersburg. Gerasimov, the head of the St Petersburg Okhranka, tried to divert Burtsev by telling Bakai that all the information concerning Azeff's supposed treachery to the SR party had been forged. Dubroskok, one of Gerasimov's agents, wrote Bakai, "I have reason to believe that spreading rumours about the persons mentioned is a trick of that rascal Gerasimov."[43] The Okhranka also forged and circulated materials to show that two other prominent SRs were secret agents of the police.

Not only the Okhranka, but the SR tried to stop Burtsev's investigation. The central committee formed a commission "to investigate rumours about a provocation under way" (that is, the Burtsev inquiries) and it found "groundless and slanderous" the accusations against the head of the Combat Organization. But the issue would not die down as the accusations against Azeff spread among the rank and file of the party, especially following the conference in August 1908 when Burtsev openly demanded that Azeff should be barred from all conspiratorial work. He threatened the party leaders with publication in the press of the materials he had gathered.

Instead, the central committee summoned a court of arbitration comprised of respected revolutionaries. Azeff believed that the proceedings could only benefit him. "I must be put to trial. Such a trial will serve as the best means to expose the falsehood of these accusations."[44] The party's principal revolutionary thinker, V.L. Chernov, agreed: "Burtsev will be crushed."[45] As the hearings of the tribunal began in Paris – a centre of SR activity – Azeff was in and out of the city. In a gesture of studied confidence, he did not attend the hearings and received all his information from friends who spoke in his defence. Members of the Combat Organization were the most insistent defenders of their chief's good name. Some insisted that they would not believe the charges even if they were shown an agent's report written in Azeff's hand. Others threatened to shoot the judges if they dared to offend their chief.

Burtsev's proof did prove to be weak. He produced only indirect evidence and, as time went on, it became clear that he had incorrectly interpreted many episodes. For instance, he attributed the "St Petersburg letter" to the Gendarme, Colonel A.N. Kremenetsky, who had been allegedly punished for this violation of regulations by transfer to a lesser post in Siberia. Azeff himself scoffed at this interpretation of events: "To betray two such fellows as those denounced in the letter, and then be 'punished' by transfer to Tomsk instead of Petersburg, and as an Okhranka chief, at that! It would be the same thing if we had sent Tatarov to work in another place and not in the capital."[46]

By the end of the hearings, the issue had become cut and dried. On Azeff's side was the moral weight and prestige of the members of Combat Organization who stood solidly behind their leader. On the other side, there were suppositions voiced by informers who came from within the Okhranka itself. Burtsev's charges now appeared, at best, mistakes or, at worst, an attempt to destroy a respected leader of the party. Burtsev said that if the trial judges ruled against him, he would have to put a bullet into his head. Backed into a corner, Burtsev put forth his most sensational proof of Azeff's treachery. Breaking a promise that he would not reveal his interlocutor's name, he said that a month before, the former director of the Department of Police, A.A. Lopukhin, had confirmed to him personally that Azeff was part of the Okhranka network.[47]

Azeff's defenders countered that the former police director's word was surely part of a police operation to destroy Azeff and wipe out SR terrorism. Azeff was in Paris at this time, where he had an aparment, but his usual self-control appeared to desert him. He said that party affairs required that he go to Berlin, but he secretly travelled to St Petersburg to persuade Lopukhin to withdraw his testimony. Neither Azeff nor Gerasimov, however, could move Lopukhin. Word soon reached Paris that Azeff was in St Petersburg, and the Okhranka failed to buttress the story he needed in order to deny his secret trip. The Okhranka in Berlin was to have provided a person resembling Azeff to check into a hotel, but the person who checked into the hotel bore no resemblance to Azeff. Furthermore, the hotel was a poor choice; the Berlin police managed it, and it was reputed to be a gathering place for spies. No experienced revolutionary would ever select this particular hostelry. When this evidence became known in Paris, Azeff's supporters lost heart.

Azeff saw his defence crumble. He reported to Gerasimov: "All fouled up! And it is all because of our visit to that friend of ours [Lopukhin]. He revealed everything I had told him and said that you had threatened him ... The bill that you sent me and that I passed on appeared to be too suspect to confirm the alibi ... Naturally, I was unable to describe the room where I was supposed to have stayed or to recall its number (for, despite my request, you did not provide me this information)."[48]

Members of the central committee and a few other senior party leaders met to decide the disposition of the charges against Azeff. A majority favoured the death penalty but feared that an execution carried out on French soil would damage the Socialist Revolutionaries' relations with the police.[49] They argued for an execution in another country, so they rented an isolated villa in the Italian Alps. The villa had a hidden passage into a cave, where Argunov was to place a rope around Azeff's neck. But even as the party made these preparations, everyone involved still hoped that the charges against the chief of the Combat Organization would somehow prove to be unfounded. Argunov described the wrenching state of affairs that confronted the SRs: "This transition from the idea of Azeff-comrade to that of Azeff-stool-pigeon was unbearable, not only for the members of the central committee, but also for those who found it the easiest thing in the world to reach for a Browning."[50]

Azeff, who had not been detained, knew about these hopes and hesitations and did not believe that the party would seize him without warning. On 24 December 1908 a party delegation called on him and gave him until the next day to confess his misdeeds. That night Azeff slipped out of his apartment and left Paris on the first morning train. In response, the central committee announced to the party membership that Azeff was to be declared an agent provocateur. Azeff's exposure seriously undercut the reputation of the Socialist Revolutionary party, and his escape raised a whole series of suspicions. Some members believed that party leaders loyal to Azeff, including Chernov, had made possible his escape.

Azeff's role led to questions for the government in the Duma. The Third State Duma launched an investigation. Constitutional Democrats and Social Democrats gathered information and prepared to question the government. A majority of the house approved an inquiry, giving the government a month to answer under the rules. Prime Minister Stolypin found it necessary to respond in the Duma even before the end of the allotted time. He spoke on 11 February 1909 with a detailed description of Azeff's career designed to show the agent's loyal and exceptional service to the government. He observed that if a revolutionary leader happened to be a police agent, it was in truth a sad story, but not for the government, only for the revolutionary party. Stolypin concluded by saying that "while revolutionary terror exists, there will always be a need for police action."[51]

Opposition speakers had acquired important information bearing on the case. The Laborite leader V. Bulat had received from the SR information on Azeff's part in various political assassinations. Deputies on the right wing insisted that Stolypin's explanation was satisfactory and opposed the opening of the inquiry. Their sentiments were echoed in the newspaper of the Octobrist party, the *Voice of Moscow*. The paper said the entire affair was designed by the enemies of the government to discredit it.[52] Newspapers on the extreme right condemned the government for paying Azeff's bills when the Socialist Revolutionaries were able to assassinate officials almost at will.[53]

Newspapers began the hunt for Azeff. One reported that he was hiding in San Francisco, another that he had been seen in Japan.[54] In reality, after his escape from Paris, Azeff had made a long journey around the Mediterranean and then settled down in Berlin. His exposure had meant the loss of his excellent salary, his value to the police, and to the revolutionaries. His wife, Liubov Menkina, who was herself a terrorist, renounced all connection with him when she learned the truth about her husband. Azeff, however, still had formidable personal resources. He appropriated the funds of the Combat Organization and put them to work. The former terrorist now began to gamble on the stock exchange and then he started a business. Azeff travelled to health resorts and even staked his money at the gambling tables. In all these pastimes, he was accompanied by a former chansonette, his old flame ever since he had lived in St Petersburg.

The one-time secret agent tried to recover in yet other ways. He wrote his wife that she and their children alone could give meaning to his life. They were the only beings whose memory he truly cherished. "For the whole world," he wrote, "I am a kind of monster, or, perhaps, a cold man, calculating in everything. In reality, I believe there is no human being more sensitive than I. I can't endure people who are unhappy, nor even read about them; I have tears in my eyes when I see the marks of suffering on peoples' faces."[55]

Again, writing to his wife, Azeff said, "Yes, I have committed an unforgivable mistake and, as a matter of fact, I could have washed away this stain of infamy long ago, had I approached my comrades at a certain moment and told them that I had done this or that, but that I have compensated for all of it with my work, so judge me now!"[56] In 1912 Azeff tried to repair this mistake and met with his accusor Vladimir Burtsev in Frankfurt-am-Main. Azeff pleaded that he should have another trial by his former comrades and that if the new court pronounced the death sentence, he would carry it out with his own hand within twenty-four hours.[57]

Azeff tried to persuade his former comrades to take what he called a "businesslike" view of his dealings with the police. He knew from experience that party leaders believed that moral principles were subordinate to the interests of the revolution. He told Burtsev to consider the comparative value of the dignitaries killed as a result of his acts of terror and of the rank-and-file revolutionaries who had to be given up to the police. In Azeff's view, the balance was so favourable to the SRs that one could only wonder that it had been achieved at such a low cost. Despite his arguments, the party refused to negotiate with him. For one thing, they well knew that an entanglement with the perfidious Azeff could lead them into yet another shadowy scheme.

Although the Socialist Revolutionary party refused to rehabilitate Azeff, soon after the beginning of the First World War German authorities had no doubt that he still deserved his reputation as a terrorist. They arrested him as a danger to the state and he spent more than two years in solitary confinement in Moabit prison in Berlin. But Azeff remained unrepentant. He complained of the brutal injustice inflicted upon him and demanded easing of the prison regime. At the end of 1917 the Germans set him free but he survived only a few months more at liberty. A severe disease, perhaps related to his harsh prison regime, caused him a great deal of suffering and he succumbed to it in April 1918.

Many legends have surrounded the name of Azeff, both before and after his death. Facts were transformed into fantasies; the dozens of revolutionaries he had betrayed became hundreds of thousands. Some versions of the career of Azeff are fantasy, but among the others there are three principal interpretations.[58] The first is the official version and its most authoritative champion was Gerasimov who still believed to the end of his life that Azeff had been "the best possible assistant," although he said he could only speak about the period beginning in 1906 when Azeff came under his control. The historian Anna Heifman concluded that Azeff acted on all occasions in the best interests of the police. But to reach this view, Heifman had to set aside all the SR sources as falsifications.

An opposite point of view comes from Rataev, the Okhranka officer who for many years had complete faith in Azeff's loyalty. But Rataev finally changed his opinion under the sheer weight of the evidence. He saw the one-time loyal agent moving over to the other camp. He divided Azeff's career into three parts: "(1) unconditional loyalty from 1892 until the summer of 1902; (2) dubious loyalty from 1902 to the fall of 1903; and (3) criminal disloyalty from late 1903 until the end of his service." Rataev was convinced that the reason for Azeff's treachery was the hypnotic spell cast on him by Gersh Gershuni.[59]

Rataev's calendar seems probable, but there are no proofs, either direct or indirect, that Gershuni exercised such an influence. Azeff was not one of those romantic young revolutionaries whose minds and hearts were under the spell of Gershuni. On the contrary, Azeff deluded and manipulated the famous terrorist, the same way he dealt with anyone else who stepped within his reach. Rataev's assessment is based largely on a confluence of events rather than on evidence from Azeff himself.

More widely held is the view that Azeff was a double-dealer, although there is wide dispute over just what his double-dealing added up to.[60] There was no question to many of Azeff's contemporaries that he had accomplices in the high ranks of the police to act as he did for so many years. This interpretation reached its grandest flights in the foreign sensationalist press when it was reported that the grand dukes of the imperial family offered Azeff millions of rubles to kill Nicholas II. The Russian press supporting the opposition suggested that Azeff was deliberately used by the government to carry out terrorist attacks in order to justify repression in the eyes of the public.

At one time or another, all the ministers of the interior were accomplices of Azeff who, supposedly stipulating that Azeff must make no attempts on their lives, offered him full freedom with respect to other high dignitaries. Another variant of the highly placed accomplices theme concerns Rachkovsky. In memoirs published in Burtsev's *The Past*, Bakai, the Okhranka defector, maintained that Rachkovsky, Azeff's "former tutor," used his agent to eliminate rivals among other police officials.[61] Authors of extravagant historical novels have skilfully reconstructed supposed clandestine meetings between the two villains where they schemed to carry out new terrorists attacks. Another twist brings Lopukhin into the centre of the attack on Azeff. Supposedly, the former police director exposed Azeff to Burtsev and to the SRS because he wished to avenge the killing of his mentor Plehve, which he discovered had been carried out by Azeff.[62]

Azeff had never been anyone's puppet, either in the police or the SR. He engaged in his parallel activities at his own risk. He withheld information systematically, he intentionally provided false data, and, most important, he was an active participant in many heinous crimes against the state. B.N. Nicolaevsky, who has written one of the most substantial books about Azeff, believed that this police agent had always behaved in accordance with what the political circumstances suggested to him.[63] When the tsarist regime seemed to him to be on the brink of collapse, Azeff embraced completely the revolutionary cause and was ready to blow up Fontanka 16 in order to wipe out every trace of his collaboration with the police. When it seemed to him that the government would be victorious, he resumed his functions as an effective secret agent. But, whatever the course of events, he did not wish to permit the destruction of the Combat Organization because the money he was getting to fund his operations far exceeded even the excellent retainer he received from the police.

All such explanations exaggerate the uniqueness of Azeff. In reality, his actions were typical of the behaviour of many secret agents and differed only in scope. It was assumed by the police that the informer's interests coincided with those of the Okhranka. But, in practice, they often contradicted one another. The agent had to look to his own interests at all times. He knew that the data he supplied, if handled carelessly, could destroy him. There were numerous instances to demonstrate this fundamental fact of his life.

In the period after 1905, Azeff found himself on several occasions in situations of near desperation. The revelations from inside the Okhranka threatened his position in the revolutionary movement; if his colleagues in the Combat Organization accepted the charges about Azeff as genuine, his life would have been at risk. In self protection, Azeff drew the necessary conclusions from police incompetence. Whereas in his first years of service as an agent he had scrupulously reported everything that he knew, in later years he began to report selectively to his Okhranka superiors. As his rise continued in the Socialist Revolutionary party, he increasingly withheld information in order to conceal the position of growing influence he truly held within the party hierarchy. He could not refuse advancement within the party without raising questions among his colleagues. To maintain his authority, he had to engage in daringly successful terrorist operations; as he rose in importance within the party he became better insulated from any doubts raised against him.

Azeff found himself in a tight position because of the nature of secret agent service. Every secret agent was charged to abide by the law; but at the same time he was encouraged to push right into the centre of the revolutionary movement. Azeff discovered that inside the revolutionary movement was no place to remain a detached onlooker. His worth as an agent depended on the prestige he enjoyed in the revolutionary world, and this prestige had to be maintained by successful terrorist attacks. For a long period, Azeff managed to keep both sides satisfied. His record as a planner of political assassinations overshadowed all misgivings in the minds of the party. On the other hand, the arrest of terrorists, whom Azeff periodically fed to the police, induced his chiefs to continue his high salary and virtual freedom of action. Until the final, convincing exposure of Azeff, both sides believed him to be their outstanding operative. One of the Okhranka's great faults was to have failed to protect its most outstanding secret agent.

CHAPTER EIGHT

Whistle-blowers in the Ranks of the Okhranka

In the decade after 1905, the Okhranka faced a new threat: whistle-blowers. Insiders who made revelations held by far the greatest power to harm the secret police because they could identify covert agents and operations and thereby render them useless.

Three Okhranka insiders and a journalist, all men, stand out in the post-1905 period as whistle-blowers. No one can know their motives certainly, and their defections at first caught the Okhranka by surprise. Its main defence was to discredit these exposers of its secret operations, in part to dissuade others from similar actions.

The first insider to gain wide public attention – as he did, with momentous effect, in 1908 – was A.A. Lopukhin (1864–1927). As the director of the Department of Police from mid-1902 to early 1905, he had headed all Okhranka operations and had enjoyed broad access to its secrets. Whether choice or force of circumstances made him a whistle-blower is open to question, but he was definitely influenced, directly and indirectly, by the three others under discussion here, the journalist V.L. Burtsev and the former Okhranka officials, M.E. Bakai and L.P. Men'shchikov.

Lopukhin advocated the rule of law as a moral imperative. But he also held that Russia would not soon achieve such governance unless critics like him helped to shape judicial and political policy, the more directly the better. Acting on liberal beliefs and intent on reforming law enforcement, Lopukhin shifted from serving the state prosecutor's office to directing the Department of Police in the two and a half years before the revolution of 1905. Then, after discrediting events and policy differences had ended his tenure, Lopukhin became a public critic of the police. His revelations of Okhranka secrets to radicals, however, led to his arrest, conviction, and internal exile in 1909 as a political criminal.

By all conventional standards, Lopukhin was a true Russian intellectual. He emerged from their traditional social source, the land-owning aristocratic class; by entering the practice of law, he chose a field attractive to his peers in the second half of the nineteenth century. But what most placed Lopukhin among the critical intelligentsia of his era were his faith in critical thinking and his confident belief that the rightness of his ideas would change the policies of the imperial government.

Bearing the name of an old and distinguished Russian family, Alexei Alexandrovich Lopukhin was born, just after the Emancipation of the serfs, into modest wealth that came from estates in Orlov and Smolensk provinces. (So small was his private income as an adult, however, that his loss of a government salary in 1905 left Lopukhin barely able to support his family. Still, as he tells it, he preferred financial sacrifice to compromising his beliefs in order to remain in government service.) In 1886, at twenty-two, Lopukhin had graduated from the Juridical Faculty of Moscow University and joined the Ministry of Justice, where a political liberal would have seen the best prospect for furthering reform and the rule of law. Promoted in 1890 to serve as assistant procurator of the Riazan Circuit Court, he moved up again to fill that same position in Moscow. As a specialist in so-called political crimes, Lopukhin worked closely with Sergei Zubatov, then head of the Moscow Okhranka. Besides their shared commitment to ridding society of dangerous subversives who deliberately incited violence, both men saw a critical parallel need: policies that encouraged popular support for the government.

In 1900 Lopukhin rose another level to serve as assistant procurator in the St Petersburg Circuit Court, and he accepted promotion to Moscow the next year as chief prosecutor of the Moscow Circuit Court. When the minister of the interior, D.S. Sipiagin, urged him to leave the Ministry of Justice to become vice-director of the Department of Police, Lopukhin declined because he differed too much from the arbitrary police methods of the director, S.E. Zvoliansky.

To help with a backlog of political cases caused by an outbreak of peasant revolts, Lopukhin became procurator of the Khar'kov Court of Appeals in 1902, just before terrorists killed Sipiagin that April. When the new minister of the interior, the redoubtable V.K. Plehve, visited Khar'kov to assess the unrest, the two men met. Testifying several years later, Lopukhin would quote from that session these pessimistic words from Plehve: "If I had been told twenty years ago, when I was Director of the Department of Police, that a revolution was possible in Russia, I would have burst out laughing; and here we are on the eve of a revolution."[1] Lopukhin says that he in turn laid blame for Russia's widespread dissention on specific social, economic, and legal inequities. In May the basically conservative Plehve named Lopukhin, an avowed liberal, as the new director of the Department of Police.

As he recalls the appointment, Lopukhin insists that he moved to the Ministry of the Interior solely on the understanding that Plehve approved his program of liberal reforms as a sound counteractive to the revolutionary movement. Confirmation comes from Prince S.D. Urusov, Lopukhin's brother-in-law, who also recounts that Lopukhin had confided within six months of his appointment that Plehve was failing him.[2] So, too, an official who served under Lopukhin in the Gendarmes felt that Plehve had merely made a gesture to "reconcile himself with liberal circles."[3]

The minister himself announced that he expected stronger law enforcement from Lopukhin. "The revolutionary parties," a French journalist quoted Plehve as saying, "are strong only because of the weakness of the police ... The former head of the police did not know his business ... I have absolute confidence that the new director of the police will do an outstanding job."[4]

As he took charge of police officers who dealt with everything from imports to liquor consumption, Lopukhin felt most concerned about two main units under him: the Corps of Gendarmes, the uniformed imperial police that openly served across the Empire, and the covert security police, the Okhranka. Lopukhin's authority over the municipal police – the third main component in the police system – was indirect.

In his version of events, Lopukhin says that the mandate he had wrested from Plehve was threefold: to pare down the number of Okhranka division offices in order to strengthen his line of command through them to the agents in the field; to restrict their political investigations to exacting legal limits; and to end one-sided "administrative" sentences by processing detainees solely through the judicial system. (The third reform also meant the automatic release of detainees when the government lacked sufficient legal grounds for a judicial trial.) In keeping with these changes, says Lopukhin, Plehve had also promised to get rid of the statute of 14 August 1881, that had granted "exceptional" powers to the local authorities to detain and investigate suspected revolutionaries. All law enforcement was to be "in conformity with the legal principles introduced by the Judicial Statute of Alexander II."[5]

These were the reforms that Lopukhin had long favoured, and all of them targeted arbitrary procedures in political cases and faulty lines of command. Too often, he held, police agents in the field arbitrarily searched and arrested suspects, thereby deciding on their own the fate of persons in their charge and, "in sum, of the entire Empire."[6] The vast organization of the Gendarmes he inherited would be hard to reform because it was part of the military forces; so the Okhranka, a smaller, more fluid force with a precise and critically important purpose, would be his starting point.

Soon after becoming director of the police, Lopukhin made several changes in staff to impose discipline and legality down his chain of command and to replace insubordinate police officers. For one thing, he insisted that Plehve replace the head of the Foreign Agency located in the Russian embassy in Paris. The incumbent was the flamboyant, free-wheeling Rachkovsky, whose operations generally proceeded without approval from St Petersburg and even included criminal acts. For example, Lopukhin had received evidence that one of Rachkovsky's agents had participated in an anarchists' bombing in Liège.[7]

Next Lopukhin named his trusted Moscow associate, S.V. Zubatov, to head the Okhranka's central office, the Special Section. Knowing that, to accomplish his reform of trying all political cases in courts of law, prosecution evidence had to come from legal searches and arrests, Lopukhin at once transferred sole authority over that police function from the Gendarmes to the security forces under Zubatov.[8]

He had Zubatov, who brought most of his staff with him to St Petersburg, name younger Gendarme officers who had not served in the old police culture to head each of his provincial "security" divisions because they were more likely to enforce his orders for legal procedures.[9] And, on the very different labour front, Lopukhin gave Zubatov the go-ahead to find organizers for a local version of his police-sponsored clubs for workers. One recruit was Father Gapon.[10]

With detection of subversives and revolutionaries his principal objective, Lopukhin acquired another trusted police veteran to head the Okhranka's plain-clothes surveillance corps. He was Moscow's leading police detective, E.P. Mednikov, who set up a school to teach legal methods of detection to his so-called outside agents. Mednikov had founded the effective flying squad of detectives in Moscow, and from there they had been dispatched to various cities around Russia to deal with groups of radicals.

There were also the inside agents, who served directly under Zubatov. These were the elite who infiltrated the secret cells of revolutionaries by posing as their confederates. And each of them, too, was under orders to break no laws. None, for example, were to fill command posts in criminal organizations because they would have to perform, or incite others to perform, illegal acts.

It was Lopukhin's insistence that the police strictly stay with the legal limits that was new, not so much the limits themselves. Under previous directors, the police had easily ignored limits to accomplish their ends. As for the seeming novelty that a liberal would agree to direct the secret police, Lopukhin took for granted that underground revolutionaries and terrorists required the government to riddle society with covert agents and informers. As Lopukhin said later in court, "revolutionary organizations make it completely impossible to get along without [the secret police]. For me, the whole question came down to the borders in which the agency can exist and operate." At the time of his appointment, he went on to say, the peasant revolts of Khar'kov and Poltava had seemed to him "the beginning of the Russian revolution."[11]

"Although I did not really consider myself suitable for directing political investigations," Lopukhin explained further, "I took the job because the Minister pointed out that a whole series of reforms was necessary. In his opinion, the "inadequacies of the existing system of political investigation required the phasing out of the security divisions, the reform of the police, and the transfer of political cases to the overview of the courts."[12]

Lopukhin's first steps to achieve this program, however, seriously weakened the police system from within, although he had no such objectives and seemed to understand only later the flaws in his own program of reform. L.A. Rataev, who had been head of the Special Section and whom Lopukhin named to replace Rachkovsky in Paris, cites Lopukhin's personnel changes as debilitating to the organization as a whole. Especially destructive was the move of Zubatov and Mednikov to St Petersburg from Moscow where they had established a police organization that could range far and wide into the provinces. Lopukhin seems to have diminished the Moscow organization without creating a comparable one in the capital.[13]

Factors beyond his control caused even more severe setbacks for Lopukhin. Plehve made no moves to win a retraction of the law of 1881, as promised; and Lopukhin himself was impelled by events to accelerate sweeping counter-revolutionary operations.

First had come massive violations of the law banning labour strikes, with the number of illegal work stoppages soaring to a record 550 in 1903 (the previous high of 215 had come five years before, followed by a 9 percent decline the next year and an even sharper drop during the recession of 1900 and 1901). Police and troops usually had to intervene, and police agents had to track down and arrest the instigators as criminals.

In light of that worker unrest, moreover, Zubatov's outreach to workers cast a black mark on Lopukhin and cost Zubatov his job in 1903. Trouble came from a workers' group that Zubatov had funded in Odessa, where a general strike erupted that July. When Plehve learned from his own agents that the Zubatov-backed group had been instrumental in fomenting Odessa's civil disobedience, the minister called Zubatov in and gave him twenty-four hours to leave both St Petersburg and government service forever. Father Gapon was one of the few to see Zubatov off when he left the capital by train the next day.

Besides the major strike in Odessa, large walkouts by workers also took place in Kiev and Nikolaev in 1903, and Lopukhin personally visited and reported on all three cities.[14] What he faulted in Odessa was typical: deplorable conditions of work and no legal means for redress by workers. Because the Ministry of Finance's system of factory inspection had broken down, he wrote, employers had been left to raise their profits by exploiting their employees. Workers for the Russian Society of Steamships, for example, had had no raise in pay for twenty years, even though their housing costs had doubled. But he also faulted local authorities for not having taken the initiative in regulating worker-owner relations.[15]

As for why the strike had become so general, Lopukhin noted that the first to walk out were the drivers and conductors of streetcars. The many other workers who relied on the transit system had abruptly come "face to face with the strike ... and all fell under its influence." These recruits, in turn, spread word of the protest far and wide. Assuming that some workers were intimidated, Lopukhin crticized the regional chief of police, General Arsen'ev, for failing to "work out a system to protect the work places of those who wished to continue to work." Rather than taking charge, Arsen'ev had decided against mobilizing more police and had only briefly detained the leading agitators. When Lopukhin arrived late in July, he said he had found Arsen'ev "in a state of complete confusion."

In his response to the strike in Odessa, Lopukhin favoured state intervention in relations betweeen workers and employers, a position, however paternalistic, that put him squarely in line with the liberalism of the future Constitutional Democratic party, with which he ultimately identified. In the same vein, he faulted the Ministry of Finance under Count Witte for its minimal inspection of factories. Without spelling out that Witte favoured industrialists in his campaign to promote economic growth, he argued that deplorable work conditions had made the strike inevitable.

Another policing crisis in 1903 was the resurgence of anti-Semitic violence that caught world attention, the worst outbreak being the notorious pogrom on Easter Sunday in Kishinev, Bessarabia. Resentment centred on the large number of labour agitators and revolutionaries identified as Jews, and complicity by local police in the mob attacks on Jews is certain. Lopukhin at once made clear that he would not tolerate such insubordination, for he felt certain that at least some police took part because they expected their superiors to approve.[16]

Given Plehve's well-known antipathy to Jews, several newspapers abroad accused Plehve by name as a prime instigator. Writing twenty years later, Lopukhin expressed his conviction – seemingly to counter a charge still believed – that "it is unjust to attribute the Kishinev pogrom to [Plehve]. His anti-Semitism is not subject to doubt, but this one fact does not justify blaming an intelligent man for an act which is not merely repulsive, but also politically stupid."[17] Lopukhin was well aware that pogroms severely hurt Russia not only by undermining her social and political stability but also by causing other governments to see her as unstable and undeserving. The foreign trade and investment actively sought by St Petersburg was clearly put at risk by anti-Semitic violence.

That summer, after his late July inquiry into the Odessa strike, Lopukhin went to France, and his letter to Zubatov from Paris in September shows that the Jewish issue also dogged him there. Writing about demonstrations against Jews that had just taken place in England, he feared that news of such anti-Semitism in the West would stir even more rancorous outbursts in Russia – "most assuredly in the press." Easing domestic tensions would consequently become "still more complicated,"[18] but Lopukhin understood the need to push ahead. In 1904 he would sit on a commission named by Plehve under Prince I.M. Obolensky whose purpose was to examine ways to remove "needlesss restrictions" on Jews. Lopukhin and some others on the commission would advocate removing all restrictions on Jews, but nothing came of the heated discussions because the war with Japan ended deliberations.[19]

From his own reading of history, continued Lopukhin, he looked to the future with foreboding; for he could expect nothing from Jews nor any gestures to them from St Petersburg, despite the strong need for outreach. Equally disquieting was evidence from his "superficial" inquiry that Jews dominated a subversive international organization on the rise in Russia: the Masonic Order. Even as he opposed pogroms and discriminatory measures against Jews, Lopukhin found it credible that his police should be on guard against a Jewish-Masonic coalition aimed at toppling the imperial autocracy[20] – although within three years Lopukhin would reject Witte's assumption that specific organizations were orchestrating the actions and demands of Jews.

Besides having to grapple with unrest stirred by the so-called Jewish question and by worker exploitation, Lopukhin was further distracted from reform efforts by a rise in revolutionary terrorism. The minister of the interior, Sipiagin, had been a victim, and the Governor of Khar'kov province had narrowly escaped revolutionary assassins just after Lopukhin became director of police. Then, a year later, terrorists succeeded in killing the governor of Ufa. With good cause, Plehve had barricaded his closely guarded Ministry building and had begun living there; he never ventured out without armed escorts. In June 1904 terrorists struck down the governor-general of Finland; the next month, Plehve was felled.

Then had come the tragedy of Bloody Sunday in January of 1905. It was soldiers, not police, who fired on the unarmed petititioners marching to the Winter Palace in St Petersburg; but their illegal demonstration (the tsar had banned all such protests) was led by Father Gapon, whose connections with the police were well known among high officials. The final blow followed the next month with the assassination of the Grand Duke Sergei. Not long before, Lopukhin had refused to spend any more of his tight budget on added security for the grand duke.[21]

At last convinced that both his reform goals and his job requirements were impossible for him to meet, Lopukhin resigned. Transferred well away from St Petersburg, but with no reduction in pay, he next took up residence as provincial governor of Estland in the capital city of Reval. Within a year, however, he was again to resign under pressure; this time he would end his government career.

What led to his downfall was the October 1905 country-wide general strike that included Reval. As Lopukhin tells the story, when the walkout at Reval's gas plant shut off fuel for city street lamps, "the dregs of society took advantage of the darkness" to prey on the innocent. With too few police for adequate patrols, Lopukhin had asked the Reval city council to organize a citizens' militia to work with the police. The invitation to workers to take part, however, elicited their demand for a guarantee that Lopukhin would not jail their leaders, as the previous governor had done during a strike eight months before.

In talks with the chief of provincial gendarmes and Reval's prosecutor, Lopukhin was dismayed to learn that the earlier strike leaders remained in jail but had never been charged. When he next proposed to release jailed workers as an "act of justice" and good faith, the prosecutor and the Gendarme chief adamantly opposed any such "concession to the mob."[22]

Once again Lopukhin independently took a stand for the rule of law. Using his executive power as governor, he released the detainees on his own authority just an hour before the first patrol by citizens began. Within two days, however, the outraged prosecutor and Gendarme chief had summoned additional troops from St Petersburg to supplement those already in the area. When news of the arrival of new troops on the streets prompted the workers to stage a big protest demonstration and cry betrayal, continues Lopukhin, the "military commander ordered the troops against the crowd ... and more than 100 persons were killed or wounded."[23]

Summoned within a week to St Petersburg, Lopukhin there learned from the new minister of the interior, P.N. Durnovo, that he could choose resignation or dismissal for having "given authority to revolutionaries." Lopukhin demanded and got an offical review of his action. Despite being subsequently informed that the committee had found against him, Lopukhin claims to have believed otherwise because no final report ever reached him. But, rather than appeal further, Lopukhin says he "gave the whole thing up as a bad job and departed [government service] completely."[24] It was precisely because that severence in late 1905 left him in financial difficulty that Lopukhin says he did not make a public issue of his case. Despite "considerations of principle ... and the complete injustice done to me," he explained, "exposure from my side would be ascribed to motives of revenge that would sicken my moral sense."[25]

Durnovo had astutely avoided giving Lopukhin the legal grounds for appeal that would have resulted had he forced him out for freeing the jailed radicals or for failing to prevent the fatal clash between troops and citizens. The radicals' release must have angered the minister, but he knew that Lophkhin held full authority to make and implement that legal decision. As for the presence of troops which had provoked the fatal clash, Durnovo would have been aware that the Gendarme chief serving under Governor Lopukhin was insubordinate in failing to get the governor's approval for outside reinforcements, a request that Lopukhin would have denied because it would have violated his agreement with the workers. What stood out was Durnovo's decision to reject rather than champion Lopukhin. Whereas Lopukhin blamed unrest on arbitrary governance and held that the rule of law would bolster popular support and restore order, Durnovo blamed officials with liberal views like Lopukhin for deepening unrest by refusing to deny radicals the benefits of law. Those benefits of freedom and protection, argued Durnovo, should not be accorded to those who threatened the state.

Lopukhin's resignation came as the revolution of 1905 wound down, while social tensions remained high, and as the new post-October government headed by Count Witte struggled to impose order. To profit from the former police director's expertise, claims Lophukhin, Witte twice interviewed him early in 1906. (This explanation refutes the unconvincing claim by Witte in his memoirs published in 1920 that Lophkhin had initiated the late January meetings in order to complain about his old enemies, Rachkovsky and Trepov.) To win crucially needed foreign loans, says Lopukhin, Witte felt that he had to convince "Jewish banking circles" in Europe that the autocracy was actively helping Jews in Russia. What advantages should he grant native Jews, Witte purportedly asked, and with which worldwide Jewish organizations should he negotiate?[26]

How surprising that Witte, with "his mind, his great practical and political experience," scoffed Lopukhin, "could have such a purely commonplace idea about the existence of some kind of Jewish political centre for a world cabal, with secret links through which it could direct Jewery all over the world." After rejecting these beliefs, said Lopukhin, he advised Witte that granting special concessions to Jews ran counter to the just goal of equality under the law for all citizens. Moreover, the State Duma, not Witte, should address making Jews fully equal. Where the government could and must act was to stamp out pogroms by threatening local officials with dismissal if any such violence occurred within their jurisdictions. Too often, he emphasized, extremist anti-Semites in government were directly involved.

Then Lopukhin says he made two serious charges: he knew of plans for a pogrom in Kiev in just twelve days and of pamphlets printed by a press in the Department of Police being distributed to incite it – as they were designed to do all across Russia. When Witte demanded proof, Lopukhin said he obtained incriminating pamphlets from the source the very next day, "so certain were its directors of the legality of their operation and so little concerned were they with conducting a conspiracy."[27]

As for background, Lopukhin reported learning the press runs had begun after the October Manifesto when Rachkovsky, as vice-director of the department, had ordered a Gendarme officer, M.S. Komissarov, to hire two printers and supervise their ongoing production of anti-Semitic pamphlets. That very night, advised Lopukhin, Witte should go with witnesses to ban the printing in mid-production and report his action to the press. In turn, the Council of Ministers should order the public prosecution of those responsible, to publicize widely the government's total opposition to the pogroms. If Witte took these special steps alone, argued Lopukhin, he could guarantee "the success of the Russian loan abroad."[28]

Within three days of delivering the pamphlets, Lopukhin met with Witte again, expecting a further exchange on government policy towards Jews. But this time, he says, Witte pointedly confined the talk to the fight against revolutionaries. Here, too, he faults Witte for assessing reforms as ineffectual and police repression as the only workable response.

Failing to win a ringing public condemnation of police anti-Semitism from Witte, Lopukhin proceeded to get one at a session of the first Duma through a sitting member – his brother-in-law, Prince Urusov.[29] The official reply to that body came on 8 June 1906 from the minister of the interior, P.A. Stolypin; "its avoidance of the truth," says Lopukhin, prompted him immediately to inform Stolypin, an acquaintance since school days, of facts he seemed not to know. Writing from Munich on 14 June, Lopukhin first justified his own role in initiating the public discussion and condemnation of the involvement of government personnel in pogroms: "Only a State Duma informed by the press has sufficient strength once and for all to stop the enormous threatening danger to the state of the systematic preparation by the authorities of pogroms against Jews and others."[30] Then he described the production, contents, and distribution of police pamphlets; named Rachkovsky as instigator; and told of the substance and consequences of his talk with Witte in January.[31]

Although he knew that Witte had at once ordered the pamphlets stopped, continued Lopukhin, he had since learned that Komissarov had merely moved the press out of police headquarters to his own apartment, with no interruption in publishing. Moreover, the police were guilty of another subterfuge. Stolypin should know that his 20 April dismissal of Rachkovsky as head the Special Section of the Department of Police had been nullified by Rachkovsky's "superior." Through written instructions, that official had authorized Rachkovsky to continue to oversee not only "all the Okhranka divisions" but also the "orientation of all the affairs of the Department of Police," with full power to "call on all the social forces of the organization."[32]

Recalling just such insubordination while he was director of police, Lopukhin contrasted his inability to confirm the collusion of local police in the 1903 pogrom in Kishinev with his ability to do so after

retirement. The reason was clear: "All power, in fact, has been transferred from above to below by the Statute on Security [of March 14,
1881]."[33] That law designed to improve security throughout the
Empire had effectively empowered persons in the lower ranks of the
police and Gendarmes to act independently of the central authorities.

On his return to Russia, Lopukhin met with the prime minister (the
tsar had named Stolypin to the post in July 1906), but the "explanation that followed between Stolypin and me on the subject of my letter
left no room for doubt that Stolypin had consciously distorted the
truth in his statements before the Duma." Moreover, Stolypin scoffed
at Lopukhin's charge spelled out during their discussion, that Azeff
filled a top role in the Socialist Revolutionary party. When they parted
in enmity, says Lopukhin, he warned Stolypin that, "if I found out
that Azeff was still an agent of the Russian police, I would take
measures to expose him."[34]

Because his police tenure disqualified him from resuming the practice
of law or joining the Constitutional Democratic Party and running for
office, Lopukhin found himself writing for the press to support his
family; and his most saleable subject was police misconduct. One
publisher printed a collection of his pieces as a book in 1907.[35]
Included there was an historical analysis of why Russian police had
come to operate outside established law.

About the time his book appeared, Lopukhin was establishing a
new career as a representative of Russian commercial interests, including those which dealt with European companies. His fortunes improving, he holidayed abroad in 1908, only to face the issue of Azeff once
again through Vladimir Burtsev, an emigré journalist who was a critic
of "provocation," whether by the government or by revolutionaries.[36]
What Burtsev condemned was subterfuge designed to incite the enemy
to brutal acts in order to cause public horror to redound against that
enemy. Double agents, or agents provocateurs, were a prime tool.

As Burtsev tells it, he had talked with Lopukhin in Finland earlier
that year, but Lopukhin had gone only so far as to agree to discuss
provocations at some later date when he was abroad.[37] He had therefore managed to confront Lopukhin on the Paris-Berlin train on the
afternoon of 5 September 1908, and pleaded for help in exposing an
especially dangerous agent provocateur. Burtsev then proposed to tell
what he knew about a presumed Okhranka operative and asked
Lopukhin merely to confirm or deny what was said. His method was
designed to ensure, he said, that "if at any time [Lopukhin] had to
answer for his conversation with me, then he could say with absolute

validity that he had made no revelations, that I knew everything without him, and that he could not disclaim that which I had told him in a private conversation."

Lopukhin, according to Burtsev, remained coolly non-commital until he learned for the first time that Azeff had not only headed the Socialist Revolutionary Terror Brigade that killed Plehve and the Grand Duke Sergei but had actively plotted and expedited both assassinations.[38] Lopukhin himself, during his 1909 trial, would testify that Burtsev's revelations so meshed with what he already knew and so repelled him that he felt morally compelled to help stop Azeff from shedding more blood.[39] These motives aside, Lopukhin appears to have confirmed Azeff's police role to Burtsev more because of long-held convictions than because Burtsev's evidence finally convinced him of Azeff's perfidy. That is, what Burtsev presented was merely indirect and circumstantial proof from a whistle-blower of relatively low status in the Okhranka – M.E. Bakai.

Bakai had first reported Okhranka misconduct to Burtsev in 1906, when Burtsev still published his leftist journal, *The Past*, in St Petersburg. Although Burtsev was initially sceptical of the police gossip offered by Bakai, the editor had gradually pieced together that Okhranka agents who infiltrated revolutionary groups were prodding them, even helping them, to commit criminal acts. When the Okhranka arrested Bakai early in the morning of 31 March 1907 for the political crime of telling Burtsev confidential information about the police, Burtsev transferred himself and *The Past* to Paris and engineered from abroad Bakai's successful escape from his sentence of internal exile so that he could join him.

Charges against the Okhranka, compiled by Burtsev and Bakai from yet other informants, began appearing in Burtsev's Paris journal to cause what the head of the Foreign Agency, A.M. Harting, called "extremely depressing circumstances" for his work. Harting therefore approached officials at the Paris Prefecture of Police about forcing Bakai to leave the country, and learned that they would deport no one without cause. At their suggestion that he devise a sound pretext for such action, Harting telegraphed the Okhranka in St Petersburg for help, but to no avail.[40]

In the memoir he wrote for *The Past*, Bakai said that his introduction to the Okhranka had come in 1900 when he served the underground paper, *Southern Worker*, as a member of the outlawed Socialist Revolutionary party. Under psychological pressure from the Okhranka, Bakai had betrayed the printing plant and put himself into the hands of the police. By 1902 Bakai was earning his living in Warsaw as an Okhranka officer. Not until the aftermath of the 1905 revolution, claims Bakai, did he realize that the political investigations of the Okhranka were "base." By then he deplored the Okhranka's recruitment of informers from all levels of society. Hearsay evidence from "hooligans and prostitutes" that no court under the judiciary would admit, he wrote, was used by the Okhranka as grounds for searches, arrests and, as he himself experienced in 1907, for convictions in closed proceedings.[41]

Although Bakai's information cast a dark light on the Okhranka's secret operations, Burtsev's main campaign to expose agents provocateur suffered a credibility problem for lack of strong evidence. When he added to his list the name of Azeff, a Socialist Revolutionary tribunal in Paris summoned him to prove his charges. Again, they found his proof too weak. At this juncture, Burtsev had determined to return with testimony from an ex-director of police that Azeff was an Okhranka agent. He repeated to the tribunal both Lopukhin's testimony and his name – both still hearsay evidence.

Within a fortnight, Lopukhin learned what Burtsev had done when Azeff himself called the on ex-director at his St Peterburg apartment. Azeff had come to implore for a convincing denial from Lopukhin to the SRs. Ten days later, the head of the local Okhranka, Gerasimov, claiming purely altruistic concern for an agent who had left the police six months before, advised Lopukhin that, "to save Azeff, I ought to ... 'lie,' even if [the SRs] interrogated me with the muzzle of a pistol to my head." Then, when Lopukhin had refused, Gerasimov had shifted to threats. Should Lopukhin address the SR tribunal, warned the chief, the Okhranka "will know everything that transpires ... and at that time we will know how to proceed."

His own reaction, swears Lopukhin, was strong revulsion at the "placing on me of the obligation to protect an agent of the police who was, in my eyes, undoubtedly a criminal." Moreover, Azeff and Gerasimov together had left him with fears he had never felt as director of police: "the prospect of aggressive actions against me, even threats to my life."[42]

Gerasimov gives a somewhat different account of his exchange with Lopukhin and says that he inferred that Lopukhin had then already "gone too far" to back down because he "already decided to betray Azeff." As proof, Gerasimov claims that Lopukhin had told him that, although he would not appear before the revolutionary tribunal itself, "I tell you frankly: if [its representatives] ask me, I will tell them the truth. I am not accustomed to lying."[43]

A critical event now followed on 10 December 1908 when Lopukhin was visiting London on business. That afternoon, he says, he found three Socialist Revolutionaries at the door of his hotel room and admitted them. When they asked him to confirm or deny Azeff's role as a police agent – such confirmation was necessary for the tribunal to make a decision, they said – Lopukhin replied in the affirmative. To their query about whether he had met with Azeff as director of the police, he answered that he had, twice. Had Lopukhin seen the agent recently? Replying that he had (in his St Peterburg apartment), he described Azeff's main features. Did Lopukhin as director know the names of all the terrorists? Answer: some. Did the department keep a list of known terrorists? Lopukhin said it did not. One visitor then put forth three revolutionary code names and asked if Lopukhin had heard of any of them. Answer: one.

Then, insisting that the conversation return to Azeff, Lopukhin says that he made a strong plea that Azeff's life be spared, but got no reply. When the visitors instead thanked him for his service to the party, Lopukhin demanded that they speak only of his service to mankind.[44]

By his own admission, Lopukhin said more in London than he had said to Burtsev. Under no duress and certainly with no gun at his head, he had freely chosen to betray police secrets useful to the SRs.

Lopukhin's revelation that Azeff had worked for the police, a fact which became widely known, destroyed the Socialist Revolutionary party in Russia,[45] on the one hand, and infuriated tsarist officials, on the other. Harting, as head of the Foreign Okhranka, insisted to his superiors on the first day of 1909 that the government publicly excoriate and even punish Lopukhin as a traitor lest others with damaging secrets see him as hero they must emulate.[46] Eighteen days after Harting's telegraphed recommendation arrived in St Petersburg, a large contingent of Gendarmes in bullet-proof vests made a showy early morning arrest of Lopukhin at his apartment. Charged with betraying a state secret to an organization he knew to be criminal, he was arraigned for an open trial that would convene in March and attract enormous publicity in the press.

During the pre-trial investigation, Lopukhin was asked why he had betrayed state secrets to Burtsev rather than take his suspicions about his own Okhranka agent to a superior. Lopukhin says that he replied that he had gone, in vain, to Stolypin, who accused him of being a "revolutionary." But, with no witnesses to corroborate the time and content of the conversation, the court ruled the testimony inadmissable during the trial. Because in 1909 Stolypin was prime minister, Lopukhin argues, "I am convinced that the dominant aim of my arrest and prosecution was to deprive me of the possibility to name Stolypin as a protector of Azeff." (He saw the court's subsequent sentencing of him to a remote area as serving the same end.)[47]

On 11 February, Stolypin responded in the State Duma to an interpellation on the exposure of Azeff (as deputies on the left shouted objections) by saying that he had read the materials gathered in the preliminary judicial investigation in the Lopukhin case. He then made the pre-trial judgment that there were "no facts in hand for accusing Azeff of so-called provocations." It followed that Burtsev likewise had provided Lopukhin with no substantiated facts that could justify exposing Azeff. Thus the government had to prosecute Lopukhin or face "complete chaos in the state system."[48]

Other detractors of Lopukhin argued that the former police director had cooperated with Burtsev to exact revenge against two old foes.[49] That is, because he had persuaded Plehve to fire Rachkovsky in 1902, Lopukhin believed that Rachkovsky had enjoined his protégé, Azeff, to conspire with fellow SR terrorists to kill Plehve in 1903, and then, to bring down Lopukhin, Rachkovsky had arranged the grand duke's assassination, again through Azeff and the SRs. Therefore, in 1908 Lopukhin had used Burtsev to hurt Azeff and his protector, Rachkovsky.

A.T. Vasiliev, who would later head the Department of Police, was among those who held that "there was no serious basis whatever" for trying Lopukhin under a paragraph of the criminal code that made collaboration with illegal, seditious organizations a criminal act; he claimed to know that four of the judges at the trial had strong misgivings about the verdict. Finally, he said that the prosecutor, W.S. Korsak, "confessed to me quite frankly how difficult he found it to bring Lopukhin's conduct within the scope of the paragraph cited."[50]

Predictably, A.Ia. Passover, Lopukhin's defence lawyer, argued before the court that his client had done nothing to violate the law cited against him. At no time had he sought out or consorted with anyone in the SR party, nor had he volunteered information to Burtsev or the three SRs who unexpectedly confronted him. Affirming facts that another person uttered on his initiative did not constitute conveying those facts to him. (According to I.V. Gessen, also a jurist, Passover privately described Lopukhin's being charged as a revolutionary as a "crude grotesque." Gessen himself blamed Stolypin, who wanted vengeance for the loss of an agent he "valued highly.")[51]

In his own deposition prior to the trial, Lopukhin made this argument: "I am not a revolutionary and not a socialist, and I reject force as a means of political struggle ... In accordance with my religious convictions, I have no sympathy with any kind of killing and I condemn a party which includes killing in its system of struggle. Therefore, for me, the very idea of participation in the Socialist Revolutionary Party is impossible."[52]

The trial of Lopukhin took place on 28–30 April 1909 before the Special Bench for the Adjudication of State Crimes of the Governing Senate.[53] The judges, all with equal voice, were six senators (one of whom, Voronov, presided in the capacity of chief justice), and four representatives from Russia's legal classes, or estates (two marshals of the nobility, a city mayor, and a rural elder). All through the sessions, members of the government, the public, and the press filled the courtroom and spilled into nearby corridors. Newspapers provided lengthy, florid accounts. Lopukhin was calm, advised *New Times*, but his "small frame is lost on the large bench ... where not so very long ago sat criminals, arrested on the signature of Lopukhin for those crimes for which he is now accused." At the trial's end, his wife was described as exhausted; his other relatives, as noticeably nervous.[54]

In their collective ruling, the judges found Lopukhin guilty as charged and sentenced him to five years hard labour, a harsh penalty. Lopukhin told the press, "For me, hard labour is better than emigration. I will not run."

On appeal, the full Cassation Department of the Senate reduced the punishment to five years of internal exile in Krasnoiarsk. In 1912, with two years yet to serve, Lopukhin received a grant of amnesty and restoration of his civil rights. A year later he became the assistant director of the Moscow branch of the St Petersburg International Commercial Bank.

When the Provisional Government came to power in 1917, Lopukhin gave written testimony to its Extraordinary Investigating Commission. In that brief, he mainly described his dealings with Stolypin and focused especially on the consequences of his own futile efforts to persuade two chief ministers to act responsibly against illegal police activities. Lopukhin seized an opportunity to put on the record his version of the Azeff scandal: that the autocratic government had subjected him to an expedient trial in 1909 to prevent a full public airing of police improprieties and any hint of the complicity of the chief minister.

In all of these experiences, Lopukhin faced in acute form a dilemma familiar to Russian liberals during the reign of Nicholas II: can one remain loyal and obedient to a government that violated its own laws? The response of Lopukhin was to claim that the demands on an intellectual to serve truth and justice far outweighed his obligations to the existing order. To Prime Minister Stolypin, on the other hand, Lopukhin was one more liberal official so preoccupied with the flaws in the autocracy that he lost sight of paramount need to fight lawless revolutionaries with every possible means.

Unquestionably, Lopukhin held firm to liberal principles that conflicted, again and again, with autocratic rule – a problem that confronted many of his like-minded peers. However foolhardy, prone to martyrdom, or hungry for fame he may have been, Lopukhin stood firm for the rule of law. An intellectual fully schooled in the law, he was able to judge clearly the issues before him and he foresaw probable consequences of his actions. His personal sacrifice on behalf of legality underscored an unresolvable conflict betwen liberal and authoritarian political ideas in the late imperial period.

By using an open trial to condemn and punish Lopukhin for betraying Okhranka secrets, the government hoped to discourage any more such whistle-blowing. But the effect was just the opposite for Okhranka official L.P. Men'shchikov, who was already an anonymous purveyor of secrets. In May 1909, just two months after Lopukhin's conviction, this twenty-year security veteran fled to the West and methodically proceeded to disclose the contents of the hundreds of Okhranka documents he had previously sent there.

As "Ivanov," Men'shchikov had begun in 1905 to mail abroad tantalizing bits of inside information damaging to the Okhranka. His purpose, he would claim, was to prepare the way for openly exposing Okhranka wrongdoing on a grand scale. It was this long-term goal that had caused him, in April 1887, to begin informing the Okhranka about the activities of revolutionaries.

Quantitatively, Men'shchikov was the champion whistle-blower of his time. By his count he gave Burtsev and the revolutionaries the names of at least 350 inside agents of the Okhranka, including one hundred who infiltrated the Social Democratic party and the Jewish General Workers' Union (the Bund), twenty-five who posed as Socialist Revolutionaries, and seventy-five who posed as Polish revolutionaries. Putting truth and fairness first, he says, he never made disclosures without full documentation, just as he preferred to give them directly to the revolutionaries who were at risk rather than speak through the sometimes expedient and self-interested Burtsev. Once openly a whistle-blower in the West, he published his exposés himself, for his own profit and to supplement his own private pension plan.

As for his earlier years, records show that the police arrested the seventeen-year-old Men'shchikov in February 1886 on the charge of subversive activities alleged by an informer for the Okhranka who later became its chief – Zubatov. Men'shchikov, in his memoirs, denies ever having been a radical activist,[55] but contends that his brief stay in jail convinced him to "sacrifice my honour" by working for the police so that he could discover its secrets and use them to destroy it from within.[56]

In April 1887 Men'shchikov became an informer for the Moscow Okhranka, as had Zubatov before him, and both men climbed through the ranks.[57] Zubatov, who in 1902 was to become the head of the Special Section in the Department of Police in St Petersburg, thought highly enough of Men'shchikov to make him second-in-command in Moscow by the winter of 1902–3. Men'shchikov had earlier accepted a special assignment to pose as a revolutionary in order to infiltrate the Marxist Northern Workers' Union in Voronezh, Iaroslavl, Kostroma, and Vladimir. (There and elsewhere during his career, according to a police document, intelligence that he gathered enabled the Okhranka to "liquidate" thirteen major revolutionary groups.)[58]

In June of 1903 Men'shchikov joined Zubatov's elite Special Section in St Petersburg under Lopukhin; and, despite Plehve's firing of Zubatov in July 1903 and Lopukhin's having to step down in February 1905, Men'shchikov stayed in place. He wrote his first anonymous letter to the SRs in the fall of 1905, making the same charge that Lopukhin was making: that an Okhranka inside agent was performing criminal acts as an SR terrorist.[59]

A report in the Okhranka files that evaluated Men'shchikov in 1906 praised him unconditionally and described him as bold, resourceful, adroit, tactful, analytical, and a skilled combatter of smugglers and subversives.[60] At least one colleague of that period dubbed him "The Pen" of the Okhranka for his skill in writing intelligence reports. Another, writing after Men'shchikov's defection, remembered him as "accurate and pedantic" to a fault and a loner who "spent all his free time at home."[61] To yet another, Men'shchikov was a "typical intellectual" who never joined "the after-dark orgies of the other Okhranniki."[62] Then there were those who, after his defection, clearly recalled Men'shchikov's drive to "penetrate to the very core of political operations" and to know all names, including code names, of the persons involved.[63]

Men'shchikov was removed from the capital to the hinterland in January 1906 to head the Okhranka section in Finland. Afraid that he had come under suspicion as an exposer of Okhranka secrets, he continued to mail the copies he made of police documents to addresses in Western Europe for safekeeping. Should agents of the Okhranka arrive to search his house, he had kerosene at hand to set fire to his papers.[64]

Once Lopukhin had been sentenced, early in 1909, for aiding revolutionaries, Men'shchikov knew that he could avoid the same fate only by going abroad. On the pretext of needing a rest, he got approval for an extended leave with regular monthly pay and moved that fall to southern France. Using documents he had previously sent to the West, he continued his secret exposure of Okhranka double agents, aware that his attempts to remain anonymous would eventually fail. Suspicion was likely to fall on him not only in connection with the exposure of Azeff, but also with that of a female SR double agent, Zinaida Zhuchenko. As Men'shchikov well knew, his evidence about Zhuchenko had first alerted the SRs in Paris to her role as a police agent and then sent them to Burtsev in February 1909 to seek her exposure.[65]

Zhuchenko had first become a police agent in 1893 and served the next year under Zubatov. While an informer, she was caught in the group arrest of the radical circle she had joined; to maintain her revolutionist pose, she spent time in Butyrki prison and began a five-year term of exile in Siberia. In April of 1898 she made a daring escape to Europe, doubtless with help from the Okhranka. For the next seven years she reported on "fellow" Socialist Revolutionaries in Germany, returning home in 1905 to take part in SR agitation in Moscow that included robberies (called "expropriations" by the revolutionaries).

In 1909, Azeff's exposure caused Zhuchenko to expect exposure herself so that she, like Men'shchikov, left Russia to return to the West. But, unlike him, she left a relatively safe haven to risk her life to go to her son, then ill in Germany, to deflect possible SR reprisals against him. Were she herself killed, her Okhranka pension was to go to him.

By the summer, Burtsev had tracked her down. He sent a letter requesting an interview, and their meeting took place in August. Sensing the futility of denials or silence, Zhuchenko unrepentently admitted her role as an Okhranka agent. For her, the Okhranka and all its agents remained necessary, heroic, and noble. A published condemnation of Zhuchenko as a provocateur inevitably followed, one that Zhuchenko described as a "public discrediting directed to 'break the butterfly on the wheel.'"[66] There were no attempts against her life.

Men'shchikov meanwhile was extending his disclosures by confiding in individual revolutionaries, including the Menshevik V.I. Gorev. To him, testifies Gorev, Men'shchikov provided the code names of Okhranka agents within the Social Democratic ranks and gave advice on how to discover which persons they were.[67] In addition, Men'shchikov and Gorev together analysed an Okhranka report – provided by Men'shchikov – on the second Congress of the Russian Social Democratic Workers' party with the purpose of identifying the Okhranka infiltrator who was its source. Deducing that the spy resided in Rostov, they correctly surmised him to be Dr Jacob Zhitomirsky, a trusted Bolshevik agent of Lenin. Although Burtsev conveyed to Lenin this solid assumption, Lenin kept full faith in his comrade until proof of Zhitomirsky's allegiance to the Okhranka emerged after the fall of the tsarist government in 1917.[68]

As more and more persons learned that Men'shchikov was compromising the Okhranka to its enemies, in September 1910 Men'shchikov published a telegram in the Paris daily *Le Matin* revealing his true identity. Newspapers in France and Russia commented at length, especially on the unsavoury moral practices of the Russian imperial government. The Okhranka braced for yet more damaging revelations.

In the last decades before the revolution, Lopukhin, Bakai, Burtsev, and Men'shchikov effectively removed from the Okhranka's team of inside agents a large number of key players. Their revelations further hurt the Okhranka by discreditng it in the eyes of the public at home and abroad. Few people took exception to the use of infiltrators who merely sought intelligence about the plans of the revolutionaries, but many deplored their provoking or participating in crimes and violent acts.

CHAPTER NINE

The Assassination of Stolypin

Of the many problems that plagued the Okhranka throughout the thirty-seven years of its history, two tragically came together on 1 September 1911 when twenty-four-year-old Dmitry Bogrov mortally wounded the head of both security and government, Prime Minister and Minister of Interior P.A. Stolypin. Once more did a double agent (in this case, Bogrov) double-cross the Okhranka; and once more did a loyal officer (in this case, N.N. Kuliabko, the Kiev Gendarme chief who gave Bogrov access to Stolypin) undo security measures by violating basic rules of procedure. The consequence was disaster for the state and the Okhranka alike.

Dmitry Bogrov, the turncoat assassin, came to maturity in Kiev preparing to follow in the footsteps of his affluent lawyer father, an assimilated Jew who owned the apartment building in which the family lived on Bibikovsky Boulevard. Politically, the senior Bogrov struck others as moderately liberal and the whole family was caught up in politics. Further to the left was an elder cousin of Bogrov named Sergei Evseev who espoused revolutionary radicalism as a Social Democratic emigré; Evseev's subsequent dedication to the Bolsheviks reportedly enabled him and the woman he married to enjoy a personal relationship with Lenin. When Dmitry was in the last class of the gymnasium, Sergei was already well-known in the revolutionary underground and among the Social Democratic emigrés. Perhaps to match this cousin, Bogrov claimed to support the terrorist Maximalist wing of the Socialist Revolutionaries by the time he finished his secondary studies with honours in the spring of 1905.

Enrolled next in the Juridical Faculty of Kiev University, Bogrov was sent by his parents to study in Munich in late 1905, just as the waning revolution made imminent a government crackdown on dissidents. He did not complete his degree in Munich but resumed his Kiev studies in late 1906, having read deeply, he claimed, in the works of the anarchists Michael Bakunin and Peter Kropotkin.

By December Bogrov had aligned with a covert cell of espoused anarchists only to offer his services to the Kiev Okhranka in February 1907 as an informer against them. According to his testimony after he shot Stolypin, Bogrov did so out of disillusionment with fellows who, in his words, had been "plundering more than they had been implementing the ideas of anarchism."[1]

Another who would testify in 1911 about Bogrov as a fledgling spy was Kuliabko, the Gendarme who took command of the Kiev Okhranka at the close of 1906.[2] A youthful thirty-three with the comparatively low rank of a retired lieutenant, Kuliabko now commanded several Gendarme generals because the Kiev Okhranka controlled the entire governor-generalship of Kiev, which included several provinces, each of which had its own Gendarme command. In August 1909 he was named to the Separate Corps of Gendarmes with the rank of captain and after less than a year became a lieutenant-colonel.

What Bogrov told him at their initial interview towards the end of 1906, according to Kuliabko, was that, while abroad earlier in the year, "he had lost 1,000 or 1,500 francs at cards, that it was a debt of honour, that he had no money because of his father's miserliness, and that he hoped that I would give him an opportunity to pay the debt in exchange for the services rendered to me." During that same first encounter, continued Kuliabko, he gave Bogrov "75 or 100 rubles in advance and we came to an arrangement" – one that would subsequently provide Bogrov with 100 to 150 rubles a month.[3] The story Bogrov told about his father's stinginess might be suspect, although he may have wished to conceal his gambling from his family. Bogrov senior was actually a generous man who gave substantial sums to charities. He fully supported his son's education and gave him 100 to 150 rubles a month in pocket money. Bogrov's father also offered his son capital to start his own business. Those who would see Bogrov as a revolutionary from the beginning of his contact with the Okhranka would argue that he concocted the gambling story in order to explain his approach to the Okhranka. His brother Vladimir also believed that Dmitry approached the police as "a continuation of his revolutionary work."[4]

Despite Kuliabko's assertion that he first met with Bogrov towards the end of 1906, his claims are disputed by contrary evidence. Dmitry Bogrov testified later that he first began to serve the Okhranka in the middle of 1907. However, he also said that he joined a group of anarchists towards the end of 1906 and after two months, disillusioned with them, went over to the service of the police. Okhranka records list Bogrov as a collaborator for the first time in February 1907, and this would seem to be the most certain time for the commencement of Bogrov's informing.

Most important to Kuliabko and the Okhranka following Stolypin's death, of course, was to establish in their own defence that Bogrov, as agent "Alensky," had proved truly useful to the state in the four years prior to his fatal defection.[5] There was thus strong cause for the police in their reports to exaggerate Bogrov's assistance in the arrest of 102 persons suspected of revolutionary activity from April 1907 to the beginning of 1910. (Three were sent to hard labour, one to prison, twenty-seven to Siberian exile, and sixteen placed under police surveillance.)[6] Among other arrests linked to Bogrov were those in early 1908 of Naum Tysh and German Sandomirsky, two anarchist-communists from the Paris-based "Stormy Petrel" group who had come to Kiev the previous fall to energize the anarchist cell to which Bogrov belonged. Sandomirsky would remember in 1926 his positive reaction to the Bogrov he knew during their brief collaboration, saying that he had then confidently ranked Bogrov as the sort who "will not fail one."[7]

The Kiev (or southern) group of anarchist-communists led by Tysh and Sandomirsky was arrested in December 1907. The members languished in the Kiev prison for fourteen months while the judicial investigation took place. A trial then followed and the accused received sentences of hard labour. The longest, for eight years, was that imposed on Sandomirsky.

Well-informed about the activities of the anarchist-communists, the police knew the password of an anarchists' conference late in 1907 in Kiev: "The tyrants are feasting, let us impede their feast." Tysh and another member, Peter Liatkovsky, were convinced that Bogrov had betrayed them, but Sandomirsky defended his friend and only later concluded that he had been the betrayer. His reasoning had been that Bogrov knew certain resolutions taken by the conference, but the police did not. Had he been an informer, Sandomirsky believed, Bogrov would have passed these resolutions on to the police and they "could have been important accusatory material against all of us."[8]

Bogrov's part in the destruction of the group is therefore not entirely clear. During his own deposition in September 1911 following his assassination of Stolypin, he neither supported nor rejected the idea that he was responsible for the fall of the Kiev anarchist-communists. In police documents the arrest of the group was credited to information that Alensky (that is, Bogrov) had provided. As an active member of the group, Bogrov would have been in a position to supply the police with evidence of its activities, but as a secret agent he would have been protected throughout the judicial investigative proceedings because of the Okhranka's established practice of guarding its secret sources of information. It is therefore possible that any evidence linking Bogrov to the trial would have been excluded in order to protect the agent. The evidence against Bogrov's betrayal of the revolutionaries is not especially strong and the record of the Okhranka, written later to demonstrate Bogrov's superiority as an agent, is suspect but seems likely to have some foundation. In any case, someone did it and Bogrov had the best opportunity.

There were two instances when Bogrov engaged in betrayals in 1908 while he was in Kiev, but each showed him capable of betraying either side. The first began with a communiqué from Kuliabko to the director of the Department of Police on 25 July 1908 that credits Alensky with having turned over correspondence smuggled out of prison by members of the Borisoglebskii group of SR Maximalists (a group operating independently from the Stormy Petrel organization of Tysh and Sandomirsky) regarding terrorists involved in manufacturing and distributing explosives.[9] Three years later, at his trial, Bogrov would contend that he had "purposefully" not learned the address of the explosives manufacture and had therefore told Kuliabko "only that the terrorists were setting up a laboratory somewhere in the Podol' [a suburb of Kiev]."[10] He had deliberately avoided providing enough information to make possible a police raid on the laboratory.

In the same year Bogrov betrayed the revolutionaries to the police a second time. He reported the Maximalists' plans to arrange the escape from prison in Kiev of Naum Tysh and other prisoners early in September 1908. Bogrov had discovered the prearranged code used by investigators over the telephone to order the prisoners brought from the prison for interrogation. He planned with others to order the prisoners brought and then attack the escort on the way and free their comrades. Bogrov had concluded arrangements with the stirring words, "Failure is possible. Then, I will be the first to die."[11]

Bogrov told the police about the plot. Acting on Bogrov's information, they arrested the plotters, Bogrov among them, and held him from 10 to 25 September 1908. He claimed later that his arrest had been contrived: "In order to prevent the crime it was necessary to arrest the participants the night before and, in order to hide my role as agent, I was also fictitiously arrested by the police."[12] Almost as soon as the police released him, Bogrov again went abroad and remained there until April 1909, although he made two brief trips back to Russia during this period. While abroad, he had told the editor of an anarchist newspaper that it was necessary to kill either Nicholas II or Stolypin.

Bogrov visited St Petersburg either on his way back to Kiev or on a trip north after he had returned to Kiev, and he told members of the SR party that he intended to kill Stolypin. He met with Socialist Revolutionaries, according to their testimony, during the days of the Orthodox Trinity, that is, late May or early June 1909. He looked up Egor Lazarev, an old populist, who was living legally in the capital as a journalist. Lazarev recalled later that he knew nothing of Bogrov when he appeared in St Petersburg. He listened to this complete stranger with astonishment. "I have made up my mind to kill Stolypin," Bogrov told Lazarev. "How did he annoy you?" Lazarev says he asked Bogrov, trying not to show his surprise at this declaration. Bogrov gave no explanation, but said he wanted no help, "only the sanction of the central committee of the Socialist Revolutionary party of the terrorist act which he planned." Bogrov said he could not do the deed on behalf of the anarchists, because they had no party. Lazarev did not encourage the self-appointed assassin: "Participants [in terror] should be party members, reliable and loyal people, personally familiar, at least, to the members of the central committee who are in charge of the Combat Organization. What you suggest is an extemporaneous act."[13]

Lazarev said he formed a negative assessment of Bogrov and decided he would not even submit his proposal to assassinate Stolypin to the central committee of the Socialist Revolutionary party. He did not wish to implicate the party in actions carried out by a person he saw as unpredictable, especially one who was not a party member. (Following the assassination in 1911, the central committee issued a denial that the party was in any way involved.) Still, questions linger, particularly because the meeting between Lazarev and Bogrov had lasted for six hours. Lazarev admits to having delivered a lengthy lecture to Bogrov, who listened attentively, on the entire history of the terrorist movement in Russia, beginning with the People's Will and the assassination of Alexander II.

A number of police documents also credited Alensky with an especially important accomplishment when he was again back in Kiev in the fall of 1909 and attending law classes. He had informed the Okhranka about a conspiracy to assassinate the tsar. The affair began on 12 September 1909 when a twenty-eight-year-old woman arrived in Kiev who, according to her passport, was a Swiss citizen named Elena Lukiens. Bogrov had received information from abroad that her real name was Julia Merzheevskaia (Lublinskaia). She was known among the emigrants for her readiness to spend her considerable legacy in support of the Socialist Revolutionaries. Bogrov gained the confidence of the young woman after she arrived in Kiev; he learned that she had been ordered to assassinate Nicholas II while he was on a visit to Sevastopol on 5 September 1909 (that is, a week before she had arrived in Kiev). She was to conceal a bomb in a bouquet of flowers and wait for the tsar to pass along the embankment. The attempt on the life of the ruler failed to materialize, however, because Merzheevskaia missed her train and arrived in Sevastopol after the departure of the tsar.

Under specific instructions from St Petersburg, Kuliabko kept Merzheevskaia under close surveillance. Bogrov spent a lot of time with Merzheevskaia and passed on to Kuliabko all the letters that she asked him to mail for her. The police finally decided in October to arrest Merzheevskaia. A medical examination of the suspect led the police to the conclusion that she was insane. The government did not indict her but instead sent her to Siberia for five years under an administrative order. Vladimir Bogrov later insisted that Merzheevskaia's condition was evidence that his brother was using her to solidify his position with the Okhranka and knew all along that Merzheevskaia was no threat to the tsar.[14] Kuliabko reported to the director of police that the revolutionaries abroad, having suspicions of Bogrov, sent Merzheevskaia as a means to test him.[15] If Kuliabko believed that Merzheevskaia was a decoy to flush out Bogrov, he had unnecessarily inflated her importance and had treated her as a genuine threat to the tsar in his correspondence with St Petersburg. His cautiousness may have been an over-reaction to harsh criticism of the security division under his supervision several months before by General Gerasimov.[16] Lieutenant-Colonel M.Ia. Belevtsev, who investigated the case for the Okhranka in 1912, was dubious about Bogrov's role in the matter. He believed that the case "had been inflated by 'Alensky' in order to emphasize his own value as an agent."[17]

In the fall of 1907, before the downfall and imprisonment of the Sandomirsky-Tysh group, the first doubts about Bogrov appeared among the revolutionaries, but they were no more than vague rumours.[18] The next year, as the position of the Kiev anarchist-communists grew worse as a result of arrests, Naum Tysh accused Bogrov openly of provocations. Others had suspicions of Bogrov and even blamed him for embezzling funds from the group. Word began to filter out of Lukianovskaia prison that comrades in the cells suspected that Bogrov had been responsible for putting them there. As was common among the revolutionaries, the party in Kiev summoned a court to deal with these charges. The members of the court actually visited the prison to gather information from Tysh and others and invited Bogrov to make a submission in his own defence. Although investigating the charges, the court did not find against Bogrov.

Bogrov took steps to make certain that those who were attacking him remained in prison.[19] The foiled escape attempt in September 1908 had served this purpose, as Bogrov admitted in 1911. No one was therefore able to make a certain case against Bogrov; he was probably saved by suspicions that there were several agents among the Kiev revolutionaries and betrayals could not be absolutely attributed to any single person.

Bogrov himself contributed to this atmosphere by accusing others of informing to the police. A few anarchists – who frequently took matters into their own hands – finally decided to settle with the man they suspected of treason to the cause. The anarchist "Belousov" (P. Svirsky) tried to find Bogrov to assassinate him, evidently late in 1909 or early in 1910.[20] Bogrov's departure from Kiev in April 1910 for St Petersburg may have been connected with his fear of remaining in Kiev. He had graduated from the university in Kiev in February 1910 and now had his law degree in hand. Having become a target, Bogrov developed a sudden interest in a career in the capital.

Bogrov received support from Kuliabko, the Kiev Okhranka chief, who commended him to his counterpart in the capital, Colonel M.F. von Kotten. Bogrov was immediately put on the roster of von Kotten's secret agents and began to receive a salary. Bogrov had so little to do, however, that he told von Kotten that he felt guilty for taking the money. Von Kotten might have believed that Bogrov would become useful over time, for a newly arrived informer would know little about the activities of the revolutionary underground. Or, more likely, von Kotten was responding to his colleague Kuliabko who asked for refuge for an agent in trouble.

Installed in St Petersburg in an unrewarding bureaucratic position, enrolled as a secret agent but hardly in a position to make a contribution, constantly alert to make certain that he had not been followed by his enemies in Kiev, Bogrov found himself increasingly disgruntled and uneasy. His father did manage to place him for a time as an assistant to a secretary in one of the numerous departments in St Petersburg. Bogrov also made some attempts to plead criminal cases, but seems to have attracted no clients. He wrote ironically to a relative during the time he was in St Petersburg: "I have only two or three hours a day when nobody is bothering me and when I am absolutely alone and these are my reception hours as a solicitor."[21] He seems to have wanted to break out of a stultifying existence, for he returned to Kiev briefly in November and then went to Europe, where he travelled from December 1909 to February 1911. In Kiev he seemed despondent and wrote a friend on 1 December 1910: "By and large, I am sick and tired of everything, and I would like to do some eccentric thing."[22]

Looking back on Bogrov's life at that time, some have concluded that he was feeling remorse for having betrayed comrades in Kiev. Others have concluded that he felt driven to break spectacularly with a life that he now found repellant. Yet others believe that Bogrov had already made his choice of a target in 1909. He is quoted as having said, "Only the tsar is more important than Stolypin. As for the tsar, it is next to impossible for me to get to the tsar alone." As for the prime minister, an acquaintance quoted Bogrov as saying in the spring of 1910, "I hate a man whom I have never seen. Who is that? Stolypin. Maybe this is because he is the most clever and gifted man among them, the most dangerous enemy, and all evil is rooted in him."[23]

Bogrov's vehement dislike of Stolypin has been ascribed to his Jewish origins. Many Jews felt that the prime minister, because he was a Russian nationalist, opposed Jews. Solzhenitsyn in *August, 1914: The Red Wheel*, wrote that Bogrov hated Stolypin because of his nationalities policy and determined to act because he was a Jew. Solzhenitsyn also says that Bogrov decided to take revenge against Stolypin for the long history of anti-Semitism in Russia.[24] But no one in the Bogrov family had shown any powerful commitment to the cause of Jews in Russia; neither had Dmitri Bogrov. His grandfather, G.I. Bogrov, was a well-known writer (*Memoirs of a Jew*) who belonged to the assimilationist trend. Not long before his death, he and his Lutheran wife were baptized in the Russian Orthodox Church. Bogrov's father was not baptized, but his brother Vladimir adopted Christianity in 1908. Nominally Bogrov belonged to the Judaic religion and was registered in official documents as Mordecai, but his parents gave him the Christian name, Dmitry.

Moreover, none of Bogrov's statements about Stolypin point in the direction of resentment based on Jewishness as a motive for the assassination. Bogrov had targeted Stolypin as the main representative of the reactionary political course of the government. Nor does the Jewish factor enter at all into Bogrov's work as a secret agent. Because of the great number of Jews among the anarchists in Kiev, Bogrov actually betrayed a number of them to the police. Bogrov remembered the pogrom of 1905 in Kiev, not for reasons of vengeance, but because he wished to prevent the repetition of such an event. To this extent, he did identify with Jews. During his interrogation, he said that he had given up the idea of regicide because "being a Jew, he considered that he had no right to commit an act which would entail fatal consequences for Jews and which would cause their rights to be infringed."[25]

No one gave Bogrov's talk about his intention to kill Stolypin serious attention. Nor has evidence surfaced to show precisely when he decided to act; he was still talking about it and seems not yet to have made a decision in the summer of 1910. Whether he could have anticipated it or not, he did come face to face with Stolypin at the St Petersburg municipal water purification plant before leaving the capital for Kiev. This encounter could well have been a complete surprise. Back in his home town, Bogrov spent about six weeks with his parents at the family dacha near Kiev from late June until 5 August. His parents went abroad a week later and after some days his brother Vladimir and his wife left to live in St Petersburg. Bogrov was alone in the city in the large family apartment. During the coming year he seemed possessed and rushed around from place to place. Although only twenty-three, he had turned completely grey and looked much older than his years. In mid-August 1911 he was still working and actually wrote his father with some enthusiasm over a business deal (which included bribing someone) that he anticipated concluding.[26]

By the time the tsar arrived in Kiev in the last days of August 1911, fundamental problems remained in the functioning of the security system in the city. Two years earlier, in 1909, General Gerasimov had conducted an inspection of the Kiev Okhranka and issued a damning report of the organization under Kuliabko: "Officers do not concern themselves with agents at all, they are handled by the Chief of the Department of Police and the senior detective, Demidiuk. There is no work with the agents, no guidance."[27] Gerasimov quizzed Demidiuk about his knowledge of the charters of the revolutionary parties and received no answers. He then asked him if he knew what anarchy was. "I do not know," Demidiuk answered. Gerasimov ordered him dismissed on the spot.[28] But the order either was never carried out or later rescinded, because Demidiuk was still in the same position at the time Bogrov assassinated Stolypin.

Other serious lapses appeared in an information sheet on the Kiev Okhranka compiled in December 1910. One serious error had occurred in January. Kuliabko had reported to St Petersburg that there were no Social Democratic organizations in the city. The Department of Police responded and, according to an internal report, "sent Lt.-Col. Kuliabko leaflets and secret documents proving beyond any doubt the existence in Kiev of a serious Social Democratic organization. It has 15 workers' circles, a students' faction, a propagandists' group, and a printing house publishing a magazine and leaflets."[29] Moreover, three secret agents were operating within the Social Democrats but were providing very little information. One, who was receiving 100 rubles a month, was sending in no reports at all. Investigators of the work of the Kiev Okhranka also faulted Kuliabko for failing to respond to requests for information from the capital; he had ignored nine straight requests during one period and had only answered the tenth. Eighteen months after Gerasimov's inspection, the Kiev Okhranka had still not restored discipline, and an accounting checkup showed that 1,300 to 1,600 rubles a month were being wasted. An unusual list of code names in Kiev suggested the local secret agents' frivolous use of funds: "Liqueur," "Vodka," and "Beer."

Although there was ample evidence against Kuliabko as head of the Kiev Okhranka, he had influential friends in St Petersburg who had smoothed his career path and now insulated him from disciplinary action. Colonel Spiridovich was a relative and M.N. Verigin, the vice-director of police, a close friend. Kuliabko had, accordingly, risen rapidly in the Okhranka. In 1909 he held the rank of captain, but less than a year later was promoted to lieutenant-colonel. Prior to the festivities in Kiev, Spiridovich had reported to the commandant of the palace on the services of Kuliabko: "The [Kiev] Okhranka is well informed about all local affairs; [has] absolute awareness, absolute control."[30] When his colleagues arrived in Kiev to supervise security operations for the tsar's visit, Kuliabko responded with a festive restaurant dinner for his guests where a popular chanteuse provided the entertainment. The chief of the city police had on his desk the following morning a report from a local constable: "Returning to the Hotel Europe in a cab towards morning, Mr. Verigin fell from it near Nikolaevskii street."[31]

Nicholas II and other dignitaries were to appear in Kiev at the end of August and the beginning of September 1911 to unveil a memorial to Alexander II. The Okhranka had begun preparations for the imperial visit, to include Prime Minister Stolypin, in the spring of 1911. Such preparations were familiar to the secret police because they preceded every imperial journey in Russia and abroad. Rachkovsky, as head of the Foreign Okhranka, had specialized in such planning abroad and had won high favour for his work in the security detail. His long experience had acquainted him with the appearance of his quarry, their methods and psychological characteristics, and whether they were planning an operation. He made certain that the enemies of the tsar could not get close enough to do him harm, but no one in Kiev had the knowledge of Rachkovsky.

Planning the security for the tsar and the other officials in Kiev fell to Lieutenant-General Pavel Grigorievich Kurlov. As deputy minister of the interior and the commander of the Gendarmes, he was head of the Empire's police and security system. Kurlov had had something of a checkered career, most of the time in executive positions rather than as a working security specialist. He began his career as an officer in the Mounted Guards regiment and, following graduation from the Military Juridical Academy, served in the Department of Law of the armed forces.

Kurlov then moved into the civil administration. The tsar named him governor of Minsk and then of Kiev. His career almost foundered when a disturbance broke out in Minsk and he sent troops who fired on a crowd and killed fifty people; this was widely seen as an excessive use of force, and the revolutionaries prepared to take revenge against Kurlov. In the winter of 1905–6, Zinaida Zhuchenko, the Socialist Revolutionary who was also an Okhranka agent, reported to the Moscow division that the party had ordered her to transport a bomb to Minsk for the assassination of Kurlov. What should she do? The deputy chief of Moscow division at that time, von Kotten, a former artillery man, defused the bomb and directed Zhuchenko to transport it to Minsk. She did; it was thrown by a revolutionary and actually hit Kurlov on the head, but did not explode. The perpetrators were arrested and hanged.[32] This event, showing Kurlov on the front line against the terrorists, strengthened his reputation as a defender of the regime. Kurlov continued to rise in the government and later became governor of Kiev, a more prestigious post. Later, after Kurlov was investigated for negligence in the killing of Stolypin, the tsar wrote him: "Thank you. I never doubted the loyalty of General Kurlov."[33]

In March 1907 Kurlov was named new vice-director of the Department of Police under M.I. Trusevich. When the chief of the Main Department of Prisons was killed by terrorists, Kurlov took his place, but this was only a brief side-step in his career. In January 1909 he returned to the Ministry of the Interior as deputy minister under Stolypin, who as both minister of the interior and prime minister largely left the running of the ministry to Kurlov.

Kurlov arrived in Kiev on 14 August to manage the imperial visit with his two assistants, M.N. Verigin and Colonel A.I. Spiridovich. Verigin was a fairly young man, only thirty-three, and belonged to a wealthy aristocratic family. He had graduated from a privileged school and had the rank of a gentleman of the tsar's bed chamber, but his career at Fontanka had proceeded very slowly. Kurlov, however, liked him and raised him to be one of the vice-directors of the Department of Police.

Colonel Spiridovich, on the contrary, was a seasoned Gendarme. He had contributed to solving a number of political cases and was one of the scholars of the Okhranka. He had written several thorough and well-documented books about the revolutionary movement and had developed a course to instruct Gendarme officers in the history and activities of the revolutionary parties. He was currently serving as chief of security of the imperial palaces and so had a number of police agents under his authority. Spiridovich also knew Kiev well because he had served there for three years as head of the Okhranka.[34] N.N. Kuliabko was designated to assist the officials from St Petersburg. He was married to Spiridovich's sister and had earlier graduated with him from the Pavlovsky Military College.

To pay for the security of the tsar and other high officials in Kiev, the government had allocated 300,000 rubles to the Gendarmes. Typically for a tsarist visit, overall planning and management was in the hands of the central authorities who, however, relied on the local Okhranka, Gendarmes, police, and military. Prior to the arrival of the dignitaries, the Gendarmes and local police swept Kiev clean of suspicious persons. They arrested thirty-three individuals merely on suspicion of membership in the Socialist Revolutionary party. The police checked on everyone who lived along the route of the tsar's journey through the city and ordered owners of buildings to lock their gates and to allow near windows and on balconies only trustworthy people known to them personally.

To assist the Kiev police, the Department of Police dispatched 189 detectives from the capital. The department also summoned the armed forces to assist in securing the city. Along the forty-three-kilometre route from Kiev to the nearby town of Ovruch, one of the places on the tsarist itinerary, soldiers and mounted guards were stationed in staggered rows every five metres. Within Kiev itself the authorities summoned into being a so-called people's guard which consisted of several thousand members from local Black Hundreds' organizations.[35]

Security officials issued special passes to various planned festivities. Altogether, there were twenty-six different categories of passes given on the basis of reliability. Only the most trustworthy individuals were to obtain passes permitting them to be near to the dignitaries. The security of Nicholas II was the top priority of the security forces, but the police also mounted a heavy guard at the house of the governor-general, where Stolypin was to stay. Security agents were evident everywhere and "in all the corridors, leading to the entrance-hall, police agents in civilian clothes were on duty around the clock. There were chairs for them everywhere. Agents were also guarding all the staircases inside the house."[36]

Police officials had seemingly taken all precautions, but even then there were slip-ups. Agents brought a suspicious person seized on the streets to the Okhranka headquarters on the morning of 26 August. Before they managed to search him he took a pistol from his pocket and shot himself. The person who had caught the attention of the police was Alexander Murav'ev, whom some later linked with Bogrov.

Bogrov learned of the suicide several hours after it had occurred and approached the senior detective, Demidiuk, to tell him that he had information that might throw light on it. Demidiuk told Kuliabko, who in turn asked Bogrov to drop by his home later that day. When Bogrov arrived, Kuliabko was hosting a dinner for his visiting police colleagues. The Okhranka chief asked his agent to put his information on paper in an adjoining room.

Kuliabko, perhaps smarting under the humiliation suffered by the local security forces, decided to offer a counter-example to show his own effectiveness. At the close of the dinner, Verigin recalled, Kuliabko said that "an interesting man had arrived, was in the next room, and he suggested to me and Colonel Spiridovich that we should listen to what he had to say."[37] The police officials, on the strength of this recommendation, received Bogrov, whom Kuliabko identified as a trustworthy and valuable secret agent. Kuliabko had violated long-standing Okhranka policy that only the controlling officer of a secret agent could know his identity. This was only one in a series of mistakes, many of them violations of procedure, attributable to Kuliabko.

Bogrov now gave the outlines of a conspiracy. He told the officials that a year earlier in St Petersburg he had met a certain "Nicholai Iakovlevich." The lawyer S.E. Kal'manovich and the journalist Egor Lazarev had made the introduction; both men were known to be associated with the Socialist Revolutionary party. Bogrov said he had presented himself as a revolutionary, but he was actually under the orders of Colonel von Kotten, the chief of the St Petersburg Okhranka.

Later, in Kiev, Bogrov continued, a messenger arrived from Lazarev, contacted the Socialist Revolutionary underground, pronounced a password, and inquired to whom he could turn to find out more about the underground revolutionary activities of Bogrov. Bogrov said he then received a letter from Nicholai Iakovlevich asking whether there had been any changes in his political convictions. A month earlier, Nicholai Iakovlevich turned up at the Bogrovs' country cottage near the village of Kremenchug not far from Kiev. He wondered if Bogrov could help him find a secret apartment for three persons already in Kiev and a motorboat for a run on the Dnieper river. Bogrov said he understood from this conversation that the visitor and the others already in Kiev were preparing an assassination of a high-ranking official. A month had passed since that time and Bogrov said that when he learned about the suicide at the Okhranka headquarters, he concluded that it might somehow be connected with a planned terrorist attack.

Spiridovich and the others listened attentively: "All three of us had the impression that the information should be taken seriously and that the terrorist act ... concerned the person of the Emperor."[38] The three officials reported what they had learned to Kurlov, who sent police to Kremenchug in the hope of finding the mysterious Nicholai Iakovlevich. A check with von Kotten confirmed that Bogrov worked for him in St Petersburg and had met Lazarev and Kal'manovich, but St Petersburg had no knowledge of any Nicholai Iakovlevich. Von Kotten did not go on to explain that Bogrov had done little for the Okhranka while he was in the capital; his cryptic response to Kiev might have been because of his deep dislike of Kurlov and Verigin.

Security officials now proceeded in the belief that Bogrov had made contact with mysterious terrorists about whom no one else had any information. Officials in Kiev seem to have overlooked Okhranka stress on corroborating information from independent sources. They put Bogrov's apartment under surveillance in the event that terrorists would make another attempt to reach him, but Kuliabko seems not to have asked Bogrov why, if Nicholai Iakovlevich had visited the Bogrov dacha a month earlier, his trusted agent had not informed him of that contact until the day of the dinner.

After several uneventful days during which the tsar arrived and began a round of festivities, Bogrov on 31 August phoned the Kiev Okhranka and said that Nicholai Iakovlevich had arrived at his apartment the previous night. The police, it seems, had mounted the surveillance only during the day and had missed the visitor. Bogrov had learned from his guest that either Stolypin or Leo Kasso, the minister of public eduction, would be the target of the assassination attempt. Nicholai Iakovlevich had asked Bogrov to obtain a pass to attend the Merchants' Garden for an outdoor fete in honour of the tsar. He also asked Bogrov to note detailed descriptions of the two ministers, a rather peculiar request since both officials were well-known public figures and Stolypin's portrait was widely available for sale on the streets. Kuliabko promptly sent Bogrov a pass and the agent attended the fete, but he later claimed that he was unable to get near to the dignitaries because of the press of the crowd.

At the Merchants' Garden where Stolypin was also visiting he was surrounded by the crowd and Bogrov could not get near him. Bogrov was carrying a Browning pistol in his pocket, suggesting that he was stalking a quarry. The next day was 1 September and very likely seemed to him to be a final chance to get close to the prime minister. During the day, before the opera, he left a letter to his parents: "I cannot act differently, and you know that for two years I have been trying to give up the past. But a new, quiet life is not for me; anyway, I would have come to the same end, as now."[39]

Kuliabko testified later that when he had first learned that the terrorists had set Bogrov the task of gathering identifying information about the dignitaries, he was struck by the absurdity of the assignment. He concluded that the terrorists suspected Bogrov and were attempting to divert him from their operation. There was good reason, accordingly, to send Bogrov to the Merchants' Garden and to the Opera House the next day. "The idea had flashed across my mind that those tasks were just a blind for Bogrov, and ... the pretext of observing would make it possible for them to attempt an assassination without his knowledge."[40]

Kuliabko's attitude towards Bogrov now seems influenced by his conviction that the "terrorists" who had supposedly arrived in Kiev were suspicious of their contact. The request to Bogrov to obtain a ticket was based therefore on Nicholai Iakovlevich's belief that Bogrov was in contact with the Okhranka. How else could this undistinguished person have secured a ticket? In this way, Kuliabko reasoned, Nicholai Iakovlevich, believing that Bogrov was working for the Okhranka, wished to give Bogrov an assignment in order to divert him from the "terrorists'" actual target. Kuliabko would want to play along with the request of Nicholai Iakovlevich so that he would not conclude that the Okhranka no longer trusted Bogrov.

On the night of 31 August, Bogrov appeared at Kuliabko's apartment with a written report about Nicholai Iakovlevich, now allegedly residing in his apartment. "There are two Brownings in his luggage. He says that he has not come [to Kiev] alone, but with a certain 'Nina Alexandrovna' who will be at the Alensky Palace tomorrow between noon and 1 p. m ... I think that this young woman 'Nina Alexandrovna' has a bomb. 'Nicholai Iakovlevich' has said that there can be no doubt about the success of their enterprise, and he hinted at mysterious, high-ranking protectors."[41] Kuliabko now grew alarmed because of Bogrov's report that the terrorists might have accomplices in the Department of Police. It was now the night before a series of events to be attended by the tsar.

Early in the morning of 1 September Kuliabko reported what he had learned from Bogrov the night before to the governor-general, F.F. Trepov, and to Kurlov. Kurlov met with Stolypin and urged him to be particularly cautious, but Stolypin seems not to have shared the anxiety of his subordinates. Kurlov recalled, "in concluding our conversation, he said that the information about the supposed malefactors was not serious and he would not believe it even if a bomb was found."[42]

At 11 a.m. Bogrov appeared at Verigin's room at the European Hotel to inform him that the terrorists had postponed their meeting until evening on Bibikovsky Boulevard. At 3 p.m. the security officials gathered at Kurlov's to review arrangements. Kurlov said later that he had been puzzled by the change in plans by the terrorists, but he, too, thought that they might suspect Alensky of Okhranka ties. "It occurred to me that the malefactors could conceal many aspects of their plan from 'Alensky' and that by meeting on Bibikovsky, situated not far from the route to the theatre, they could make it necessary for 'Alensky' to accompany them and take part in the terrorist act, at least as a witness, in order that he would be unable to betray them at the last moment."[43] At this meeting, the officers decided that Bogrov would give a pre-arranged signal to police observers who would then arrest the entire group.

Nicholas II and his retinue had returned from manoeuvres for an afternoon dinner. The program of festivities for the evening was very full, and the group left at 4 p.m. for the race track, where there was to be a review of boy scout units followed by races for the Emperor's Prize. By 8 p.m., the races concluded, the tsar and other members of his party arrived at the Opera House for the performance of the *Tale of the Tsar Sultan*. Instead of arriving in a carriage, Stolypin came by automobile and entered the theatre unnoticed by a side entrance.

Bogrov himself understood that the Kiev Okhranka, especially Kuliabko, were negligent during the period from 26 August to 1 September and to some extent he was induced to see how far he could go in carrying out his poorly formulated plans by the surprising lack of attentiveness among security officials. In his deposition to Lieutenant-Colonel A.A. Ivanov, a Gendarme officer, on 4 September 1911 he said that "Kuliabko could have taken note of the fact that I was not behaving in a conspiratorial manner, that I dropped in during the afternoon to the Okhranka, that I telephoned there from my apartment, that I sent a messenger there, that I went to the European Hotel (where all the okhranniki were staying), and, finally, decided openly to sit in those places designated for the merchantry in the theatre, where a questionable person could not get a ticket."[44] But by 1 September, security officials believed that Bogrov was a trustworthy agent and that he alone could keep them apprised of the terrorists' movements.

Once the dignitaries were safely inside the theatre, the governor of Kiev, A.F. Giers, said that he had breathed a sigh of relief: "There was no need to worry about the theatre because the members of the public permitted entry had been thoroughly screened."[45] Officials agreed that the inside of the Opera House was safe. Security officers had checked in advance the entire premises. According to the document of inspection required of the police, Gendarmes had examined the floor, checked the velvet boarding of the barriers, and had even examined the crystal chandeliers to make certain that the terrorists had not managed to prepare them to fall on the audience.[46]

Bogrov was among the "thoroughly screened" public. Just how he managed to get a ticket is unclear. Later, Bogrov said that Kuliabko had offered him a ticket and he had readily accepted it. Kuliabko first testified that Bogrov had requested the ticket and he had granted it, with the permission of Kurlov and his aides. Kurlov, however, said that he had not known that Bogrov would be at the theatre. Confronted with Kurlov's testimony, Kuliabko changed his first version and said that he had probably misinterpreted the words of his chief and he accepted full responsibility for the ticket. Who authorized it, if anyone, or why has never been explained. Kuliabko appears to have acted on his own.

Bogrov himself provided the reason for receiving the ticket. At 6 p.m. he called Kuliabko on the phone and told him that the meeting on Bibikov had been cancelled, that Nicholai was planning to go to another apartment, and that he wanted Bogrov to go to the Opera House to gather information on Stolypin. The agent asked for a ticket which he received from Kuliabko at 8 p.m. by messenger. Bogrov had now provided himself with a reason to be at the theatre rather than on Bibikov Boulevard. In his deposition on 2 September, after the shooting, he said: "I, for the most part, calculated that Kuliabko, surrounded as he was by bustle, would not pay much attention and would give me the ticket because of his confidence in me."[47] Kuliabko probably reasoned that, although Nicholai was supposedly under watch in Bogrov's apartment, he might slip out (none of the detectives staked out there had ever seen him) or other SRs known to Bogrov might appear at the Opera House. There was good reason, accordingly, to send Bogrov to the theatre. "The idea had flashed across my mind that those tasks were just a blind for Bogrov, and that sending him to the theatre under the pretext of observing would make it possible for them to attempt an assassination without his knowledge."[48]

One hour before the curtain was to rise, the Kiev Okhranka had delivered to Bogrov ticket number 404 in the eighteenth row of the orchestra. As chief, Kuliabko was therefore responsible for admitting Bogrov to the Opera House and in so doing he committed the fatal error. In permitting his agent entry, he had violated the Department of Police circular of 3 October 1907 which prohibited the use of secret agents for external surveillance. He also broke the "Instructions concerning the protection of royal persons" which prohibited police informers from being in the vicinity of the tsar. It turned out that Kuliabko had committed similar offences on previous occasions. In 1907 he had admitted a female agent into a theatre to point out terrorists who were preparing to assassinate General Kurlov, who was governor of Kiev at the time. Two years later he had permitted informers to be present for the same reason during a visit of Nicholas ii to Poltava.[49]

At the first intermission of the opera, the Kiev Okhranka chief sent Bogrov back to his apartment to see whether Nicholai Iakovlevich was still there. Bogrov returned within minutes with the assurance that his guest was still there. Police constables guarding the theatre did not want to readmit Bogrov because he now had a used ticket, but Kuliabko intervened and walked his agent into the theatre arm-in-arm. During the first interval of the second act, Kuliabko and a number of Gendarmes gathered in the foyer to compare notes. As they were talking, Kuliabko recalled, "we heard shouts and loud cracks. Our first impression was that part of the theatre had crashed down because of overload. General Kurlov and I rushed into the hall."[50] Colonel Spiridovich was already there: "I had rushed into the hall, reached Prime Minister Stolypin by running over the chairs, went over to the criminal who had been apprehended and brandished my sabre at him."[51]

Stolypin had been hit by two bullets while standing near the barrier to the orchestra pit while speaking to Baron V.B. Fredericks, the minister of court, and to I. Potocki, a land-owner. Giers, the governor of Kiev, said:

It looked as thought Peter Arkadievich did not understand what had happened. He bent his head and looked at his white frock coat, which had already started to soak with blood on the right side, under his chest. Moving slowly and firmly, he put his hat on the barrier near his gloves, unbuttoned his white frock coat and, looking at his blood-soaked vest, he waved his hand as though signalling, "Everything is over." Then he dropped heavily into a chair and said clearly and distinctly, in a voice which was heard by all those standing near him, "I am happy to die for the tsar."[52]

Bogrov, the wielder of the pistol that had shot Stolypin, was in the hands of a crowd of opera-goers who were pummelling him. Colonel I.I. Ivanov of the Gendarmes pulled the terrorist away from the crowd and threw him over the barrier. Kuliabko ran up, looked into his blood-smeared face and said hoarsely, "That is Bogrov." He ordered Gendarme Captain P.T. Samokhvalov to go immediately to Bogrov's apartment to arrest everyone hiding out there. Samokhvalov rushed off, gathered up several agents on duty near the entrance to the Bogrovs' building, and together they burst into the apartment. All twelve rooms were empty. "Where are your terrorists?" Samokhvalov asked the senior police agent, S.I. Demidiuk. "Now it is clear that he has been deceiving us," answered the detective.[53]

Within minutes, an interrogation began in the smoking room of the Kiev Opera House. G.G. Chaplinsky, the procurator of the Kiev Court of Appeals, who was at the opera, took charge, and entrusted Colonel Ivanov with the interrogation. Chaplinsky recalled that during the interrogation, a police officer entered the room and "said that he had to take Bogrov to the police department immediately on the orders of Kuliabko. I told him that Bogrov would not be taken from the theatre."[54] Chaplinsky's abrupt rejection of the request resulted from one of Bogrov's first utterances under interrogation: "I invented everything that I told Kuliabko."

Throughout the evening the interrogation of Bogrov continued, and he described his actions in detail; he was subjected to three more sessions over the next few days until 6 September. The principal interrogators were the chief of the Kiev detectives, V.I. Fenenko, and Colonel Ivanov. Ivanov recalled that the proceedings did not go smoothly because Bogrov "was nervous and constantly digressed, bringing up extraneous subjects."[55] Over these few days, Stolypin was still alive. One bullet had only superficially injured his left arm, but the other had lodged in his chest. More than one newspaper suggested that a kind of divine miracle had saved Stolypin: "Hope lifts everyone. Stolypin was saved by the patron of Kiev and Holy Russia Vladimir in the form of the order [that is, a medallion worn by Stolypin], shaped like a cross, which the bullet hit and, having broken it, altered its fatal course toward the heart."[56]

On the following morning, 2 September, Stolypin asked for a mirror, looked at his tongue and smiled, "Well, it looks as if this time I will pull through."[57] The medical bulletins, however, proved too optimistic. The bullet had become embedded in his liver and an urgent operation was unsuccessful. In the evening of 5 September, Stolypin died of his wounds.

Bogrov's case was transferred from the District Court, a civilian tribunal which operated according to the Judicial Reform of 1864, to the district military tribunal. The district courts were viewed by many officials as too lenient with terrorists; there would be no such fears with the military court. These courts had received many terrorists cases since the early 1880s when they had been named as an option in political cases. Bogrov's trial took place on 9 September in the Pechersky citadel, where he had been held during the inquest. The prosecutor was from the military justice administration, Lieutenant-General M.I. Kostenko. Bogrov declined to have a lawyer named on his behalf and conducted his own case. Kostenko recalled that "during the trial Bogrov behaved properly and completely calmly. When he spoke, he mainly addressed the onlookers who included the Minister of Justice Shcheglovitov, the commander-in-chief of the garrison, his assistant, the governor of Kiev, the marshal of the nobility, the commandant, officials of the civil and military procurators' offices."[58]

No one else was present; as in all trials in the military court system, in contrast to the civil system, neither the public nor the press were admitted and no jury sat for the proceedings. There was only a single session: it started at 4 p.m. and ended at 9:30 the same day. The judges then held a consultation for thirty minutes and announced their decision. The court condemned Bogrov for premeditated murder of Stolypin and sentenced him to death by hanging.

On the night of 12 September, three days after the verdict, judicial officials entered Bogrov's cell to take him out to execution. According to one of the jailors, the condemned man said, "The only happy moment in my life was the moment when I learned that Stolypin had died."[59] Delegates of local Black Hundreds' organizations were present at the execution. They wanted to make certain that there was no substitution for Bogrov. At 3:02 a.m. Bogrov was prepared for hanging and, according to many eye-witnesses, he behaved courageously. The actual hanging was botched when Bogrov broke loose from the rope and a second attempt had to be made. According to the executioner, Bogrov rasped, "Scum."[60]

Executed at the age of twenty-four, Dmitry Bogrov remained inexplicable to his contemporaries. Commentary about him since has tended to fall into sharply divided positions. He was a frightened provocateur who was unable to extricate himself from his dual roles as a police agent and a Socialist Revolutionary terrorist and finally lashed out at his main tormentor, the government. Or conversely, he was one of the most successful SR terrorists and deserved a monument in his honour.

During the investigation, Bogrov insisted that he had accomplished the assassination without any outside assistance. The investigation did not prove otherwise, and the court convicted him as a lone terrorist with no suggestion that he was part of a larger conspiracy. There had been eleven other attempts to kill Stolypin, but they all failed, although they were undertaken by well-equipped and experienced terrorist groups. Because of these failures, many believed it impossible that a single gunman could have penetrated the security cordon around Stolypin; there must have been assistance of some kind. Doubts persisted about the fullness of the investigation, partly because of many rumours and tales about additional evidence.

Several witnesses gave evidence that seemed to suggest a wider conspiracy, perhaps including an attempt on Nicholas II. One witness said that he had seen Bogrov on a horse on 29 August attempting to cross the tsar's route. Another insisted that Bogrov, posing as a photographer, had attempted to approach the tsar's stand on 1 September at the race track. But the facts seem to be that Bogrov did not own a horse and that he had been in his apartment, not at the races, on the day of the tsar's visit.

Several spectators at the theatre on the night of the shooting of Stolypin testified that Bogrov had hesitated following the firing of his pistol. What was the meaning of this act? A right-wing newspaper thought the hesitation showed Bogrov's expectation that a confederate was lurking in the crowd ready to kill the tsar should the monarch approach his prime minister "because of his profound magnanimity."[61] Another bystander reported that he had seen a suspicious-looking person try to switch off all the lights at the electrical switchboard, but an electrician had driven him off. This suggested to some that there had been an accomplice ready to turn off the lights to give Bogrov a chance to escape the blacked-out theatre to a waiting car.

A.V. Zenkovsky, the prime minister's deputy, said he heard from F.F. Trepov, the governor-general, that "on the day of Stolypin's assassination Bogrov had lunch with a well-known enemy of the monarchy, Lev Trotsky-Bronstein, in the restaurant Metropol close to the opera theatre. The search for Trotsky after the assassination produced no results."[62] At that moment, Trotsky was at a congress of Social Democrats in Vienna and was about to make a speech when the news arrived that Stolypin had been shot.[63]

Other leads hinted at others' involvement. The Department of Police focused considerable attention on the Socialist Revolutionary party and especially the Maximalists. The police had known that in the winter of 1910 the terrorist Boris Savinkov was preparing an attempt against Stolypin. Savinkov failed in this venture and, fleeing to Paris, continued to try to organize, said a police report, "an assassination of the sacred person of the Emperor or Secretary of State Stolypin."[64]

Additional leads suggested connections between Bogrov and others. Alexander Murav'ev (who also went under the name Vasiliev and more recently carried a passport of the peasant Viziukov) had been arrested some days before the assassination. His arrest, according to the theory, had prompted a change in roles and Bogrov came forward to carry out the shooting that had been assigned to Murav'ev.[65] Witnesses testified that the two were acquainted and that Murav'ev had visited Bogrov's flat in August 1911.[66] The Kiev Gendarmes reported to the Department of Police that it had proof of Murav'ev's role in the crime.

Another possibility developed when Bogrov said at his trial that around 15 August 1911 one of the anarchists approached him "and said that I was definitely recognized to be a provocateur, and he threatened to publish the information and to bring it to everyone's notice. That disheartened me because I have many friends whose opinions I value."[67] The implicating of the anarchists was new and at variance with what Bogrov had said at his interrogations.

Bogrov said he was told that he had until 5 September to rehabilitate himself by performing a terrorist act. The anarchists would kill him if he refused. Bogrov said it did not cross his mind at the time to assassinate the prime minister. He had thought of the Okhranka chief in Kiev, Kuliabko, and he said he had assassination in mind when he called on Kuliabko at his apartment the night of 31 August. But he could not bring himself to kill him in his own apartment when he greeted him warmly in his dressing gown. "If Kuliabko had been in uniform I would have killed him," Bogrov testified. He had no clear plan, said Bogrov, when he arrived at the theatre on the next evening, 1 September. "I chose Stolypin because he was in the centre of everyone's attention. If anyone had questioned me, I would have left, but no one did so I fired twice."[68]

Although Bogrov changed his personal statement, his testimony did not influence the verdict of the district military court. But the inconsistent testimony of the accused prompted an unusual development; the government was still not satisfied that it had truly established the facts of the preparation of the assassination. The authorities questioned Bogrov in prison on the day following his conviction; the interrogation had nothing to do with the judicial process, but was conducted by Ivanov of the Gendarmes. Bogrov now gave names and nicknames of anarchists who had urged him to commit the crime. He identified their photographs and gave his opinion as to where they were located. He further told of two anarchists' underground locations, one for weapons and the other for a printing plant.

These new revelations did not satisfy the Gendarmes. They had in the meantime arrested the anarchist Peter Liatkovsky, but over the course of six months of interrogation had found no evidence of a link between the anarchists and Bogrov. Finally, they released Liatkovsky. Following the revolution of 1917, however, Liatkovsky revealed that he had met with Bogrov prior to the assassination. Bogrov had complained about the suspicions of other anarchists that he was informing for the Okhranka. Liatkovsky said he told Bogrov there was only one way to "rehabilitate" himself. Bogrov responded, said Liatkovsky, "So, I should go right now, and at the cross-roads kill the first policeman I run into? Is that rehabilitation?" As they parted, Bogrov said, "that as far as he knew, there will be military manoeuvres in Kiev. Nicholas, and certainly Stolypin, will attend them; he planned to reach the latter through his connections with the Kiev group. [He said] that I and the other comrades would still hear about him."[69]

Still, Liatkovsky's casual comment to Bogrov is not proof that the anarchists had threatened Bogrov with death if he did not assassinate a higher state official. Bogrov claimed that he had actually received the threat from an anarchist, "Stepa," whom he had known through underground work in Kiev and later in Paris. There was a Stepa, V.K. Vinogradov, who had been sentenced to fifteen years in a hard labour camp for the assassination of a military officer, but he had escaped from Siberia. Vinogradov was capable of killing Bogrov and it could be that Bogrov was more afraid of him than what might befall him following the assassination of Stolypin. He might prefer to redeem himself in the eyes of the anarchists and end his life as a martyr to the revolution rather than as a martyr to the cause of the authorities.

Still, more persuasively, Bogrov would likely not have been provoked to act by the threats of a single anarchist. If Stepa made threats against Bogrov, the Stormy Petrel group in Paris, of which he was a member, conducted no investigation into the allegations against Bogrov. Such an investigation would have been certain, in response to serious charges against Bogrov, before action could be taken. Another element casting doubt on Bogrov's story about Stepa is the Okhranka record. There is no evidence that he was in Kiev prior to the assassination of Stolypin; the last police record on him noted that he was about to leave for South America.

Bogrov's statement that he first planned to assassinate Kuliabko and then could not bring himself to commit the deed when he met him at his apartment does not stand up either. Because Bogrov had ready access to Kuliabko, who trusted him, he would not have required a prolonged period of preparation, but could have killed him easily. In telling the story, Bogrov would appear to have been trying to strengthen his contention that he acted because of anarchists' threats.

Differences in Bogrov's testimony between the interrogation and the trial resulted from the death of Stolypin. The prime minister was still alive when the bulk of the pre-trial interrogation took place. His death changed Bogrov's position because it became certain that he would be condemned to death. Bogrov immediately abandoned the pose of an inflexible fighter against the autocracy and began to show himself repentant and more forthcoming. By adding to his testimony facts that had the ring of truth to them, Bogrov, while he could hardly hope for mercy, probably thought he could delay the execution for many months while the additional investigation took place. The Gendarmes would not want to lose their main source of detailed information about a conspiracy. Bogrov had obviously committed the assassination, but the police by their unusual post-trial interrogation might still be able to identify co-conspirators and Bogrov seems to have tried to encourage their expectations.

Bogrov's gambit, however, did not distract the authorities for long. The trial lasted only six hours and the execution followed three days later. Such speed was unusual in capital criminal cases of this kind. I.P. Kaliaev, the assassin of Grand Duke Sergei Alexandrovich, was executed three months following his conviction. E.S. Sazonov, who had thrown the bomb that killed Plehve, escaped execution altogether and was sent to hard labour. The speed in carrying out the sentence gave rise to suspicions that the government wished to remove Bogrov from the scene quickly because he possessed information that might implicate persons in the government. At the least, as long as Bogrov lived he was a reminder of the ineffectiveness of a police system whose officers took pride in their abilities in the fight against terrorism.

Public criticism of the police had commenced right after the shooting of Stolypin. To soothe public opinion, Nicholas II ordered an investigation of the officials who had been charged with the protection of the dignitaries during the festivities in Kiev. He named Senator M.I. Trusevich to lead the investigation. Trusevich, as a former director of the Department of Police, appeared to have the requisite professional experience to conduct a searching inquiry. Officials who had been political allies of Stolypin welcomed the naming of Trusevich because he had lost his police directorship partly as a result of the actions of General Kurlov, who would be one of the subjects of the inquiry. Trusevich, it was believed, would have no reason to spare his former colleagues.[70]

Trusevich's investigation led to a second inquiry under the chairmanship of Senator N.Z. Shulgin. The First Department of the State Council twice discussed the investigation and the result of these efforts bore out Trusevich's thorough methods. The Ministry of Justice decided to try in a court of law Kurlov, Verigin, Spiridovich, and Kuliabko for "inaction by responsible authorities which caused consequences of great importance." The indictments or accusatory documents were ready in January 1913 when Nicholas II ordered the proceedings against three of the defendants halted. The Kuliabko case did proceed and he was sentenced to sixteen months in prison; the tsar reduced the penalty to four months.

This equivocal – some said scandalous – conclusion to the Stolypin assassination raised questions about official concealment of some kind of involvement in the assassination by higher officials. By 1911 there were several different groups who blamed Stolypin for a series of political and policy mistakes and even for constitutionalist tendencies.

Several months before the trip to Kiev, in March 1911, conservatives had openly begun a political offensive against Stolypin. They had seized upon a draft law which aimed to introduce the elective district assemblies (zemstvos) into the Western provinces. Right-wing members of the State Council led by P.N. Durnovo, the former minister of the interior, and V.F. Trepov, managed to reject the draft law. They had acted with the consent of the tsar and had voted down the draft law as an expression of mistrust in the prime minister. Stolypin, however, determined to rescue his legislation, threatened to resign unless Nicholas prorogued the Duma for three days and issued the Western Zemstvo bill under Article 87 of the Fundamental Laws, which permitted the tsar to promulgate legislation under emergency conditions. Stolypin had used Article 87 blatantly and thereby provoked widespread criticism of his unconstitutional ways. Liberals in the State Duma, who had been consistent defenders of constitutional development in Russia, dropped their support of the prime minister. Stolypin had also persuaded the tsar to use his special powers to banish his opponents from the State Council, and members of the right were furious at this high-handed action. Nicholas was a reluctant participant in Stolypin's manoeuvres and resented Stolypin's forcing him into a difficult position. Officials at court echoed the feelings of their imperial master. As the political storm intensified, Stolypin told his friends that he fully expected to be summoned to the tsar to be dismissed as prime minister.

This conflict earlier in the year gave rise to the idea that Stolypin's many enemies would try to find some other way to get rid of him. The assassination seemed to be the logical outcome of the hatreds generated among Stolypin's opponents.[71] Firmer evidence supports the allegation that the leadership of the Okhranka played a role in the killing of the prime minister. V.N. Kokovtsov told the tsar that, at least on the part of General Kurlov, there was more involved than criminal negligence. There is no record of what Kokovtsov had in mind, however.

More persuasive was A.I. Guchkov, the leader of the Octobrist party, who insistently claimed that the Okhranka was involved in the assassination. He announced his suspicions during a debate in the Third State Duma and he repeated them after the revolution of 1917 when he had emigrated to Western Europe.[72] Some historians have supported Guchkov's conclusions. The general suspicion has been that highly placed persons in the Okhranka manipulated Bogrov for their own purposes; these officials in turn were said to be acting to fulfil the wishes of those above them. Avrekh, for instance, declares that "they knew perfectly well, that they were fulfilling the secret wish of the court and camarilla. Certainly, there was risk in that but the game was worth the candle."[73] Other historians, admitting that there was much that was inexplicable in the actions of police officials, have found no hard evidence of an official conspiracy but have agreed that the Okhranka lost control of their agent while conducting a risky operation to flush out terrorists.[74]

Guchkov did not name the officers against whom he made his charges, although it was widely believed that he had Colonel Spiridovich in mind. Spiridovich went so far as to request permission of his superiors to challenge Guchkov to a duel. The argument for Kurlov's involvement usually rests on his ambitions and those of his subordinates to move up the official ladder and their view that Stolypin stood in their way. An anonymous police memorist writes: "It was rumoured that General Kurlov, as an ardent monarchist, was appointed as deputy Minister of the Interior over the objections of the late prime minister in order to create a counter-balance to his liberal aspirations. Kurlov's adherents, when Stolypin was still alive, were not ashamed to say that in the near future Kurlov would be the Minister of the Interior, M.N Verigin, the Director of the Department of Police, General Spiridovich, Governor of St Petersburg, and Lt. Col. Kuliabko, chief of the palace secret service, etc."[75]

Even more extravagant rumours flew through the press, especially in Finland where the papers were less susceptible to government pressure on Russian matters. Some publications said that a conspiracy of Gendarmes was not completed because General Spiridovich was unable to silence Bogrov by running his sabre through him right after the shooting of Stolypin.

Senator Trusevich had before him all of these versions and more. He testified in 1917 after the February revolution that he had commenced his investigation in the belief that Kurlov was the principal plotter in Kiev. Then, in rejecting this thesis, he decided that "his only motive could have been his career. But he would then destroy himself with the assassination because, as he was in charge of the guard and the assassination was committed in his presence, the chances of then being appointed to the post of the Minister of the Interior were sharply decreased – he would have been cutting the ground out from under his feet in this way, and he did just that."[76] What Trusevich had in mind was that, following Stolypin's death, A.A. Makarov was appointed minister of the interior, and Kurlov had to resign.

Another motive assigned to Kurlov was financial. It was claimed that he had covered his own personal financial problems by uncontrolled expenditures on the security measures. Kurlov did have financial problems because of a divorce and his marriage to Countess Armfelt. He had rather complex finances, had taken loans and given promissory notes, but he did manage to give a full accounting for his expenditures in Kiev. The record was clear: Kurlov had overcharged the treasury by 65 kopecks.

Kurlov as deputy minister probably schemed against Stolypin, but he clearly had no rational reason to want to assassinate his chief. To an outsider, the long chain of Okhranka and police errors might seem premeditated. However, no secret police or security official had a motive or was connected with a conspiracy by Trusevich's investigation.

The weight of the evidence comes down to Bogrov acting on his own. His reasons lay in a chain of events which were rooted in the system of political investigation long conducted by the Okhranka. Bogrov was an example of the risks involved in the Okhranka's methods of recruiting and maintaining a corps of secret agents. Some of them went to work for the Okhranka reluctantly or they changed their allegiance and dreamed of ways to get even with the secret police.

Treachery is endemic to any secret agent system, and the Okhranka was hardly an exception. The major difficulty it faced in getting to the bottom of the Bogrov case was the compartmentalization of the police structure. Various officials and departments frequently did not share what they knew with others, and the key requirement for the effectiveness of the police was not fulfilled. Compartments necessary to preserve secret information in this way blocked information from passing to those who could have used it. Kuliabko, as an example, in sending an inquiry about Lazarev and Kal'manovich to the St Petersburg Okhranka did not reveal his source of information. Von Kotten surmised that Kuliabko did not wish to reveal Bogrov's name to him, and confined himself to a limited response. If he had described in detail the peculiar behaviour of Bogrov in the capital, it might have alerted Kuliabko to risks associated with Bogrov. When Trusevich reported to the tsar, referring to the failure to pass this information among officers, he wrote that these "unusual relations" appeared to be the result of "persecution" of von Kotten by Spiridovich and von Kotten believed that anything he said would be used against him in some way by his enemies.[77]

Other errors by Gendarmes resulted in Bogrov getting close to Stolypin. The police did not put him under surveillance, did not check his apartment where the alleged terrorists were supposedly in hiding, allowed him into the theatre, and permitted him to roam freely around it. Kuliabko was ultimately responsible for most of these errors, but the main responsibility lay with Kurlov who selected his subordinates according to the principle of their personal devotion to him.

PART FOUR

The Political Police and the Jewish Question

CHAPTER TEN

Protocols, Masons, and Liberals

During the last years of the Empire, a climate of conspiracy bred fears in many that covert plotters against the tsar, even broad groups of them, were insidiously subverting Russian society. Probable conspirators of this sort, especially for extremist right-wing politicians, were Jews as a whole, Masons as a whole, and Liberals as a whole – or all of them together in a sinister coalition.

As guardians of state security, the directors of the Okhranka necessarily investigated such possibilities. Conclusive evidence shows that, despite their awareness that some Russian Jews were revolutionaries and that Masons abroad used revolutionary language, most security officials dismissed the idea that either the Jews or the Masons collectively posed a threat. With respect to the so-called Liberal faction, however, the Okhranka misjudged both the intentions and strength of this legal group that openly presented its program for change. And in their determined use of counter-measures against this political opposition, predictable though it was, Okhranka leaders further eroded the order they sought to preserve.

Many historians today contend that the Okhranka did target the Jews collectively as revolutionary conspirators at the turn of the century, and, as a prime piece of evidence, they point to the fraudulent *Protocols of the Elders of Zion*, whose precise origins remain a mystery. But, even as no concrete evidence has come to light about when, where, and by whom their drafting took place, solid data on the actual publication of the Protocols before the revolution explode the thesis of Okhranka involvement. Only six different printings are known in Russian before the revolution, merely one of which can remotely be linked to the government. These, along with the documented censorship decision in 1905 on the infamous Nilus edition, provide convincing evidence of non-involvement by the Okhranka or any other government agency.

Details about those few printings are the logical beginning point for this discussion; the bibliographical findings used here are those of Boris Nicolaevsky, who examined all six separate versions.[1] Nicolaevsky first cites an undated, unsigned hectographed copy of a manuscript in Russian written by three different hands that he found, missing some pages, in the rare books collection of the Lenin Library.[2] Its title read: "The Ancient and Continuing Protocols of Meetings of Zionist Elders"; below it appeared the subtitle: "The Root of Our Impoverishment." On the basis of textual evidence, Nicolaevsky judged it to predate every printed version that he found.

As Nicolaevsky and others have verified, the first known publisher was P.A. Krushevan, an outspoken anti-Semite and the owner of a small-circulation and short-lived daily newspaper called the *Banner* (*Znamia*) in St Petersburg. In its pages, during late August and early September of 1903 (the only year when the *Banner* met its daily schedule), there appeared a purported translation of policy formulated during sessions of the "World Union of Freemasons and Elders of Zion." Entitled "The Jewish Program for World Conquest," it was prefaced with editorial assurances that the tract conveyed a true warning, whether its original was an authentic Zionist document or an allegorical configuration. If the latter, the *Banner* argument went, the tract then had to be an apocryphal warning by an "obviously ... very intelligent person" who had correctly deduced that the Jews had "plans of conquest."[3] Because, like most newspapers in the two capitals since 1865, the *Banner* was not subject to preliminary censorship, Krushevan was able to publish the Protocols freely.

Raising no questions about authenticity, S.G. Nilus published a lengthier version of the Protocols in late 1905. Planning to circulate it as a small book, Nilus submitted his manuscript in mid-1905 to the Moscow Committee on Press Affairs for the censorship review still required with respect to all works of 160 or fewer pages; his chosen title at this stage – "The Triumph of Israel, or the Coming of the Anti-Christ as a Political Possibility (The Protocols of the Meetings of the Elders of Zion), 1902–1904" – seems to have implied that the alleged meetings took place in the years just previous.

On 28 September 1905, Moscow censor S.I. Sokolov rejected the short book in a thirteen-page critique. Explaining that the manuscript depicted the so-called Elders of Zion plotting to subvert existing governments through "hellish" liberal politics and revolutionary acts, he warned that its publication could "lead to the annihilation everywhere of all Jews without exception, the mass of whom are undoubtedly unaware of the plots of the Zionists." Appropriate authorities should, however, examine the manuscript to decide if it warranted investigation.[4]

In its ruling, the Moscow Committee on Press Affairs agreed that, because it might sow discord if widely read, the Protocols tract could not be circulated as a short book. But the committee also ruled that, because it conveyed "doctrines ... of the Zionist sect" that were, to them, self-evidently "extreme and insane," the Nilus manuscript could be published as part of a long book, assuming that it would only attract a small audience.[5] These same censorship records show that the committee had in hand the ten chapters of the book that Nilus had published in 1902, most of them devoted to apocalyptic prophesy – in convoluted and nearly impenetrable prose – that Christ would return within the next few years.[6] Even a cursory reading of that text shows the doctrines of Nilus himself to border on the extreme and insane, and that fact surely caused the committee to assume that only a small group of fanatics would buy a thick book by Nilus.

Upon receiving the committee's decision, it should be noted that Nilus could rightly have insisted on permission to publish the Protocols as a short book under the book regulations then in effect.[7] That is, censorship approval of works entirely comprised of material already legally published was virtually automatic so long as that material, once circulated, had not provoked a post-publication ban by the state. No such censure had followed the 1903 publication of the Protocols in the *Banner*. But apparently Nilus did not know about or care to use that particular regulation. Or perhaps neither he nor the Moscow Press Committee knew about the obscure prior publication of the Protocols tract, so unnoticed had it been. Had police officials been backing the Nilus manuscript, on the other hand, they would certainly have brought this regulation before the committee, were such a tactic necessary to cause it to approve the publication of the Protocols as a small book.

Taking no exception to the Press Committee decision, Nilus proceeded to publish the Protocols as an addendum to his book of 1902. Given its 1905 imprint, the resulting revised edition, entitled *The Large in the Small and the Antichrist, as a Near Political Possibility*, came off a press registered to the Committee of the Red Cross at Tsarskoe Selo during October, November, or December.

In this version of his book, Nilus did not specify the time of the alleged Protocol meetings, and perhaps he dropped his earlier "1902–1904" allusion (in the title that headed his mid-year censorship submission) after belatedly learning that the *Banner* had described the meetings as past history in 1903. Moreover, Nilus himself ruled out any such recent historical referent by electing to specify in his book that 1901 was the year in which he acquired a manuscript of the Protocols through an unnamed friend. As for its pedigree, Nilus describes the manuscript as an extract copied from a thick book in a Zionist archive hidden in France and explained that it had somehow been stolen from the Freemasons by an unidentified woman.[8]

In December 1905 appeared the lone edition of the Protocols with a link to the government – a brochure entitled *The Root of Our Misfortune* that was printed on presses belonging to the St Petersburg Military District. Although censorship approval (on 9 December 1905) was denoted on an initial page, nowhere did the name of the publisher appear. Nicolaevsky thinks it significant that Grand Duke Nicholas Nicholaevich, later commander-in-chief, was head of the military district, but a subordinate could easily have put this very slim work through the press. The number of copies is unknown, but their format, as a brochure of only a few pages, meant that they had little durability. Except for one curious alteration, shifting the onus of conspiratorial blame to the Masons by describing the "excerpts from ancient and contemporary protocols" to be those of the "Elders of Zion of the Universal Society of Freemasons," this brochure, maintains Nicolaevsky, effectively republished the Protocol tract that had appeared in the *Banner* in 1903.[9]

The year after the brochure was published, the Protocols again appeared, this time in *Accusatory Speeches. Enemies of Humanity*, a 1906 book by G. Butmi, a leading member of the anti-Semitic Union of the Russian People. His publisher was the St Petersburg Institute for the Deaf. Nicolaevsky says this version is the same one put out on the press of the St Petersburg Military District and he cites the date given for the first time of its translation from French into Russian as 1901. He also quotes these words from Butmi's introduction: "The Zionism of Herzl, joined to the Masons in 1900, spread throughout Russia and became the chief instrument in a plot to spread internal rebellion, which is now tearing apart our homeland ... in accordance with the plan of the Elders of Zion."[10] In 1911 and again in 1917, Nilus republished his version of the Protocols. They first appeared under the title, *The Great and the Small. The Coming of the Antichrist Is Near and the Reign of the Devil on the Earth*. The second was published as *What Is Close Is Here at our Doors. "Who Is there Who Does Not Believe that It Is at Hand?"* For both printings, he used a Russian Orthodox press at the Troitsky-Sergeevsky Monastery, near which he appears to have been living. In the 1917 edition, Nilus for the first time named his source of the Protocols manuscript as Tula land-owner and neighbour A.N. Sukhotin; again for the first time, he claimed to have learned that the Protocols were completed at a 1879 Zionist Congress in Basle under Theodore Herzl.

These six are the only known printings of the Protocols in Russian prior to the Bolsheviks' assumption of power; their small number, their conspicuous sponsorship by extremists, and their small impact on the public makes a point. That is, had the Okhranka, in the last two decades of the Empire, decided to use the Protocols to defame the Jews, its top security officials would have ensured their wide circulation through accessible and respectable small books or pamphlets, just as they would have contrived and publicized respectable endorsements that were, in fact, conspicuously absent. Never would they have favoured the right-wing printings that actually appeared, so sceptical about them and indifferent to them was the public as a whole.

Against this circumstantial evidence that the Okhranka itself did not spread or promote the Protocols must be weighed the available testimony of individuals who claim direct or indirect knowledge about the genesis and dissemination of that fraudulent tract. All of these recorded attestations date from 1921 or later, and few are first-hand.[11] Contradictions abound within this collective whole, as will be shown by a summary of the allegations of each testament in chronological order of their utterance or entry into the public domain.

First among these is the report by one Isaac Landman in the *American Hebrew* on 25 February 1921 of an interview with Princess Radziwill, "a writer of note on matters Russian and European and a member of an old Russian family." According to Landman, the princess conveyed to him three pieces of information from her personal knowledge. First, initial forgers of the Protocols were secret police agents acting under orders from the head of the Third Section, General "Orgewsky,"[12] who planned to use the fraudulent document to convince Alexander III that the assassins of his father in 1881 were Jews bent on ruling the world. Secondly, Orgewsky lacked entrée to the tsar and entreated help from the head of the Okhrana, or Palace Guard, General "Tcherewine" (Adjutant-General P.A. Cherevin), who refused any part in the plot but who retained a copy of the Protocol draft and later included it in his unpublished memoir, the original of which he gave to the tsar and a copy of which he gave to the princess as one of his "dearest" friends.[13] And finally, "following the Japanese War and at the beginning of the first Russian Revolution [defeat abroad and turmoil at home were clear by March 1905, but not until September did Japan sign a peace treaty] ... Russian secret agents and police officials, Grand Duke Sergei at their head," recovered the never-used Protocols draft from an official file and ordered subordinates to enlarge and modernize it.

The princess claimed personally to have "handled" this second draft "several times" while she lived in Paris ("I am now referring to the years 1904 and 1905"). Her means was one "Golowinsky" (Matvei

Golovinsky), a friend's son, who, during social calls, proudly handed it about as his joint project with "Manasewitch-Maniuloff" and "Rachkowsky" to prove a "Jewish conspiracy against the peace of the world." The princess remembered that it was "in French, all handwritten but in different handwritings ... on yellow-tinged paper," and she clearly recalled that "a huge blot of blue ink" stood out on the first page. She later "heard that this same manuscript was incorporated by Sergei Nilus in his famous book" but knew nothing of Nilus or his work.[14]

One week later, another article in the *American Hebrew* presented corroborating statements from Mrs Henrietta Hurlbut, an American who claimed to have been with the princess (again no dates) when Golowinsky displayed his manuscript. Besides reporting that Mrs Hurlbut recalled the same details about the manuscript, including the blue blot, it emphasized that she was an anti-Semite who admitted having later read the Nilus book for its own sake only to recognize it, unexpectedly, as "my old friend Golowinsky."[15]

Bearing the date April 1921, the next testimony is an unpublished typed document signed by F.P. Stepanov. There he attests to having acquired in 1895 – from a neighbour, A.N. Sukhotin – a handwritten Russian manuscript that he understood to be a translation of a French-language copy of the original Protocols. Sukhotin's source, claimed Stepanov, was an unnamed woman who had secretly copied a French-language manuscript held by acquaintances in France. Contending that the original document for all these copies was a bona fide record of actual meetings of the Elders of Zion, he states that he made hectographed duplicates of his own Russian-language copy and that one of these reached Nilus in 1897.[16]

In the next month, on 14 May, an article linking Rachkovsky to the Protocols appeared in *Evreiskaia Tribuna* (*Jewish Tribune*), a newspaper published in Paris. Its French author, A. du Chayla, claimed to have been a guest in Nilus's home in 1909, and there to have read a French-language manuscript of the Protocols written in several hands and bearing a conspicuous blue blotch on its first page. Nilus purportedly told du Chayla that he had received it from a long-time resident of Paris named "Madame K," whose source was "a Russian general," whom, when pressed, he named as Rachkovsky. Du Chayla depicted Nilus as a failed magistrate and inept landholder and as a religious zealot who constantly carried the manuscript out of fears that the Jews meant to steal it.[17]

Evreiskaia Tribuna on 26 August continued the discussion through a signed article by Sergei Svatikov, a Menshevik sent by the Provisional

Government in 1917 to investigate and close down the Foreign Agency. In it Svatikov identifies Madame K as a friend of Nilus, one Madame Komarovskaia, and – in expressed support of Radziwill and Hurlbut – agrees that Rachkovsky ordered Matvei Golovinsky to rewrite the Protocols. He offers no proof for these identifications, but he dates the residence of Golovinsky in Paris as 1890–1900 and his employment as an Okhranka agent as 1892.[18]

In his fuller account in an unpublished manuscript from this same year, Svatikov says that he interviewed Foreign Agency detective Henri Bint both in 1917 and 1921 and learned from him that Rachkovsky planned to hone a more readable and compelling Protocols tract in 1905. Allegations credited to Bint sharply contradict the princess's timing of events; first, that what inspired Rachkovsky to take up the pseudo-document for the first time was the Protocols text that Nilus published in 1905 (censor Sokolov recommended in September that authorities examine it); and, second, that Rachkovsky initiated his project to "deepen" the Protocols without informing his superiors in the Police Department (Rachkovsky did not rejoin the department until July 1905).[19]

To prove that Rachkovsky had undertaken the embellishment project in 1905, writes Svatikov, Bint claimed personally to have taken part by obeying a directive that year from Rachkovsky at the Department of Police (thus in July or later) that sent him to a bookdealer in Frankfurt to order specific anti-Semitic books, all of which he picked up and then mailed from Paris to Rachkovsky at the Police Department in St Petersburg. According to Svatikov, Bint believed that Rachkovsky intended to publish the revised Protocols to incite Russians against the revolutionaries, not against the Jews. To support his contention, Bint in 1921 had shown Svatikov several contrived pamphlets – all devoid of anti-Semitism – that Rachkovsky had, on his own initiative, published in Paris before 1902 to accomplish that same aim.

Proof that the Protocols were a forgery rested on an entirely different kind of evidence in a series of articles in *The Times* of London in August 1921. The newspaper's Constantinople correspondent argued that striking similarities, too many for chance, showed conclusively that the Protocols were based on an 1864 political tract by French lawyer Maurice Joly that expressed, in the voice of Machiavelli, despicable political practices that the reader could readily associate with Emperor Napoleon III. The correspondent, whose name was Graves, demonstrates how alike are the words of Machiavelli in Joly's satire and the words of the Elders of Zion in the Protocols.[20]

All of these data from 1921 were aired, with no significant additions, by du Chayla and others at a "trial" of the Protocols in Berne in October 1934; the next month the *American Hebrew* reprinted its own 1921 translation of du Chayla's Paris article of 1921. In turn, to hear from a witness so far silent, the journal sent du Chayla's article to Nilus's son Sergei (hereafter young Nilus), then living in Poland, with a request for his commentary; young Nilus replied in an eight-page typed letter dated 26 March 1936.[21]

Anti-Semitism does not come up in his 1936 letter to the *American Hebrew* but, because the son is likely to reflect his father, it is relevant here to cite the offer that young Nilus would make four years later in a letter addressed to Nazi leader Alfred Rosenberg, the future commissar of Germany's Eastern Occupied Territories and a spokesman for Nazi racist ideas. As a resident of Poland, in March 1940 young Nilus would volunteer to provide assistance to Rosenberg in his handling of the Jews – and it is hard to imagine that young Nilus hoped to make life easier for them.[22]

As for the 1936 letter, young Nilus mentions at one point that his father had died six years before in Soviet exile, but he mainly rebuts du Chayla's "inventions" about the Protocols. He insists, for example, that his father could not have acquired the Protocols from Rachkovsky through Madame Komarovskaia because he himself had witnessed his father's receipt of the French-language manuscript from Sukhotin in 1901, when Sukhotin had specified his source as a "widow of a noble in his district, who had found it after his death in his desk." These alone were the Protocols that his father had translated and published in 1905, claimed young Nilus; for all the many times they had come before his eyes, he could not recall ever having seen a blue blotch on their front.[23]

Again to rebut du Chayla, young Nilus described his father as a religious, non-mystical, and scholarly landlord who enjoyed continuous prosperity up to 1917. As for biographical details, he recounts that, in 1883, at the age of nineteen his father had fled to France with his equally well-to-do, but married, thirty-eight-year-old cousin; that they returned to Russia with infant son Sergei a year later to face the wronged husband's adamant refusal to divorce; that, but for another stay of some months in France just before the tsar made twelve-year-old Sergei legitimate in 1895, they henceforth shared a comfortable life together in Russia until the Soviets intervened; and that Nilus had added to this happy household in 1906 the woman that he married with the blessing of the mother of his only child.[24]

Of relevance to the Protocols is young Nilus's statement that, following his parents' return to Russia in 1895, his father had closely associated with three Stepanov brothers: Michael, Nicholas, and Philippe (Filip, in Russian).[25] For it was F.P. Stepanov who, fifteen years before young Nilus' letter, swore that Sukhotin had given him the Protocols in Russian translation in 1895, and a copy had reached Nilus in 1897. Young Nilus also testified that his father chose to provide his translation of the Protocols to "Mr Gringmut" for a series of articles in his *Moskovskie Vedomosti* newspaper that young Nilus claims to remember reading as they appeared in "winter 1902–1903." Because the only known printing of the Protocols before 1905 was in Krushevan's *Banner* in the fall of 1903, young Nilus seems to misremember precise details, as would be fully understandable. But no matter what he knew of that first publication or when he learned of it, young Nilus would logically insist that his father was the source for it, if only to reinforce that his father alone held a singularly rare copy of the Protocols.[26]

During the two years following young Nilus's letter to *American Hebrew*, V.L. Burtsev, the investigative journalist well known for his spy exposures in the decade before the revolution, completed his book on the Protocols that appeared in 1938. He devotes much of it to line-by-line comparisons – which go well beyond the examples of parallel wording listed by *The Times*' reporter Graves in 1921 – to prove that the Protocols are based on Joly's 1864 satire. In the remaining pages, he comments on what happened once the Protocols were fabricated.[27]

He testifies, for example, that one of the last Okhranka chiefs, S.P. Beletsky, told him in 1918 that he had never considered injecting the Protocols into the trial of Beilis, the Jew charged with ritual murder in 1911–13. Quoting a conversation that took place when the two men shared a Bolshevik jail cell, Burtsev remembers these words of Beletsky: "Although several persons proposed to us to use the 'Zionist Protocols,' we fully understood that this meant destruction of the entire case. They were such an obvious forgery."[28] Burtsev similarly quotes former Okhranka agent Manasevich-Manuilov, whom Princess Radziwill alleged in 1921 to have worked on the Protocols. This time remembering a private conversation from before the revolution, Burtsev recounts that Manuilov dismissively referred to the Protocols as a pseudo-document that "only an idiot could believe."[29]

Burtsev also quotes a written statement that he solicited in 1934 from a former Okhranka official who claimed to have investigated the Protocols for Stolypin in 1908. This official, identified as "Globychev," a one-time chief of the St Petersburg Okhranka, would appear to be the general who took command of the capital Okhranka in February 1917 – Major-General K.I. Globachev.

According to Globachev, an unnamed but opportunistic Foreign Agency agent in Paris drafted the Protocols sometime between 1896 and 1900, the latter being the year in which, "unbeknownst to his immediate superior" (this phrase absolves Rachkovsky, then head of the Foreign Agency), he forwarded his forgery to a St Petersburg Okhranka official named Colonel Piramidov. Although Manasevich-Manuilov and others then commenced efforts to channel the forgery to the tsar, testifies Globachev, success came only in 1905 through D.F. Trepov (who became court commander in November 1905) and V.F. Dzhunkovsky, at the time assistant to the governor of Moscow province.

Nicholas II, claims Globachev, found the Protocols plausible; he did so just as a surge of anti-Semitic disinformation from such right-wing groups as the Union of the Russian People coincided with a terrible outbreak of pogroms. Faced with a tract that was very likely yet more such disinformation,[30] Stolypin ordered an investigation of the Protocols in 1906. The resulting report by two Gendarme officers, identified by Globachev as Martynov and Vasiliev, labelled the Protocols fraudulent and cited, as support, testimony to that effect received from Rataev in Paris and Harting in Berlin (both held those Foreign Agency postings only until July 1906).[31] Upon reading that report, the tsar purportedly issued this order: "Get rid of the 'Protocols.' It is impossible to defend something sacred by dirty methods."[32]

All these various facts became known to Globachev, he says, during his own inquiry in 1908, also ordered by Stolypin; although Burtsev relates no reason from Globachev for that second probe, it would have followed the 1907 publication of the Protocols by the Union of the Russian People's spokesman, Butmi. As for his own summation of the Protocols, Globachev found them a fake and ruled out the involvement of any high officials.

Burtsev himself agreed that the Protocols had been forged but held high officials fully responsible. He retells and endorses the details of origin related by Princess Radziwill in 1921 – as he does her explanation of the reworking of the 1881 manuscript in 1905 by Golovinsky at the behest of Rachkovsky. He offers no proof for any of these details. His justification for accepting them as truth, rather, was his own conviction that top policy-makers in the Department of Police consistently sought to exploit endemic anti-Semitism in their campaign against revolutionists. By casting a blanket of blame on Jews for political agitation, labour strikes, and revolutionary terrorism, the police imagined they could stir Russians more effectively to become passionate supporters of the tsar. The Protocols, argues Burtsev, fitted perfectly into that design: they portrayed the Jews as conspiring to rule the world by internally ruining all existing social orders through every possible disruptive means, whether political, economic, or religious.

On the contrary, it can be argued that both documentary evidence and logic refute the commonplace assumption that high officials consistently and deliberately made scapegoats of the Jews. Some individuals within the government favoured that policy and effected it whenever they could, but the position of the tsarist government by 1900 was to curb anti-Semitic violence in Russia, not to promote it.

The two final testimonies in this discussion come from the papers of A.S. Spiridovich that were added to the archives of Yale University in 1962. As head of the palace security guard from 1906 to 1912, Spiridovich knew Rachkovsky personally; the statements that he left on the Protocols divorce Rachkovsky from any involvement on the grounds that he was never anti-Semitic: "First, his secretary was the Jew Gol'shman; his chief assistant was Gekkel'man; not one of his reports was anti-Semitic; and he even did not remark on Jews as the leaders of the revolutionary movement." Spiridovich also writes: "We have full reason to declare that Nilus gave the 'Protocols' to Krushevan for publication in *Banner*. Nilus sympathized with Krushevan and his activity ... and I would not be surprised if sometime it is shown that he, Nilus, was the author."[33]

The second statement in the Spiridovich papers is from Rachkovsky's son, Andrei Petrovich, who claims never to have heard of either Nilus or Golovinsky. Thus he "completely reject[s] any connection between Rachkovsky and Nilus," but allows that Golovinsky could have been an agent. Rachkovsky himself was permanently terminated from police work in July 1906 and died three years later; no record has emerged of any comments by him on the Protocols to any investigator or acquaintance or in any writings of his own.

These, then, are the testimonies of "witnesses" and "investigators" of the Protocols, any or all of whom may have lied, misremembered, or otherwise distorted the genesis and dissemination of this pseudo-document. Given the textual proof from Graves and Burtsev about the genesis of the Protocols from Joly's 1864 satire, of course, no one can believe the contention of Nilus, Butmi, and the like that an original copy of the published Protocols rests in a secret archive of Zionist plotters.

The question here is about involvement by the tsarist secret police. The testimony of Princess Radziwill is pivotal, for she claimed to possess a copy – one that has never materialized – of the original Protocols drafted under orders from the head of the Department of Police in the 1880s, and, in addition, to have handled and read the manuscript of the "modernized" version ordered by Rachkovsky in 1905. That blue-blotched 1905 manuscript written in French in several hands is, therefore, the one piece of empirical evidence to tie the

Okhranka to the Protocols. The princess says that she held and read it some time after March of 1905 and heard from its possessor that Rachkovsky was involved.

Du Chayla claims that he, in 1909, held and read the Protocols – allegedly the very ones that had provided Nilus with the text for his 1905 edition – as a blue-blotched French manuscript penned by several persons; he alleges that he heard from its possessor that Rachkovsky was its source. If the blue-blotched manuscripts described by Radziwill and du Chayla within three months of each other in 1921 are one with the French-language manuscript that young Nilus confirmed in 1936 that his father possessed, however, that particular manuscript could not have reached Nilus in time to provide the text for his 1905 book. That is, Nilus had to have used a copy acquired before March 1905 – and that was most certainly true for publisher Krushevan who printed the Protocols in the *Banner* in 1903.

Officials allegedly recovered an old copy of the Protocols from their files in March of 1905 and sent it to Paris for revision in hand-written French (apparently necessary for a document purportedly from a French archive) – a process that would have taken six weeks of work at a minimum. To have transformed the alleged 1905 manuscript into the text that he gave to the Press Committee no later than September 1905, Nilus first would have required sufficient time to ponder and translate it and then, as required by press regulations, yet more time to send his translation to a printshop for typesetting, type-correction, printing, and collation. All of that preparation for his censorship submission would have required much more than four months.

In any case, copies of the Protocols had to have been available in Russia well before 1905. The *Banner* version of 1903 is sufficient proof in itself, but there is also the statement of Stepanov that he made hectographed copies in 1895 and the testimony in Burtsev's book from Globachev that a St Petersburg Okhranka officer received a copy from a Paris agent in 1900. If Nilus held the blue-blotched manuscript that Princess Radziwill alleges to have read in Paris in 1905, it had to have been a supplementary copy that reached him after he prepared the text for his 1905 book.

The real origins of the Protocols remain a mystery; so far no substantive evidence identifies the anti-Semite or mere opportunist, Russian or French, police or private, who fabricated them in the 1880s or 1890s. Nor is there clear proof about who channelled the pseudo-document to people in Russia likely to feel moved to publish it. The couriers, for their part, had the option of representing the tract as artful disinformation designed to defame the Jews or, as purportedly happened with respect to Nicholas II and Nilus, as an authentic Zionist document proving a Jewish conspiracy.

When the document did appear in print in Russia in 1903, 1905, 1908, 1911, and 1917, hard facts about its publication conclusively rule out police involvement. No doubt some persons in the Okhranka and the Police Department at large advocated the publishing and wide circulation of this disinformational tract in order to stir popular anger against the Jews, but their advice did not cause police officials to take measures to ensure wide circulation of that contrived text or to promote wide belief in its authenticity. It has already been pointed out that the actual publishers were extremists who had no credibility beyond the small ranks of their like-minded peers. As the record also shows, those same extremist publishers accomplished their small press runs and even smaller circulations with no support from the police or any government sector.

Discussion of the Protocols has so far centred on the Jewish question, even though that pseudo-document targets both Masons and Jews as co-conspirators bent on world domination. The discussion that follows, then, will examine to what degree the Okhranka focused attention on possible conspiratorial activities against the throne by Russian Masons. But because the concerns of the Okhranka about the Masons centred on their being liberals, to examine the response of the Okhranka to the Masons in the last two decades of the Empire requires examining its response to liberals as a whole.

Liberals who were Masons had, after all, figured strongly in the failed coup attempt of 1825 against the tsar by the Decembrists; the ban that Alexander I had declared against them even earlier, in 1822, had remained in effect through every successor up to Nicholas II. A modest change had come with the loosening of state strictures following the revolution of 1905, when the government had not excluded the Masons from its legislation of 4 March 1906 that permitted individual, non-governmental societies to exist, so long as each had first been examined, approved, and registered by local authorities.

Similarly, only months earlier, P.N. Durnovo, the minister of the interior, had responded to alarms voiced by Foreign Minister Lamsdorff about the "spreading influence in the West of Masonry" by rejecting his proposal for an investigation of the influence of Masonry on international relations,[34] although Durnovo's main objection to such a study, no doubt, was its unwieldiness.

Notable among those who sought unsuccessfully to revive Masonry in Russia at that point was a liberal professor of juridical history,

M.M. Kovalevsky, who returned to Russia in 1905 after fifteen years of self-exile in France. Having joined the Masons in Paris because of their international connections and their dedication to social and moral betterment, Kovalevsky hoped to foster liberal change at home by prodding like-minded individuals to organize Russian lodges. One eminently desirable liberal he vainly tried to recruit for this endeavour was Paul Miliukov, the future leader of the Constitutional Democratic party.[35]

No figures are available on the precise number of Masonic lodges that actually existed in Russia from 1906 to 1917, but very few appear to have won approval from local authorities. Given the justly earned liberal reputation of Masonry, after all, some high police officials strongly opposed even its limited reintroduction into Russia; one was M.I. Trusevich, in 1907 the director of police, who vowed in a letter to the Warsaw governor-general that he would devote all his energies to prevent the spread of what he saw as an international conspiracy to subvert monarchical government.[36] Another was the head of the Special Section in 1908, E.K. Klimovich, who voiced the same dire description of the Masons in reply to an inquiry from a subordinate.[37] Permitting liberals to form associations made no sense to police officials troubled by an already-restive society, given that placing informers in each (a difficult task in liberal groups) was seen as the only means to monitor them.

Okhranka officials had begun expressing their concerns about liberals as agitators against the autocracy well before the 1905 revolution, and two examples from 1902 are reports by L.A. Rataev, then head of the Special Section. In the first one, dated 11 February, Rataev deplored that a number of such groups "were almost exclusively operating on a legal basis and were completely elusive for the organs of surveillance."[38] To compensate, he called for the establishment of what he called "observation points" (meaning small security divisions) in particularly difficult areas.

Three months later, the newly appointed police director, A.A. Lopukhin, implemented Rataev's recommendation. Rataev issued a second report that pointedly blamed this heightening of security measures on liberals within the upper classes and the intelligentsia. Through their publications, congresses, reading rooms, and Sunday schools for workers, he protested, these skilled manipulators of opinion were drawing "well-meaning" and intelligent allies into their movement by, for example, unfairly accusing the government of "monstrous brutalities" against student demonstrators. Anywhere such "serious people" organized, he wrote, a "revolutionary mood and ... movement" inevitably developed.[39]

Lopukhin himself issued both directives and an explanatory circular about the new investigative posts in Vilna, Ekaterinoslav, Kazan', Kiev, Odessa, Saratov, Tiflis, and Khar'kov.[40] Lacking sufficient security personnel to head them all, he necessarily appointed a number of Gendarmes; again forced by circumstances, he required each head to recruit and train his own secret agents, both internal and external. As for their oversight, none were to undertake arrests or investigations, except in an emergency, without higher approval from the Gendarme provincial commander. To fund them, Lopukhin increased the budget allotments for secret agents in the eight cities requiring posts and did the same for special units previously in place in St Petersburg, Moscow, and Warsaw.[41]

Upgrading the new posts to make them better conform to his reformist plans, Lopukhin reorganized each in June 1903 as a local unit within the Okhranka. They would proliferate to as many as seventy-five in the remaining years of the Empire – that is, as a full-fledged security division (okhrannoe otdelenie, which became abbreviated, in common usage, as "O.O.") responsible directly to him through his Special Section.[42] His directive this time enjoined his heads to pay "special attention ... so that [agents] do not themselves engage in political crimes"; and he spelled out much more precisely the rules and procedures for their searches, arrests, and inquiries, all aimed at detecting both criminal subversion by revolutionaries and dangerous but legal agitation by liberals.[43]

A follow-up report in September by one of Lopukhin's subordinates in the police secretariat, M.G. Trutkov, described the creation of the scattered O.O.s as urgently required to fight disorders that had overtaxed the Okhranka's flying squad of security agents. Admitting that all police agents were finding it more difficult to deal with highly effective agitators who kept their activities just within the limits of the law than with blatantly criminal terrorists, he decried the indiscriminate local arrests in the previous year that had put the government in a bad light and also made overcrowded jails into planning and recruitment centres for further rebellion. Placing the new units directly under the Special Section, wrote Trutkov, ensured their being better supervised by "a completely intelligent person." In the mere three months since the changeover, he claimed, improved methods and results were already evident.[44]

The high level of education at this time among personnel in the Security Section seems to have been a common source of pride to Okhranka officials, no doubt in part because it made that staff a match for the liberals. Police Department official M.S. Komissarov, for one, would echo Trutkov's very words about them in his testimony to the Provisional Government's Extraordinary Investigating Commission in 1917. Many "intelligent people, all ... university and law graduates," he would stress, gave the Special Section "an unusual, specific character."[45]

Readily apparent to that well-educated Security Section in 1904 and 1905 was an all-out campaign by the liberals to unite all segments of Russian society behind their program: a freely elected constituent assembly to establish a western constitutional government based on respect for the law, universal suffrage, freedom of conscience and organization, and freedom of the press. First to use this strategy were the liberals who founded the Union of Liberation in 1902, who also pressed for improved conditions for industrial workers and their families.

The "banquet campaign" of the liberals in late 1904 prompted resolution after resolution in keeping with their program. An Okhranka informer at the liberal dinner in the Hermitage Restaurant in Moscow on 14 December, for example, reported that the "radical part of society" had there resolved to demand the immediate summoning of a constituent assembly.[46] Despite the ban on non-government labour organizations, the Union of Liberation in 1905 was encouraging members of the educated professions to form their own unions with the goal of uniting with like groups of workers.[47] In May of that year the Okhranka took note that fourteen such professional groups had formed the Union of Unions to build a broad coalition to demand liberal reform.[48] Rachkovsky, as head of the Special Section, in July ordered police surveillance over the professional unions and the use of "administrative measures" against them to frustrate their objective of promoting democratic ideas.[49] Four months before, an analysis from the St Petersburg Gendarme administration had reported that the All-Russian Congress of the Union of Lawyers had declared "full solidarity with the revolutionary parties with the objective to establish in Russia a new state order based on a universal, direct, equal and secret ballot."[50]

To the dismay of the Okhranka, the educated upper class was consorting with revolutionaries in an uprising that no agency of government could stop. In the midst of it, one more typical dispatch went out from the Special Section to all governors, police chiefs, and Gendarme commanders calling for better intelligence reports, no delays in decisive preventative actions, and closer monitoring of the public mood.[51] But even some local police and members of the Gendarmes would insubordinately join in the demands for change by year's end.[52]

Two years after the 1905 revolution had ended, the Okhranka still kept a close watch on the liberal section of the opposition. But it now recognized that its leadership of the working class had been displaced by that of the Socialist Revolutionaries and, more particularly, the Social Democrats.[53] However, in its fight against political conspiracies that operated covertly, the mandate of the Okhranka was to detect every sort of opposition. Fears that liberals would use Masonic lodges for this purpose were still taken seriously by some Okhranka officials.

The first of two somewhat laughable counter-Mason manœuvres took place in 1908, but its haphazard conduct, like that of the second in 1910, conveys the limited degree of concern felt within the Okhranka about the threat posed by Masonry. At centre stage before the public in the 1908 caper was a poseur inside the Moscow lodge who helped confirm, for pay, its conspiratorial nature.

Reporting to his chief at the Special Section, E.K. Klimovich, in November 1908, Moscow Okhranka chief M.F. von Kotten found it necessary to explain privately the virtues of one James Percy, an outspoken Mason within his bailiwick who claimed to be a Londoner who wrote for American and English periodicals. In fact this grand secretary who served Grand Master P.A. Chistiakov of the Astreia lodge of Moscow was an Okhranka infiltrator named Ivan Fedorovich Persits, a man doubly adroit "as an insinuator and in pursuit of his own financial advantage." He posed no security risk, wrote von Kotten, because the lodge affair that involved him could easily be ended in "two or three months."[54]

On 13 November so-called James Percy had come to public attention by disingenuously telling *Veche*, a right-wing Moscow broadsheet, that English Masons had laid the groundwork for spreading Masonry in Russia because they considered it ripe for their promotion of liberal government. What these Masons really had in mind, *Veche* angrily commented, was the corruption of the Russian people, a view echoed by several other papers. At the end of December, through Persits, the police timed their search of Chistiakov's apartment to coincide with a secret and therefore illegal meeting in progress. Requiring no other grounds for an administrative ruling, the Department of Police banned this group of Moscow Masons as a conspiratorial organization. As for Persits, *New Times* used his real name in a story in January 1909 reporting his arrest and probable expulsion from Moscow in connection with an illegal meeting that, "according to some information, was Masonic."

Later that year, P.G. Kurlov became assistant minister of the interior and thus overseer of the Police Department. He was strongly fearful of a Masonic conspiracy, and would secretly take steps in 1910 to initiate the second notable counter-Mason operation.

Kurlov's choice for the mission was a minor official in the Second Secretariat who spoke several languages and boasted a gold medal from an elite lyceum in St Petersburg, one V.K. Alexeev. Sent first to Brussels in October 1910, Alexeev picked up a letter of introduction to the secretary of the Anti-Masonic Association, Abbot J. Tourmantin, and proceeded to Paris to query him on the French Masonic lodge, the Grand Orient. Surprised by the abbot's indifference, Alexeev filled his first report to Kurlov with quotes from the Grand Orient's newspaper, *Revue Masonnique*. Although one commentator there described the Russian government as an "embarrassment among civilized nations," Alexeev admitted to finding no evidence of Masonic plots against it.[55]

After next finding the abbot's assistant receptive to a 500-franc "loan," Alexeev proceeded to discover from the abbot that his price for a full disclosure about Masonry in Russia was 500,000 francs, the cost of bribing three high Masonic officials. When Kurlov replied that he could agree to pay informers only a small annual retainer with additional payments for each document provided, Alexeev stood by the initial proposal, even as he submitted a bill for 2,000 francs for his own princely expenses for cabs, theatre, cigarettes, valet, and numerous "suppers for two" during his failed six-week foray that ended that December.[56]

Just over a year later, in January 1912, the abbot addressed a letter to the minister of the interior, A.A. Markov, inquiring whether his request for a "significant sum of money" had ever been satisfied and whether Russian officials still refused to undertake "something in Russia against the Freemasons." Apparently having written to let the minister know that he had so far received nothing but deserved something, the abbot did win a small retainer for supplying several subsequent reports of what proved to be useless political speculation.[57]

Alexeev had meanwhile taken up the pursuit of conspiratorial Masons in St Petersburg and filed a report on the meeting of twenty such suspects at the Museum of Inventions and Improvements on 11 March 1911. He cited as chief propagandist among them one V.V. Arkhangelskaia-Ovchinnikova, whom the Okhranka identified as a radical feminist with a graduate degree in historical philosophy from the University of Paris.[58] Alexeev freely talked with her and she seems to have delighted in convincing him of Masonic power. She may have been the one who caused him to report that fall that Masons had a role in Stolypin's assassination and that Grand Orient had worked through "revolutionary committees in fulfilling a plan that was only in embryo."[59]

After reading the reports of Alexeev in the Okhranka file on the Masons as the new Police Department director in 1912, S.P. Beletsky dismissed the conspiracy findings as baseless. When Grand Duke Nicholas Nicholaevich, the army commander, subsequently asked him to inquire into Masonic influence on the officers of the guards' regiments in St Petersburg, Beletsky again found no evidence of subversion by Masons and this time characterized the members in Russia as mere "occultists."[60]

Taking just the opposite stand was a secret Okhranka circular in 1915 to the heads of all agents in the field. It emphatically warned that new efforts to subvert the state, church, and monarchy were under way through the organization of Masonic lodges disguised as merely occult, philosophical, scientific, and graphological organizations. These particular subversive groups all had ties to Masons abroad and were insidiously spreading oppositional propaganda to new recruits in their private meetings. Clearly implied was the need for informants to penetrate all such groups.[61]

What the Okhranka did not then know and would never discover, surprisingly enough, was that truly secret groups modelled on Masonry but having no links to it had taken form by this time as meeting places for dedicated liberals at the very highest levels.[62] Created wholly outside the Masonic organizational framework to serve a purely political purpose, these symposia convened to debate liberal policy plans in the homes of members. They kept no record or membership lists. N.V. Nekrasov, a member of the left wing of the Constitutional Democratic party and a close ally of Miliukov, is credited with starting this unique organization. Rejecting ritual and admitting women, it grew to become a network of very small local and provincial lodges under a grand council, whose national congress framed broad policy resolutions but placed no obligation on individual members to accept them as required. Its purpose was to hold democrats and liberals together to act in concert with Miliukov, who, it so happened, rejected repeated offers to join.[63] Only some three hundred people belonged to this intimate liberal fellowship by the time of the February revolution in 1917, not one of them an Okhranka informer.[64]

One liberal deliberately kept in the dark about these new lodges was Prince D.I. Bebutov, whom some organizers wrongly suspected of having ties with the police because he met with Manuilov-Manasevich, a questionable figure believed to have connections with the secret police. The anti-government political activities of Bebutov, rather, had caused the Okhranka to consider him a security risk; it opened a file on him when he donated 10,000 rubles to the Kadets.[65] When Manuilov was asked by the Extraordinary Investigating Commission of the Provisional Government in 1917 about Bebutov's service to the police, Manuilov knew of none.[66]

After September 1915, when hopes ended for cooperation between the autocratic government and the centre coalition of the Duma called the Progressive Bloc, the liberal lodges allied with Miliukov's efforts to preserve the monarchy under a new constitutional order; when that effort failed in the collapse of the tsarist regime, they supported his creation of the Provisional Government in 1917 as a transitional body to a new Russian democracy, with founder Nekrasov and fellow members Alexander Kerensky and M.I. Tereshchenko filling cabinet seats.[67] (Assertions that several members of the government were Masons are without foundation.)

Kerensky later expressed his vehement dissent to the "absurd" thesis of some critics that the lodges' secret activities had unseated the tsar, and he summed up all their efforts as "directed toward the establishment in Russia of a democracy based on broad social reforms and on a federal state order." Revealing that he joined the network just after his election to the Fourth Duma in 1912, he also explained that the lodges ensured secrecy by keeping no membership lists or written records.[68]

Prince V.A. Obolensky, a leading Kadet and member of its Central Committee from 1910 to 1917, likewise came forward after the revolution to speak about the liberal network as a former member. He made the point that, although the members of the secret group had been united in their rejecting revolution before February 1917, subsequent fractious disagreements on policy had caused it to fall apart.[69] He could remember only one Bolshevik within the ranks and few Jews, none in leading positions. Accordingly, this Masonic-like organization was not Masonic, although it was decidedly secret and organized for democratic political purposes.

Fears about the liberals in the last years of the Empire rested on the decisive role of that political grouping (whose most widely known expression was the Union of Liberation) in promoting a popular movement in the 1905 revolution. As articulate and skilled organizers of the popular unions and societies that spread widely and as advocates of an influential reform program, liberals did pose a formidable threat to the intransigent autocracy. Where the Okhranka failed badly as a gatherer and analyser of intelligence, however, was in not recognizing that the autocracy could and should have worked with the liberals to modernize the political structure of the Russian Empire.

Not only did the Okhranka remain in the dark about the existence of the liberal "Masonic" organization led by Nekrasov, but it also failed to penetrate the inner councils of the main liberal parties, the Kadets, the Octobrists, and the Party of Popular Freedom. The ability of the Okhranka to send dozens of undetected secret agents into the ranks of the Social Democrats and the Socialist Revolutionaries contrasts sharply with its anaemic effort to place observers among the liberals' leadership.

In its basic form, the Okhranka was a fighting organization to combat terrorists and revolutionaries; its speciality was combatting conspiracy against the government. It had become expert and highly successful in this assignment by establishing a wide network of secret agents. But the Russian liberals were neither secret, conspiratorial, nor interested in organizing violence against the government, although they often expressed their sympathies for radicals and even terrorists. They published newspapers which discussed and promoted the parties' policies. The liberal parties had no subversive aims, although confidentiality was often imposed for their most delicate gatherings, as, for instance, meetings of party central committees.

To plant spies among the inner group of party leaders proved impossible. The leaders of Russian liberalism had been well acquainted with one another for years. No agent could get close to them and none would think of informing the police about confidential meetings and conversations with his colleagues. The most important Okhranka agent reporting of the liberals was an Austrian national by the name of I.I. Drilikh, who worked for the liberal Moscow daily, *Russian Word*. Drilikh was assigned to get to know the reporters and writers who covered the liberal movement and to learn from them what the major parties were planning. He was regularly debriefed by the head of the Moscow Okhranka himself, A.P. Martynov, who much enjoyed their long conversations ranging widely over the Moscow cultural scene. Other liberal publications were also targets, but these efforts ultimately yielded some completely inaccurate appraisals of the liberal movement.

The Okhranka warned its networks on 2 September 1914, just after the beginning of the First World War, that the lull in revolutionary activity was only because of a temporary rallying to the cause of the nation against the common enemy. The leadership of a renewed opposition would be the same as over the past decade. It would center on the left-wing of the Kadets, who had by its political activities since 1904 "created a favourable basis of propaganda and agitation for clearly revolutionary ideas." The Okhranka told its network, "the Kadets under the flag of the 'Constitutional Democratic Party' hide their republican goals."[70] These warnings to the political police came only one week after the Kadets had joined other oppositionists in the State Duma to promise suspension of the struggle against the autocratic regime while the Russian Empire faced the Central Powers in war. The Okhranka dismissed such professions and insisted that liberal leaders, while "externally professing loyalty are secret leaders of revolutionary organizations." The idea that the Kadets were revolutionaries aiming to bring about a violent overthrow of the imperial government is the predominant theme of all Okhranka reporting and instructions, beginning in 1905. This thesis is not entirely at variance with what the liberals intended, but the Okhranka proved to be wide of the mark in assessing the main objectives of Russian liberals, especially the Constitutional Democrats.

Two characteristics of the Okhranka appear to be responsible for a lack of objectivity in assessing the Kadets and their intentions. First, a number of high officials believed in the revolutionary intentions of the liberals and periodically issued statements of their own warning police officers and agents about them. Second, with such political certainty constantly emanating from St Petersburg, it would have been the unusual agent, indeed, who would have reported a view of the liberals that he knew in advance his superiors did not wish to hear.

Instead, the Okhranka, desperate to stop a rising tide of public hostility against the old regime, hurt the autocracy further by finding enemies where they did not exist, such as among the Masons. As for the Jews, the Okhranka as an institution saw the folly of targeting them, and did not, as is often thought, issue the *Protocols of the Elders of Zion* to blame the troubles of the autocracy on the Jews. Still, the Okhranka was unable to control some of its own officers or other sections of the government who saw in anti-Semitism a means of focusing popular discontent against a convenient target.

CHAPTER ELEVEN

The Tsarist Police
and Pogroms

This chapter assesses the extent of police involvement in pogroms – a Russian word meaning mob assaults against Jews and other minority groups. The mob brutality that the term describes was most pronounced between 1881 and 1905 and struck critics everywhere as a brutal throwback to a distant past and proof of the barbaric policies of the Russian autocracy. Tsarism stood convicted of employing violence against its own citizens, especially those of Jewish nationality.

Critics assigned the lion's share of blame to the imperial police, who were said to have forsaken their role as the enforcers of law and order in the Empire and actually instigated mob criminal assaults, perhaps in fulfilment of a diabolical plan to direct popular anger from conditions of Russian life to Jews and other minorities. Assuming the vast powers of the imperial government, and arguing from the scope and ferocity of the pogroms, critics often concluded that they could only have happened with police involvement.

Among the disturbing charges against the imperial police has been the claim that it deliberately incited one part of the population against another – an act that was a violation of the Empire's own criminal code – and this continues to be a widely accepted view among historians. Recently, for instance, in describing the Baku riots in 1905 pitting Azerbaijanis against Armenians, Audrey Alstadt-Mirhadi writes, "As was the case in the pogroms against the Jews elsewhere in the Empire, there is clear evidence of instigation by agent provocateurs. In Baku the goal was to divert energy and attention from the labor movement."[1] A clear implication of this statement is that the government deliberately incited mob action as a weapon in the struggle against the left.

Other chapters have assessed several episodes in Russian history where the security police have been charged with illegal operations and have argued that these complex political and social events did not, on the evidence, occur because of deliberate police actions directed from above. The discussion below takes up the controversial issue of the pogroms.

Local police and Gendarmes sometimes contributed to pogroms because they did not act swiftly enough; at other times individual policemen took part in anti-Semitic activity. High officials sometimes pridefully expressed their anti-Semitism, but there is no evidence pointing to deliberate actions by high police officials, including those in the Okhranka, designed to incite Russians and others to attack Jews.

In the early 1880s, several weeks after the assassination of Alexander II, an unprecedented series of events occurred in Russia. They took the form of massive social turmoil with a powerful anti-Semitic undercurrent. A series of anarchic pogroms broke out against Jews. Coincidentally, this happened when the newly established Department of Police was in the first stages of setting up the security divisions, but the latter had nothing to do with the pogroms.

In the spring of 1881 in the provinces of the Pale of Settlement[2] – the required place of residence for the Empire's Jews – a series of shocking pogroms occurred. The first occurred on 15 April in the city of Elizavetgrad, and the wave of agitation spread to other cities: to Kiev on 26 April, to Anan'ev on 27 April, and to Kishinev on 29 April. From the cities, the agitation flooded into nearby villages.

In Elizavetgrad district the pogroms engulfed twenty-five settlements, and in Kiev district, forty-two. In May pogroms broke out in Odessa, Nikolaev, Alexandrov, and Romny. In November a second pogrom took place in Odessa, followed by one in December in Warsaw. In the spring of 1882 there were signs that there would be a repetition of the previous year. In March there was a second wave in Anan'ev, in June-July in Borispol, Dubossary, and Pereiaslavl. According to official figures, 259 pogroms took place in 1881–2, 219 of them in villages and hamlets. In 1883 clashes took place in Rostov-on-Don, Ekaterinoslav, Krivoi Rog; and in 1884 in Nizhnii Novgorod. Robbery of Jewish homes and businesses and massacres of the Jews themselves were characteristic of these events. Although these regions had a history of clashes between Jews and non-Jews – they had been lacerated by strife in the sixteenth and seventeenth centuries – these events of the 1880s were different.

Massive pogromist upheavals were entirely new; the government had not foreseen them and responded sluggishly. The authorities failed to halt the spread of violence from one village to the next. After studying these events, Samuel Dubnow, the historian, concluded in 1909 that they demonstrated advance knowledge by the government and showed that the police were coordinating the pogroms. How else could one explain that "in a well-organized state over the course of an extended period, the government, knowing each time about the pogroms under preparation, permitted itself to be caught unawares and did not take any preventative measures."[3] Even the head of the Kiev Gendarmes, V.D. Novitsky, wrote that the three-day anti-Semitic pogrom in 1881 in Kiev was the responsibility of the governor-general, A.R. Drentel'n (an earlier head of the Third Section). Local authorities, explained Novitsky, sabotaged the orders of M.T. Loris-Melikov, the minister of the interior, to take decisive measures to prevent pogroms. The commander of the Corps of Gendarmes, P.S. Vannovsky, ordered the military to preserve its neutrality and informed it in advance that any soldiers who used a bayonet or a whip against those participating in a pogrom would be prosecuted before a court. But, Novitsky asserted, Drentel'n changed these instructions after the pogromists were on the move and he had been knocked down by them in the street.[4]

Because the wave of pogroms began so soon after the assassination of Alexander II, contemporaries quickly concluded that the murder of the tsar had produced the outbreaks. In the opinion of many opponents of the autocracy, the pogroms were an answering blow of the conservatives to the liberal statesmen of the era who had hoped to introduce consultants from the upper classes into the government. Named as the spiritual encourager of this trend of anti-Semitism was K.P. Pobedonostsev, with the main organizers said to be the minister of the interior, Count N.P. Ignatiev, and the director of the Department of Police, V.K. Plehve. The anti-Semitic views of the new tsar, Alexander III, his top police officials, and members of his closest circle took the form of anti-Semitic legislation. But the tsar and his advisors were also firm believers in the necessity of restoring order after the tumultuous 1870s; they had no wish to incite vast elements of the population to a form of popular upheaval.

As for the pogromists themselves, they believed firmly in the rightness of their cause and in their actions. They drew support from anti-Semitic newspapers and often inflamed the mood of unlettered groups by reading aloud excerpts from these publications. Volunteer agitators expounded on the theme that decrees issued by the tsar allowing anti-Semitic activity were being suppressed by disloyal subordinates. Rumours easily spread through the Russian cities and into the countryside and officials reported them to St Petersburg. In September 1881 the governor of Chernigov province reported to the minister of the interior: "The Tsar Alexander Alexandrovich [Alexander III] – it is being said from mouth to mouth – is not a real tsar, because he still has not been crowned and therefore he cannot send out a ukaz to kill the Jews, but only to destroy their property. After his coronation, then he will send out a ukaz to slaughter Jews, because they killed his father and drink our blood."[5]

Some officials made known their anti-Semitic views and thereby fed the widely held idea that St Petersburg approved assaults against the Jewish population. Count Ignatiev, who led the Interior Ministry early in the reign of Alexander III, spoke as if he sympathized with those who participated in the pogroms when he told a rabbi in St Petersburg that "Jews themselves are guilty of the pogroms: by siding with the nihilists they deprive the government of the possibility of protecting them from violence."[6]

Police officials in the provinces knew about the viewpoint of the ministerial leadership; it was not necessary that such information pass along official channels. The police chief of Elizavetgrad, I.P. Bogdanovich, recalled that for several weeks before the pogrom in his city he entertained a guest from the capital, a state secretary whom he does not name. The official visitor expressed himself reservedly, but clearly defined the borders of possible connivance:

If, God forbid, a Jewish pogrom should occur, you will not be guilty, you would not be involved in it, and you do not have it in your power to foresee ... an unexpected explosion ... of popular indignation ... the economic basis, exploitation ... finally, even religion, well and if they begin to rob rich Russians, Germans, this is already another problem ... then this is entirely negligence and the police are guilty.[7]

Alexander II's assassination is sometimes seen as a cause of the outbreaks of violence against Jews because of alleged belief that the Jews were responsible. Although agitators made this connection to incite mobs, there is no factual support for it. Jewish participation in the first populist circles was practically non-existent. Jews made up only 4 percent (about the same as the Jewish proportion of the general population) of those prosecuted before the courts at the end of the 1870s for involvement in political crimes. At the time of the pogrom in Kiev in April 1881, rumours circulated among the crowds that a Jewish woman, one Gesia, had killed the tsar. But Gesia Helfman, a member of People's Will, was not among the group of bombers on the Catherine Canal, and the grenade which killed the tsar was thrown by a Pole, I.I. Grinevitski.[8]

The ease with which right-wing agitators manipulated the so-called Jewish question to rouse elements of the population attracted revolutionary populists on the left of the political spectrum. Some were prepared to follow the lead of the anti-Semites. The historian Iu.I. Gessen describes their thinking in this way: "There is information about the role of some members of the People's Will Party who considered the pogroms an aspect of the revolutionary upheaval: that the movement which would be easiest to direct against the Jews, could then be turned against the gentry and government officials. Proclamations were prepared which were summons to attacks on Jews."[9] The executive committee of the People's Will did issue such proclamations on 30 August 1881 but they were not distributed widely.

Some officials, and more particularly, peasants, small merchants, and assorted thugs might deceive themselves about the role of Jews in the assassination of the tsar. But such views do not prove the participation of leaders of the government or the police in the organizing of pogroms. A later writer, Hans Rogger, doubts that such a cautious government leader as K.P. Pobedonostsev, the procurator of the Holy Synod and a close advisor to Alexander iii, would risk arousing popular emotions. Pobedonostsev understood that an aroused pogromist mob could easily slip out of control. As for Ignatiev, he assumed the post of minister of the interior only after the beginning of the pogroms. Soon after taking office on 6 May 1881 he issued orders to local authorities: "Such violations of order ought to be not only suppressed but foreseen: for the first duty of government is ensure the security of the population from any kind of violence and savage arbitrariness."[10] A year later his successor, Count D.A. Tolstoy, warned police who participated in pogroms that "those found guilty will be dismissed."[11]

V.K. Plehve, the director of the Department of Police, could hardly be single-handedly responsible for the pogroms. In any case, as Rogger points out, the accusors of Plehve have never produced a single piece of convincing evidence to support their claims.[12] Aronson, who has studied the pogroms of 1881, rejects the version that police authorities and the Holy Druzhina, the volunteer detachments who swore to protect the tsar, stirred up the pogroms. He explains that the pogroms of 1881 usually spread from the cities to the country, and that they were started by seasonal workers who were returning to their homes. These workers travelling by rail were joined by peasants working in industrial enterprises and both acted from motives of economic frustration. The latter saw Jews as their main competitors in business. Having begun in a few cities, the violence spread to many more villages. The pogroms, says Aronson, were a sorry response to conditions of modernization and industrialization in Russia rather than an expression of ancient national and religious hatreds.[13] The expanding railway network had provided a means to spread anti-Semitic agitation in the same fashion that it would later encourage the strike movement.

Department of Police leaders in St Petersburg had no part in stirring up the pogroms. Local agitators played a major role and they took advantage of social and economic discontent. But this is not to say that no policemen participated in the pogroms; an assessment of individual regions turns up evidence that some police officers, acting on their own, participated in pogroms.

After the pogroms in the Pale of Settlement in the early 1880s, the government formed commissions to investigate the life and occupations of Jews. There were fifteen provincial commissions (one for each of the provinces of the Pale) and one Higher (the Pahlen) Commission. The main objective, although it was not announced, was to find out why Jews, who made up about 10 percent of the population of the Pale, could not get along with the Russians, Ukrainians, Belorussians, and to a lesser degree, with the Poles. The commissions' materials testify to the existence of serious social tensions in those areas where the Jewish populations lived. According to the guidelines for the studies, which defined the quality of life, Jews had an undoubted advantage over other inhabitants of the Pale. At the same time, it must be said, that Jews could be considered well off only against the background of the unfortunate Russian countryside. The repressed majority of Jews dragged out an impoverished existence.

But even in the Pale, and to a certain extent outside of its borders, there flourished a stratum of Jewish financiers, merchants, and industrialists. Precisely in these areas, which had developed intensively in the second half of the nineteenth century, Jews of energy and talent found rewards. They conducted one-third of the trade and industrial enterprises in the Pale. According to statistical information gathered in 1884, in the fifteen Russian provinces of the Pale, 31.3 percent of the merchants of the First Guild were Jews, and in the ten Polish provinces their percentage was 61.7 percent. Among the merchants of the Second Guild, 53.6 percent in the Russian provinces and 65.4 percent in the Polish provinces were Jews. In the main cities the figures were even more pronounced; in Vilnius, 77.5 percent, in Belostok, 78.3 percent, and in Kovno, 80.6 percent. Jews were prominent in the wine business. They ran 55.3 percent of the distilleries, 89.9 percent of the wineshops, 77.8 percent of the taverns, 67.5 percent of the pothouses, and 52.5 percent of the inns. The high percentage of Jews in this sphere of commerce was to become explosive because it fed an anti-Semitic claim that they made the Russian people into alcoholics. Less pronounced was the presence of persons of Jewish origins as operators of industrial enterprises. According to data from 1855, Jews owned 31 percent of the factories in the Pale.[14]

A supplemental cause contributing to tensions between Jews and others was the competition among artisans. In the Pale there were 301,560 Jewish artisans. They had long maintained guild organizations and cooperative societies that had helped them survive in an hostile environment. A former rabbi, Ia. Brafman, wrote about these: "For the Jewish artisans, there was always the brotherhood and the *kahal*; it follows that in the struggle between the artisan-Jew and the artisan-Christian the first ought to get along and come out as victor – one could not resist the many."[15]

High numbers of Jews in the financial world, the result of a whole series of historical, social, and psychological causes, furthered the development of anti-Semitic feeling. Jews were accused of monopolizing trade, occupying themselves as money-lenders, and taking bread from Russian artisans. Some high officials were ready to draw the conclusion that poverty among Russian peasants was the result of economic well-being on the part of Jews. In his report about the condition of the Jews, Count Ignatiev said, "Thanks to cohesion and unity, they [the Jews], with few exceptions, directed all their forces not to improving the productive strength of the state, but primarily to the exploitation of the impoverished classes of the surrounding population."[16]

In May 1882 Ignatiev proposed "temporary rules" which prevented persons of Jewish religious beliefs from settling outside of the cities and small towns of the Pale and from buying or leasing land. Ignatiev's alleged purpose was concern about the security of Jews, who were subject to violence from the peasants. But the true objective of this reform was actually dictated by the wish to protect the rural population from unfair commercial intermediaries, and it led to the further isolation of the Jewish population. The restrictive legislation was widened by a subsequent law which prevented free movement of Jews, this time inside the Pale. Other measures restricted Jewish membership in the liberal professions, in local government, and applied special censorship measures to Jewish publications.

Ignatiev's temporary rules only intensified social tensions. Jews were expelled from the rural areas, and the amount of land leased by them contracted by almost seven times. According to land ownership data in the census of 1897, the Jewish population by that time held only 3.29 percent of the land. At the same time those of Jewish origin continued to be a major presence in commercial activity. I.M. Bikerman writes, "Jews make up almost three-quarters (72.8 percent) of the trading class; but in some parts of the Pale and in certain sectors of trade the percentage is even higher. In the northwest region of one thousand traders 886 are Jews, of a thousand in the bread trade, 930 are Jews, which is to say that almost the entire bread trade is in Jewish hands."[17]

A new development was the appearance of large number of Jews who worked as hired labourers. Figures show 392,000 individuals (or 8.04 percent of the population in this category), the majority of them apprentices who were confined to the traditional guild system. At the beginning of the twentieth century factory workers numbered 45,000 persons and 92,000 were unskilled workers.[18] In the industrial south, where there was a good deal of unemployment, replacement workers from this pool were viewed with hostility.

Government measures, taken in response to the pogroms of the 1880s, actually intensified the tensions between Jews and the rest of the population in the Pale of Settlement. This was the principal result of restricting the movement and economic and professional activities of Jews.

These tensions boiled to the surface in the Pale once more in the terrible pogroms in Kishinev and Gomel in 1903. Although largely confined to these two cities, these outbreaks were much crueller than the disturbances of the early 1880s. The difference in their character foreshadowed the period of immense upheaval through which Russia was about to pass. Social and economic factors again predominated. In the province of Bessarabia, of which Kishinev was the capital, Jews made up 37.4 percent of the urban population, and in Mogilev province, where Gomel was a principal city, the Jewish part of the population was 52.6 percent. Trade to a significant degree was in Jewish hands.

During the two decades after the massive pogroms of the 1880s, the Jewish population adopted new attitudes towards the Russian imperial state and society. Attacks on Jews and restrictive legislation served to politicize them. Between 1892 and 1902, of the 1,178 persons who were subject to police inquiry for participating in populist revolutionary organizations, 181 were Jews, and of the 5,047 investigated from Social Democratic circles, 1,180 were Jews.[19] Jews by no means dominated the revolutionary movement, but their proportion was much greater than their number in the population as a whole. Jews committed themselves not only to radical causes, however, but were a diverse group in Russian life, both politically and socially.

Anti-Semitic propaganda in Russia, however, made no distinctions, but lumped all Jews into a single, undifferentiated mass which allegedly aimed to subvert the Russian Empire. One of the principal figures behind the propaganda against Jews was a native of Kishinev, P.A. Krushevan, the editor of the short-lived St Petersburg paper, *Banner*.[20] In Kishinev he published *The Bessarabian (Bessarabets)*. Local Jews accused him of inciting the pogroms in Kishinev through the columns of his paper, and one Pincus Dashevsky, a professed Zionist, attempted to assassinate him with a dagger. Krushevan also fanned latent anti-Semitism among the businessmen of Kishinev. One of the merchants, another anti-Semite named G.A. Pronin, published inflammatory articles and instigated the Russian and Moldavian populations to violence against "aliens." His exaggerations of national and religious differences resonated especially among conservative clergy of the Russian Orthodox Church. Pronin himself was in contact with John of Kronstadt, an Orthodox priest widely known for his anti-Semitic sermons. He sent messages to Pronin which included accusations against Jews.

Turmoil commenced in Kishinev on 6 April 1903, the first day of the Orthodox Easter celebration; Jewish Passover had taken place one week before. According to superstition, these days were especially dangerous for Christian children, since Jews were said to use their blood for religious rites. Immediately prior to the pogrom, rumours spread that in neighbouring Dubossary a ritual killing had taken place. In Kishinev itself a rumour spread that a Jewish doctor had attempted to extract blood from a young serving girl. These false rumours triggered the destruction of a synagogue and massive looting of Jewish homes. Towards noon on 7 April the first killing occurred and by evening thirty-eight Jews and four Christians were dead. By mid-afternoon the governor, R.S. von Raaben, issued orders to the police and military and by evening they had largely suppressed the pogrom.

Groups opposed to the government laid the blame for the Kishinev pogrom on the authorities and, in particular, on the minister of the interior,[21] although accusations against V.K. Plehve did not appear in the press; the censorship forbade specific accusations against state officials in print. But they circulated anyway, and appeared openly in foreign newspapers. An alleged confidential letter from Plehve to von Raaben reached the English papers. The letter made reference to the struggle of the Christian population against its enemies, but the letter was a forgery by an unknown hand. The prose, for one thing, is not Plehve's; nor was it Plehve's administrative style to send private letters to subordinates. This would have been especially so in the case of von Raaben, who did not enjoy Plehve's confidence. In any event, documents show that Plehve, having received news of the pogrom from the local authorities, undertook all measures possible under the law to restore order. He also reported to the tsar about his supplementary measures: "Despite the summoning of the military and the arrest of more than 60 rioters, disorders continued. The governor requested authority to impose measures of strengthened security. I approved his request by telegram."[22]

Following the pacification of the outbreak, Plehve secured the tsar's agreement to dismiss von Raaben because of his poor handling of the disturbances. He sent his director of police, A.A. Lopukhin, to Kishinev to investigate the conduct of the local authorities at the time of the pogroms. Lopukhin did not discover any traces of premeditated preparation of the pogrom, but he concluded that the events could not have taken place without the participation of the lower police ranks.[23] The Gendarme officers seemed to be duplicitous. Two days before the pogrom, the head of the Kishinev Okhranka, Baron Levendal', had sent a telegram to St Petersburg reporting that a tense atmosphere had developed in the city. He complained that the chief of the police had not taken preventative measures against a possible disturbance. At the same time, Levendal's good relations with local anti-Semites such as Pronin were well known. Lopukhin suspected that the Gendarme officer simultaneously had favoured the pogromists and moved to cover himself by the advance warning to his superiors in St Petersburg based on suppositions.

Actions of the local police contributed to the allegations about Plehve, but the minister frankly condemned the police in a report to Nicholas II. Plehve forthrightly and accurately recognized that insubordinate policemen subject to his ministry were a key element in the pogroms. He wrote: "Because of the disorganization of the rank and file of the police, who were not under authorized control, all these excesses were carried out with impunity. This even more encouraged and aroused the thugs. The ranks of the police, not having taken preventative measures, turned out to be completely powerless to oppose the disorders."[24]

A somewhat different view of the events came from Prince S.D. Urusov, who replaced von Raaben as the governor of Bessarabia. He concluded that from somewhere high in the Ministry of Interior a hint might have been passed down to the local authorities on the desirability of using force against the Jews. This hint "rolled down the stairway" of the Corps of Gendarmes and was seen as an order when it reached bottom. On the other hand, despite Urusov's belief, police hostile towards Jews could easily have acted without any hints. Prince Urusov also found that much social tension at the local level was the consequence of the anti-Semitic legislation of the imperial government, which the police were supposed to enforce: "I must note that the hatred of the police rank and file toward the Jewish population was intensified by ... the completely senseless and unachievable objectives of the legislation on Jews."[25]

Pogroms in Kishinev led to events in Gomel. The widespread anger following the Easter outburst especially roused young Jews in Gomel to protect themselves and their people. They now believed that they could not depend on the police. Jacob Shumatsky, a member of the Jewish labour union, the Bund, recalled: "After the Kishinev pogrom, the Executive Committee of the Bund took up the question of self-defence."[26] There was widespread agreement on this course of action and because 28,000 Jews lived in a city of only 47,000, they were confident of their ability to protect themselves.

Gendarmes later insisted that detachments of Jewish youth began target practice in the spring in the outskirts of the city and that stores of small arms were being accumulated in the synagogues. The authorities insisted that the Jews of Gomel were the instigators of the disorders. Major-General Baron Medem reported to the assistant minister of the interior and commander of the Corps of Gendarmes, von Val': "Sensing the complete powerlessness of the police and knowing their numerical superiority over the peaceful Christian population, lately the defiant Jews challenged the masses of the people, and even the Russian intelligentsia in the government including the officers, who are serving in the Gomel infantry regiment, were subjected to some incidents and assaults."[27]

A trifling argument over a barrel of herring at the merchants' building was the pretext for the clash of 29 August 1903. Around five thousand Jews quickly gathered on the square and shouts were heard to revenge the Kishinev pogrom. Troops arrived and restored order with difficulty. The head of the provincial Gendarme administration, Colonel Poliakov, expressing a view rather typical of the police, telegraphed on 4 September to St Petersburg about the initial fighting: "The Jews, armed with knives, daggers, revolvers, and various clubs, trying to scuffle with the Russians, were held back by the troops, and fired at the soldiers from under fences and from garrets."[28]

These opening events were called "the Russian pogrom." This phrase was meant to underscore that a reverse pogrom had taken place and that the Russian and Belorussian populations were aggrieved. The police chief of Gomel, Raevsky, tried to prevent further confrontations, but the lower ranks sympathized with the Christian population. A former police officer, Solov'ev, emerged as a leader of the mob during a scuffle in the public market. The chief of police was unable to persuade Okhranka leaders to take action, so he turned to the Gendarme captain Dudkin and asked him to set up surveillance over the railway shops located in the city. It was there, according to local police reports, that the workers were organizing to take revenge on the Jews. The reports from the Gendarmes were not alarming: "The Gendarmes assured me that in the workshops all was tranquil and that there was no reason to expect disorders."[29] The police chief nonetheless readied his men.

On the afternoon of 1 September the workers began to move into the city from the shops on the outskirts, but they were held back by a detachment of police under the chief himself. Captain Dudkin later reported that the police chief acted arbitrarily because the workers were merely headed for dinner and had no criminal intent. Then rumours swept the workshops, allegedly spread by Gendarme non-commissioned officers, that the Jews in the city were cutting up their wives and children. The workers became highly agitated against the Jews and anyone whom they considered their accomplices. According to the testimony of the commander of the company, who had been summoned to the workshops, the shout went up in the crowd, "Give us the chief of police. We will make short work of him."[30]

The police and the company of soldiers restrained the crowd without difficulty, but an unknown assailant wounded the assistant police chief Brzhovsky in the back. Accompanied by the shout of "the Jews have killed the assistant chief," the mob sacked the houses and shops of Jews. Nine people were killed, five Jews and four Russians.

In the Gomel pogrom, the Gendarmes clearly behaved differently from the local police; Gendarme soldiers incited the mobs, and the local police attempted to restrain them. The attitude of the governor was completely prejudicial, and the Gendarmes could perhaps have drawn their inspiration from him. He reported to Plehve afterwards, "This entire 'Bund' and these social-democrats, they are all Jews. True, there were instances when Christians took part in these events, but they took sides because of the violations of others – the Jews were the ones who started it." He said that his ordering of strict police measures over the Jews "will not prevent an additional new explosion of national hatred if the Jews themselves do not change their relationship with the Christians."[31]

Local officials in Gomel typically assumed the worst of the Jews and insisted that they were responsible for the pogrom, but there is no evidence that higher officials in St Petersburg gave encouragement to the pogrom.

Two years later another series of pogroms struck the Russian Empire, occurring in widely scattered cities. In February bloody carnage erupted between Armenians and Azerbaijanis in Baku. In April 1905 the Jews of Zhitomir and Simferopol were attacked, in June there was a pogrom in Nizhnii Novgorod, and in July in Kerch. The scale of these attacks was larger than before. In Baku, according to official data, 232 persons were killed. Each of these bloody battles was comparable with the worst of the pogroms of the previous decades. Taken together, they exceeded anything that the country had seen to that point.

All the outbreaks of violence in that month developed according to a kind of archetypal pattern. The Manifesto of 17 October, which granted the citizens of the Russian Empire basic civil liberties and a new legislative assembly, proved to be the stimulus. As news of the Manifesto spread, meetings and demonstrations began throughout Russia. Numerous speakers hailed the end of despotism in the first days following the Manifesto, but the revolutionary euphoria began to give way to a sobering up. A kind of massive movement of the heretofore "silent" masses produced an outpouring of support for the traditional patriarchal order. For one thing, massive popular demonstrations – which included anti-Semitic elements – expressed indignation at the scorning of the symbols of the autocracy such as tsarist monograms, portraits of Nicholas II, and busts of his predecessors. Of particular irritation to the anti-Semites was the evident satisfaction of the Jewish population which viewed the Manifesto, prematurely as it turned out, as the long-awaited arrival of equal rights. Every placard seemingly paraded by Jews, every Star of David put on show, only prompted more rumours.

Rumour mills turned out rash words attributed to Jews. Kievans spread the story of a person of "non-Russian visage" who put on his head a frame from a portrait of Nicholas II and declared, "Now I am the tsar." Odessites spread the story of Jewish bragging to their Russian acquaintances, "We, the Jews, gave you God, and now we will give you a tsar." Other rumours concerned outrages against sacred objects of the Orthodox Church by persons said to be Jews.

Responding to the demonstrations mounted in favour of the Manifesto were "patriotic" parades with marchers carrying religious banners and portraits of the tsar. Local government officials, conservative merchants, and priests of the Orthodox Church organized them. In some cities there were clashes between rival demonstrations; in others, armed detachments, manned by members of illegal parties, fired on their opponents. Some patriotic demonstrators responded to the summons of their leaders and turned into pogromists. Peasants in the nearby urban areas simply followed the example of the inhabitants of the cities. They smashed commercial shops and set fire to farmhouses rented or owned by Jews.

Although there is no precise record of all the pogroms in the fall of 1905, virtually all contemporaries accept fairly high figures for injury, death, and destruction. The maximum figure is that 660 villages, towns, and cities were disturbed by pogroms; at least four thousand people were killed and ten thousand injured. According to calculations based on figures recorded by the Department of Police, the Ministry of Justice, the press, and other sources, between 18 October and 1 November 1905, pogroms occurred in 358 population centres (108 cities, seventy suburbs and smaller towns, and 180 villages). There were 1,622 people killed and 3,544 wounded. These data are not exhaustive. The greatest number of deaths occurred in Odessa, which registered 618 dead and 561 wounded. Next was Ekaterinoslav (88 and 231), Kiev (68 and 301), Tomsk (68 and 86), Kishinev (53 and 67), Minsk (52 and 100), and Baku (51 and 83). Pogroms also occurred in other cities far from the Pale, such as Kursk, Tver, and Iaroslavl.[32]

In the fall of 1905 anti-Semitic pogroms were entwined with assaults on members of other minority groups and it is possible to establish the national groups of about two-thirds of the people who suffered death or physical harm from the pogroms. Of these, 58.4 percent of the dead and 42.6 percent of the injured were Jews. The rest were Russians, Ukrainians, Belorussians, Armenians, and others. Those who seemed to be enemies of the autocratic order were also deemed vulnerable by the pogromists. Their targets included the democratic intelligentsia, liberal political activists, and students from the higher and the secondary schools. All this was clear, for example, in a telegram from the Gendarme Lieutenant-Colonel Subbotin about the events in the town of Nezhin: "The people roamed the streets looking for any Russian democrats, dragged them from their apartments, forced them to stand in front of portraits publicly, to swear oaths, to join processions, and to sing hymns. The people sobbed. Jews were not present."[33]

Some newspapers, following the explosion of violence, concluded that only the government had the power to set in motion such a powerful, spreading series of events. The liberal South Russia (*Iuzhnaia Rossia*) declared: "The very scope of the Russian-wide organization of the counter-demonstrations with all of their scandalous variations shows that this was the business of the authorities, who had the means to arrange it; it was not done by feeble private organizations."[34] The opinion was widespread among those in opposition to the government that the assistant minister of the interior and supervisor of the police, Dmitry Fedorovich Trepov, was the prime instigator. He now rivalled Plehve as a candidate for a tsarist official who instigated pogroms, since Plehve, having been assassinated in 1904, could no longer be blamed for events at the end of 1905.

Trepov had already earned the enmity of anti-government groups. One of four brothers, he had spent his entire career in government service. He completed the Pazheskii Cadet Corps and served in tsar's household troops, but his real love was police work. Even as a boy, his favourite activity was to play policeman. A boyhood chum remembered that "he arranged toy figures, gave them assignments, positioned them to catch thieves, and to arrest members of criminal organizations."[35] Anecdotes abound about Trepov's tragicomic passion for order and a zealousness that exceeded the bounds of common sense.

Trepov received his first major assignment in 1896 when he became the police chief of Moscow. He was summoned to St Petersburg at the beginning of 1905 where he was to be named to the active army in the Far East. An attempt was made to assassinate him before he could leave, but he had earned a reputation in the capital for maintaining order in Moscow. Events now worked in favor of Trepov's promotion up the ladder of the imperial security system.

Following Bloody Sunday on 9 January 1905, the government fell into disarray. The opinion was widespread that the minister of the interior, Prince S.D. Sviatopolk-Mirsky, lacked the capacity to deal with deepening public turmoil. High officials sought a decisive military man to unite the security apparatus of the government to fight the revolutionaries, who were seeking to capitalize on popular discontent. A number of candidates were considered, and the influential court official A.A. Mosolov proposed his kinsman, Trepov. The minister of the imperial court, V.B. Frederiks, supported the nomination and the tsar named Trepov. Nicholas II's uncle, Grand Duke Sergei Alexandrovich, the governor general of Moscow, considered Trepov his protégé and wired him, "I remember everything, I am with you in spirit, God help and protect you. Sergei."[36] On 11 January 1905, two days after the massacre on the streets of the capital, Trepov became the governor-general of St Petersburg and, in April, he was named assistant minister of the interior and commander of the Corps of Gendarmes. As head of the police apparatus, he was now one of the Empire's most powerful figures and, because of his authority over the police, perhaps even more powerful than the new minister of the interior, A.G. Bulygin.

But the October Manifesto brought an end to Trepov's career. His detractors have asserted that the one-time favourite of the palace could not reconcile himself to the new constitutional order and so decided to "slam the door" before departing. On 14 October, Trepov ordered the troops of the capital garrison, "Don't use blanks and don't spare the bullets." When his kinsman Mosolov learned about these instructions, he asked Trepov: "Don't you understand that after this you will not be called Trepov but 'Gen. Don't Spare the Bullets?'" Trepov answered: "I know this and I know that this will be a dishonourable nickname, but otherwise I cannot face my own conscience. The military have to overcome their fear, for they had begun to turn sour."[37]

Although employing repressive policies against the popular disturbances, Trepov believed they were necessary only for a limited period. At the time, Nicholas II proposed to Trepov that he assume powers of a military dictator. But Trepov advised the tsar that it was impossible to rely purely on force to deal with the popular revolution. He argued for concessions. On the night of 16–17 October, Trepov, having just become familiar with the contents of the still unpublished Manifesto, wrote to the tsar: "Freedom of the press, of conscience, of assembly, of organization must be granted."[38] At this moment Trepov, because of his enormous influence at court, was a key figure in endorsing the October Manifesto. Far from being a reactionary and pogromist, he was one of the main founders of the new constitutional system.

Trepov relinquished his post right after the pogroms of the October Days. The news of his departure produced a widespread sigh of relief and the value of Russian securities rose on international markets. But Trepov did not abandon political life and the tsar named him commander of the imperial court, from which position he was said to exercise the powers of a dictator.[39]

At first the new commander enjoyed the complete confidence of the tsar. But he soon aroused Nicholas II's dissatisfaction by engaging in confidential negotiations with the liberal opposition about the possibility of forming a government of well-known public figures. In the eyes of the revolutionaries, on the other hand, Trepov was responsible for the organization of the pogroms during the October Days. Accusations against Trepov's reactionary influence undoubtedly encouraged terrorists to hunt him right up to his death from a heart attack in September 1906. No existing evidence, however, supports the allegation that Trepov sought to discredit the program of civic freedom granted under the October Manifesto, or that he played some kind of hidden role and secretly organized the pogroms.[40]

Supporting the theme of this chapter, the case of Trepov shows that the alleged pogromists at the centre of power were not guilty of inciting one part of the Russian population against another. It must be said that local police were sometimes inciters of pogroms, but not on orders from St Petersburg and higher police officials. There is no proof of any kind that a plan existed to use pogroms to rally support against revolutionaries and in favour of the tsar; indeed, there are many instances of Okhranka and Gendarme officers acting in timely fashion against mob violence.

Yet another cause helps to explain the disturbing effects of the publication of the October Manifesto on the population of imperial Russia. The document was written hastily, in secret, and therefore with no public or internal governmental discussion of the momentous issue of constitutional change. The Manifesto, a brief document, was moreover couched only in general terms; the spelling out of its principles was to come later.

Unforeseen consequences resulted. The sudden, unexpected news of this sharp turn in political life threw provincial authorities into confusion. Communications throughout the huge expanse of Russia were difficult under the best of circumstances, and a general strike during October had interrupted rail and telegraph traffic and the publication of newspapers. Acting with unaccustomed speed in the preparation and publication of the Manifesto, the government had taken no steps at all to prepare local officials for what was an overturning of the established constitutional order. The viceroy of the Caucasus, Count I.I. Vorontsov-Dashkov, requested a coded telegram from the capital confirming whether freedom had actually been granted. The governor-general of Irkutsk, Count P.I. Kutaisov, said that news of the Manifesto "spread around the city by rumour." Over several days, while still overseer of the police, Trepov had no communications at all with a majority of Russian cities. The Gendarme administrations and the city Okhranka detachments were unable to control local populations. Typical of the messages which began to stream into the Department of Police was that of the head of the Odessa Okhranka: "Normal life has come a stop ... we have no communications with our secret agents and the detectives are not on the job."[41] One of the consequences of the social storm of 1905 was a widespread breakdown of police authority partly because the central authorities had no contact by telegraph with local administrators and police officials.

During the revolutionary demonstrations which followed the publication of the Manifesto, crowds subjected uniformed police to verbal and physical abuse. In Vilnius, Jews tried to free one of their fellows who had been arrested for shooting at a police officer. Troops rushed to the scene of the fracas and killed or wounded forty people.

In some cities located outside of the Pale the issue of the police served as a direct cause of a pogrom. Following the Manifesto, the Kazan' city council voted to stop financing the police and created instead a "people's militia" made up of a number of students and members of illegal parties. The militia confiscated arms from police stations. On 21 October a patriotic demonstration turned against the militia, and its members took refuge in the building of the city council. The building was in turn surrounded by troops. According to the local paper, the governor of the province appeared and, "standing in the council chamber, he declared that if they did not leave the building within 15 minutes with their hands in the air, he would order a salvo of artillery."[42] In the ensuing skirmish, troops killed eight militiamen and captured the rest.

Similar events took place several hundred miles from Kazan' in the Siberian city of Tomsk. Judicial documents about a pogrom there give the following account: "Deputies of the town council and mayor Makushin appeared before the governor, Azancheev-Azanchevsky to tell him that they had fired the chief of police, stopped paying the policemen, and were organizing a militia. The governor agreed to the dismissal of the chief of police but said the question of the militia would have to be referred to the provincial administration."[43]

Defying the governor, the city council quickly organized a militia; this action prompted additional turbulence in the city. On 20 October a crowd of citizens approached police headquarters, demanded a portrait of the tsar, and set out to settle accounts with the militiamen. A detachment of militiamen had taken refuge in the administrative building of the Siberia railway, and the crowd, joined by soldiers, besieged the building. They then set fire to it and "many, who had appeared at the windows, escaped on to the roof and slid down the water pipes. The soldiers, on the side of the people, shot them with their rifles."[44] The majority were railway workers who had been caught up accidentally in the mob assault on their building.

Virtually everywhere in different cities the police made no secret of their negative response to the Manifesto. A police official in Zhitomir addressed local citizenry: "Did you know that they have declared freedom of conscience, word, meeting, and the inviolability of the individual?" He gave his own answer: "I will still break all of you like dogs, while you get your freedom."[45] Some police could be found among those who fanned nationalist tensions. On the streets of Irkutsk a policeman of Italian origin was told by another local policeman, "Those who are for the Russian people, come to this side of the street."[46] In Simferopol a senior policeman, S.N. Ermolenko, slashed to death several Jews who had gained entrance to the police station.[47]

But not only individuals among the police joined the pogromists. There were cases when wholesale defections from police departments occurred. One example took place in Kiev. Rafal'sky, the vice-governor, reported to Trepov about conditions in the city: "From time to time one encounters police officers engaging in open looting of Jewish stores. They are apathetic and indifferent to the consequences."[48] In Kiev to investigate the pogroms, Senator E.O. Turau detected an indifferent attitude toward the chief of police, Tsikhotsky. When he showed up on the streets a crowd of pogromists yelled, "Hurrah." When he demanded that they disperse, the thugs laughed and egged one another on and one said, "Don't be afraid, you fool, that's his little joke." But Tsikhotsky was unable to guarantee the security of the fashionable district of Lipki, where the wealthy had their homes, any more than he was the poor districts. Furthermore, according to Turau, a police officer named Pirozhkov of the Podol' district urged Kievans to attack Jews. When searches and arrests of pogromists commenced after the pogroms, the rioters complained, "You ordered us to rob, and now you are searching us."[49]

In Odessa, police incitement of pogromists was even more evident. This port on the Black Sea which had attracted a variety of national groups was a centre of social tensions. National divisions meant that in addition to traditional competition between traders and artisans, there was rivalry among groups of workers. Russian workers saw organized groups of Jewish and Armenians artisans especially as competitors, since they were in a position to monopolize job opportunities in large firms and at the port. Under the conditions of economic recession at the turn of the century, the incursion of Jews into non-traditional places of employment aroused strong resistance from Russians who were accustomed to filling certain kinds of jobs. This tension led to attacks by Russians even on Jews who were no actual threat to them.[50]

Already in the summer of 1905, prior to the October Manifesto, the port city of Odessa had became an epicentre of revolutionary events. The city authorities painfully endured the humiliation of the three July days when the mutinous battleship *Potemkin*, lying in the harbour, held the city in the sights of its 12-inch guns. After the mutineers sailed away to take refuge in Rumania, the head of the Odessa city administration, D.B. Neidgardt, ordered immediate instruction in sharpshooting and issued small arms to his officers. According to military testimony, "the policemen were practising by shooting at stuffed figures on which were scrawled the words 'striker' and 'student'."[51]

As fall approached, the city of Odessa became more tense by the day. The police chief reported on 16 October, the day before the Manifesto was published, that "among Jews the rumour has spread that in Petersburg and Moscow beatings are taking place on the streets every day, that there is a resulting shortage of bandages and that Gen. Trepov will be killed any day now."[52] A clash in the university in

Odessa left four policeman and one Gendarme wounded. The police arrested 214 people, 197 of them Jews.

On 18 October news of the Manifesto arrived in Odessa. Neidgardt pulled 853 of his men from their posts and left the city in the hands of detachments of self-defence militia composed of student and Jewish youth. On the following day, when patriotic demonstrations began, the chief again sent the uniformed police into the streets. Senator A.M. Kuz'minsky, who investigated the pogroms in Odessa later, said that the police had fired into the air to drive the self-defenders from the streets, and then pointed out to soldiers the buildings where they took refuge. "Many police officers," he reported, "acted in concert with other policemen and frequently led crowds of hooligans." The commander of the military district Baron Kaul'bars declared to the administration of the city that it was impermissible that police were taking part in the disorders, but he noted at the same time, "We are all one in spirit with the pogrom." Neidgardt, to whom a Jewish delegation turned for help, answered even more cynically, "You wanted freedom. Well, there's your freedom."[53]

Police discipline collapsed in other cities. In the town of Orsha in Mogilev province, a police constable, Rakovsky, assumed leadership of a crowd of thugs, and local police appear to have participated in the killing of two Jewish defenders. The head of the Mogilev provincial Gendarme administration in the city of Minsk, Poliakov, testified that Gendarmes tipped off the pogromists. When Jews set off by train from Minsk to Orsha to help defend the local Jewish community, the Minsk Gendarmes warned local police. When the defenders arrived on the train various pogromists, including policemen, awaited them with the words, "Well, look the democrats have come on the train and we will deal with them." In the words of a witness, "They killed people like cattle." Twenty-four defenders lost their lives.

The bloodiest beatings took place in the first three or four days after the Manifesto and they continued sporadically over the next two weeks in individual villages. The police began to restore order only after the turmoil was well under way or after the pogroms began to abate. A very few officials were decisive when the tide was in full course. Among them was Stolypin, at that time the governor of Saratov, who returned from vacation during the pogrom and ordered the army to fire volleys at the pillagers. There were cases where police stood against their colleagues who had joined the pogromists. In Rostov-on-Don, for example, the Gendarmes from the railway detachment fought against police who had sided with the pogromists.

Another level of the conflict among the police authorities showed up between chiefs and their subordinates. In the city of Ryl'sk in Kursk province the assistant district police officer gave a speech from which, in the words of a pogromist, "we were to understand that it was necessary to organize a pogrom." However, the district chief called on local citizens to restore order. "Volunteers came forward and soon a group of 30 citizens with shouts of 'hurrah' moved against the pogromists, who quickly dispersed."[54]

There were also cases when the initiative of the local police organs did not receive support from higher authorities. Captain Razmarits requested the following from the Volynia staff of the Gendarmes: "Would it be possible in case of anti-Semitic pogroms, about which there are many current rumours, to allow local inhabitants of the Volynia border area to pass over to Austria without regular documents?"[55] The St Petersburg command flatly turned down this request to bend the rules to permit temporary residence in Austria in the interest of protecting lives.

No high imperial police official played a major role in the October pogroms but evidence shows that individual units of the low ranks participated in some of the pogroms and even incited them. The main actors were local citizens, peasants, and soldiers whose rifles decided the course of events on the streets. The majority of those who were killed and wounded were victims of shooting by soldiers. The fundamental guilt of the local police was that they often held aloof or secretly sympathized with the pogromists, but the central police administration and the Okhranka neither had a policy to incite pogroms nor did they do so.

CHAPTER TWELVE

The Beilis Case and Damage Control

In 1913 a Jewish workman named Mendel Beilis attracted world attention when he went on trial in Kiev for the ritual murder of a Christian boy, and this chapter examines the role of the imperial government and its political police in the prosecution. The main thrust of official involvement from St Petersburg was to limit the damage this unfounded case would cause both to public order and to government credibility.

In March 1911, anticipating a threat to public order, Kiev's chief of Gendarmes warned superiors about local pamphlets that urged vengeance against Jews for a boy's death attributed to ritual murder. By mid-April the minister of the interior began using the "intensified security" statute of 1881 to deal with that crime and its contingent dangers to the state.

It was for security reasons, consequently, that officials used the 1881 law in late July to confine Mendel Beilis and his son at Gendarme headquarters through a temporary detainment that could not, under that same law, exceed fourteen days. On the twelfth day they released the son and remanded Beilis to the Kiev civil police for indefinite custody under an arrest warrant issued by the procurator who headed the murder inquiry. Intending the first incarceration as protective custody for Beilis in light of the tense state of affairs in Kiev, this arrest by the Interior Ministry acting through the Okhranka entrapped the state in a no-win dilemma in the Beilis affair. Eventually, the minister of justice, I.G. Shcheglovitov, himself faced the serious political quandary of having to decide between two evils: allowing a baseless trial or cancelling it in the face of anti-Semitic political agitation. He chose to continue due process in the expectation of exonerating Beilis while winning a public declaration from the jury endorsing the existence of Jewish ritual murder practices.

Most commentaries on the trial cite it as a prime example of how reactionary high officials prevailed over moderates in their deliberate campaign to make Jews, rather than the government, the target of public hostility. A failing, discredited regime, the argument goes, sullied justice to save itself. Among the first to put forward that view were journalists covering the trial in 1913. These words were from *The Times* of London: "It is daily becoming clearer that under forms of law a momentous political struggle is being fought out. This is not the Beilis case. It is possibly a final fight for existence on the part of the innermost powers of reaction against all the modern forces in Russia."[1] *Russian Word (Russkoe Slovo)* of Moscow, the largest daily in Russia, implied at the conclusion of the trial that the prosecutor had manipulated underlying anti-Semitic feelings among the jurors who, lacking grounds to convict Beilis, had yet slandered Jews in general. *Word* declared that "progressive society" was unanimous in applauding the acquittal and in condemning the government for letting the trial take place.[2]

In a denunciation of the tsarist regime that Soviet censors surely welcomed, A.S. Tager, who had served as an investigator for the Extraordinary Investigating Commission of the Provisional Government, in 1933 placed full blame for the Beilis trial on the malicious anti-Semitism of the government.[3] In 1935, in its own translation of Tager's book as *The Decay of Tsardom,* the Jewish Publication Society of America added an introduction which argued that, as deliberate policy, the tsarist regime portrayed its opposition as "a Jewish movement calculated to make Jews the masters of Russia" – the very point that Jewish organizations were then making in order to discredit the fraudulent *Protocols of the Elders of Zion* as a propaganda weapon framed by the Okhranka.[4]

Three decades later, in 1967, Maurice Samuel reiterated the scapegoat thesis in his *Blood Accusation.* Contending that "the Beilis case was manufactured by Russian governmental authorities expressly to inflame the populace against the Jews," Samuel describes the trial as an attempt to "arrest and turn back the forces of progress" and as the "last convulsion of an ancient tyranny."[5] And in 1986 Hans Rogger has narrowed the scope of that thesis to argue that a few high-ranking anti-Semites, especially Shcheglovitov, reacted opportunistically and viscerally to the Beilis case. This coterie did not work out a deliberate plan to stir hostility against Jews, he says, but rather set about manipulating the trial to "see how far they could go in imposing their cynicism and madness on the state."[6]

Mendel Beilis did suffer incarceration and trial in the city of Kiev because he was a Jew, but to blame an anti-Semitic conspiracy within the government is to ignore political and security factors that strongly influenced the course of the case. In the first place, most state officials under Nicholas II, whatever their prejudices, opposed actions that could arouse pogroms against Jews. Such actions were enormously disruptive to public order, turned Russian Jews into revolutionaries, and generated European hostility that hurt Russia politically and economically.

Likewise seen as a liability by many officials were the discriminatory laws, inherited by Nicholas II, which served to limit the movement of Jews and their access to property, higher education, professions, and public life. Because of those laws, most Russian Jews were required to live in the Pale; consequently, it was there that most of the few large-scale outbreaks of anti-Semitic violence took place, all before 1906, that marred the reign of Nicholas II. Proposals within the government to grant full rights to Jews received serious consideration under Nicholas II, with backers of that reform including such high officials as S.Iu. Witte, the long-time finance minister who served as prime minister in 1905–6. Another champion was Stolypin who, after becoming prime minister in 1907, began pressing his Council of Ministers to end all laws directed solely at Jews; he was still working for that change when the murder took place that led to the Beilis case.

Although no pogrom-scale attacks on Jews had occurred during those first four years of Stolypin's tenure, fears of a recurrence caused the Okhranka to keep the Gendarmes constantly alerted for anti-Semitic strife and fully informed on past outbreaks. Thus, when anti-Semites in Kiev circulated fliers to decry the killing of the boy Iushchinsky as Jewish ritual murder, security forces already had in mind one previous flashpoint: the rumours of Jewish ritual murder that had set off the infamous Easter pogrom in Kishinev in 1903.[7]

The slashed corpse of twelve-year-old Andrey Iushchinsky, in what was his old neighbourhood about six kilometres from the quarters that his family then occupied, was found on 20 March 1911. Besides the question of who had killed him, investigators would ponder why the corpse was left, fully exposed, in a cave frequented by children close to Jewish property just as Passover began and why it bore some forty cuts – all ingredients for the faking of a Jewish ritual murder.

On the day of the funeral one week later, a band of anti-Semites known as the Double-Headed Eagle Society broke the law against inciting violence by scattering fliers that called for violence against Jews for their ritual murder of Iushchinsky. Although the police detained one member, Nikolai Pavlovich, for questioning about the offence, he was released within days for lack of evidence. By then another member, nineteen-year-old Vladimir Golubev, had forwarded the illegal flier to sympathizers in the capital.

At least one local copy reached Kiev's chief of Gendarmes, who sent the text to Okhranka headquarters in St Petersburg. Among its inflammatory lines were these: "Every year before their Passover, [the Jews] torture to death several dozens of Christian children in order to get Christian blood to mix with their unleavened bread (*matza*) ... The official doctors found that before the Sheenies tortured Iushchinsky, they stripped him naked, tied him, and then slaughtered him, stabbing him in the principal veins in order to get as much blood as possible."[8] The pamphlet did not, as it stated, reflect the official forensics report that was released later and which showed that the multiple stab wounds were inflicted after death.

High officials had more cause than their fear of pogroms to pay close attention. They also knew that the principal supporters of the imperial government – conservatives who championed the tsar, the Orthodox Church, and who were strong Russian nationalists – would tend to label the pamphlet credible, so that their leaders would condemn the government for failing to act against Jews in a criminal case. Of further concern, the imperial government especially needed calm in Kiev because the tsar was to visit that city early in September in the company of his family, Prime Minister Stolypin, and dignitaries. In the spring of 1911, security officials were already taking steps to ensure calm and to protect the tsar during the state visit.

Meanwhile the civil police, who held exclusive authority to conduct the initial investigation of civil crimes, proceeded to talk to persons close to the victim, none of them Jews. Hearing that the boy had suffered domestic beatings, they detained his mother and stepfather for questioning and searched their home. Not only could the parents have known about the cave close to Jews from their previous residency, but they could also easily have transported the corpse to that site, given that the state of the body and of the cave confirmed that the boy had died elsewhere.

Three weeks after the funeral, the governor of Kiev, A.F. Giers, expressed concern to St Petersburg that critics were condemning the Kiev police for their seeming indifference to the possibility of ritual murder. On 13 April, Giers wired P.G. Kurlov: "There is growing conviction among the right-wing organizations that the murder is being covered up by the government."[9] Kurlov responded on behalf of the prime minister, Stolypin, the same day: "It is vital to take the most decisive measures to maintain order; a pogrom must be avoided at all costs."[10] The Interior Ministry therefore was aware of the murder in Kiev and its implication for public order as early as 13 April. The

Department of Police at once took steps to strengthen the work of the investigation. It sent several top detectives to Kiev, and Lieutenant-Colonel P.A. Ivanov of the provincial Gendarme administration also was ordered to join the investigation.

By this time, the assistant procurator of the Court of Appeals in Kiev, G.G. Chaplinsky, had wired the Justice Ministry about rumours of a pogrom to take place on 17 April. Although that day proved peaceful in Kiev, the next day was marked by two significant developments in St Petersburg. In the first, rightist deputies met to frame a Duma interpellation for later that month (29 April) to condemn the ministers of justice and interior for failures in the Iushchinsky inquiry and the Kiev police for not focusing their murder investigation on Jews. In the second, responding for the government, Shcheglovitov ended control of that probe by local police by ordering Chaplinsky to take charge.[11] Shcheglovitov met the tsar the same day and may have told him about the developments in Kiev. The highest officials of the realm now knew about the murder investigation in Kiev as of 18 April and were aware of its implications for security.

Civil law dictated that the police alone conduct the preliminary investigation (*predvaritelnoe doznanie*) of a civil crime, just as it empowered them to hold in temporary custody persons linked to or affected by the case – whether to question such detainees, protect them, or restrain them from flight. By law, the police in turn had to convey all their findings to a local prosecutor, who alone could use them, should he deem them sufficient, to order the police to make whatever arrests he authorized. Once the police arrested someone, authority over the case shifted to the prosecutor.

Then commenced the judicial inquiry (*iuridicheskoe sledstvie*) conducted by the judicial investigator (*sledovatel'*), an officer of the court under the supervision of the prosecutor, who could also call on the local police and Gendarmes for assistance. This investigative phase served to establish grounds for an indictment; and that order came only from a panel of judges when a majority of its members ruled the grounds in hand sufficient to justify trying the suspect before a judicial court.

In ordering Chaplinsky to head the Iushchinsky murder investigation prior to any arrest, the justice minister preempted the normal authority of police who served the minister of the interior. By necessity, therefore, the minister of the interior had to have known about and approved or even ordered that preemptive act.

To intervene in the Iushchinsky case, Stolypin used a statute in wide use by the government: the law enacted on 14 August 1881 to deal with revolutionary dangers. In the main, that statute required the minister of the interior to declare a security emergency and then impose a period of "strengthened" (*usilennaia*) or "extraordinary" (*chrezvychainaia*) security, whenever and wherever he saw the state in peril and to effect, throughout its duration, any measure of "security" that he saw as necessary.[12] The law itself specified, for example, that the interior minister could, on security grounds, give broader discretionary power to the state's security police by extending to two weeks the maximum length of time that Gendarmes could detain someone on their own authority for security reasons.

Whether to use the 1881 law openly or secretly was another decision for the interior minister, and he quite logically had to choose secrecy in April 1911. Any public declaration of strengthened security just after the Iushchinsky murder would only have heightened popular anxieties and made tensions worse. Then, too, Kiev may already have been secretly under strengthened security because of the tsar's impending visit. A public declaration of emergency legislation would have undercut the tsar's claim as beloved by a loyal people.

After Chaplinsky took control of the murder investigation, however, Kiev's special security became evident to those who knew the precedent set by past orders to local procurators to commence a judicial inquiry prior to an arrest. Each previous order had resulted from the invocation of strengthened security by the interior minister, just as each concerned a case that he had deemed security-related. Moreover, behind each of these shifts from the norm lay the assumption that a prosecutor, being far better schooled in the law than were police, would more rigorously enforce legal standards during an investigation. Strict standards were essential should a security-related case go before a civil court; for the criminal code banned from judicial deliberations any evidence obtained through illegal searches, seizures, or interrogations. Placing the prosecutor at once in charge guarded against losing a security-related judicial case merely because police laxness had made crucial evidence inadmissible. By naming Chaplinsky, moreover, the minister of justice had at once openly drawn in yet other skilled personnel – the multi-purpose Gendarmes; for only a prosecutor heading a judicial inquiry could summon them, as did Chaplinsky, to help local investigators resolve a civil crime.

Again to stress a point central to this book, Gendarmes served openly on one level as conventional police in imperial service, and in that capacity they sometimes took orders from local or provincial authorities. On a higher level, as security police who acted both openly and covertly to safeguard tsar and state, they answered only to the Okhranka or its superiors. In addition, but only on the rare occasion of an insurgency or war, the minister of war could make them full-time soldiers under his command. With respect to the Iushchinsky case, after mid-April 1911 the Gendarmes performed sometimes as conventional police, sometimes as security police, and sometimes as both at once. They did so because the minister of the interior required full use of their skills and powers to get the state safely past all the political snares contingent to the boy's killing.

No security concerns would have stemmed from the murder had not anti-Semites in Kiev raised and then intensified their charge that Jews had killed Iushchinsky for ritual reasons. But because that lie spread widely through rumours, broadsheets, the anti-Semitic press, and the Duma, as security chief, Stolypin had to take immediate measures to prevent or blunt adverse reactions that could, in his view, hurt the state. Close surveillance might even disclose, as the minister must have recognized, that foes of the state or of Jews had feigned ritual murder to serve their ends. Should either possibility prove true or should any politically disruptive plot be found, the minister would then have had to decide whether security would best be served by judging the perpetrators judicially or administratively.

This case would become increasingly politically charged throughout its duration. Just as continuously in effect, therefore, was the authority of the interior minister to influence its handling at every stage. Today, more than eight decades after the jury's verdict in Kiev, Western commentators unanimously condemn its handling and place most blame on the justice minister's anti-Semitism. This study, in contrast, relates that case's evolution to the interior minister's use of intensified security. Given that pivotal factor in effect as of mid-April 1911, subsequent developments and actors in what became the Beilis affair appear in a new light.

Notable first is a major development of early May 1911: the arrival in Kiev of the emissary from the minister of justice, A.V. Liadov. Later, in 1917, he would link his trip to pressing for adroit handling of the Iushchinsky murder case following the Duma interpellation, to ensuring calm for the September state visit of the tsar, and to ordering a meeting with Double-Headed Eagle members as part of the murder inquiry.[13] Liadov arrived in Kiev by train on the morning of 2 May and departed to return to the capital on the evening of 5 May.

Liadov well knew that his superior, Shcheglovitov, was not acting independently but responding to constant direction from Stolypin and other high officials of the Ministry of the Interior, including the assistant ministers Kurlov and A.A. Makarov (a future minister). Liadov remembered occasions when Makarov would write to the Ministry of

Justice to say that he was "especially concerned" about an acquittal because someone had complained.[14] In fact, it was Stolypin who dominated Shcheglovitov and caused him to fear accusations of weakness in political cases. As the Iushchinsky case unfolded, the influence of the Interior Ministry over the Justice Ministry became paramount.

Liadov bluntly told Golubev, the Double Eagle leader, that it was not in the interest of his organization to initiate a pogrom. "Why?" Golubev responded. "Because," said Liadov, "the governor-general [F.F. Trepov] has told me that the Sovereign will come here for the dedication of the monument to Alexander II. If some of your colleagues initiated a pogrom and disorders break out in Kiev, then you will not see the ceremony, and it will be your fault. Would it not be more important for you to see the Sovereign?" Liadov quotes Golubev's answer: "Such an idea never entered my head. I promise you (this brought a smile to my face) there will be no Jewish pogrom."[15]

Liadov himself, then, was under orders from Shcheglovitov, but carried out a mission primarily for the security chief, the minister of the interior, who held first responsibility to maintain order and keep the tsar from harm or humiliation. It therefore follows that Liadov ultimately served the interior minister by conveying orders from St Petersburg that both the Iushchinsky case and the Eagle faction receive special handling lest either provoke disorders.

Another reason for Liadov's trip was the Duma interpellation that took place on 29 September; for, during that inflammatory session, conservative deputies predicted a pogrom in Kiev unless the police seized "the Jew who is guilty of cutting up a Russian child and taking his blood."[16] Leading the attack was G.G. Zamyslovsky, a lawyer, who would team up with the prosecution at the Beilis trial. S.P. Beletsky, then director of the Department of Police, would name Zamyslovsky in 1917 as the prime instigator of the trial itself.[17] Zamyslovsky had been a public prosecutor and had risen to deputy prosecutor of the Court of Appeals in Vilnius. His life took a turn, however, when he won election to the Third State Duma and emerged as a chief speaker for the right wing. He was intensely interested in the Beilis case and had made several trips to Kiev prior to the trial. His anti-Semitic speeches would do a lot to stir up public opinion on the Beilis trial.

The Duma outcry came as no surprise, of course, because throughout April anti-Semites in Kiev and St Petersburg had made clear their anger over the seeming indifference of police investigators to widespread charges of ritual murder. Given the state of the corpse when found, they argued, investigators should detain Jews as suspects, not the dead boy's kin.

In light of this dissatisfaction, questions arise today about why the purportedly anti-Semitic Chaplinsky, the Kiev prosecutor in charge of the case, did not use his new authority over the investigation to implicate Jews at once, as he could have in the ten days before the interpellation. Chaplinsky, in the first place, was not an anti-Semitic crusader who wished to condemn Beilis because he was a Jew; but he was prepared to use the judicial system to appease anti-Semites in Kiev. Perhaps the justice minister, in his mid-April order, required Chaplinsky to maintain the status quo until an emissary from the capital arrived to clarify St Petersburg's intervention. Possibly that intervention itself, being extraordinary, convinced Chaplinsky to defer any initiatives pending counsel from the capital. At the very least, he had to have deduced that St Petersburg was interjecting some control over the local handling of the Iushchinsky case because that case affected its interests.

It follows, therefore, that Liadov most likely went to Kiev right after the interpellation to enable the autocracy to win full credit centre stage for a prompt show of goodwill to anti-Semites, thereby avoiding a pogrom in Kiev. In what would therefore have been an orchestrated political move, not until early May did Liadov deliver the directive from St Petersburg that investigators in Kiev hear and then test the demands of the Eagle faction.

Other key figures in the investigation (including Kiev's chief judicial investigator V.I. Fenenko and Chaplinsky who remained silent throughout) attended a 5 May meeting that Liadov held with members of the Double Headed Eagle Society. And it was there that Golubev gave a new direction to the investigation by stressing a fact that was obvious to all: a Jewish estate owned by one Zaitsev was near to the cave where the corpse was found. More startling, he alleged that a "Jew named Mendel" who worked on the estate had since "behaved in a queer way" by "giving the children candies and asking them not to tell the police anything"[18] – that being the first mention of Mendel Beilis that is documented in records related to the murder of Iushchinsky. Six days later Chaplinsky reported to the justice minister that Fenenko had inspected the grounds in question with Golubev. "Nothing suspicious was discovered on the Zaitsev estate," he wrote, "and we did not find the basements that Golubev had mentioned" – a reference to allegations by Golubev about a probable murder site.[19]

With their concession to anti-Semites made and St Petersburg duly informed, investigators resumed their inquiry by focusing on Iushchinsky's kin and another set of non-Jews – namely, four thieves and their adjunct, Vera Cheberiak. A possible link between the gang and Iushchinsky was the bond between him and Vera's son – a bond that might have caused the victim to walk six kilometres on his own, if he did so, to revisit his old neighbourhood rather than go to school. Plausibly the motive for the gang to kill the boy was to silence someone who had learned of their crimes at Vera's home or through Vera's son. Investigators also reasoned that the gang could have faked a ritual murder and left the corpse where it would quickly be found near Jewish-owned property both to divert suspicion from themselves and to set off a pogrom to facilitate their thievery. Suspicion of Vera and the gang heightened, moreover, as investigators gradually confirmed that Iushchinsky, on the day he disappeared, had spent time in her quarters, which were located near the cave.

Because no hard evidence to link anyone to the crime would ever be found, opportunity plus plausible motive would emerge as circumstantial grounds for detainments, interrogations, and actual charges in the case. The cause of death and condition of the corpse would also figure prominently in the ongoing debate over whether or not a ritual murder had taken place.

More than two months after Liadov's visit to Kiev, even as Vera and her son continued to deny any contact with Iushchinsky on the day he disappeared, a lamplighter named Shakhovsky came forward to testify that he had seen young Cheberiak with the victim in Vera's neighbourhood on the day in question. Then, on 20 July, during what was his third interview over two weeks, this witness went much further to make a first-time claim: that young Cheberiak had told him three days after the disappearance of Iushchinsky that a black-bearded man had menaced the pair in the Zaitsev brickyard during their last outing. According to the official report, the lamplighter next announced to chief judicial investigator Fenenko: "I think this Mendel took part in the murder."[20]

One day later Fenenko again questioned young Cheberiak, but still the boy denied being with Iushchinsky. Because his manner caused the chief investigator to assume that Vera, whom he most suspected, was cowing her son into speaking as he did, Fenenko recommended the redetainment of Vera for further questioning (as would happen) and another interrogation of young Cheberiak once he and his mother had been separated. On that same day, 21 July, prosecutor Chaplinsky detailed these very developments to the justice minister who happened to be at his estate in neighbouring Chernigov province.[21]

Surely of immediate concern – to murder investigators and security officials alike – was the sudden elevation of the Jewish factor and all its contingent ramifications. Investigators at the same time had good reason to disbelieve the latest account of the lamplighter; for, while this witness based his accusation against Beilis on hearsay to which he gave grave significance, he had not mentioned an exchange of words of any sort with young Cheberiak all through two earlier interviews. Investigators consequently had to have seen the possibility that persons bent on blaming a Jew for Iushchinsky's death were marshalling witnesses against Beilis. The humble lamplighter made a likely candidate, especially since he must have been bragging widely about his importance to investigators and his imminent third interview.

Within thirty-six hours of the lamplighter's implication of "Mendel," in any case, Gendarmes had taken Beilis and his adolescent son into custody and detained them at Gendarme headquarters in Kiev under Article 21 of the statute of 14 August 1881 for intensified security. The detentions make sense, as will shortly be shown, as an intensified security measure. Those commentators who mistakenly contend that Chaplinsky ordered the detentions to make way for his subsequent arrest of Beilis base that assumption solely on the juxtaposition of the two events. They also have no basis to condemn him for staging a pre-dawn raid and detaining his clearly innocent son, as well.

Simply put, Chaplinsky did not order those measures. Security officials alone could use the 1881 law, just as they alone could order detainments at Gendarme headquarters. Moreover, had Chaplinsky wanted Beilis detained in late July for any reason, he himself had full authority to order the civil police to take him into temporary custody – as he did at that time with respect to Vera Cheberiak.

Orders for detaining Beilis and his son, then, came not from Chaplinsky but the governor-general supervising Ukraine and neighbouring provinces of the Russian Empire, an official subordinate to the Ministry of the Interior. This was F.F. Trepov, who had been among those who urged Liadov to see Golubev early in May; and because he had powers under the statute of the 1881 statute to do so, Trepov could have ordered the detainments on his own. Chaplinsky later described the course of events in the following way: "The governor general called me and asked me to receive the chief of the security division [Okhranka] on an extremely important matter. Kuliabko [the chief] appeared, effected a conspiratorial air, and declared that he was required to detain Beilis, but that he was concerned that he might interfere with the investigation. To my question under what law will he detain Beilis, Kuliabko declared, that in light of the tsar's trip he had special authority."[22] Tager dates this meeting as 29 July 1911.

Chaplinsky is not the only witness to the fact that security considerations were behind the arrest. Fenenko, the judicial investigator who opposed the indictment of Beilis, later said that the Kiev Okhranka arrested Beilis "as a security matter." He went on: "I do not know the exact reason for the security division's arrest [detainment] of Beilis."[23]

Of central importance, therefore, to the Beilis case was the accused's detainment not by the local police, who could have been directed to have done so by the prosecutor, but by the Kiev Okhranka or security division under orders from the governor-general using, as was necessary under the law, Gendarme officers. Testimony that this was a security matter therefore comes from two witnesses on opposite sides in the Beilis case, Chaplinsky and Fenenko. What is argued here is that an official or officials under the minister of the interior ordered the two detentions to protect the state because the autocracy could be severely undermined were Beilis and his son left as targets of pogromists just after a second witness had accused the elder Jew of killing a Christian boy. More particularly, security officials feared that were Beilis left at large, fanatics who would almost certainly make Beilis an issue or their target for violence could likely trigger a pogrom in the critical period before the tsar's state visit.

For these reasons, then, security officials imposed protective custody on both Beilis and his most vulnerable child. As for why the seizures took place under cover of darkness, that common precaution by security police served to hide from the public a seemingly arbitrary act that could not, for security reasons, be explained, even to Beilis or to the Gendarmes who carried it out.

To be sure, anti-Semites in the security ranks or elsewhere could have recommended the two detentions on security grounds, while actually urging them as a means to ensnare Beilis. But, as explained before, that same end could have been accomplished routinely by having the municipal police rather than the security police take Beilis into temporary custody – whether for questioning, to prevent his flight, or even to protect him. But under the 1881 statute, Gendarme officials could, on their own authority, hold persons in temporary custody for security reasons for no more than fourteen days. It follows, then, that the detentions on 22 July of Beilis and his son provided only a fourteen-day solution for the problem of keeping them safe to prevent a pogrom. On the other hand, whereas the interior minister could extend the security-related detention of someone suspected of a security crime, neither Beilis nor his son fit that category. Thus, under the 1881 law, the Gendarmes could not keep these two in custody beyond the two weeks that ended on 5 August.

Of great importance here, actions by Chaplinsky in the same period after the lamplighter testified on 20 July led to the transfer of Beilis from Gendarme custody into the custody of the local police on 3 August. That is, on 22 or 23 July, Chaplinsky went to Minister Shcheglovitov at his Chernigov estate. From there he telegraphed the Kiev Gendarmes, according to Tager, to ask: "Has Mandel been arrested?" (Although the correct word would have been detained, the telegram confirms that Chaplinsky expected Beilis to be in security detention by that time.) Back came the reply, which has to have been sent after the detainment in the early hours of 22 July): "Mandel has been arrested under the law on state security" – "Mandel" being used in all likelihood to avoid specific identification of Beilis.[24]

On 1 or 2 August Chaplinsky, again in Kiev, convened the main persons involved in searching for Iushchinsky's killer, including N.N. Brandorf, the prosecutor of the Kiev Circuit Court, who returned from a two month holiday on 1 August. There he asked Fenenko, as chief investigator, to recommend the arrest of Beilis as a murder suspect; but Fenenko refused, citing insufficient grounds. Consequently Chaplinsky himself ordered the arrest, which took place 3 August, when the son went free. Beilis says in his memoirs that as Fenenko took him into custody, he said, "Beilis, it's not me who brings an accusation against you, but the prosecutor."[25]

Precisely when and why Chaplinsky decided to arrest Beilis is impossible to determine. Some conjecture, with no direct evidence, that Shcheglovitov ordered him early on to find a Jew to charge. Events themselves make it far more probable, however, that Chaplinsky went to Shcheglovitov for backing for the arrest, perhaps initially proposing it during talks of late July 1911.

Another unknown is whether the late July talks were already planned, but their critical timing makes it altogether likely that Chaplinsky rushed on his own to Shcheglovitov in order to seize a sudden opportunity. And his main motives can have been anything from hopes to ingratiate himself with his minister to genuine belief that the arrest of Beilis would still anti-Semitic agitation in Kiev. It is also possible that Chaplinsky believed that Beilis committed the crime or that the prosecutor was a virulent anti-Semite. The evidence presented here, however, calls these last two alleged motives into question.

What does seem clear is that Chaplinsky saw the Gendarme detainment as an opportunity for his arresting Beilis and he went to Shcheglovitov to explain to him his next steps and to secure the minister's agreement. No one immediately knew that Beilis had been seized by the security police, but when that became widely known within days, it served to implicate Beilis in the crime. Chaplinsky must have felt the warm glow of acclaim from the Kievan anti-Semites at this juncture and he would confidently press Fenenko in November 1911 to complete the judicial investigation and move to indict Beilis.

Chaplinsky, the prosecutor of the Kiev Court of Appeals, had begun to play the central role in the Beilis affair in Kiev. Perhaps for that reason, most commentators on the Beilis affair class the prosecutor with the fanatical anti-Semites. Chaplinsky had a completely different view of the matter. When the anti-Semitic organizations had initially blamed the murder on religious fanatics, Chaplinsky said that he "couldn't understand how in the twentieth century in a town such as Kiev a case like this could originate."[26] The prosecutor had even acted against Black Hundred agitation in Kiev over the murder and had asked that the saying of the office for the dead at Iushchinsky's funeral be banned in order to remove a cause for demonstrations against Jews. For his efforts, Chaplinsky had found himself under attack from extreme rightists in the Third State Duma. But with the arrest of Beilis in early August he no longer suffered criticisms from anti-Semites. Chaplinsky possibly shared the anti-Semitism of many imperial officials, but his primary motives in the Beilis case were political. And he was ready to brush aside evidence pointing to Beilis's innocence in an effort to appease anti-Semitic agitation in Kiev.[27]

But the prosecutor's role in the Beilis affair reveals another motive. Whereas the detention of Beilis was unquestionably an intensified security measure, the civil arrest and eventual prosecution of Beilis also make sense as an opportunistic assertion of authority by Chaplinsky in order to advance himself. That is, Chaplinsky expected to please not only Shcheglovitov but also Prime Minister Stolypin (who, being the minister of the interior, was absolute executor of the law of 14 August 1881 and could dictate to other ministers on any security-related matters).

Inevitably, many assorted mindsets other than Chaplinsky's influenced the handling of the Iushchinsky case from the arrest of Beilis onward. Not only was there a widespread outcry in the Duma and newspapers of the day that ritual murder was wholly implausible, but a number of key officials throughout the government also held that view. But, as for the role of the officials who are the focus of this book, the ensuing discussion will show that, once Beilis had been arrested, security officials commenced mainly a reactive role whereby they vainly attempted to stop the prosecution. They would fail for lack of an alternate course of action and because the government had stumbled into a no-win political dilemma.

Grounds for the arrest of Beilis were, in any case, cobbled together by Chaplinsky, who had the discretionary right to deem them sufficient. And very likely a part of that effort was the dispatch of investigator N.A. Krasovsky to the Zaitsev brickyards on 29 July (just five days before the arrest) to affirm, as Krasovsky did, that ovens there were large enough to accommodate a murder.[28] What resulted was a warrant that cited Beilis as a probable participant in the probable ritual murder of Iushchinsky on the basis of findings by investigators to that time, vacuous though they were. Chaplinsky used the only remotely credible grounds available to him – findings that supported the cause of death as ritual murder. And, in using those grounds, Chaplinsky publicly aligned himself with those who considered ritual murder plausible.

As to the immediate security implications of the arrest of Beilis on 3 August 1911, the Gendarmes would have to set Beilis free on 5 August because that was the fourteenth day of the detention. In the rapid developments of 1–3 August, in any case, Chaplinsky would have reached an agreement with the Gendarmes to transfer Beilis from their custody to that of the Kievan police.

It was, evidently, during her detention at this time, that Vera Cheberiak at last concluded that Iushchinsky had visited her quarters on the day he had disappeared and then gone out into the neighbourhood with her son, Zhenya. In this same late July, early August period, Zhenya felt so ill that Fenenko could not interview him again.[29] The boy's decline to near death caused officials to release Vera on 14 July and on 8 August Zhenya died, as did a younger sister a few days later. Rumours that poison had killed them both entered the extensive press coverage about the case, which had by this time attracted national and international attention. Many newspapers also printed the report from the Bacteriological Institute on 10 August that Zhenya had died from his illness.

With the release of Vera about a week before Chaplinsky went to see Shcheglovitov in Chernigov, the authorities had only Beilis under custody and the most promising witness in his favour was now dead.

Chaplinsky's judicial investigation proceeded to what might seem an inevitable conclusion: the indictment of Beilis in January 1912 on little evidence. But it was a panel of judges of the Court of Appeals in Kiev, acting under the division of powers in the judicial reform of 1864, who decided in favour of the indictment, not Chaplinsky. There is no evidence available to document the thinking of the judges or the possible outside pressures that might have influenced them, but they were also free not to indict. Fenenko, still the chief judicial investigator, used these same five months to search for evidence against Vera Cheberiak; but, according to Fenenko's testimony in 1917 (when circumstances made it politic to have resisted the trial of Beilis),

Chaplinsky repeatedly placed obstacles in the way of that effort because he wanted Beilis indicted.[30]

Events such as the assassination of Stolypin and the hurried trial and execution of his murderer, Bogrov, likely influenced the thinking of Chaplinsky and the Kiev judges on the Beilis case.[31] The release of Beilis at a time when a Jew had murdered the head of a Russian nationalistic government would have aroused enormous resentment among anti-Semites. Here was yet another argument to let the Beilis case run its course. Kuliabko sent a coded telegram to Beletsky on 6 September and reported that in view of the Iushchinsky murder and the attempt on Stolypin (who survived for several days despite his wounds) local authorities had taken preventive measures to forestall an expected pogrom.[32]

When the vote came on the indictment on 20 January 1912, Chaplinsky was in St Petersburg where he must have discussed the case with officials in the Ministry of Justice and, perhaps, with Shcheglovitov himself. Announcement of the indictment in turn set off world-wide reactions. The imperial government now had no choice but to conduct the Beilis case in the full glare of international publicity.

A lawyer, A.D. Margolin, headed a group of prominent persons of Jewish origin organized to help Beilis and his family. One obvious defensive measure was to carry out a parallel investigation of the murder of Iushchinsky; for this purpose, Margolin secured the help of Fenenko. By law, the judicial investigator could not cooperate, but he did so covertly. Margolin also turned to a journalist, S.I. Brazul'-Brushkovsky, who had been conducting his own investigation. He had already concluded that the key to the mystery was in the hands of Vera Cheberiak.

Brushkovsky arranged for Margolin to meet Cheberiak in the city of Khar'kov in the eastern Ukraine on 7 December 1911. Vera Cheberiak later insisted that Margolin, who had been introduced to her as "an important gentleman" from St Petersburg and a deputy of the State Duma, had proposed that she assume responsibility for the crime for a payment of 40,000 rubles. "You need not be afraid," she said Margolin told her, "at the worst the best lawyers will defend you or we'll give you clean papers and nobody will ever find you."[33]

Margolin and his committee, in the meantime, continued their investigation. They recruited the former police officer Krasovsky and he found two assistants, Sergei Makhalin and Amzor Karaev, whom he had known for their "good connections in the underworld." Krasovsky probably did not know that Karaev was a secret agent of the Kiev Okhranka, with the code name of Kavkazsky. Before long, however, the Okhranka fired him because although "part of his information was of a rather serious nature ... upon checking it turned out that this information had been obtained as a result of provocative activities and blackmail."[34] Also let go at the same time was Karaev's close friend and fellow Okhranka secret agent Makhalin, who found himself abruptly unemployed because of the mistakes of his colleague.

On 28 January 1912, just as Chaplinsky returned to Kiev, A. Shredel', the head of Kiev provincial Gendarmes, sent a confidential criticism to the vice-director of the Department of the Police, Kharlamov, that Chaplinsky had submitted false evidence against Beilis to the judicial panel. He referred to a finding (not dated) by Fenenko that a note purportedly found on the body that appeared to incriminate Beilis had actually been faked by a certain local policeman.[35] A fortnight later, in mid-February, Shredel' sent a second letter marked "absolutely secret." He referred to his having full control over the Beilis investigation, by which he meant a second, security-related investigation by the Gendarmes.[36] The local police agencies were, in the meantime, continuing their investigation.

Two of his assistants, Shredel' explained, had connected associates of Vera Cheberiak with a number of local robberies and had established that their crimes and their contacts with Vera had stopped after the murder of young Iushchinsky. Shredel' saw these facts as circumstantial evidence implicating the gang in the murder, and he faulted the local prosecutor for failing to proceed with criminal charges against them. He warned: "The charge against Mendel Beilis in the murder of Andrey Iushchinsky, because of the insufficiency of evidence gathered against him and the universal interest in the trial, which has acquired almost European-wide notoriety, can bring enormous troubles for those who permitted the hurried completion and one-sidedness of the investigation."[37]

A follow-up letter from Shredel' on 14 March deplored that the evidence against Beilis was "indirect." A single hearsay witness (the lamplighter Shakhovsky) said Zhenya Cheberiak had told him that he had seen the murder victim the night before his death and that he thought he saw a man resembling Beilis – one with a black beard – grab the boy, but he could not make a positive identification. Shredel' again faulted Chaplinsky for his blindness to the thieves associated with Cherberiak.[38]

Much the same intelligence shortly went to the assistant minister of the interior in a secret letter from the governor of Kiev, Giers. In his April communiqué, Giers said that he expected Beilis to be acquitted and that the impact on Russia would be "extremely distressing."[39]

This absolute certainty about an acquittal expressed by the provincial chief of the Gendarmes and the governor in Kiev underscores the weakness of the case against Beilis – a case that the prosecutor would have to argue before observers and journalists from around the world. When the jury inevitably pronounced Beilis innocent, supporters of the government would feel "distress." The flimsiness of the evidence would make the imperial government appear incompetent or viciously anti-Semitic to liberals and moderates, whose opposition would mount. On the right, the loss of the case would cause those bent on censuring Jews to regard the government as ineffectual, if not incompetent, and this group might instigate pogroms. As both officials argued in their letters of January through April, proceeding to trial was a no-win situation.

These grave doubts were now supported in another quarter. Results from the private investigation, which had been continuing for about six months, strongly supported ending the proceedings against Beilis. On 5 May 1912 Brazul'-Brushkovsky acquainted the Gendarme Colonel Ivanov with the results of the private investigation and later that month publicized his findings in *The Kievan* (*Kievlianin*). The paper was edited by the conservative D.I. Pikhno, a member of the State Council, and something of an anti-Semite himself. When Brushkovsky's findings appeared in this paper with its impeccable right-wing credentials, the defenders of Beilis took heart. Margolin saw the influence of this article as extraordinarily important: "It was inconceivable that the newspaper thought of as a stronghold of the government and conservatism, let alone anti-Semitism, should have revolted against the violation of justice and the arbitrary rule of Shcheglovitov's ministry."[40]

Brushkovsky had obtained evidence by collaborating with Krasovsky, the dismissed police investigator; his most important finding was a purported confession from Vera Cheberiak's brother. The reporter was now firmly convinced that Vera Cheberiak and members of the gang of thieves – Peter Singaevsky, the brother, Boris Rudzinsky, and Ivan Latyshev – had murdered Iushchinsky because they feared that he had already or was about to betray them to the police. The reporter concluded that the bandits had lured the boy into Cheberiak's flat, and had then "gagged him, started to torture him to make him confess that he had gone to the police."[41] Then they killed the boy, wrapped his body in a carpet, and after several days, took it to the cave not far from Cheberiak's flat.

The letters of Shredel' and Giers had gone to the Ministry of the Interior. Despite that ministry's uneasiness about a trial, the Justice Ministry pushed ahead, still following the lead of Chaplinsky. The Kiev prosecutor had lost none of his conviction about Beilis and wrote on 28 May to Liadov, Shcheglovitov's deputy. Many "who occupy important positions have tried to convince me that the Beilis case ought to be stopped, that such is the wish of our minister, etc."[42] Chaplinsky said he was prepared to proceed with the trial despite arguments against it.

One of those who opposed Chaplinsky, Lieutenant-Colonel Ivanov, on 12 August sent a summary of Brushkovsky's findings to the police director, S.P. Beletsky. He argued for the release of Beilis and the laying of charges against Cheberiak and the gang of thieves. The Kiev Gendarmes were making it clear in St Petersburg that proceeding with the trial would make the government look worse than releasing Beilis. Chaplinsky did not, however, act on either recommendation and declared that "the judicial authorities cannot be toys in the hands of scoundrels."[43] Shcheglovitov was not so obdurate, however, and, responding to the criticism, instructed the chief judicial investigator of the St Petersburg Court of Appeals, N.A. Mashkevich, to review the case. As well, Kuntsevich, a police official, had been sent to Kiev in the summer of 1912 to evaluate the evidence. He returned to the capital to report that he found insufficient cause either to prosecute Beilis or to show evidence of ritual murder.[44]

Defenders of Beilis now believed that they knew the truth of the murder of Iushchinsky, and Brushkovsky's evidence would provide the basis for the courtroom defence. But the journalist's findings do not support the conclusions of Tager in his book, *The Decay of Tsarism*, that the initiators of the trial "knew the true murderers and concealed them."[45] The case is too complex to justify a claim that a group of officials deliberately conspired to promote a miscarriage of justice because of outright anti-Semitism. The investigator Mashkevich did not accept the evidence of Brushkovsky and did not have confidence in the participants of the second investigation. But he also committed a serious error when he accepted Vera Cheberiak's testimony to him that Iushchinsky and three other children playing in the brickyard were chased by two Jews dressed in peculiar clothes. Then she said, "Mendel Beilis caught Andrusha by the arm and led him in the direction of the ravine." Cheberiak made this statement for the first time sixteen months after the murder at a time when she was defending herself from the accusation of murder. Her statement turned out to be the principal finding of Mashkevich's inquiry into the case.

Well before Ivanov's communiqué to Beletsky in August, yet another political factor was figuring into the case, for the trial was scheduled for the fall of 1912, just as elections for the Duma took place. Again, the Interior Ministry took the lead in deciding a course of action. On

3 May Makarov (now minister of the interior) recommended to the justice minister that he postpone the trial in light of the intense public interest it had generated at home and abroad. Taking the position of Shredel' and Giers, and using almost identical language, he stated flatly that Beilis would be acquitted "because of the impossibility of proving his guilt"; and defeat for the government prosecutor, he continued, would impart to the "Russian population a very distressing impression," a consequence he did not define in concrete terms. He went no further than to say that delaying the trial would help to "protect Russian electors from heavy shocks."[46]

Minister of Justice Shcheglovitov responded by directing the president, or chief judge, of the Kiev Circuit Court to "satisfy the request" of Makarov to defer the trial.[47] The elections to the Fourth State Duma in the fall of 1912 were conducted under tranquil conditions, and produced a conservative legislative assembly comparable to that of the Third Duma. The government's working with more nationalistic groups in the Duma appeared to be paying political dividends. Shcheglovitov already knew about the revelations that the Kievan journalist published in May, for Brushkovsky had already explained his position to the Kiev prosecutor that previous January.[48] The minister knew the case was weak, but he stood firm all the same, choosing to defer rather than dismiss the case against Beilis. Shcheglovitov saw graver repercussions in a dismissal.

Concluding that Chaplinsky could not produce the evidence against Beilis that he had promised, the government began to devise a different strategy to win some semblance of victory. The trial was now to be held in the fall of 1913 and that postponement gave more time to the prosecution. The charges against Beilis remained, but the prosecution now concentrated on demonstrating that Jews practised ritual murder. This new strategy, carried out under the authority of the minister of the interior, N.A. Maklakov (who had replaced Makarov in February 1913), emphasized political factors and involved virtually no effort to convict Beilis. Even before the trial began, Maklakov had said to Zamyslovsky in the lobby of the State Duma building that the conviction of Beilis was impossible because of the weak evidence. Zamyslovsky was quoted by a newspaper as having replied: "Let him be acquitted; it is essential for us to prove the ritual character of the crime."[49]

The government could not therefore abandon its prosecution of Beilis and appear to be caving in to critics on the left. As to why the state wished to prove ritual murder, Beletsky, the head of the Department of Police, later testified that political motives were dominant in the conduct of the trial and cited another factor: Maklakov, his superior, he said, had united with the minister of justice on the "necessity of arranging the judicial case" against Beilis as a way to thwart the movement in Russia, favoured by Stolypin, to grant broader civil rights to Jews.[50] On the one hand Maklakov, like Stolypin, strongly opposed pogroms; on the other hand, unlike Stolypin, he took a stand against changing the legal status of Jews, precisely because he felt that unrest would inevitably result. No one questioned that some person or persons had inflicted stab wounds on the body of the murder victim. A centrepiece of the prosecution case would now be to show that the wounds were made in order to gather blood for purposes of ritual.

Maklakov's subordinate, S.P. Beletsky, the director of the Department of Police, in the summer of 1913 summoned one of Russia's top criminal investigators and the head of the Moscow detectives, A. Koshko, to St Petersburg and asked him to review all the documents in the case, copies of which were on file in the capital. Koshko first met with Beletsky, who directed him to meet with Shcheglovitov. Installed in a temporary office, Koshko worked about a month on the materials, making copious notes, and then prepared a report for the minister of justice. Shcheglovitov also discussed the matter with him in a final interview.[51]

Koshko told Shcheglovitov that his review of the materials had not changed his early impression that "the investigation was conducted incorrectly, one-sidedly, and, I would say, with prejudice." Several circumstances were especially notable. Expert testimony showed that the boy had been killed before his body was moved to the cave in which it was found. Koshko told the minister that he would not have arrested and prosecuted Beilis on the evidence. In the discussion, Shcheglovitov granted that Beilis might not be guilty.

When Shcheglovitov then pressed him on the issue of the ritual murder, Koshko answered that such an event was unprovable on the basis of the evidence. He said that even if there had been a sect of ritual murderers, they would hardly have picked Kiev for their deeds because it was a centre of anti-Semitism, monarchism, and right-wing political organizations. Any such event, if known, would have inevitably produced a massive swell of opinion against Jews. In his experience, Jews were universally afraid of provoking pogroms, because recent such events in south Russia were still fresh in their minds. Koshko reasoned that such persons would not have picked a boy as well known as young Iushchinsky because his disappearance would immediately attract attention.

As Koshko elaborated his argument and the evidence to support it, Shcheglovitov's face, he recalled, grew steadily darker. Finally, the minister rose to his feet and left the room without offering his hand. His last words to the Moscow detective were that he regretted having turned to him for help. He hoped the jury in the Beilis case would "shake you and your Judophile views."[52]

Beletsky, who had organized Koshko's visit, must have hoped that the experienced detective's critical assessment might focus on elements of the case that would strengthen the prosecution. Despite the disappointing results of Koshko's assessment, the justice minister nonetheless adhered to the course of carrying the trial through to a verdict. The ritual murder had become the centrepiece of the government's case in the absence of evidence against Beilis. Both the prosecution and the outcome of the trial showed the influence of this view. To strengthen the prosecution team, Shcheglovitov ordered to Kiev to argue the government's case O.Iu. Wipper, the deputy public prosecutor from the St Petersburg Court of Appeals. Chaplinsky had now been completely eclipsed and others headed by Wipper presented the prosecution's arguments.

As the course of the trial was set, Beletsky, acting under orders, gave assistance to the prosecution. He obtained from abroad through the Foreign Okhranka, at Zamyslovsky's request, a copy of a rare book purporting to give evidence on ritual murders. When the prosecution wanted information on an earlier ritual murder trial in Saratov, a Gendarme brought volumes of materials from St Petersburg. These efforts were to assist the prosecution in proving ritual murder.

Political dilemmas continued to surround the Beilis affair through 1912 and into 1913. The justice minister himself knew that the acquittal of Beilis was almost certain. Chaplinsky recalled that Shcheglovitov said, "the most desirable outcome would be for the court to stop the case. There would be no regrets, no trouble, and a load off everybody's mind."[53] A close acquaintance of the minister said, however, that Shcheglovitov believed that the case had progressed too far to turn back: "The case was given publicity and took such a turn that it is impossible not to refer it to the court; otherwise people would say that Jews bribed me and the government."[54]

Some conservative leaders were beginning to believe, however, that the government was losing prestige because of the Beilis affair. One such figure was D.I. Pikhno, the editor of the influential newspaper, *The Kievan.* Pikhno had assigned a reporter, M.I. Trifonov, to investigate the Beilis case and the editor maintained interest in it right up to his death in July 1913. Trifonov had a number of discussions with Pikhno on the Beilis investigation and describes them but does not date them.

Trifonov's recollections confirm that the justice minister decided to go ahead with the trial despite his doubts. Shcheglovitov, he says, had believed initially that Chaplinsky could fulfil his promise to produce the evidence to support a conviction of Beilis for ritual murder. When Chaplinsky failed to do so, Shcheglovitov found it necessary "to go to court because the affair had already created a great storm." Pikhno, says Trifonov, learned in his last conversation with Shcheglovitov (seemingly in 1913): "[The minister] has already understood that the case for ritual murder is shaky, that Chaplinsky had not fulfilled the hopes he had placed on him, that it was essential to dispose of the affair by means of its public examination in court, and that he saw no other way out of the situation that had been created."[55] Shcheglovitov and Pikhno were acquainted and the minister asked the editor to have a talk with Chaplinsky. Pikhno then reluctantly, again seemingly early in 1913, met with Chaplinsky, and told him, "I have nothing more to say to you. I warned you in time, but now it is too late. You have cooked this gruel, now you will have to eat it."[56]

When Pikhno died, his stepson V.V. Shul'gin came to similar conclusions about the Beilis case, although earlier as a member of the extreme rightists in the Third Duma he had signed the interpellation on the ritual murder two years earlier. As the trial began, Shul'gin wrote a lead article criticizing the machinations of the judicial authorities. Before the press authorities of the Ministry of the Interior could confiscate the edition, half of it had been sold. The Kiev governor, N.I. Sukovkin, who had replaced Giers in 1913, reported to St Peterburg that the confiscation had been the first one in the fifty-year history of the paper and "drew more attention to Shul'gin's article than it was worth."[57] The article did become a sensation. Shul'gin's colleagues on the right attacked him and Chaplinsky brought a successful libel suit against him.

Public controversy intensified as the day approached for the opening of the trial on 25 September 1913. Public order was of first concern to police officials. Beletsky ordered all governors to prevent disorders, and the provincial administration in Kiev reported back early in September about their extraordinary pre-emptive measures.[58] One precaution was sending police units into the Jewish sections of the city and to the square in front of the building that housed the court, as well as the imposition of special security measures on the court itself. In addition, the authorities in Kiev had summoned mounted police from the district to help patrol the streets, and ordered three hundred Cossacks from the Kiev military district. Banned outright were all forms of agitation, and police agents were under orders to monitor the "activities of all right and left organizations" alike.[59]

On 17 September Beletsky ordered close monitoring of the jury to detect any influences on it "of persons who are interested in the case for one reason or another." The Kiev procurator should be kept informed about the mood of the jury and Beletsky said he wanted detailed accounts by telegraph for reports to the minister, Maklakov.[60] Shredel' organized a special unit of detectives to protect the persons of Beilis, the St Peterburg prosecutor, and the controversial right-wing member of the Duma, Zamyslovsky. The governor had received advance approval to impose martial law on the province if necessary.[61] Shredel' summoned to Kiev thirty-two extra detectives from surrounding cities. As well, he ordered into the jury room Gendarme officers in the disguise of court attendants to listen to the discussions of the jury – a clear violation of privileges of the jury.

Beilis appeared briefly in the dock for the first time on the opening day of the trial on 25 September 1913, thirty months after Iushchinsky's murder and twenty-six months after his arrest. By this time, because of the massive publicity surrounding almost every aspect of the case, the event had attracted universal attention. Both sides had tried to use the press to their advantage and the enormous publicity had hurt Beilis.

Possible effects of the trial on extremists continued to preoccupy officials in the Ministry of Interior. Maklakov took energetic steps. When the governor (whom Maklakov had summoned back to Kiev from the resort of Biarritz) sought permission on 9 October to detain all right-wing leaders, Maklakov responded: "It can be done but only as an extreme measure. If exhortations and warnings do not work and agitation to incite pogroms continues, those responsible will be arrested."[62] Anticipating that news from Kiev could have disturbing influence elsewhere, Maklakov on the following day reminded subordinates throughout Russia that it was their duty "to forestall any emergencies, let alone pogroms in general."[63] The authorities also attempted to head off actions on the part of Jews that might provoke disorders. Shredel', the chief of the provincial Gendarme administration, reported to the governor on pro-Beilis agitation in the press and by means of leaflets. "Undoubtedly," he concluded, "all these attacks are the result of clandestine direction from the Jewish bourgeois intelligentsia, the representatives of the powerful 'kahal.'" Shredel' said that such publicity would only promote the idea among Jews that they were being persecuted. He advised the governor to warn the Jewish leadership that these publications might lead to a pogrom, and Sukovkin called in Rabbi Gurevich of Kiev and asked him to exercise his influence to calm Jewish young people.[64]

Some observers thought the prosecution had scored an early victory by securing a jury sympathetic to its cause. The writer V.G. Korolenko described the jury as "seven peasants, three from the petit bourgeoisie, and two low-ranking officials" and considered the composition "exceptional" for a university city.[65] From the first, however, the police department official P.N. Liubimov, who reported daily to Beletsky, understood that the social composition of the jury would work against the prosecution. He predicted an acquittal. Two or three jurors were quite "conscious" and they "will be able to lead the illiterate peasants wherever they wish."[66]

Assisting the prosecutor, O.Iu. Wipper, three attorneys appeared as civil plaintiffs representing the interests of the victim, in this case the relatives of Iushchinsky. Initially, the relatives were reluctant to bring an action against Beilis, but Kievan Black Hundred members had insisted to Alexandra Prikhod'ko and other relatives that they sign the applications. Two of these attorneys, Zamyslovsky and A.S. Shmakov, played a highly visible role in the proceedings, emphasizing their anti-Semitic views.[67] The prosecution also faced formidable courtroom opponents. Beilis's backers had assembled an experienced defence team led by N.P. Karabchevsky, one of Russia's leading criminal defence lawyers, and V. Maklakov, a leader of the Constitutional Democratic party and Duma deputy. He wound up on the opposite side of his younger brother, who was minister of the interior.

Aiming to show that a ritual murder had taken place, the prosecutors wished to demonstrate that neither Iushchinsky's family nor the gang of thieves had committed it. In the course of presenting their case, they found that they were constantly running up against arbitrary and suspect actions on the part of the police in Kiev. Liubimov reported that "an unpleasant aspect of the trial is that both the public prosecutor and the civil plaintiffs (especially Zamyslovsky) and the defence repeatedly bring up the illegal actions of the police that had taken place when Krasovsky and Mishchuk, trying to outdo one another, were beating Iushchinsky's relatives within an inch of their lives." Liubimov said he received the impression from the proceedings that the police of Kiev were on trial.[68]

Zamyslovsky and Shmakov took especial aim at the case built by the journalist Brazul'-Brushkovsky, who had concentrated on the gang of thieves. They also exploited the weaknesses of the witnesses for the defence; some of them had been badly prepared and their testimony actually drew laughter from onlookers. Colonel Ivanov was a reluctant witness called by the defence, which very likely did not expect much from him. He believed Beilis innocent, but as a Gendarme under orders, he could not give testimony that would discredit the prosecution. In any event, he testified as a loyal employee of the tsarist state and Gruzenberg, on the side of the defence, thought he was a "dishonourable witness."[69]

What little the public prosecutor brought up against Beilis rested on the state's contention that the Zaitsev estate, where the brickyard was located, was a centre of "Hassidim" in Kiev. To obtain blood for the consecration of a new chapel there, one Faivel Shneerson and two priests from the "tribe of Aron" had come briefly from abroad to participate in a ritual slaying. The prosecutor in turn alleged that Beilis took part by seizing Iushchinsky in the brickyard and carrying him to the unlit brick ovens where the sacrificial rite had taken place.

To convince the jury of their main argument, that a ritual murder had taken place – never mind where or by whom – the prosecution summoned to court a number of expert witnesses from the fields of medicine, psychology, and theology. Because the Kiev pathologist who had first examined Iushchinsky's remains had since died, the prosecution called Professor D.P. Kosorotov from St Petersburg. The Department of Police paid Kosorotov 4,000 rubles from secret funds of the Ministry of the Interior.[70] Kosorotov testified that the condition of the corpse and the depth and angle of cuts showed torture and deliberate extraction of blood. (The defence predictably countered this testimony with its own pathologists, who offered entirely contradictory opinions.)

Beletsky, acting under Maklakov's orders, provided another prosecution witness by having the Gendarmes and Okhranka agents scour the Russian Empire to find an expert on Hebrew and Jewish history who would testify in court to a history of ritual murder. The man they produced was a Catholic priest and former professor of Hebrew in a Catholic academy in St Petersburg, Justin Pranaitis. Although his superiors had sent him to Tashkent for reasons of ecclesiastical discipline, Pranaitis could be of use because he had published in 1893 a virulent anti-Semitic tract, *The Christians in the Jewish Talmud, or the Secrets of the Teachings of the Rabbis about Christians*. It was Pranaitis, consequently, who testified during the Beilis trial that his own careful historical research confirmed that Jews since the Middle Ages had been sacrificing Christian children as a religious rite. He said that the gag in Iushchinsky's mouth and the thirteen stab wounds in his temple marked the murdered boy as the victim of such a rite.[71]

An expert from St Petersburg Theological Academy, I.G. Troitsky, countered for the defence. He pointed out that Pranaitis had mistranslated the texts in question and that one passage that he alleged to be about ritual murder "referred in fact to the slaughter of cattle but in no way to the slaughter of people."[72] So incompetent did Pranaitis prove to have been on the witness stand that the prosecutor must have been desperate to have called him. Wipper may have simply been going through the motions because his courtroom strategy had been dictated in advance from St Petersburg. This would also explain why he devoted so little time before the court to argue that Beilis was guilty.

One of the Gendarmes stationed in the jury room in the uniform of a court attendant reported on the jury's bewilderment: "How can we try Beilis if he is not spoken of at the court sessions?"[73] But the prosecution had already decided that the prosecution of Beilis was a lost cause, and directed its efforts to the issue of ritual murder.

The prosecution stayed with this strategy. The concluding speeches of the civil plaintiffs dealt mainly with charges against the Jewish people as a whole and not against Beilis. Even Wipper developed the same theme, a fact commented upon by the police officer D'iachenko, who wired to Beletsky that "the main deficiency of [Wipper's] speech was the anaemic description of Beilis's activities."[74]

The end result was that the jury acquitted Beilis even as it gave the minister of the interior a victory that satisfied the anti-Semites. That result came when the judge put only two questions to the jury, and their ordering confirms the primary importance placed on the question of ritual murder. The first point to decide, instructed the judge, was whether Iushchinsky "had been killed in such a manner as to inflict upon him great suffering and to drain his body of blood?"[75] The jury was ordered to proceed to the second question only if it answered affirmatively to the first.

The second question centred on Beilis. Was it he, asked the judge, who committed the murder described in question one, so doing "with premeditation and stimulated by religious fanaticism in agreement with other persons who remained undiscovered?" The verdict sought by the prosecution, then, was that someone had committed ritual murder that involved religious fanaticism. Nowhere in the instructions was the word Jew mentioned; but anti-Semites could easily read that into the verdict.

That verdict affirmed that a ritual murder had taken place but that Beilis had not done it. The minister of the interior, working with the minister of justice, had brought about what he saw as the best possible outcome in an impossible case; by highlighting ritual murder he had avoided outbreaks of violence and, in particular, pogroms. Contrary to fears among the police, the verdict of not guilty did not cause public disturbances. As Beilis was released following twenty-seven months in captivity, the police chief of Kiev said to him: "I have been almost lowered by anxiety. I have been responsible for you and order in the town for the last two months. I had to be on guard to prevent any contingency. Let me assure you it's no easy matter to keep an excited crowd in check. I am genuinely pleased to hear that you are free."[76]

High officials were also happy to have the trial behind them. They had counted on just such an outcome for political and security reasons. The verdict satisfied them by appeasing anti-Semites while it relieved them of dealing with the outcry that would have followed the conviction of Beilis. The Gendarme officer Liubimov suggested the Department of Police continue the murder investigation, but he found no interest in the pursuit of the killers of Iushchinsky. In December 1913 V.F. Dzhunkovsky, the assistant minister of the interior, told Shcheglovitov that an English detective had arrived in Kiev to continue the investigation. The information turned out to be incorrect, but Shcheglovitov responded that he had no intention of pursuing the murder case. He wrote Dzhunkovsky that the Ministry of Justice had no new evidence in the matter and that "it would be highly expedient to stop the search." He said the detective should be warned "that his actions are likely to stir up local passions which might result in his exile from Kiev."[77]

The imperial government, over the last two decades of the nineteenth century and the first several years of the twentieth century, believed that it faced a serious threat to its stability in the so-called Jewish question. Although numerous students of this issue have taken the position that the Russian government was guilty of deliberately fomenting violence against the Jewish population of the Empire, an investigation of actual policies does not support the conclusion. To be sure, a great number of imperial officials from the tsar on down can be said to have been anti-Semitic. But there were also powerful officials such as Witte and Stolypin who sought to solve the Jewish question and help economic development by gradually integrating Jews into the mainstream of Russian life. Above all, they wished to avoid providing excuses for anti-Semitic outbreaks.

The Beilis affair brought the issue of anti-Semitism to the surface before a world audience and compelled officials of the imperial government to work out a strategy to emphasize ritual murder when it became absolutely clear that they could not and should not convict Beilis. In other words, their prime goals of avoiding pogroms and general disaffection forced them to prosecute in a way that would placate anti-Semites, avoid pogroms, and at the same time exonerate Beilis.

PART FIVE

The Decline of the Okhranka

CHAPTER THIRTEEN

The Struggle for
the Okhranka

Okhranka record-keeping reached an apex in 1916 as security files bulged with reports from informants hired to keep watch virtually everywhere. As challenges to the old regime mounted, security officials fell back on saturation infiltration to sow discord and distrust among opponents of the government in order to keep them from uniting. In 1917, evidence from police files that this principle had been in effect for years would provide the grounds for one more report by the Provisional Government, that of the Extraordinary Investigating Commission, on autocratic corruption.

Among the police officials included in that exposé were two very different policy-makers from the closing decade of the Empire: S.P. Beletsky and V.F. Dzhunkovsky. Both came to their police posts after long but quite different service in the government and with strongly contrasting philosophies, and a discussion of their disagreements and interactive administrations aptly closes this study of political investigation under Russian governments.

In reporting to the Extraordinary Commission of the Provisional Government in 1917, its investigator, I. Iodlovsky, summarized the dominant policies of the Okhranka from 1907 to its dissolution in February 1917. Quoting directive after directive, he documented his argument that the political police had shifted primarily to using informers and provocateurs once it had created the local security divisions, or O.O.s, in 1903. Stolypin, he argued, had confirmed that shift from predominantly external operations to those that were predominantly internal by approving police circulars of 10 February 1907 and 19 January 1911.[1] Although he makes too much of orders that necessarily addressed worst-case circumstances, Iodlovsky effectively shows that duplicity and underhandedness became common in Okhranka operations.

The last police director, A.T. Vassilyev (September 1916 to February 1917), would label the attitude of the Provisional Government investigators naive in their assumption that the use by police officials of paid informers within "prohibited political organizations" whom they guaranteed "immunity from arrest" constituted a crime for which those same officials should be prosecuted. Such covert means were legitimate, he argued, taking the standard but defensible position of the Okhranka, because those means alone could effectively counter criminal conspirators against the legal order.[2]

Expanding its informers' network was one Okhranka response to an intensifying of revolutionary activity, including a wave of terrorism and so-called expropriations or bank robberies to fund radical parties that continued largely unabated after the revolution of 1905. Reliable police figures show that there were nine thousand persons, including great numbers of state officials, killed and injured in terrorist attacks during this period. From early 1908 until mid-1910 there were an additional 7,600 casualties throughout the Empire. Violence spread and drew sustenance from the support of terrorist acts against the autocracy by almost all political parties. Terrorists claiming to be acting for a proliferating number of obscure groups became more criminal in character and their assaults more casual, wanton, cynical, and murderous. Criminals and psychologically disturbed persons found their way into political terrorism. Often they only vaguely connected their acts with political objectives.[3] This epidemic of terrorism required the Okhranka to focus anew its energies on extending its informer network.

What follows are examples – not all of them Iodlovsky's – of typical post-1905 orders for intensifying the very operations that Iodlovsky condemned. The first is from July 1908 when M.I. Trusevich, as police director, called for yet more secret agents who were to expedite the arrest of subversives by promoting what he euphemistically called an "ever sharper narrowing" of their programs – that is, by provoking them to commit criminal acts.[4]

That same year, S.E. Vissarionov (vice-director of the police and head of the Special Section from 1908 to 1912) expanded the range of his agents to include local government institutions and private warehouses where revolutionaries might obtain arms.[5] Making a virtue of the psychological impact of blanket surveillance, he expressed confidence that resultant distrustfulness would become so strong that "no conspiracy will ever seem sufficient."[6]

By 1910 N.P. Zuev, director from 1909 to 1912, was placing security spies within the Gendarme units that watched the railways (that is, some of his internal agents were to conduct surveillance on some of his external agents) and within the regular military; he singled out the Lithuanian-Polish Socialist party and the Pan-Islamic movement for penetration.[7] A year later he was warning his agents to watch closely the "radical intelligentsia" who were bent on reactivating the unions of 1905. It seemed to him that the Social Democrats and the left-wing liberals within the Kadets were forming an expedient political alliance to build a massive opposition.[8]

As the number of strikes in 1911 grew, Vissarionov directed the Okhranka to spread a still broader blanket of secret agents throughout the workforce to prevent a re-enactment of the 1905 revolution, when organized groups of labourers and professionals had united to form so broad a front that the government was forced to accede to their demands.[9] In June of the next year, the director of police, S.P. Beletsky, flatly ordered that every union of workers in the country contain an internal agent. By September he had included all educational institutions and prisons; by October, "all oppositional and revolutionary spheres, especially those of students, peasants, railway workers, soldiers, and sailors."[10] When V.F. Dzhunkovsky became Beletsky's superior in April 1913 he set about reducing the Okhranka's infiltration corps. But the following year he had to face new security problems with the outbreak of war with Germany in July. At that point, even he could see the need to place agents among the Mensheviks and Bolsheviks to sabotage any union between those two oppositional and increasingly powerful factions.[11]

Beletsky brought his all-out emphasis on infiltration back to the fore in September 1915 when he replaced Dzhunkovsky as assistant minister of the interior. Under his watch, the director of police, E.K. Klimovich, sounded an alarm to his ranks in July 1916 about the anti-government sentiments reported by an informer within the Central Executive Committee of the privately organized War Industries Committees. Although this network of business leaders had purportedly come together to help the war effort, he warned, its Central Committee had taken a subversive stand for "freedom of coalition" and its vote to encourage workers to join together in whatever form – social, cultural, or educational – could win them the requisite approval of local authorities. Here was an effort to organize the working mass against the state order, contended Klimovich.[12]

Three months later and only four months before the fall of the tsar, yet another director of police, Vassilyev, was demanding that his investigative units "systematically broaden" their secret agent operations. He also directed that no one in the network fail to submit written reports. Unless the Security Section received raw data, its analysts could not make the best use of agents and informers – or judge who were slackers, as was so easily the case in secret operations.[13]

Beletsky, then, epitomizes the quintessential spy master who became the principal figure in the tsarist secret police in the last years of the regime. He personally guided major operations, adopted all known methods of investigation, and surrendered himself to his work with all the enthusiasm of one newly converted to a faith. Beletsky seems to have wanted to prove that he was exceptionally qualified for his high post, for he was one of only a few officials outside the upper class who had succeeded in ascending to a high rung on the administrative ladder in a bureaucracy overwhelmingly dominated by the gentry.

Having successfully completed a law degree at Kiev University, Beletsky nonetheless had to struggle for every advantage that went to others by right of birth. He began his service career as a junior assistant in a government office and after thirteen years had managed to climb only to senior assistant. A change in his life came when he became absorbed in an activity outside his official duties, the altruistic work of the Red Cross. He worked on various committees and commissions under the patronage of various high government personages and their wives. Beletsky was the scrupulous and conscientious fulfiller of work that tended to bore those in charge, such as keeping financial records, maintaining correspondence, and filing materials. For his later career, his most important assignment was to work on a commission assuring food supplies to the population under the chairmanship of the marshal of the nobility in Kovno, P.A. Stolypin. Stolypin was impressed by Beletsky's attention to his responsibilities, and when he became minister of the interior he appointed Beletsky to the post of vice-governor of Samara province. In June 1909 Stolypin summoned Beletsky to St Petersburg as vice-director of the Department of Police.

Although Beletsky was completely new to the world and staff of the police, because of his connection with Stolypin he soon found himself dealing with highly delicate matters. He prepared for Stolypin's signature an answer to Count S.Iu. Witte on the participation of police officers and Black Hundreds' agitators in the attempt on Witte's life. Beletsky recalled that it fell to him "to concoct formal responses that appeared to be responses, but carefully nuanced to be neither two nor one and one-half, as it was said."[14]

In the Department of Police, as vice-director, Beletsky had responsibility for the financial section and he was chairman of the legislative commission which had been charged with preparing reforms of the police. The vice-minister, A.A. Makarov, supervised this work. When

Makarov moved up to become minister he named Beletsky, who once again had performed well in a subordinate's role, head of the Department of Police (Beletsky actually filled this role from December 1911 but formally received the designation of director only a year later). Beletsky immediately displayed his staggering capacity for work. He was at his desk from early in the morning until late in the evening. If his minister required a report quickly, then Beletsky would sit through the night to study a thousand pages of documents and would present a detailed summary in the morning.

In the eyes of his colleagues and acquaintances, Beletsky was an exemplary person, who perhaps transgressed by his excessive currying favour from higher-ups. Beletsky considered himself an excellent father and, along with two daughters of his own, raised an orphaned girl. However, on one occasion, Makarov said, not without reason, that his subordinate was irreproachable as long as he held him in check.

Until he became director of the Department of Police, Beletsky hardly ever encountered issues of political investigation; as vice-director, management problems had occupied his time. From such a man, whose formative experiences had been outside the police system, who threw himself into the preparation of the reforms of the police, one might expect a fresh approach to the police system and its bureaucratic routines. No such reaction came from Beletsky. The new director took a narrowly official position towards secret police work, to the corps of detectives, to managing the affairs of the department. His colleagues and subordinates began to refer to him as the "All-Russian detective" and the "poet of the police trade." Beletsky actually revelled in his position as head of the Empire's secret police. He sent experts abroad to study all the latest police methods, summoned the first conference of the heads of his detective divisions, and promoted the use of the latest scientific methods for struggling with criminality. He was the pioneer in Russia of the use of listening devices.[15]

With great zest for his work, Beletsky plunged into matters that previous directors preferred to avoid. He personally controlled the most important secret agents, went forth into the streets of Petersburg to meet with informers and agents in conspiratorial apartments, and dictated instructions to them. Having studied all the fine points of the revolutionary underground, and being personally acquainted with the leaders of the main parties, Beletsky employed the ancient principle of divide and conquer. He staked a great deal on exploiting the schism between the Bolsheviks and the Mensheviks, although subsequent development showed that isolating the Bolshevik party had a quite different result to the one the director of the Department of Police anticipated.

Beletsky's Malinovsky operation was the result of the Okhranka's policy to widen the divisions in the Russian Social Democratic Workers' party and thereby weaken its ability to lead the opposition against the government. By 1910 the Okhranka believed that it had broken the terrorist wing of the Socialist Revolutionary party. The secret agency had made possible this triumph and Beletsky in 1912 came up with the idea of using the method of infiltration – which had been successful against the illegal SRS – against the Social Democrats operating within a legal organization, the State Duma. His chosen agent would be Roman Malinovsky.

Malinovsky, a Russified Pole, had a criminal record. He had served a prison term for burglary from 1899 to 1902 and, upon release, had joined the workers' movement and risen rapidly through its ranks. He became a founder of the St Petersburg Metal Workers' Union and, in 1907, its secretary. Malinovsky attracted a following among the workers because of his fiery speaking style and bold attacks against the government. He was one of those figures in the early twentieth century who sensed the influence of the masses, developed the qualities of a spell-binding orator, and knew how to sway the thinking of a large audience.

Following his term in jail, Malinovsky joined another organization, the Okhranka. Okhranka agents knew a lot about him and told him that they understood that he was hardly a believing revolutionary, but rather a tribune of the people who sought acclaim. Beletsky planned to further Malinovsky's true ambition for public attention and influence. After a period of reflection, Malinovsky agreed to serve as a secret agent.[16] His rise as police agent paralleled his upward climb in the Metal Workers' Union. The value of his reports soon vaulted Malinovsky to the status of a privileged agent. He was permitted to inform on his comrades directly by telephone rather than at meetings in conspiratorial apartments. The Okhranka had so much confidence in him that it did not subject him to the periodic psychological assessments that controlling officers undertook during a debriefing. The Okhranka scrupulously protected Malinovsky and carried out the arrests of those he denounced with great care in order to avoid compromising him. Eventually, to protect his connection with the St Petersburg Okhranka, the police exiled him from the city to avoid exposure.

Malinovsky merely moved to Moscow and resumed his double career. He was "arrested" on the streets of the city and, while under detention, became a regular agent of the Moscow Okhranka after negotiating personally with its head, P.P. Zavarzin.[17] His value to the police had become even greater because of his rise in the Russian Social Democratic Workers' party. The two rival factions of the party, the Bolsheviks and the Mensheviks, were competing for influence among the workers. Malinovsky was thoroughly familiar with this struggle because he had earlier led the fight to beat back the Bolshevik takeover of the Metal Workers' Union. Beletsky put great value on Malinovsky's knowledge of inner-party affairs and especially his ability to evaluate accurately information about the party received from the Foreign Agency. Malinovsky's information would now be used in another way. Beletsky said later that he instructed Malinovsky "to use all possible means to promote the divisions in the party."[18]

Malinovsky was not left on his own to promote this objective. The Okhranka came up with a fresh idea for the use of its agent: Malinovsky was to run for election to a deputy's seat in the State Duma as a representative of a workers' curia in Moscow; the Okhranka intended to make certain that he won the election. Beletsky says that A.P. Martynov, the new chief of the Moscow Okhranka, first raised the idea with him in 1912 as the elections approached for the Fourth State Duma. A.T. Vassilyev, who would later be the last chief of the Okhranka, said that this "trifling affair" was entirely the idea of Beletsky.[19]

No matter who thought of the idea, Beletsky liked it; but, before going ahead, he first sought approval from his superiors: "I spoke by telephone with Zoltarev [vice-minister of the interior]. Zoltarev met with Martynov and said that it was necessary to put the question to Dzhunkovsky [then Moscow governor]; if Dzhunkovsky agrees to push ahead, we will explain to him what Malinovsky offers as an agent ... In any case, Dzhunkovsky was informed and with the permission of Dzhunkovsky, Malinovsky was put through the Electoral Commission."[20]

Guided by Beletsky, the Okhranka instructed Malinovsky to leave the Mensheviks and join Lenin's Bolsheviks. Malinovsky soon became a rising star in the more radical faction and was elected to the Moscow central committee. He was no longer required to report on his comrades, only to keep Beletsky informed about their latest planning. Other Okhranka agents in the Moscow Bolshevik organization now had responsibility to inform on the membership of the faction.[21]

The most brilliant phase of Malinovsky's career as a secret agent lay ahead. As Moscow delegate to Lenin's Bolshevik Congress in Prague in January 1912 (the Okhranka bought his train ticket), Malinovsky knew that Lenin planned to name his own party central committee in place of the united party committee that had been elected at the last Social Democratic party congress. Working at Lenin's side, Malinovsky won election to the Bolshevik party central committee and was nominated to stand at the next election for the State Duma. Malinovsky had not only become a leading Bolshevik, but would emerge as Lenin's chief spokesman in Russia just as the workers' movement was taking on a new direction.

Following the revolution of 1905, the government had largely confined workers to restricted forms of organization. But with industrial expansion speeding up in 1910, factory workers gained new confidence and pressed demands on their employers. Then, a single event caused the workers' movement to become even more radical. In April 1912 troops fired on striking miners at the Lena goldfields in Siberia. Protests and demonstrations swept through the industrial centres of European Russia. Three-quarters of a million workers went on strike in 1912 and the number increased in 1913. Both the Okhranka and the Bolsheviks now saw good reason to elect Malinovsky to the Duma. The Okhranka wished to splinter the resurgent workers' movement and Lenin wished to bring it under his control.

Beletsky cleared the way for Malinovsky's election. He arranged to expunge Malinovsky's criminal record and issue him a new passport. For nomination, the law also required work for one employer for at least six months. When Malinovsky fell into conflict with the foreman of the Moscow textile plant where he worked and claimed his job was at risk, the Okhranka ordered the arrest and detention of the foreman for four months until Malinovsky had been elected to the Duma. By this time, Beletsky had assumed personal control over Malinovsky and met him in the private dining-rooms of the most expensive restaurants. Beletsky or another Okhranka officer reviewed Malinovsky's speeches, some of which Lenin had written. Beletsky and Malinovsky co-authored Bolshevik statements, and Malinovsky supplied his chief with party documents for copying.

Beletsky and his collaborators had violated the election law when they purged Malinovsky's record. They had arbitrarily arrested and detained the factory foreman who had threatened Malinovsky's job. Vissarionov said later that this was an extremely unusual Okhranka operation; no other agent had received so much attention. When Dzhunkovsky was asked later if he knew that Malinovsky did not have the right to be elected, he replied, "If I had the information about Malinovsky, then of course he would not have been." [22]

A.M. Eremin, who headed the Special Section, had early doubts about the operation, amd events would confirm them in the course of 1913. It was not that Malinovsky was threatened with exposure, but that he began to appear to some officials in the Okhranka (although not to Beletsky) to be helping the Bolsheviks more than the government. For two years Malinovsky remained as the principal spokesman for the Leninist group in Russia, both as leader of the Bolshevik faction in the Duma and the chief public spokesman outside of the Duma. The Bolshevik newspaper *Pravda* also promoted the Leninist message; it was edited by another Okhranka secret agent, Miron Chernomazev. Vissarionov said he believed that Malinovsky had gone over the other side. "When I began to read his speeches in the Duma, I came to the conclusion that it was not possible to work with him any longer."[23]

When V.F. Dzhunkovsky became assistant minister of the interior in April 1913 he at once took steps to trim the sprawling system of secret agents that, to him, exceeded good order and legality. As he tells it, he found Beletsky unsympathetic to this change. But Beletsky was so entrenched in the department that Dzhunkovsky could not bring about his resignation until January of the next year. He would later emphasize their differences over appropriate security operations.

Because Beletsky likewise recognized the disparity of their views, contends Dzhunkovsky, this incumbent police director had deliberately "overtaxed me with pettiness, sought my agreement on trifles, in order to distract me from the main things, the essentials." In turn, maintains Dzhunkovsky, when he had confronted Beletsky with his "criminal" and "corrupting" use of secondary students as informers against their fellow students – the basis for police arrests following demonstrations in St Petersburg in April 1913 – "Beletsky could not prove to me the necessity of it." Dzhunkovsky had consequently banned the practice only to discover some Gendarmes ignoring that prohibition. Believing that "this happened with the participation of Beletsky," Dzhunkovsky immediately took the "extreme measure" of firing the Gendarme offenders.[24]

Dzhunkovsky claims also to have taken exception to using Gendarmes placed within the military as informers. He especially deplored that the spy network included military commanders, some of whom required the secret agents in their ranks to distribute radical pamphlets and to provoke disturbances to justify the arrest of suspected troublemakers. Although the minister of war, V.A. Sukhomlinov, seemingly favoured these "horrors," Dzhunkovsky once more ordered a ban on established practice even as he doubted its effectiveness.[25]

Other immediate reforms claimed by Dzhunkovsky were his new procedures that put an end to Gendarme abuse of passengers on trains, that limited perlustration solely to letters bearing on national security, and that mitigated the exile system, which he personally opposed because it intensified opposition. Using the authority he held, he said, he often shortened the periods of exile recommended by the Special Conference, "never refused a request for independent travel to the place of exile [the convoy and transit system was harsh] ... and almost never refused to substitute deportation abroad for exile, seeing in this no danger for the state."[26]

Two months after assuming office, he had convened a conference in Moscow of police subordinates to promote legality in their operations; just a week later, he ordered the elimination of all but the most essential security divisions (those in St Petersburg, Moscow, and Warsaw remained, and several in outlying regions were reduced to observation posts). That fall, the indefatigable Dzhunkovsky inspected his far-flung police empire, the farthest outpost of which was the Foreign Agency in Paris, then covertly headed by A.A. Krasil'nikov.[27] As Dzhunkovsky took pains to emphasize, he had "legalized and properly arranged" Krasil'nikov's presence in Paris as something else – that is, as an official sent from the Russian Ministry of the Interior to consult with crime specialists in its French counterpart.[28]

By arranging a seat in the Senate for Beletsky, Dzhunkovsky made way in January 1914 for a new director of police, A.V. Brune de St Hippolite. Within six months, a new but temporary deterrent to subversive acts and agitation – the outbreak of war against Germany – caused Brune to frame a prescient analysis of the political future.[29]

Revolutionaries were momentarily biding their time, he wrote, lest their usual disruptive activities outrage the bulk of the population that had patriotically rallied behind the tsar. Their long-term objectives remained the same: to help place Kadets in the most important government posts because the liberals were certain to broaden the political freedoms of "the word, organization, and assembly" and thereby enable the revolutionaries to expand their "socialist propaganda and agitation." Already the liberals had aided the revolutionaries by fomenting a resurgence of workers' organizations which, because of the recent influx of peasant "green workers" and women into the factories, had tilted towards the radicals. When the time was right, the revolutionaries would use that support from the working masses to trample autocrat and liberals alike in order to seize power and impose socialism. Meanwhile the Okhranka's agents must help to stem that tide by reporting fully on the currently dominant opposition – the Kadets and the newer liberal party backed by powerful businessmen, the Party of Popular Freedom.[30]

On 6 September, not long before this analysis of the opposition as a whole, Brune had issued a directive expressing his narrower and immediate concerns about conciliatory signs among the revolutionary factions of the Social Democratic Labour party, and especially between the Bolsheviks and Mensheviks. He had consequently ordered all his internal agents within the party to prevent reunification by any possible means – the very assignment that Beletsky had given Malinovsky.[31]

But Malinovsky, the flamboyant Bolshevik known for his speeches in party and government councils alike, was not among the police agents who received Brune's October directive; for, although he was still secretly on full pay from the Okhranka, he had gone into retirement abroad, having abruptly resigned on 4 May from the Duma. How that sudden change came about is still open to conjecture. According to the account left by Dzhunkovsky that puts himself in the best light and contradicts Beletsky's version of events, Beletsky had at no time during his use of Malinovsky informed or consulted Dzhunkovsky, knowing that he would never tolerate the illegal chicanery of manipulating state politics. Therefore, maintains Dzhunkovsky, he had remained in the dark until April 1914 when Brune discovered Malinovsky's records in the voluminous files he had inherited.[32] Claiming outrage that a police agent was serving in the Duma, Dzhunkovsky says that he had immediately ordered Malinovsky to tender his resignation to the president of the Duma, M.V. Rodzianko, and to leave Russia, albeit with a 6,000-ruble annual pension that equalled his previous police salary. Rodzianko testifies that he learned the reason for Malinovsky's departure only several days later from Dzhunkovsky, who asked him to keep the matter confidential.[33] (Dzhunkovsky probably broke confidentiality because he felt Malinovsky's role would sooner or later become known and thought it best to be forthright with Rodzianko at the outset.)

Another plausible explanation, however, is that Dzhunkovsky primarily found the political timing right for Malinovsky's retirement in the spring of 1914. Because the crowd-pleasing Malinovsky was then a big factor in the Bolsheviks' rising influence among the workers, the strange departure of this icon would disconcert the public and make it easy for the Okhranka to spread misinformation (or even the truth) about Malinovsky to demoralize the Bolsheviks and to repel their potential supporters.[34]

Lenin, finally admitting in 1917 that he had been in error in defending Malinovsky, said nonetheless that the Bolsheviks had benefited enormously from Malinovsky's work. But when, following the revolution, Malinovsky foolishly presented himself to the Bolsheviks as a supporter cruelly blackmailed into working for the Okhranka, he was summarily executed. As for the summation of the Malinovsky affair by Dzhunkovsky, the former assistant minister conjectured merely that the "Department of Police received little advantage, [and] more likely it distracted Beletsky from serious matters."[35] As for why he did not prosecute Beletsky for criminally securing the Duma post for Malinovsky once he knew about it, Dzhunkovsky plausibly replied, "I simply did not want a scandal."[36]

Whatever happened, the indignation professed by Dzhunkovsky over the Malinovsky affair is thoroughly consistent with his reformist stance against the Okhranka's excessive and illegal use of informers and secret agents. Moreover, if he and Beletsky were in fact strongly at odds over Malinovsky's departure, Dzhunkovsky gave Beletsky yet another issue to use against him later, in addition to their purported differences over cutbacks in Okhranka personnel.

By the time Malinovsky resigned, Dzhunkovsky had reduced security forces by sufficient numbers to trim 500,000 rubles, by his estimate, from the Police Department budget for 1914. Most of his projected savings had come from eliminating security divisions, but he had also reduced the guards at Fontanka 16, for example, and halved the one-hundred-man contingent that protected the tsar's mother, the Empress Maria Fedorovna. In further restraint, he was requiring subordinates to obtain approval in advance for any costly operations.

Insisting that the budget in effect when he became overseer of the police was exorbitant, Dzhunkovsky contends in his memoirs that the funds that the government made available to the Ministry of the Interior for security operations in 1913 exceeded 5 million rubles, about 1.5 million of them from the tsar's discretionary secret fund of 10 million rubles. There were also many security expenditures outside the Interior Ministry, such as the salaries paid by the Justice Ministry for six guards for its minister; likewise there were expenditures by the Ministry of the Interior not officially within its security budget that largely belonged there, as in its payment of 208,000 rubles for "strengthening" Gendarme units in the provinces.

Listing the total amount of Interior's official security budget for 1913 as 3,966,105 rubles, Dzhunkovsky specifies that just over one-fourth, or 1,034,663 rubles, went for protective services (688,180 to the Okhrana that secured the palace and its surroundings, and 346,483 to the St Petersburg chief of police to provide personal guards for the imperial family and high officials). Two-thirds, or 2,667,942 rubles, went for domestic political investigations (1,984,524 rubles to security divisions or O.O.s, 608,500 to railway Gendarmes, and 74,918 to agents directly under the Security Section). Finally, the remaining 6.6 percent, or 263,500 rubles, funded operations outside Russia by the Foreign Agency.[37] Included in the expenditures beyond the official budget and paid for by the tsar's secret funds were 800,000 rubles for extra security during celebrations for the three hundredth anniversary of the Romanov dynasty. Some 700,000 additional rubles, then, went for still other extraordinary security costs incurred at the option of high officials.

Whatever initial savings Dzhunkovsky accomplished at the start of his 1914 budgetary year, his cutbacks became a necessity when the outbreak of war in July forced him to maintain his budget cuts for that year and the next. They survived his departure into 1916. General figures for 1914, 1915, and 1916 show a stabilizing of expenditures for political investigation. The budget for 1914 was 3,348,192 rubles (74 percent of all expenditures for the Department of Police); that of 1915 was 3,327,638 rubles (73 percent of the total); and that of 1916 was 3,543,317 rubles (72 percent of the total).[38] Assuming, which is likely, that these figures include the Foreign Agency, they all show reductions of about 500,000 rubles in each annual budget after the 1913 budget, thus appearing to bear out the savings that Dzhunkovsky reports in his memoirs.

The figures given by the Menshevek Sergei Svatikov, however, appear to show that the budget for political investigation was rising again in 1916. He cites two allocations by the director of police for 1916, the last year of the Empire, showing outlays of 2,701,394 rubles for domestic political investigations and 261,000 rubles (782,477 francs) for investigations abroad – about the same as Dzhunkovsky cites for the 1913 budget for the two categories.[39] This suggests a return in 1916 to 1913 levels for political investigation.

After the revolution of 1905, the network of secret agents had widened enormously. As the pride of the Okhranka, it was considered the most effective means for struggle with the collective forces of the opposition. However, there were those who believed that the army of secret agents had grown much too large. In their opinion it was ineffective, corrupt, and cost too much. The conflict between those who wished to widen this favourite instrument of Russian political investigation and those who wished to curtail it appeared in sharp outline in the conflict between Beletsky and Dzhunkovsky.

Dzhunkovsky tried to reform the Okhranka, to cut its budget, and to deliver it from those who opposed the changes. He appeared to achieve a major victory in his program to reform the police when he removed Beletsky and put an end to the operation which had installed the secret police agent Roman Malinovsky as a member of the State Duma. Beletsky, however, the next year assumed the post of assistant minister of the interior and took into his hands control over the police. The cause of this strange reversal of events is to be found in the huge influence of Rasputin and Beletsky's adroit use of this influence in his own interests.

CHAPTER FOURTEEN

Police Officials and Rasputin

Internal divisions within the imperial political police appeared in sharp outline during the final three years of the regime, especially in two efforts to save the autocracy by those two very different police masters: Dzhunkovsky and Beletsky.

Rasputin, the Siberian peasant who became spiritual counsellor and political advisor to the tsarina, made their task impossibly difficult, given that this main enemy of the throne derived his power from his relationship with Alexandra. Whereas the Okhranka had waged effective clandestine warfare against various external enemies – in the underground, over the vast reaches of the Empire, over the continent of Europe – in Rasputin it encountered for the first time an enemy who had the support of the imperial consorts.

How, then, could the masters of the political police deal with this threat to the monarchy? Each man used his own proved methods of political policing: Dzhunkovsky attempted persuasion and Beletsky used intrigue. But Rasputin confounded both of these experienced police administrators, who became increasingly alarmed over the influence of Rasputin at the imperial court. Neither, despite their ability to call on the resources of the Department of Police and the Okhranka, could rescue the autocrat from himself.

Rasputin would not have risen to a top position in the palace but for the long-standing Russian practice of heeding and supporting a few individuals regarded as "God's fools" – that is, psychologically impaired persons looked upon as saintly because of their seemingly divine insight and gifts of prophecy. They were supported by charity from the faithful of the Russian Orthodox Church.

Many cathedrals became renowned precisely because one could meet the "blessed" on the church porch. A number of aristocratic families had their own resident prophets. Heightened interest in mysticism at the beginning of the twentieth century made the influence of these people easier in St Petersburg high society, where spiritualistic seances were a constant distraction. God's fools fit into these diversions because of their own claims to special spiritual insight. Spiritualism, whether because of the influence of St Petersburg society or as a result of her own private searchings, shaped the outlook of Tsarina Alexandra Fedorovna. Although German by birth, as a granddaughter of Queen Victoria she was tutored under the queen's supervision until she was fifteen at the English court by a demanding Englishwoman, Miss Jackson. She did well in her studies and spoke English as well as German, her native language. She absorbed little English scepticism, however, and welcomed to the tsarist residences several of the "blessed."[1] One of them was Grigory Efimovich Rasputin-Novykh.

Rasputin was a common family name in Siberia, where Grigory was born in the village of Pokrovskoe, Tobolsk province, in 1864 or 1865 into a peasant family.[2] As a boy, Rasputin ploughed fields, worked in a fisheries artel, and served as a coachman. Like most peasants, he married early and showed a taste for delinquent behaviour. One villager later claimed to have caught Rasputin in an act of petty thievery and to have rendered him unconscious with a blow from a fence post.[3] Once Rasputin faced charges before the village assembly as a horse stealer, but was acquitted for lack of hard evidence.

When he was about thirty, Rasputin informed his family that he had undergone a sudden religious conversion. His sceptical relatives responded with laughter, for that change of heart during a day of hard labour on a threshing crew was an excuse for him to drive his shovel into a pile of grain and take off, wandering aimlessly alone from one monastery to another. By his own account, he went from Siberia to Kiev and later completed a pilgrimage to far Mount Athos in Greece and even to Jeruselem.

He never took holy instruction, nor was he ever more than marginally literate; although he could recite the gospels by heart, many observers seriously doubted the sincerity of his belief in the Orthodox faith. Some contended that he had joined one of the strangest of the Siberian religious groups, the *khlysty*,[4] but the Tobolsk Consistory investigated that charge and could find no evidence to support it.

Rasputin first appeared in St Petersburg in 1903 or 1904, when he was about forty. Nonetheless, he presumptiously called himself "starets" or elder – a non-canonical title of respect commonly accorded to aged monks – because he claimed the powers of a clairvoyant and a healer. Claims that supposedly respected doctors confirmed cures by Rasputin in cases pronounced as hopeless do not stand up to scrutiny.

Rasputin became the protégé of several highly placed churchmen, the most important of whom were Feofan, rector of the St Petersburg Ecclesiastical Academy, and Hermogen, Bishop of Saratov, and a member of the Holy Synod, the state's supervisery body of the Russian Orthodox Church. Another churchman who supported Rasputin was Iliodor. This crowd-rousing monastic had become acquainted with Rasputin in 1903 at the very beginning of his career. For several years he gave support to the starets, inviting him to Tsaritsyn where Iliodor preached, and he travelled to Pokrovskoe to be Rasputin's guest. Only after several years of close relations with Rasputin did Iliodor finally understood the true nature of the starets.

Through Hermogen and Feofan, Rasputin entered into some of the drawing rooms of the capital's aristocracy in 1904 or 1905 as a simple peasant from the countryside. At some point, he met members of the imperial family. The Grand Duchesses Stana and Militsa, daughters of the Duke of Montenegro and related to the Romanov dynasty, "discovered" the rustic Siberian. They introduced Rasputin to Grand Duke Nicholas Nicholaevich, the uncle of Nicholas II, and they recounted stories of Rasputin's miraculous abilities to their circle. Eventually, the imperial couple learned of Rasputin.

Rasputin met the tsar on 1 November 1905, and Nicholas wrote in his diary: "I met with a man of God Grigory from Tobolsk province."[5] Meetings thereafter occurred from time to time. When Rasputin was in the capital, he was sometimes invited to the tsarist residence where he might converse with Nicholas and Alexandra. In later years, to the horror of the imperial couple's attendants, he addressed Nicholas II as "Papasha" and Alexandra as "Mamasha." They respectfully called him "Our Friend" and in correspondence always used capital letters. Most important, Nicholas and Alexander became convinced that the prayers of the starets could ease the suffering of the heir to the throne, Alexis, who suffered from hemophilia. According to his daughter Maria, Rasputin first appeared to heal the tsarevich sometime in 1906 during a crisis when the family physician believed the imperial couple's son might die.[6]

By 1908 Rasputin stood out from the crowd of "God's people" at court, but only after the beginning of the First World War did Rasputin's power become genuinely significant, although his influence on the royal couple was not equal. The tsarina fell completely under the powerful influence of Rasputin, but Nicholas from time to time showed his anger with Rasputin. However, Nicholas repeatedly granted reprieves to Rasputin, having persuaded himself that he was not permitting outside interference in his personal life.

What can be called the "Rasputin circle" increasingly intruded into the sphere of governmental affairs. This circle, which had come to include Alexandra's lady-in-waiting, Anna Vyrubova, and several distinguished ladies, became the talk of the capital. It was said that the "Rasputinites" were deeply depraved. There are many legends about the sexual activities of Rasputin, but one should approach them with caution. For instance, it was said that Rasputin had intimate relations with Vyrubova, but no evidence supports such claims.

Along with the women in Rasputin's circle, there appeared some businessmen and even government officials. As a result, Rasputin's apartment became filled with a crowd of petitioners during his reception hours from 10 a.m. until 1 p.m. Not only the poor but the wealthy and important wished to see the tsarist favourite. One witness to these events left the following impression: "There is an officer in the brilliant uniform of one of the guards' regiments who modestly waits his turn. Here is a man with fat jowls coming into the reception room accompanied by a manservant in a fur cape. He is clearly some kind of banker on an urgent mission."[7]

Even the prime minister, Stolypin, seems to have had a meeting with Rasputin as early as 1906. In response to the urging of the tsar in a letter of 16 October, he had invited the starets to meet his daughter who had been injured in the dynamite blast at his summer home on Aptekarsky Island.[8] Rasputin complained that the minister initially was his "best friend" and then became his enemy.

Rasputin's meetings with great numbers of petitioners came to the attention of the police. According to A.V. Gerasimov, its chief until 1909, the St Petersburg Okhranka began surveillance of Rasputin's apartment toward the end of 1908 at the prodding of the commandant of the imperial court, V.A. Dediulin. He feared that under the guise of one of Rasputin's "blessed," a terrorist might get near the tsar. Gerasimov also ordered a watch on Rasputin wherever he went and conveyed his detectives' reports to the prime minister about Rasputin's unsavoury acquaintances and immoral behaviour.[9] Gerasimov first reported sometime late in 1908 to the prime minister about Rasputin, and says that Stolypin did not know of his existence at that time,[10] but he may well have forgotten the name of the Siberian peasant who had visited him two years before. P.G. Kurlov, the assistant minister of the interior, recalled after the revolution of 1917 that Stolypin on one occasion invited Rasputin into his office. After the departure of the starets, the prime minister told Kurlov, "We are going to have trouble with him."[11]

Stolypin then reported to the tsar during an audience at the summer palace at Tsarskoe Selo. His report was the first time a high official tried to convince Nicholas to banish Rasputin. In response to a question from his daughter, he responded that he found it "impossible to do anything" by reporting the misconduct of Rasputin to Nicholas. As proof, he quoted a recent response of the tsar: "I agree with you, Peter Arkadeevich, but it is better to have ten Rasputins than one hysterical Empress."[12]

Stolypin made plans secretly to remove Rasputin from St Petersburg on his own responsibility by first ordering the starets detained and then exiling him from the capital. He wanted the operation carried out in the most complete secrecy. However, Rasputin managed to get wind of police intentions to detain him and instead concealed himself for several weeks in the mansions of his friends where the police could not gain access. Then, when Rasputin departed for his home village, Stolypin hoped for a lessening of Rasputin's influence on the tsar. But the prime minister could not block Rasputin from access to the imperial family. A close assistant of the prime minister later claimed that he had advised him, "You are a strong, talented man, you can do much, but I advise you not to challenge Rasputin and his friends, for you will break yourself on them."[13]

For Rasputin was parlaying his influence into a political role. At the end of August 1911, just prior to the assassination of Stolypin on 1 September, he stopped by Nizhnyi Novgorod and proposed to the current governor, A.N. Khvostov, the post of minister of the interior, the portfolio still held by Stolypin, the prime minister. As Khvostov tells it:

I, in the first place, ordered the police chief Ushakov, a decisive man of commanding appearance, to escort Rasputin to the train leaving for Petersburg, and, in the second place, upon taking leave of him, told Rasputin that if I was needed by the tsar, he himself would make this proposition to me, having summoned me to himself or having raised the question during my last personal report, and that I could not look on him, Rasputin, as a general-adjutant sent to me by the tsar with an order of this kind.[14]

Rasputin perhaps made that proposition because he knew that the tsar was thinking about replacing Stolypin as prime minister and minister of the interior.[15] On the other hand, the contention by some of Rasputin's contemporaries that the starets knew Stolypin's assassin, Dmitry Bogrov, and through him had a hand in the assassination is wholly unsupported by the evidence and altogether unlikely.[16]

S.Iu. Witte, one of Stolypin's predecessors, recalled that G.P. Sazonov, a journalist on the left who moved to the right following the revolution of 1905, approached him in late July 1911 about becoming prime minister once again. Sazonov was a close collaborator of Rasputin's and the starets had lived in his house during his first stay in the capital. Sazonov told Witte that he was conveying the views of the tsar who wished to replace Stolypin. Witte dismissed out of hand both Sazonov and his message.[17]

Stolypin could not prevent Rasputin's ascendancy; his many successors as minister of the interior were equally frustrated in their attempts to remove Rasputin from the centre of imperial power. The first of them, A.A. Makarov (who held the post from September 1911 to December 1912) had to deal with a starets-related scandal in December 1911. It involved Bishop Hermogen, Iliodor, and another of God's fools, Mitia Kozelsky, each of them having his own scores to settle with Rasputin.[18]

Iliodor, the Russian Orthodox priest, stood out vividly among this trio. As a leader of the right-wing Union of the Russian People, he had been a constant political nuisance for Stolypin, for he preached publicly that Nicholas II was surrounded by Judeo-Masons and that the prime minister was the chief traitor of the lot. Such extremism might have appeared merely amusing had Iliodor not been able to sway great crowds of listeners, especially lower-class women. Huge crowds assembled at the gates of the monastery at Tsaritsyn outside of Moscow where Iliodor delivered his fiery sermons. Stolypin had to divert a great deal of time and energy to his political combat with the "mad monk" – his label for Iliodor.

Iliodor, Hermogen, and Mitia had enticed Rasputin to Hermogen's residence, confronted him in January 1911, and demanded that he swear never again to cross the threshold of an imperial palace. Rasputin fled his enemies, but his influence with Nicholas had already grown to such a degree that he had no difficulty retaliating against them. At Rasputin's bidding, Hermogen was banned from participating in the Holy Synod's sessions. Dediulin, the imposing commandant of the court who had initiated the surveillance of Rasputin in 1908, delivered a personal order from the tsar in December 1911 exiling the bishop from St Petersburg to a monastery in Russian Poland and was ready to use force to expel him from the capital.[19] Nicholas II's order created a ticklish dilemma. Many believers were horrified by this treatment of a bishop.[20] Officials were fearful that Bishop Hermogen would resist. The Department of Police decided to send two Gendarme officers in civilian clothes to arrest Hermogen and carry out the deportation. The tension eased, however, when Hermogen agreed to offer no resistance.[21]

Pacifying Iliodor was not so simple. Even his political opponents expressed the view that the tsar had treated him arbitrarily. Although incarcerated in a monastic cell, he took his vengeance by ordering his underlings to release letters of the tsarina in his possession addressed to the starets. Rasputin then declared that these letters had been stolen by Iliodor when they were still friends. Alexandra had written the starets: "How painful it is without thee. My soul is at rest only when you, teacher, are by my side and I kiss your hand and put my head on your shoulder."[22] These phrases, which originated in the tsarina's feelings of religious exaltation, gave rise to a great deal of speculation about the close relations of Rasputin to the imperial family.

Makarov, the interior minister, was distraught as hundreds of copies of the duplicated letters passed from hand to hand in St Petersburg. Dealing through a lengthy chain of intermediaries, Makarov managed to acquire the originals and return them to Nicholas. Kokovtsov, who had replaced Witte after the prime minister had been assassinated, recounts that Makarov told him: "The Sovereign blanched, unsteadily drew the letters from the envelope and, seeing that the hand-writing was that of the Empress, said, 'Yes, this is a genuine letter.' and then opened the drawer of his writing table and in a completely uncharacteristic gesture, sharply tossed the envelope in."[23]

As a result of the episode with the letters, the tsar ordered Rasputin briefly barred from court, and Makarov lost his position as minister of the interior. As for Iliodor, he was deprived of his religious office. He had failed to dislodge Rasputin in 1912 but was purportedly behind an assassination attempt two years later by one of his "spiritual daughters," Khioniia Guseva, a former lover. She stabbed Rasputin in his home village of Pokrovskoe as he was about to enter a church, and managed to inflict serious wounds. Knowing that the police would link him to the stabbing, Iliodor had to flee abroad, where he wrote the book, *Holy Devil*, to excoriate Rasputin in print.

Rasputin's wounding caused Dzhunkovsky to place him under police guard and close surveillance – an opportunity he seized to document Rasputin's unseemly behaviour and shady contacts. Nicholas II himself ordered N.A. Maklakov, the interior minister, "to prevent the repetition of such atrocities," so that on 30 June 1914 Maklakov directed Dzhunkovsky to establish a continuous protective watch on Rasputin and his contacts.[24] Dzhunkovsky added his own objective: "I had in mind to obtain certain data which would permit me to bring accusations of illegal activity against him."[25]

At least four experienced agents henceforth monitored Rasputin, code-named "The Dark One," around the clock: two as bodyguards, two as covert agents. The domestics who worked in Rasputin's apartment also served the secret agency, and Dzhunkovsky stationed yet another agent in Rasputin's home village. From their daily reports emerged proof that their quarry in his own haunts "behaved disgracefully, got drunk, led a licentious life" and then feigned "gentle meekness and piety when he was at Tsarskoe Selo."

There was little turnover among the agents and detectives who surrounded Rasputin despite the tedium of their assignment. Rasputin's neighbour in the same stairwell recalled that "the agents played cards at the entrance constantly because they had nothing else to do."[26] When he was in a good mood, Rasputin would invite his minders into his kitchen, and even carry on political discussions with them. He insisted, for instance, that in 1905 it had been "still too early" to grant a constitution to Russia. The agents recorded Rasputin's comings and goings, questioned first-time visitors about their purpose, and entered all such data in brief, factual reports. Frequent visitors were distinguished by code names. Rasputin's varying condition and mood were routinely described.[27]

As required by Okhranka practice, officials at the highest level evaluated all such reports. Dzhunkovsky hoped to assemble sufficient discrediting evidence to convince the tsar to break with Rasputin. A large part of the problem, contended Dzhunkovsky, was the baseness of capital society that surrounded him in St Petersburg where so many courted Rasputin and so few resisted his demands that he felt "nothing but contempt" for those he used.[28]

Dzhunkovsky observed that even Maklakov, his superior, seemed "confused" with respect to the starets, but had at least once stood up to Rasputin by refusing to appoint a subordinate that Rasputin had urged on Nicholas through the tsarina. The candidate was a minor official whom Rasputin had chanced to meet in a railway station and decided to transform into a provincial governor. Whether or not that slight to Rasputin figured in Maklakov's subsequent dismissal on 5 June 1915, his successor as minister of the interior, A.A. Khvostov, did elevate Rasputin's feckless candidate to the governorship of Tobolsk.

Because all too many lackeys like Khvostov blindly obeyed the tsar, contended Dzhunkovsky, getting rid of Rasputin could not in itself correct the crisis whose first cause was Nicholas's thralldom to Alexandra. But perhaps a report proving Rasputin a scoundrel might cause Nicholas to assert his own authority against his wife's misjudgments.

In the spring of 1915, after nearly ten months of surveillance, Dzhunkovsky suddenly had grounds to suspect serious malfeasance behind a salacious evening spent by Rasputin at the Yar Restaurant in Moscow on 26 March, given that one participant was a broker of sleazy deals and sometime journalist, N.N. Soedov. The chief of the Moscow Gendarmes, A.P. Martynov, had sent the barest intelligence on that event, perhaps fearing that he himself might be held accountable were any such details to reach the tsar. By demanding agent reports from Martynov's files, Dzhunkovsky learned that Rasputin had not only ridiculed Alexandra on the night in question but had also behaved like "some kind of sexual psychopath" with respect to the women who served food and drink at the Yar Restaurant. The agents also reported that Soedov had organized the dinner to entice Rasputin into arranging, in exchange for a share of the profits, a contract to sell the army large shipments of underwear.[29]

Late on the evening of 1 June, with evidence in hand that went beyond Soedov and the restaurant debauchery, Dzhunkovsky personally made a case to the tsar that his hospitality to Rasputin threatened both the dynasty and Russia itself. The assistant minister felt confident that his family background and credentials as a long-standing loyalist and state servant added weight to his arguments, and he left the encounter gratified that Nicholas had not raised his usual objections to interference in his personal affairs and had even agreed to receive further intelligence about Rasputin.

When, only four days later, the tsar replaced Maklakov with Duma member N.B. Shcherbatov, Nicholas took that step to mollify a growing opposition in the Duma soon to be called the Progressive Bloc that had made clear its dislike of the obdurately conservative Maklakov.[30] Thus could Dzhunkovsky rightly see that change as no threat to himself, just as he could revel in the tsar's having stopped receiving Rasputin – a conspicuous change noted by everyone at court that lasted all through June and July.[31]

By early August, however, Alexandra had left Nicholas with no choice but to remove Dzhunkovsky from his police post and once more to show respect for the "holy fool" whom she revered as the saviour of their son. She had sent V.N. Sablin, her aide-de-camp, to Moscow to persuade those present at the Yar event to change their testimony to the effect that they had witnessed a conventional dinner party devoid of misdemeanours of any sort. Then, by insisting that her husband accept Sablin's findings over those of Dzhunkovsky, she effectively made Dzhunkovsky's continuance impossible. One of the witnesses explained to Colonel P.P. Zavarzin, chief of the Moscow Okhranka, why he changed his initial testimony: "We understood that Rasputin truly was powerful and to dispute with him therefore made no sense; further, it seemed improper to inform on someone whose hospitality one had enjoyed."[32] The result was entirely different from the earlier investigation. It turned out that Rasputin with his friends had enjoyed a modest supper and had left the restaurant quietly. All the conversations about financial machinations were laid to the intrigues of Dzhunkovsky. Friends of the tsarina had thwarted a police operation based on credible evidence offered by a trusted servant of the throne. Others were to conclude that other means would have to be used to remove Rasputin from his position of influence near the imperial family.

At the end of April 1915, as Dzhunkovsky was compiling his dossier on Rasputin, Prince M.M. Andronikov, an aristocrat who made it his business to keep in touch with the great houses and the ministers and matters at court, told Beletsky about coming changes in the cabinet and the possibility of his returning as police director.[33] Andronikov later informed Beletsky that he had proposed Khvostov as interior minister, that the tsarina had interviewed him and had had a favourable impression. The so-called period of ministerial musical chairs was about to begin – a strange time of rapid shuffling about of highly placed officials. These changes took place during a series of setbacks in the war against the Central Powers. The opposition Progressive Bloc was gathering in the State Duma behind a demand for a new government to serve with the approval of the Duma.

Privy to the tsarina's counter-attack against Dzhunkovsky, and possibly a party to it, was Beletsky, Dzhunkovsky's implacable enemy since being dismissed by him from the police directorship in 1912. Beletsky, who became secretly associated with Rasputin towards the end of 1914 (he had concealed the connection from his wife, who opposed any meetings with Rasputin), possessed an unquenchable ambition and great skill at advancing himself. After his tangled dismissal as director in February 1912 and appointment to the Governing Senate in July 1914, Beletsky, just barely forty years old, was restless in his honourable exile.[34] He now intended to avenge himself against Dzhunkovsky and he capitalized on his talent for manœuvre. One proof that Beletsky hungered for revenge was his publication of a pamphlet under a pseudonym that accused Dzhunkovsky of complicity with revolutionaries.

Seeing Dzhunkovsky's initiative against Rasputin as a risk-laden venture that could easily be turned against the assistant minister, Beletsky set about demeaning Dzhunkovsky in order to replace him. A logical first step was to enlist allies of Rasputin to his cause and to mend his own bad relations with the starets. These had stemmed from the negative reports that he had widely distributed, while police director, against Rasputin. Beletsky therefore had cultivated Anna Vyrubova, in order to impress upon her that his intimate knowledge about intrigues within the Department of Police made him the perfect appointee as assistant minister of the interior.[35] He stressed that he would guarantee the security of Rasputin when he regained control over the the police.

Beletsky also sought support for his reappointment from a man he had known since 1913 – Prince Andronikov. Surviving by his contacts in fashionable and official St Petersburg, the prince affected an air of insouciance. He liked to boast that, as a youth, although enrolled in the prestigious Pazhesky Corps of Cadets by his father, he had managed not to qualify for the final year and so by the age of eighteen had accomplished absolutely nothing in life. He nonetheless acquired a position in the Interior Ministry and highly placed persons received Andronikov in all the great houses and major offices of the capital. The cause of Andronikov's popularity was obvious: he had been one of the first to grasp the possibilities of friendship with Rasputin, who became a frequent guest in his apartment. Spiridovich, the Gendarme officer, learned that Andronikov had hung a huge portrait of Rasputin in his study and that he had said about the self-styled holy man: "He's a clever *muzhik*, v-v-very clever. And cunning. Ah, how cunning he is. And it is possible to do business with him. And because it is possible to take him in hand, we should try it."[36] Beletsky viewed Andronikov as means to "get through to every minister,"[37] and made him central to his calculus of influence.

Another ally in restoring Rasputin to favour and promoting Beletsky was Aleksei Nikolaevich Khvostov. Khvostov belonged to a wealthy and influential gentry family. His uncle Alexander Alekseevich Khvostov, would succeed him as minister of the interior within four months. A.N. Khvostov's views put him on the extreme right of the political spectrum. Whatever government post he filled, Khvostov maintained close relations with Black Hundred organizations and was the only provincial governor who wore the badge of the Union of the Russian People for official receptions at the tsar's residence. In 1912 he had been elected a deputy of the Fourth State Duma and became chairman of the extreme right fraction. Khvostov made no distinction among his administrative, legislative, and political activities and used them all to advance his views and achieve his ambitions.

No one doubted Khvostov's numerous talents; he was, moreover, a man of wide education. But he completely lacked scruples. State Secretary S.E. Kryzhanovsky, for instance, wrote that Khvostov was a "violent, almost instinctually primitive man."[38] The minister himself liked to say that he was a person "without a restraining centre."[39] One of his subordinates remembers a man of gargantuan appetites: "Even the appearance of Khvostov was Falstaffian. Over the years his corpulence widened hypertrophically ... Bulging out in every direction, his fat quivered when he walked."[40]

As this party of Beletsky, Andronikov, and Khvostov jointly conspired to oust Dzhunkovsky in order to restore Rasputin and elevate Beletsky, Nicholas must have been independently pondering a momentous change that he would shortly effect despite disapproval from all sides: that of removing himself from St Petersburg to join his army at military headquarters near the front. He must have seen this option at least in part as a means to absent himself from the troubles stirred up at court by his wife, over whom he had absolutely no control.

In any case, Nicholas had not yet announced that he would go to the front when, in late July 1915, he bowed to his wife once more by agreeing to the reappearance of Rasputin as an intimate advisor and companion. He agreed to remove Dzhunkovsky as assistant minister of interior, a decision that Rasputin had to have known by the time he left St Petersburg in early August to visit his home village in the company of his usual police bodyguards and surveillance agents.

While in the capital Rasputin's friends were working on his rehabilitation, the starets himself continued to create new scandals in his home territory, and he made no effort to show himself as being reformed. On 9 August, in a drunken state, he repeatedly disputed with the captain and passengers on board the steamboat from Tiumen to Pokrovskoe. With difficulty, the crew forced him back into his cabin. So many passengers queued up to peer through the window into the cabin that, according to the surveillance report, "at the request of the agents, the window was closed. Two hours before arrival in Pokrovskoe, Rasputin slid to the floor and lay under the table drunk until the arrival of the steamboat to Pokrovskoe. At 8 o'clock in the evening the boat docked. The agents asked the captain to loan them two crew members to help carry Rasputin onto the dock, and four men dragged him out, dead drunk."[41]

On the following day Rasputin quizzed the detectives about the events of the previous evening and expressed surprise that he had gotten so drunk on three bottles of wine. "In this conversation," added the reporting agent, "he said by the way that 'Dzhunkovsky will be dismissed from service and he will think that he is being dismissed because of me and I don't even know the man.'"[42] This was Dzhunkovsky's first news that he would soon be leaving his post. He registered his own surprise that he, an assistant minister and major-general of the imperial suite, found out about his dismissal from the detectives who were conducting surveillance over Rasputin. Six days later, on 19 August, Dzhunkovsky was summoned to the then-minister of the interior, Prince N.B. Shcherbatov, who showed him a note from the tsar: "I insist on the rapid dismissal of Gen. Dzhunkovsky." He was sent to active army service, where he served out the war and was fully convinced that he owed his departure to the influence of the tsarina.[43] Dzhunkovsky had no doubt about the consequences of Rasputin's influence but also about his inability to do anything about it. The starets had stirred up evil that "is digging Russia's grave."[44]

Shcherbatov lasted only a month longer because, on 3 September, he and several other ministers signed a letter to the tsar protesting his decision to stay near the front as supreme commander of his military forces.[45] Such a decision would take Nicholas out of the capital and leave many major political matters in the hands of his wife who, it was now widely known, was under the influence of Rasputin.

Khvostov succeeded Shcherbatov that same month as acting minister of the interior (he would become full minister that November) and, as one of his first acts on 28 September, named Beletsky as his assistant minister in charge of the Department of Police. That same day, Beletsky and Khvostov joined Rasputin at a dinner hosted by Prince Andronikov to celebrate their joint successes. Beletsky later recalled that event: "From the conversation around the table, it was clear to me that Rasputin had known about our appointments, that he had nothing against us now, and that he, obviously, wanted it known that we had received our appointments from his hands."[46]

Still in office as director of police for the first three months of his tenure was Brune de St Hippolite (3 February 1914 to 4 September 1915); but Beletsky replaced him with K.D. Kafafov (24 November 1915 to 14 February 1916), who would tell the 1917 investigating commission that Beletsky alone commanded all police affairs. As proof, Kafafov claimed that his own refusal on 9 January 1916 to distribute to governors and Gendarme commanders an anti-Semitic circular that came to him from Beletsky was summarily overruled.[47]

From 1908 to the middle of 1915, the leadership of the Ministry of the Interior and the Department of Police saw the Rasputin circle as a malignant tumour that must be excised completely. Through all the attempts to warn the tsar, including Dzhunkovsky's well-documented presentation, not one of the ministers or assistant ministers gave a thought to the idea of enlisting Rasputin as an ally. But a new stage of the relations between the secret police and Rasputin arrived with A.N. Khvostov and Beletsky.

Ordinarily rancorous, Rasputin gave no hint that he remembered his earlier grievances against Khvostov and Beletsky. At the same time, there is contradictory testimony about Rasputin's further relations with the minister of the interior. Khvostov claimed before the Extraordinary Investigating Commission in 1917 that he met with Rasputin once or twice, that Rasputin was hostile to him and that, generally, the starets served Beletsky. Beletsky told the same commission of regular meetings over dinner with Khvostov and Rasputin.[48]

Nonetheless, Khvostov and Beletsky, once installed in office, were very soon attempting through Andronikov to rein in Rasputin. They, too, found that his scandalous behaviour and associations were creating public antagonism against the throne. They first attempted to bribe Rasputin into lying low by means of monthly payments and frequent gifts, covering these costs fom a secret fund. Rasputin took the money but periodically demonstrated to the minister and assistant minister that they were not buying him. Khvostov and Beletsky had to endure Rasputin's capriciousness and adapt themselves to his rages when he called the minister "Pot Belly."

Viewing Khvostov and Beletsky as his henchmen, Rasputin showered them with notes which usually began with the words, "Darling, dearest, I need your help," or "Sweet one, help God's slave," and the like. There would follow requests, the fulfillment of which kept Beletsky busy constantly. By his own admission, the assistant minister of the interior had to immerse himself in criminal activity in order to fulfill the demands of Rasputin. Finally, Beletsky recounts, he saw his policy as a mistake.[49]

Beletsky had conducted his relations with Rasputin largely through Prince Andronikov, who had supplied his apartment as a meeting place should Beletsky wish to speak with Rasputin. But the prince and Rasputin clashed over a question of money, and a heated argument followed. This was too much for Vyrubova, and she declared that she had lost confidence in the prince.[50]

Beletsky consequently had to secure a "conspiratorial apartment" on an alleyway off the Fontanka where he could meet secretly with Rasputin. He summoned to the capital as a new go-between a deft Gendarme office, M.S. Komissarov, whose name figures in the history of the Okhranka, most especially as the initiator of the secret printing plant that turned out anti-Semitic pamphlets in the basement of the Fontanka 16 following the revolution of 1905. Dzhunkovsky, when assistant minister, had found Komissarov too ready to launch illegal schemes and had in effect exiled him to run the Gendarme post in distant, provincial Viatka. Beletsky, in contrast, brought Komissarov to the capital and assigned him to the delicate mission of dealing with Rasputin.

Assigned as bodyguard for Rasputin, Komissarov first appeared in full dress uniform before Anna Vyrubova to declare himself at the disposal of the starets. When the two men met, Komissarov put off Rasputin's usual resort to holy words for newcomers by proposing a drink. He soon arranged through Beletsky to ensure, through the capital's police chief, that the proprietors of local drinking places always served Rasputin and his entourage in a private dining room away from regular customers. As a further means of neutralizing Rasputin, Beletsky increased the number of agents around him. Besides the detectives of the St Petersburg Okhranka, Komissarov brought his own detachment of reliable police agents.[51] Khvostov and Beletsky also tried to divert Rasputin from the capital by encouraging him to go on pilgrimages. But nothing succeeded in removing Rasputin from society and from his influence on the tsarina. And his demands on the Ministry of the Interior for cash infusions and favours did not abate.

Eventually, Khvostov concluded that Rasputin must die, given that the various attempts to isolate him or remove him did not work. He even made a point of asking Komissarov: "Isn't is possible sometime, somehow, when Rasputin is drunk, to kill him?"[52] Other highly placed persons were also testing the murder option. Leaders of the right wing were telling Beletsky that as long as Rasputin lived all their propagandistic efforts on behalf of the dynasty were without effect.[53] General I.A. Dumbadze, the Yalta military governor who headed the guard at the Crimean residence of the tsar, went even further in a coded telegram to Beletsky. He asked permission to drown Rasputin in the Black Sea while he was travelling by ship to the Emperor's summer home.[54]

Beletsky instead urged his chief to show Nicholas (as had Stolypin and Dzhunkovsky) documented evidence of the scandalous behaviour of Rasputin, including the scurrilous things he had said about the imperial family. He claims to have compiled such proofs with the help of Komissarov and K.I. Globachev, the head of the St Petersburg Okhranka, only to learn that Khvostov lacked the nerve to confront Nicholas. Khvostov, for his part, said in 1917 that he had undertaken this mission, but to no avail.[55]

Beletsky says that Khvostov set in motion plans for killing Rasputin by assigning him command of Komissarov and four other agents. The officers, however, saw themselves in grave risk because they bore responsibility for Rasputin's security and would be certain targets of the tsar's wrath while Khvostov remained unscathed. The assistant minister deferred action by pointing out the flaws in the proposed methods and by stretching out the test of poison chosen for lacing Rasputin's favourite drink, madeira.[56]

In his lengthy deposition, Beletsky contended that Khvostov became privately infuriated with Rasputin in January 1916, blaming him for the tsar's bypassing him as successor to I.L. Goremykin, who was retiring as chairman of the Council of Ministers. Beletsky says he had concluded that the clumsy manœuvres of his chief, Khvostov, would lead to his downfall. He understood that it was time to line up with his more adept rival, Boris Sturmer:

I clearly saw that B.V. Sturmer would not content himself with being a premier without real power and that as a close collaborator with Plehve [former minister] would well know the secret information and range of power commanded by the Minister of the Interior and would exert all his strength to acquire the portfolio of the minister of the Interior. Therefore, foreseeing Sturmer's struggle with A.N. Khvostov, and evaluating the line-up of forces, I saw the predominant weight on the side of Sturmer."[57]

Early in 1916, therefore, the allies of a few months before turned against one another. Khvostov, having given up on the Beletsky assassination team, turned to the defrocked Iliodor, who was living in Norway under his family name, Trufanov. Excluded from the plotting of his own minister and allying himself with Sturmer, Beletsky used his office to discredit Khvostov. According to contemporaries of Beletsky, the assistant minister foiled Khvostov's plan by ordering the detainment of Khvostov's emissary in February 1916 at the border on his return from seeing Iliodor. Beletsky anticipated discrediting Khvostov and advancing his own cause with Rasputin. He says that he ordered the arrest of Khvostov's agent, one B.M. Rzhevsky, and the search of his apartment yielded incriminating evidence against Khvostov. Rzhevsky, under police interrogation, said that five fanatical followers of Iliodor were to kill Rasputin on Khvostov's order.[58]

Khvostov countered Beletsky's 1917 account by claiming that Beletsky had framed him by intimidating Rzhevsky into making false allegations against him.[59] The former minister said that Beletsky's design was to force him from office to clear the way for a successor sympathetic to Rasputin – namely Boris Sturmer – by exiling Rzhevsky to Siberia by administrative order. In attempting to distance himself from the entire affair, Khvostov sent Beletsky out of the capital in February 1916 by naming him provincial governor-general at Irkutsk in Siberia.

Beletsky's readiness to sacrifice Khvostov in favour of Sturmer did not help him, for Komissarov was in the meantime revealing Beletsky's earlier plotting against Rasputin in the Ministry of the Interior. Komissarov had told everything to a confidant of Rasputin, I.F. Manasevich-Manuilov, who passed on the details to the Rasputin circle.[60] Beletsky consequently was naive when he asked Rasputin to rescue him from the appointment to Irkutsk. He unknowingly faced an enemy and no rescue followed his meeting with the starets.

With Rzhevsky now in the hands of the Gendarmes, Beletsky, no longer on the side of Khvostov, ordered his arrest. The inquiry established that in contravention of the wartime rules on currency exports, a huge sum in foreign currency had been issued to Rzhevsky. The investigators found an unmailed Rzhevsky letter to Khvostov in the journalist's apartment. In accordance with the rule of gathering evidence, this letter was entered into the police record. Khvostov was especially agitated by this exposure of his link to Rzhevsky and an illegal act, as he said later: "What should the Gendarmes do upon finding a letter addressed to the Chief of Gendarmes? They should get it to the Chief of Gendarmes quickly ... but they opened it and filed it."[61] The investigation revealed the letter and other information to show the close connection between Rzhevsky and Khvostov.

Rzhevsky confessed that he had reached an agreement with Iliodor to organize the assassination of Rasputin. It was planned to lure the starets to meet with a beautiful woman; Rzhevsky's mistress was to play the role of the woman. Following the murder, the conspirators would transport Rasputin's body by automobile and dump it through a hole in the ice in the Neva river. The murder itself would be carried out by five fanatical followers of Iliodor from Tsaritsyn. The police had even intercepted a telegram from Iliodor to Rzhevsky with the message, "the brothers have agreed."

Khvostov in 1917 blamed the assassination plot on Beletsky. He claimed that the mission of Rzhevsky to Iliodor was for the purpose of acquiring his manuscript for the book, *The Holy Devil*, or at least to hold up its publication until the end of the war.[62] Khvostov feared the effects on public opinion of the book. Everything else was the result of the scandalous intrigue of Beletsky who, having embroiled and cowed Rzhevsky, forced him to implicate Khvostov. In the opinion of Khvostov, Beletsky was still serving the Rasputin circle, which aimed to displace him as minister in order to install its own obedient puppet. Although some facts line up in support of parts of Khvostov's version, they do not confirm that Beletsky was plotting the assassination of Rasputin.

Rasputin was shaken by the police's discovery of Rzhevsky's mission and of Khvostov's plot against him. "You see my hand," he said to a friend, "the minister has kissed this hand, and it is he who wants to kill me."[63] The minister assured Rasputin of his loyalty, but the starets had his own way of dealing with the hapless minister of the interior. Aron Simanovich, a jewel merchant from Kiev who was close to Rasputin, suggests that Rasputin had no doubt that Khvostov had tried to have him killed: "[Khvostov] tried to shift all responsibility to Beletsky and Rzhevsky; in the meantime, Rasputin had already succeeded in communicating to the tsar the actual state of this affair." Rasputin told Nicholas that he believed Khvostov, and, upon learning of this report, the minister was certain of his victory.[64] He jumped to a conclusion favourable to himself too quickly.

In fact the starets had shrewdly understood that the tsar would get rid of Khvostov quickly in order to shut off an embarrassing affair while crediting Rasputin with Christian forgiveness for asserting that he believed Khvostov. The minister was therefore caught completely by surprise when, on 3 March 1916, he received notice of his dismissal. In order to avoid a scandal, Khvostov had long since decided not to prosecute Rzhevsky, but had rather exiled him to Siberia by administrative order.

For Beletsky, it was now clear that there remained only one course open to him: to accept his honourable exile. Having been named governor-general of Irkutsk, he still had not departed for his new posting. Before leaving, on 7 March 1916, Beletsky gave an interview to a reporter from the *Stock Market Bulletin*. He obliquely laid out the story of the assassination attempt against Rasputin, underlining his main divergences from Khvostov. "I understand the struggle with the revolution, with the enemies of the state order, but it is an honest struggle, eyeball to eyeball. They blow us up and we prosecute and penalize them. But attacks from the corner, this is a return to Venice and its hired killers – and cannot strengthen but undermine and destroy statehood."[65]

Later Beletsky admitted that he was motivated not by idealistic considerations but by the wish to defend his own reputation (by shifting all responsibility on to Khvostov).[66] The result, however, was the opposite; the interview provoked extreme reactions in government circles. Beletsky was accused of carrying an internal dispute to the public and retribution was swift. The tsar dismissed him from the governor-general's post before he had departed for Irkutsk, but he elevated him to membership in the Senate with a handsome stipend.

Boris Vladimirovich Sturmer, the chairman of the Council of Ministers, who now assumed the post of minister of the interior, was widely believed to be in league with Rasputin.[67] There were secret meetings between them, fully recorded in the reports of Okhranka detectives who were protecting Rasputin. Like his predecessor Khvostov, Sturmer wished to keep his contacts with Rasputin secret and appointed Ivan Maniulov as an intermediary.[68] Maniulov had worked for over two decades in various special assignments for the Okhranka and the

Foreign Okhranka. Ostensibly a journalist, an inheritance had made him a wealthy man; he made it his business to be extraordinarily well-informed about the behind-the-scenes scandals and manœuvres of high government officials.

Manuilov's honesty was suspect. When, during his tenure as prime minister, Stolypin learned of certain financial peculations that Manuilov had engaged in, he declared, "It is time to cut off this scoundrel." Following his dismissal by Stolypin, Manuilov became a reporter for the St Petersburg paper, *New Times*, and wrote stories of the "boulevard" variety. He became acquainted with Rasputin and promptly published a story revealing that high-society ladies washed their idol in a bath house. Initially Rasputin could not abide Manuilov and made peace with him only after Manuilov reported to him the plot ostensibly engineered by Khvostov and Rzhevsky and then investigated it for Sturmer. Sturmer found an appointment for Manuilov in the Ministry of the Interior and gave him a salary higher than that of the director of the Department of Police. The logical reason was that Manuilov earned high pay for services connected with Rasputin.

In March 1916, shortly after taking office, Sturmer named E.K. Klimovich, an experienced Gendarme officer, director of the Department of Police. Klimovich had earlier headed the Moscow Okhranka and then the Special Section. But his relations with the prime minister were different from those of his predecessors. Sturmer had no patience for the reports of the director, and the result was that a discouraged Klimovich felt he had no guidance from the prime minister.[69]

After about four months as minister, Sturmer concluded that not only the police but the entire Ministry of the Interior turned out to be a disadvantageous portfolio as a stepping stone to his career. He relinquished Interior on 7 July and on the same day assumed the portfolio of the Ministry of Foreign Affairs. This position was especially influential because of the war and the conduct of diplomatic relations with allied powers. He named as his replacement at the Ministry of the Interior, also on the same day, the former minister of justice, Alexander Alekseevich Khvostov. Unlike his nephew A.N. Khvostov, who had lost this very position four months before, Alexander Alekseevich was not a member of the Rasputin circle.

Klimovich, when he first became director of the Department of Police, saw Manuilov as a petty intriguer,[70] but he failed to appreciate the importance of Manuilov's new connection with the Rasputin group. When he heard allegations that Manuilov was engaging in extorting bribes for favours, he arranged for an agent to pass bank-notes whose numbers had been recorded to Manuilov. Although Manuilov was arrested with these notes in his possession, the entire

Rasputin circle rose to his defence, having concluded that the arrest was an indirect blow against the starets.

Sturmer, responding to the demands of the Rasputin group, asked A.A. Khvostov to fire Klimovich. He categorically refused, and the rage of the group expanded to include the minister of the interior himself. According to the president of the Fourth State Duma, M.V. Rodzianko, Sturmer told Khvostov by telephone, "You have sent me bad news about the arrest of Manasevich-Manuilov, and now I am sending you some news: you will no longer be the Minister of the Interior."[71]

With the dismissal of both A.A. Khvostov and Klimovich effective that August, Manuilov walked out of the detention centre a free man. From Rasputin he learned: "While you were sitting under lock and key, Protopopov was named [minister of the interior], now Russia will stand firm here." The starets gave his summary of recent political developments: "We were mistaken in pot belly [his name for A.N. Khvostov], because he was only one of the right-wing fools. I say to you all the right-wingers are fools. Well now we have made a choice between right and left – Protopopov."[72]

Protopopov, the last minister of the interior of the imperial regime, appears therefore to have won his office as the result of Rasputin's influence on affairs of state. Alexander Dmitrievich Protopopov (who was administrative director of the ministry from September 1916 and minister from December) was a wealthy, cultivated aristocrat and a member of the Octobrist political party. He was widely seen as a politician of great promise, one of the leaders of Russian liberalism. He had emerged in the Fourth State Duma as assistant to the president, Rodzianko, a post to which he was elected by vote of his colleagues. He also travelled to Europe as a member of the parliamentary delegation to meet with European counterparts and created a favourable impression there.

For Protopopov, as for other representatives of the liberal opposition, Rasputin embodied all the sins of the tsarist regime. Nevertheless, he agreed to meet with the starets in the winter of 1915 when it was proposed to him by the Tibetan healer, P.A. Badmaev, another figure who was exercising influence in upper St Petersburg society.[73] But the healer was engaged in more than medicine and he is connected with almost every episode involving Rasputin. He eventually reconciled Rasputin with Iliodor and persuaded Bishop Hermogen to accept the tsar's decree ordering him to retire to a monastery.

Protopopov categorically rejected the idea that he was creature of Rasputin.[74] In his defence, it can be said that his behaviour in high office was influenced by a whole series of factors. He had hoped to serve as a conciliating bridge beween the Duma and the tsar, for their relations were normally quite tense. The new minister at the same time understood that kind words for the starets carried great weight with the imperial couple, and Nicholas was pleased to hear from him that he had earlier changed his opinion about Rasputin. "The tsar said," recalled Protopopov, "that acquaintanceship [with Rasputin] having begun with unfriendliness, frequently turns out to be otherwise."[75]

Among opposition politicians, Protopopov's agreement to become a member of the conservative government of Sturmer was viewed as a betrayal, especially after Protopopov appeared at a session of a Duma commission in the uniform of the commander of the Corps of Gendarmes (a position he held, of course, along with that of minister of the interior). Startled by the behaviour of their colleague, members of the Octobrist party concluded that Badmaev had induced the shift by causing a secret illness. Rumours to this effect were picked up by the French ambassador, Maurice Paleologue, who had also observed strange changes in the personality of Protopopov: "At the time of his cabbalistic operations it would not have been difficult for [Badmaev] to acquire influence over this unstable mind, this ill brain, in which there had already appeared symptoms of delusions of grandeur."[76]

Those who criticized Protopopov were right to wonder about his behaviour, but the man they labelled a turncoat had been one of the candidates of the Progressive Bloc to join the "government of popular confidence." From a formal point of view, Nicholas had fulfilled a recommendation of the liberal opposition to name ministers with the confidence of the Duma and, therefore, when Rodzianko, the president of the Duma, reported that Protopopov had lost his mind, the tsar justifiably remarked that no one had noticed that while Protopopov was still the assistant president of the Duma.

Dissatisfaction with Protopopov intensified because of his appointment in September 1916 as assistant minister of the interior of his former colleague in the horse guards, P.G. Kurlov, widely believed to have been responsible for the assassination of Stolypin in 1911. At the outset of the war, Kurlov had been posted to the civil administration of the Baltic provinces and, while there, fell under heavy criticism for failing to take adequate measures for the evacuation of Riga in the face of the German offensive. In the Duma there were even demands for Kurlov's indictment for treason; but none of this had deterred Protopopov and he had installed Kurlov as supervisor of the police.[77]

Kurlov's return from political ignominy reassured Rasputin. Before returning to high office, Kurlov had seen the advantages of a close relationship with Rasputin and had cultivated him through Badmaev. Kurlov is rare among the memorists, most of whom disassociate themselves completely from Rasputin. His prose about the starets is almost panegyrical; he cites his Christian goodness and "practical understanding of current issues, even of a governmental character."[78]

Kurlov continued a practice, of which he himself was of course a beneficiary, of appointing his cronies and collaborators to state office. When Kurlov remarked to A.I. Spiridovich that he was about to appoint A.T. Vassilyev, his friend and partner in financial matters and a former procurator, as director of the Department of Police, Spiridovich rejoined: "So that's it, Pavel Grigor'ievich. Well, he will do nothing more than sing. He will sing and play cards. What kind of director will he make, especially at the present time?"[79] Kurlov only laughed, but did not change his decision. But his naming of Vassilyev, who had no background in police work, was a serious error at a time when the government was fighting for its very existence.

But both Kurlov and Vassilyev failed to protect Rasputin, the man on whom their careers depended. The detectives responsible for surveillance were not on duty the night of 16 and 17 December 1916 – an inexplicable lapse in judgment. At Tsarskoe Selo, the imperial palace outside of St Petersburg, there was a sense of alarm over the whereabouts of the starets. Protopopov, at the behest of the palace, summoned Kurlov and Vassilyev and conveyed to them Alexandra's insistence that Rasputin be located. Kurlov first thought it important to call in Beletsky, whom he suspected of having something to do with Rasputin's disappearance, probably because of Beletsky's connection with earlier plotting.

In reality, the criminal conspiracy of that evening showed some elements of the plan worked out early in the year by Khvostov and Beletsky. The conspirators planned to drop Rasputin's body through a hole in the ice of the Neva river. In the event, the police had to use an ice saw to retrieve the body from under the ice. Other details also match exactly the affair of Rzhevsky. Rasputin arrived at the evening, having been lured by the prospect of a meeting with the beautiful wife of one of the conspirators, Prince Iusupov. He was poisoned with spiked madeira and then was shot with a revolver.

But neither Khvostov nor Beletsky had anything to do with the assassination of Rasputin. The police, after a momentary hiatus, got down to the investigation. They discovered that on the night of the murder a policeman heard a shot in the palace courtyard of Prince Feliks Iusupov. The prince was a young aristocrat who was still continuing his education in the Pazhesky Corps of Pages. He was the son of the Moscow governor-general, a close kinsman of Rodzianko, the Duma president, and especially close to the Romanov family. He had married Grand Duchess Irina Alexandrovna, a niece of the tsar. Iusupov told the police that guests leaving his mansion had shot a dog in the courtyard, and he repeated this explanation over the next two days.

These assertions did not still Alexandra's suspicions. She wrote Nicholas that on the evening of his disappearance Rasputin had told Vyrubova that "Feliks asked him to come over at night, that he was sending an automobile for him, and that he would see Irina."[80] The police established that along with Iusupov at the palace were Grand Duke Dmitry Pavlovich and the leader of the Union of the Archangel Michael, V.M. Purishkevich. For a month prior to the assassination, Purishkevich from the rostrum of the Duma had been speaking out against Rasputin and his clique, and these speeches set the plot in motion. Prince Iusupov, who hoped to rescue the prestige of the royal family, proposed to Purishkevich that he join the conspiracy.

As a result of the unanticipated complications, the conspirators left many clues of their act. They were so careless as to suggest that they believed their high positions would shield them from harsh punishment. The chief investigator, V.N. Sereda, said that "he had seen many crimes, both intelligent and stupid, but he had never before in all his career seen such sloppy behaviour by participants."[81] The investigative team for the St Petersburg Court of Appeals was in the meantime deliberately commencing its work slowly. The prosecutor, S.V. Zavadsky, recalled his conversation with the minister of justice, A.A. Makarov, when they went to view the body of Rasputin. He "confessed to the minister" that "I didn't suspect how great was my dislike of the starets." Makarov answered: "You were never a minister and therefore could never feel the hatred felt by me and the other ministers who did not want him to live."[82]

The investigation was concentrated in the hands of the Gendarmes, and by 20 December, when Nicholas II returned from the front, Protopopov was ready with a report. The Department of Police had reached the conclusion that the assassination of Rasputin was the first step in a palace conspiracy to unseat Nicholas and to put on the throne either one of the grand dukes or his son, Alexis. Protopopov reported on the sympathies expressed by members of the Romanov family for the idea of removing Rasputin physically. He offered as proof a telegram sent by Grand Duchess Elizabeth Fedorovna, sister of the tsarina and widow of Grand Duke Sergei Alexandrovich, killed by terrorists several years before. "This telegram," recalled Iusupov, "seriously compromised us. Protopopov made a copy and sent it to Tsarskoe Selo, to the Empress, and she decided that the Grand Duchess Elizabeth Fedorovna was a participant in the plot."[83] In concluding his report, Protopopov said that the majority of the grand dukes had passed to the opposition, creating enormous danger to the monarchy.

Now believing that Rasputin was universally hated, Nicholas II did not permit the legal investigation to run its course. He ordered Prince Iusupov, accompanied by a Gendarme officer, to go the estate of his parents. He sent Grand Duke Dmitry Pavlovich to serve in a military detachment in Persia. Purishkevich did not received any punishment. The tsar also expressed his disapproval of members of the government who remained silent in the face of an event that had shaken the imperial couple so profoundly. He dismissed his current president of the Council of Ministers, A.F. Trepov, and Minister of Justice Makarov. These were the last decisions taken as a result of the Rasputin assassination. No evidence turned up of a court plot against the reigning tsar. Nor did the murder of Rasputin alter in any way the steadily declining prestige of the monarchy.

For eight years, the Department of Police had wrestled with the problem of Rasputin. Officials filled one dossier after another with detailed reports from the detectives whose assignment was to observe every move he and his friends made. Fruitless attempts were made to send him permanently from the capital, and plans were advanced in the highest police leadership for his assassination. But others in the leadership tried to use Rasputin to advance their own personal ambitions, and these efforts linked the Department of Police with Rasputin. Earlier, the police had been hated, but the connection with Rasputin destroyed the respect of even its supporters.

CHAPTER FIFTEEN

Epilogue for the Okhranka

Although Okhranka agents were accurately reporting to their superiors that a discredited Russian regime was slipping into chaos in the months just before the revolution of 1917, the tsar did not receive these realistic appraisals of the chaotic condition of the country.

Okhranka agents saw a coming popular upheaval that would threaten the tsarist governmental system. The security police had ample information provided by the network of secret agents and Gendarmes; well-trained analysts in St Petersburg wrote coherent reports in which they anticipated revolutionary events. The Gendarmes reported, for instance, on the widespread public criticism of the tsarina because of her mixing in political affairs and consorting with Rasputin. One agent cited a letter to Alexandra urging her to leave the country in order to save the regime.[1] Other assessments from the Okhranka also anticipated the outbreak of a wrenching social upheaval months before it actually occurred.[2]

Gendarme officers' reports were toned down by Vassilyev, the director of the Department of Police, and were then emasculated in the reports of Protopopov. These officials, who controlled the channels of information to the tsar, remained wedded to their theory of a conspiracy among liberals against the government which was being conducted at the top levels of society. They shaped the information at their disposal to fit this picture and they persuaded themselves that the people's loyalty to the tsar was massive and unshakeable.[3]

Even as the revolution of February 1917 unfolded, Protopopov assured the army general staff that protests then taking place on the streets of the capital would soon cease. He argued that they stemmed from a brief food shortage caused when snowdrifts, since removed, had made the tracks impassable for incoming supply trains. Likewise, his reports at this juncture assured Nicholas that the army garrison in

St Petersburg (now renamed Petrograd) could easily put down any and all local disorders, whatever their cause. The failure by the leadership to prepare the military in the capital was a major miscalculation.

When, on 27 February, intensifying popular protests had proved the inadequacy of planned counter-measures by the military, the Council of Ministers rebuked Protopopov and he resigned. But just as the Council debated the question of the minister's successor, a mob seized the Department of Police building at Fontanka 16 – and in effect put an end to the Okhranka. Several days later, the Moscow Okhranka was seized when armed men arrived, dumped mounds of files in the courtyard of the building, and set fire to the archives. It is still not clear whether the pillagers were revolutionaries striking against the hated police or police agents bent on destroying incriminating documents. Destruction and the scattering of these and other official files by marauders during the February revolution and its aftermath were to create obstacles for investigators who tried to document police, and especially Okhranka, practices.

Assuming power formally on 1 March as legal heir of the tsarist regime, the Provisional Government preserved almost all of the former government departments and ministries, but immediately abolished the Department of Police and the Corps of Gendarmes. The government organized a people's militia to carry out conventional policing duties. It was believed at the time that a volunteer militia formed from the people would be able to carry out policing duties far better than the old corrupt and secret agencies with their arbitrary and illegal methods. But these expectations dissolved before the anarchy which engulfed the streets of the capital. The disorganized and untrained militia were unable to cope with the criminality and violence which accompanied the breakdown of the old order.

Russia's Romanov dynasty, which had celebrated three hundred years of existence just four years earlier, crumbled in the course of a few days of peaceful demonstrations in the wartime capital of Petrograd. Those who assumed power, however, were not the same people who brought the imperial government down. They were not from the streets but were representatives of the most Europeanized Russian political parties, the two liberal parties, the Octobrists and the Kadets. They saw their goal as directing the elemental popular movement – so far largely confined to the army in the Petrograd military district and to the streets of the capital – into legal channels. Reflecting their determination to observe the law, the new ministers declared that they would not permit summary justice to be imposed on the minions of the old regime.

Instead, the government appointed the Extraordinary Investigating Commission to inquire into criminal actions committed by tsarist ministers and other former government officials who held responsible positions. Kerensky, the minister of justice of the Provisional Government and leader of the Socialist Revolutionary party, was a principal instigator of the commission. The commission included lawyers, but it was not under the supervision of a court, as a criminal investigation would have been under the tsarist judicial system. Although the founders would not have found it so, the commission was akin to several tsarist investigating commissions employed in the nineteenth century to gather evidence to show the extent of conspiracies against the state. In 1917 the purpose was to identify a criminal conspiracy against the people by high officials in the imperial government.

Political, not judicial, criteria governed the selection of members and shaped the inquiry from the beginning. The government named a liberal Moscow attorney, N.K. Muraviev, as chairman (Muraviev, incidentally, had been subject to external observation by the Okhranka and was listed under the code name "The Fly.") Persons from the former Ministry of Justice (several had been prosecutors, including some with highly conservative views) were among the members of the commission. There were also members from the Menshevik party and the Socialist Revolutionary party and a representative from the executive committee of the Petrograd Soviet of Workers' and Soldiers' Deputies. Given the makeup of the commission, there was no certainty that it would manage to assemble information suitable for prosecutors to prepare indictments.[4] For whereas this broad investigation was to be a means to frame judicial indictments to be tried in the carry-over courts, the Provisional Government did not follow the old imperial laws that were to govern such proceedings and the preparation of indictments for prosecution. What evidence was gathered – and it was extensive – was therefore often of questionable merit.

A politically motivated investigation by the Provisional Government resulted, lasting all through the eight months of its existence. The main purpose became to show abuses of power by persons who had acted on behalf of the autocracy. The Provisional Government wanted to prove the rightful termination of a corrupt regime; the political police were, quite naturally, its special targets. Lacking precise guidelines, the commission changed its frame of reference as it proceeded. Its inquiries were to be directed at four categories of persons: civil servants; leaders and officers of the Department of Police; leading officials in the Military and Naval ministries; and "persons not in responsible positions who influenced the activity of the former government." This last vague category referred to private individuals such as Rasputin and Vyrubova and a few former officials close to the imperial family, such as the court commandant V.N. Voeikov.

From the first, the commission also had public relations responsibilities. The Provisional Government required that it keep the press informed of the progress of its work and prepare a report to be submitted to the opening session of the Constituent Assembly, to be elected later in the year. The Russian press received information from the commission and joined in the exposure of the police by printing long lists of the names of those declared to be agents of the Okhranka. Journalists described supposed secret activities of the Okhranka. Lurid rumours, never confirmed, circulated about the prospect of yet more revelations against which the Azeff affair would pale in comparison. Journalists and writers found the secrets of the Okhranka a subject of enduring interest, and some were able to conduct interviews with the former chiefs of the secret police. By mid-1917 the judicial purpose of the commission had given way entirely to discrediting the former regime in the eyes of the public. The work of preparing materials for criminal indictments was abandoned.

Other obstacles had already complicated the commission's work. The investigation proceeded on the classic principle that a law cannot be applied retroactively. Officials of the old government were to be answerable for violating the laws of the Russian Empire. Neither the Empire nor its laws any longer existed, however, and, in any event, they now lacked legitimacy because an undemocratic ruler had legislated them. How then could the former officials be charged under them? This dilemma remained unresolved.

Commission investigators inevitably focused on the activities of the Okhranka. Through testimony and documents, they plunged into the world of double agents, perlustrations, secret operations, and provocations. They opened the question of the organization of Jewish pogroms, of the Beilis trial, of the Azeff affair, and they gave a lot of attention to the activities of the Rasputin clique. Probing deeply got the commission no closer to indictments of the servitors of the tsarist regime. Secret agents who had penetrated to the depths of terrorist organizations presented an especially complex issue. The commission was unable to document violations of law by means of "provocations."[5] Finally, the investigators found it possible only to accuse the former okhranniki of small infractions of instructions and circulars of the Department of Police, an organization declared to be criminal and anti-democratic.

Investigators could not prove who had made decisions of a criminal character in the Department of Police. The commission's investigator Iodlovsky gathered an immense amount of material to show how officials had put in place a vast network of secret agents, but evidence was lacking to show criminal actions of officials whose main documented work concerned instructions to subordinates related to the defence of the state.

Appearing as witnesses before the commission were almost all the most responsible officials of the system of political investigation. Many of them had been accused of crimes, and one after another former directors of police were arrested: Vassilyev, Beletsky, Klimovich, Zuev. The arrests then reached to former ministers of the interior, Protopopov, A.N. Khvostov, Sturmer, Makarov, to the former minister of justice, Shcheglovitov, to the assistant minister of the Interior Kurlov, and then heads of the Okhranka divisions.

At first those arrested were held in the notorious Trubetsky Bastion of the Saints Peter and Paul Fortress in Petrograd and interrogated in the same casements where the Decembrists had been held in early 1826. The conditions were especially bad because the guards were soldiers of a radical regiment in the capital area, and did not conceal their hatred for the former wielders of power. The soldiers regularly conducted conversations within hearing of their prisoners to the effect that instead of a long judicial process for them, it would be better to despatch the "boorzhyi" with bayonets and throw their bodies into the Neva river running alongside the fortress.

The incarcerated former officials conducted themselves variously. Kurlov bombarded the commission with petitions to gain his freedom for reasons of ill health. Heads of the Okhranka divisions, directors of the Special Section, and even directors of the Department of Police insisted that their responsibilities never extended to making important decisions. Seemingly, the most forthcoming former official of all was Beletsky, who believed that he could save his own life only by open and complete cooperation with the investigators. His lengthy, detailed depositions were also cleverly self-exculpatory, and Beletsky pictured himself as merely a follower of orders.[6]

By the fall of 1917 almost all of those arrested in the spring had been released. Remaining in jail were only those who had been the main leaders of the Department of Police. This turn in the commission's work was related to the Provisional Government's wish to align itself more closely with the revolutionary mood of the populace, especially in Petrograd. Leaders of the liberal parties in Russia had understood for several years that they were locked in a struggle with the radical parties to influence workers, soldiers, and peasants and this struggle intensified during the summer of 1917. The unindicted former imperial police officials remained in prison lest the government be accused of surrender to conservatives.

Never to complete their work, investigators of the Extraordinary Investigative Commission abandoned their rooms in the Winter Palace several hours before the Bolsheviks occupied the building on the night of 25 October 1917. Not a single member of the Okhranka had been indicted, much less tried. The commission's papers survived, however, and may be read partly in the seven-volume work, *The Fall of the Tsarist Regime*, published in Russian by a Soviet press in 1927, and in original documentary form in the State Historical Archive of the Russian Federation in Moscow.

Oddly, the armed uprising by the Bolsheviks of October 1917 produced favourable outcomes for many of the former leaders of the Okhranka. Taking advantage of the change in power, they left Petrograd. But for those who were still in prison, the outcome was fatal. Witnesses have testified that Beletsky was terribly afraid he would be shot and procured poison in order to commit suicide. He did not succeed in taking it, however. During the days of the "Red Terror" in 1919, a group of Chekists (Bolshevik armed detachments who were beginning to function as a political police) conducted a number of former officials to Khodynka Field on the edge of Moscow and lined them up on the edge of an open grave. Beletsky tried to run and was shot by the guards. A.N. Khvostov, A.A. Makarov, and I.G. Shcheglovitov accepted their fate without stirring.

A number of Gendarme officers served in the Civil War, which began in 1918, some of them in the counter-intelligence services against the Bolsheviks and some for the new government. One of the Okhranka's best cryptanalysts left Russia for Britain where he readily broke the codes of the Soviet state until late in the 1920s.

General Denikin, the commander of the Volunteer Army in the south (one of several White armies who fought the Bolsheviks), decided to replace the discredited Gendarmes under his command with officials from the old Ministry of Justice. This decision probably weakened the already notoriously ineffective intelligence system of the Volunteer Army. Following the defeat of the White armies, many former okhranniki went to Europe, where a number wrote their memoirs – works that have been extensively cited in this book. Those who remained in Russia also published their recollections of police service. Lopukhin lost his papers to one of the searches which occurred frequently under the new regime, but he managed to publish a short memoir while promising a more detailed account in the future. This book did not appear. Dzhunkovsky was less fortunate, and did not live to see any of his multi-volumed and highly detailed memoirs appear in print. (An abridged version of these memoirs was published in 1997 in Moscow.) Because Lopukhin and Dzhunkovsky had the reputation of fighting against Okhranka illegality, they were assured a calm life under the Bolsheviks, at least in the 1920s. Lopukhin died of natural causes in 1927. Dzhunkovsky was one of those who fell during the sweeping Stalinist purges. The Bolsheviks also prosecuted some former secret agents. Malinovsky was shot and Okladsky sent to prison. Dozens of less well-known former agents were paraded before the revolutionary tribunals and sentenced to severe penalties.

From the founding of the centralized tsarist state in Moscow in the sixteenth century to its collapse in 1917, the covert practice of political investigation was a constant in Russian life. The rulers of Russia gave institutional forms to their political investigators and security agents, beginning with the oprichnina of Ivan IV and ending with the Okhranka of Nicholas II. This study shows that, given the continuities in the maturing system, the Okhranka that served in the last decades of the imperial regime was the heir of all its predecessors.

Four distinct periods of political investigations do emerge during the more than three centuries under discussion here. The first is the period when Muscovy consolidated and centralized power and then, in the eighteenth century, absorbed powerful influences from the West – especially during the reigns of Peter the Great and Catherine II. The Russian political investigation system therefore evolved as an essential buttress to tsarist power and, consequently, did not diminish during the continuing Westernization that followed Peter. Despite periodic but short-lived reforms of the police system, the security force grew ever larger and more intrusive.

The second period of political investigation coincides with the tenure of the Third Section of His Majesty's Own Chancellery, the corps of political police created by Nicholas I in 1826. Its mandate was to extirpate the liberal spirit that had surfaced in the previous year in the amateurish rebellion of the Decembrists. So effective was its anti-liberal campaign that Russia escaped the wave of revolution that struck all major Western European countries in the early 1830s and in 1848. The Third Section proved inadequate, however, against the tightly concealed, death-defying revolutionaries who launched a terrorist campaign after Alexander II had effected broad liberal reforms with respect to serfdom, local government, the judiciary, and censorship in the 1860s and 1870s.

Links between liberalization and revolutionary agitation were confirmed for many state officials when terrorists killed Alexander II in 1881, just as a reorganization of the police system was taking place, intended in part to ferret out subversives through a new breed of secret agents. The third period of political investigation, then, commences with the start of the special security corps that contained those agents

– the unit in the Department of Police that came to be known as the Okhranka. What followed was a system for political investigation with a wide-ranging network of agents and informers whose activities spanned the huge Russian Empire and even reached into Western Europe.

Yet another sudden infusion of liberalism to soften autocratic rule – the reforms forced upon Nicholas ii by the revolution of 1905 – marks the start of the fourth and final period of Russian political investigation. By this time, most police officials saw liberals themselves – no matter that they were legally organized to participate in the new legislative government – as the vanguard of revolution. In the post-1906 decade the Okhranka consequently focused on preventing a liberal-radical-worker coalition like that of 1905. Its prime method was the one that had worked before so effectively against the terrorists – the use of secret agents and many of them. The tide of opposition overwhelmed both them and the autocracy in 1917.

Among the many methods of the Russian political investigation system, then, entrenching a covert network of spies to detect enemies of the state stands in first place. Fundamental requirements of that methodology in turn shaped several shortcomings in the Russian corps of political police: its resistance to strict limitations, whether administrative or judicial; its increasing reliance on free-wheeling agents over whom it exercised no direct control; its readiness to enlist informers in every niche of society and to use secret funding for that purpose; and its visceral distrust of liberals.

Notes

chsk Extraordinary Investigation Commission of the
        Provisional Government
GAKO State Archive of the Kiev Oblast
GARF State Archive of the Russian Federation
OR RNB Manuscript Division, Russian National Library
PSS Polnoe Sobranie Sochinenii (Completed Collected
        Works)
RGIA Russian State Historical Archive
TSGIA Moskvy State Historical Archive of Moscow

CHAPTER ONE

1 Kleimola, "The Duty to Denounce in Muscovite Russia," 761.
2 Ivan's loyalists gave him the appellation "Groznyi." A good English ren-
  dition of this Russian word would be "Awesome," but it is usually translated as "Terrible."
3 "Poslaniia Ioganna Taube i Eperta Kruze," 39.
4 Horsey, "The Travels of Sir Jerome Horsey," 163.
5 Slikhting, *Novoe izvestie o Rossii vremen Ivan Groznogo*, 19.
6 Skrynnikov, "Oprichnyi terror," 38–9.
7 See estimates in Skrynnikov, *Ivan Groznyi*, 158, and Kobrin, *Ivan Groznyi*, 83.
8 Kleimola, "The Duty to Denounce in Muscovite Russia," 772–3.
9 Veretennikov, *Istoriia Tainoi kantseliarii petrovskogo vremeni*, 2.
10 Keep, "The Regime of Filaret," 343–4.
11 Telberg, *Ocherki politicheskogo suda i politicheskikh prestuplenii v
   Moskovskom gosudarstve XVII v.*, 68.

12 Lapman, "Political Denunciations in Muscovy," 156–63.

13 Ibid., 159.

14 Ibid., 201. Dewey and Kleimola, "Suretyship and Collective Responsibility in pre-Petrine Russia," 348.

15 Lapman, "Political Denunciations in Muscovy," 35.

16 There is an English translation of the code. See *The Muscovite Law Code (Ulozhenie) of 1649*, pt. 1, ed. and tr. Richard Hellie (Irvine, Calif., 1988). Chapter 2 of the code is devoted to treasonous crimes. For the distinction between political and other crimes, see *Sobornoe Ulozhenie 1649 goda*, 20–1.

17 Kotoshikhin, "O Moskovskom gosudarstve v seredine XVII stoletiia," 239.

18 *Zapiski inostrantsev o vosstanii Stepana Razina*, 112.

19 Ibid., 126.

20 Veretennikov, *Istoriia tainoi kantseliarii Petrovskogo vremeni*, 23.

21 Cherniavsky, "The Old Believers and the New Religion," 163–6.

22 Novombergsky, *Slovo i delo gosudarevo*, 2:17.

23 Semevsky, *Slovo i delo, 1700–1725*, 51.

24 Gol'tsev, *Zakonodatel'stvo i nravy v Rossii XVIII v.*, 50.

25 *Polnoe sobranie sochinenii*, coll. 1, vol. 6, no. 3984.

26 Korsakov, *Iz zhizni russkikh deiateli XVIII v.*, 137.

27 "Zakonodatel'nye akty Petra I," *Pamiatniki russkogo prava*, 8:325. For the corresponding article in the Naval Regulations (Book v, Article 2), see 490.

28 Muller, ed., *The Spiritual Regulation of Peter the Great*, 61.

29 *Russkii biograficheskii slovar'*, sv. "Fedor Iur'evich Romodanovsky," vol. 17, 1918.

30 Veretennikov, *Istoriia tainoi kantseliarii Petrovskogo vremeni*, 91.

31 Ustrialov, *Istoriia tsarstvovaniia Petra Velikogo*, 213.

32 Ibid., 529.

33 Quoted in Waliszewski, *Petr Velikii*, 383.

34 Golikova, "Organy politicheskogo syska i ikh razvitie v XVI–XVII vv., 258.

35 Veretennikov, *Istoriia tainoi kantseliarii Petrovskogo vremeni*, 111.

36 Korsakov, *Iz zhizni russkikh deiateli XVIII v.*, 325.

37 *Polnoe sobranie sochinenii*, coll. 1, vol. 15, no. 11445.

38 Samoilov, "Vozniknovenie Tainoi ekspeditsii pri Senate," 79.

39 Bolotov, *Zhizn' i prikliucheniia Andreiia Bolotova, opisannye samim im dlia svoikh potomkov*, 2:171.

40 Samoilov, "Vozniknovenie Tainoi ekspeditsii pri Senate," 80.

41 "Istoricheskie razskazy i anekdoty, zapisannye so slov imenitykh liudei P.F. Karabanovym. Tsarstvovanie Ekateriny II," 138.

42 Korsakov, "Stepan Ivanovich Sheshkovsky," 672.

43 Bil'basov, *Istoriia Ekateriny II*, 2:353.
44 Von Gel'big, "Russkie izbrannye i sluchainye liudi," 24. Gel'big was secretary to the Saxon embassy in St Petersburg.
45 Startsev, *Radishchev. Gody ispytanii. Ocherki*, 373.
46 Babkin, *Protsess A. N. Radishcheva*, 167–73.
47 Ibid., 195.
48 The empress repeatedly blocked the arrest of Novikov until "suitable reason" had been found. Papmehl, "The Empress and 'Un Fanatique': A Review of the Circumstances Leading to the Government Action Against Novikov," 684.
49 Bogoliubov, *N.N. Novikov i ego vremiia*, 420–1.
50 *Zapiski senatora I.V. Lopukhina*, 63.
51 Shil'der, *Imperator Aleksandr I*, 2:365.
52 Trotskii, *Tret'e otdelenie pri Nikolae I*, 8–10.
53 Lemke, *Nikolaevskie zhandarmy i literatura*, 9.

CHAPTER TWO

1 "Proekt g. A. Benkendorfa ob ustroistve vyshei politsii," 615.
2 Stroev, *Stoletie sobstvennoi ego imperatorskogo velichestva kantseliarii*, 16.
3 Those arrested were chained in single cells, fed little, and individually questioned by Nicholas. As usual, each penned answers to a questionnaire before interrogation by the Special Commission.
4 "Most Dutiful Report of the Supreme Criminal Court," as translated and excerpted in Raeff, *The Decembrist Movement*, 170.
5 For more on the Decembrists, see Mazour, *The First Russian Revolution, 1825 – The Decembrist Movement: Its Origins, Development, and Significance*.
6 "Ministerstvo vnutrennikh del," *Istoricheskii ocherk*, 97.
7 Information about the institutional structure of the Gendarmes can be found in Eroshkin, *Istoriia gosudarstvennykh uchrezhdenii dorevoliutsionnoi Rossii*, and Orzhekhovsky, *Samoderzhavie protiv revoliutsionnoi Rossii*.
8 In the regular scheme of military/civil crossovers, a Russian military officer could, and commonly did, assume a civil post without severing his military ties and without relinquishing his military title and uniform. Conversely, a civilian in a civil post could legitimately receive an honorary military title and, with it, the right to wear a military uniform. But never could a civilian receive a bona fide posting or rank in the armed services.
9 "Instruktsiia grafa Benkendorfa chinovniku Tret'ego otdeleniia," 396–7.
10 "Peterburgskoe obshchestvo pri vosshestvii na prestol imperatora Nikolaia. Po doneseniiam M.Ia. Foka – A.Kh. Benkendorfu," 556.

11 Ibid., 583.

12 "Proekt g. A. Benkendorfa ob ustroistve vysshei politsii," 615.

13 Lemke, *Nikolaevskie zhandarmy i literatura, 1826–1855*, 311.

14 Benkendorf, "Graf Benkendorf o Rossii v 1827–1832 gg." 109–32.

15 Koshelov, *Zapiski, 1812–1833*, 31–2.

16 "Tsenzura v tsarstvovanie Imp. Nikolaia I," 666.

17 Lemke, *Nikolaevskie zhandarmy i literatura*, 414.

18 At least one official queried by Benckendorff judged Chaadaev sane: the Gendarme general Perfil'ev. See Lemke, *Nikolaevskie zhandarmy i literatura*, 424. Perhaps Perfil'ev so replied, however, because he wanted Chaadaev tried and punished.

19 Leonty Vasil'evich Dubel't, "Biograficheskii ocherk i ego pis'ma," 501.

20 Herzen, *My Past and Thoughts*, 260.

21 Heading Perovsky's investigation was a former military intelligence officer, Liprandi, who sent informers to Petrashevsky meetings to report who attended and what they said. See Voznyi, *Petrashevsky i tsarskaia tainaia politisiia*, 55–84.

22 Dostoevsky, "Dostoevsky's Statement on the Petrashevsky Affair," 39.

23 Evans, *The Petrasevskij Circle*, 101.

24 As quoted in ibid., 105.

25 Zubarev, "Tret'e otdelenie. Otryvok iz vospominanii," 429.

26 Dolgorukov claims to have told some relatives, with respect to his new role as security chief: "You are bound to speak candidly with me; I have become the spiritual advisor of all true subjects of the tsar." Dolgorukov, *Peterburgskie ocherki*, 186.

27 Nikitenko, *Dnevnik*, 2:19–20.

28 Orzhekhovsky, "Reorganizatsiia zhandarmskogo upravleniia v sviazi s pravitel'stvennoi reaktsiei 60-kh – 70-kh godov XIX veka," 71.

29 V.A. Dolgorukov, "Otchet o deistviiakh III otdeleniia sob. imp. vel. kantseliarii i korpusa zhandarmov za 1857 god, GARF, 109/85/21, sheets 71–84.

30 Chernyshevsky, "O novykh usloviiakh sel'skogo byta,", 5: 65–70; pt. 2, 108–36.

31 V.A. Dolgorukov, "Otchet o deistviiakh III otdeleniia ... za 1858," sheets 13, 116–30.

32 Eidel'man, *Tainye korrespondenty 'Poliarnoi Zvezdy'*, 94.

33 V.A. Dolgorukov, "Otchet o deistviiakh III otdeleniia ... za 1859," sheets 16–17, 189–93.

34 Ibid., "za 1860 god," sheets 1–6, 26.

35 Ibid. "za 1861 god," sheets 19–20, 63–6.

36 "N.G. Chernyshevsky v doneseniiakh III otdeleniia (1861–62)," 108.

37 Minister of the Interior P.A. Valuev describes these events in *Dnevnik*, 1:145–6.

38 Chernyshevsky, "Pis'ma bez adresa," PSS, 10:101.

39 This Special Investigative Commission, headed by Golitsyn until 1864, would continue until Alexander's transfer of its functions and materials, in 1874, to the Third Section.

40 Instructions of 9 February 1861, GARF, 109/213/30, sheet 14.

41 Local police detained Chernyshevsky. For details of the operation, see Antonovich, "Arest N. G. Chernyshevskogo," *N.G. Chernyshevsky v vospominaniiakh sovremennikov*, 274–9.

42 See Chernyshevskaia, *Letopis' zhizni i deiatel'nosti N.G. Chernyshevskogo* for a chronicle of these events. Courts in Russia before 1864 based decisions just on the findings of investigators.

43 The Senate termed Chernyshevsky "an especially dangerous agitator" who had used *Contemporary* to subvert the thinking of the young. Chernyshevskaia, *Letopis'*, 322–3.

44 Nikitenko, *Dnevnik*, 2:441. Liberal historian Lemke would later identify those papers as an assessment by Kostomarov of Chernyshevsky's writings.

45 Every private periodical in the Empire then underwent preliminary censorship; the 1865 reform of censorship would end that screening for most newspapers and journals in the two capitals, but nowhere else.

46 "O gazete *Voronezhkii listok*," GARF, 109/1292, 1861, pt. 2, sheet 6.

47 Ibid., sheet 12.

48 Ibid., sheet 19.

49 Ibid., sheet 31.

50 V.A. Dolgorukov, "Otchet o deistviiakh III otdeleniia ... za 1865," sheets 43–6.

51 Nikitenko, *Dnevnik*, 3:26–7; Valuev, *Dnevnik*, 2:116.

52 Shuvalov to Alexander II, 12 April 1866 and 7 May [1866], OR RNB, 610/1/1, sheets 3–21.

53 Within the corps were twelve generals, 140 staff officers, 324 commissioned officers, 2,231 non-commissioned officers, 3,592 rank-and-file personnel, 761 non-combatants, and sixteen trumpeters.

54 As quoted by Orzhekhovsky, "Reorganizatsiia zhandarmskogo upravleniia," 43. This discussion of the Shuvalov administration is based largely on Orzhekhovsky's article.

55 Orzhekhovsky, "Reorganizatsiia zhandarmskogo upravleniia," 73–6.

56 As quoted by Orzhekhovsky, "Reorganizatsiia zhandarmskogo upravleniia," 76.

57 Quoted in Khitrovo, "Moi otnosheniia k shtabu otdel'nogo korpusa zhandarmov v 1871," 390.

58 Nikitenko, *Dnevnik*, 3:58–9.

59 Orzhekhovsky, "Reorganizatsiia zhandarmskogo upravleniia," 59.

60 Shuvalov had ended the routing of Gendarme district reports through provincial governors.

61 In August 1872 the Swiss police would extradite Nechaev to Russia, where he was convicted of murder and imprisoned for life.

62 For addendum details, see Szeftel, "Personal Inviolability in the Legislation of the Russian Absolute Monarchy," 2.

63 Koz'min, ed., *Nechaev i nechaevtsy*, 13–26.

64 Vilensky, *Sudebnaia reforma i kontrreforma v Rossii*, 308–9.

65 Efremova, *Ministerstvo iustitsii rossiiskoi imperii 1802–1917 gg.*, 111. Efremova says that the law gave Gendarmes "unlimited" ways to block judicial processing in security cases.

66 Bazilevsky, ed., *Gosudarstvennye prestupleniia v Rossii v XIX veke*, 1:159–220.

67 Efremova, *Ministerstvo iustitsii rossiiskoi imperii, 1802–1917 gg.*, 112.

68 Vilensky, *Sudebnaia reforma i kontrreforma v Rossii*, 317–18. Judges and prosecutors at the Senate level were strongly conservative. See Levin-Stankevich, "Cassation, Judicial Interpretation and the Development of Civil and Criminal Law in Russia, 1864–1917," 177–9, 189–96.

69 Orzhekhovsky, "Reorganizatsiia zhandarmskogo upravleniia," 61.

70 Ibid., 63–5.

CHAPTER THREE

1 Vilensky, *Sudebnaia reforma i kontrreforma*, 319.

2 Feoktistov, *Vospominaniia: Za kulisami politiki i literatury*, 311–12.

3 Vilensky, *Sudebnaia reforma i kontrreforma*, 251.

4 Pahlen, "Zapiska ministra iustitsii grafa Palena," 268–77.

5 Bachmanov to Mezentsov, 11 January 1877, GARF, 109/3/746, sheets 6–11, 15–16.

6 Miliutin, *Dnevnik*, 2:144–5.

7 As quoted by Vilensky, *Sudebnaia reforma i kontrreforma*, 248.

8 As quoted in Al'tman, "Sledstvennaia dokumentatsiia kak istochnik po istorii revoliutsionnogo dvizheniia v Rossii v kontse XIX veka," 49.

9 Miliutin, *Dnevnik*, 3:41–2.

10 "Zapiska N.V. Mezentsova o neobkhodimosti usileniia politicheskoi agentury," GARF, 109/3/694, sheets 1–2.

11 Zaionchkovsky, *Krizis samoderzhavia na rubezhe 1870–1880 godov*, 73–4.

12 Al'tman, "Sledstvennaia dokumentatsiia kak istochnik po istorii revoliutsionnogo dvizheniia v Rossii v kontse XIX veka," 50–7.

13 Novitsky, *Iz vospominanii zhandarma*, 85.

14 The People's Will security chief Alexander Mikhailov later declared at the Trial of the 20, "Mezentsov was considered the chief culprit and for that he was killed." See *Protsess 20-i narodovol'tsev v 1882 godu*, 63.

15 Bogucharsky, "V 1878 g. Vsepoddanneishee donesenie shefa zhandarmov," 151.

16 Miliutin, *Dnevnik*, 3:87.

17 *Polnoe sobranie zakonov rossiskoi imperial*, 2d ser., vol. 53, no. 58779 (1878), art. 1.

18 Zaionchkovsky, *Krizis samoderzhaviia*, 76–7.

19 Miliutin, *Dnevnik*, 3:85.

20 Zaionchkovsky, *Krizis samoderzhaviia*, 78.

21 Ibid.

22 Drentel'n to Alexander II, 28 October 1878, "Doklady gen.–leit. Selivestrova i gen.–ad. Drentel'na Aleksandru II," 135.

23 Zaionchkovsky, *Krizis samoderzhaviia*, 79.

24 Ibid., 85–8.

25 Tikhomirov, *Zagovorshchiki i politsiia*, 136.

26 Loris-Melikov to the Chief of Gendarmes, 26 February 1880, GARF, 569/1/33, sheet 2.

27 Loris-Melikov to Alexander II, 26 February 1880, GARF, 569/1/33, sheets 1–3.

28 Al'tman, "Sledstvennaia dokumentatsiia kak istochnik po istorii revoliutsionnogo dvizheniia v Rossii v kontse XIX veka," 60. The function of gathering and collating evidence had been the responsibility of the Third Secretariat of the Third Section. Later, in the new Department of Police, it would become the assignment of the Fourth Secretariat.

29 Loris-Melikov, "Osobaia zapiska o politicheskom dvizhenii v Rossii," GARF, 569/1/105, sheets 2–17. This undated memorandum would appear to have been written in 1879 when Loris was pondering the character of a new, permanent police system for Russia.

30 Perets, *Dnevnik E.A. Peretsa, gosudarstvennogo sekretaria*, 4.

31 "Zapiska st. sek. Kakhanova, M. S. o proizvodstve del po gosudarstvennym prestupleniiam...," 23 March 1880, GARF, 569/1/44, sheet 2.

32 "Zapiska...Kakhanova." Nabokov's letter is dated 18 March 1880, written as a commentary on Kakhanov's memo, sheets 7–9.

33 Loris-Melikov, "Dokladnaia zapiska o preobrazovanii politsii," 1 August 1880, GARF, 569/1/65, sheets 5–6.

34 This was the recommendation of State Secretary Kakhanov. "Mnenie Kakhanova...o vnesenii izmenenii v ustroistvo gos.-oi politsii," GARF, 1099/1528, sheet 12.

35 Shvetsov, *Provocator Okladsky*, 9; "Informatsiia...po voprosu ob ispolnenii prigovora...," 31 October 1880, GARF, 569/1/286, sheets 1–4.

36 "Zapiska P. Makova," 4 November 1880, GARF, 569/1/71, sheets 1–16.

37 Quoted by Zaionchkovsky, *Krizis samoderzhaviia*, 311.

38 *Polnoe Sobranie Zakonov Rossiskoi Imperii*, no. 350, 14 March 1881, 261–6.

39 Zaionchkovsky, *The Russian Autocracy in Crisis*, 258. A more recent study by Jonathan Daly shows that the emergency legislation can by no means be classified as an extreme reaction by the government to the

political situation. See Daly, "Emergency Legislation in Late Imperial Russia," 609–14.

40 Szeftel, *The Russian Constitution of April 23, 1906*, 150.

41 "Polozhenie o merakh k okhraneniiu Gosudarstvennogo poriadka i obshchestvennogo spokoistva," 1881, GARF, 586/1/23, sheets 1–14.

42 See chapter 11 on pogroms for a full discussion of the long-term war against them that the government began in 1881. The work of the military courts is summarized in Fuller Jr., "Civilians in Russian Military Courts," 288–305.

43 See the extended discussion and tables showing the use of the military courts under the emergency legislation in Fuller, *Civil-Military Conflict in Imperial Russia*, 113–19.

44 "Istoricheskii ocherk organizatsii i deiatel'nosti Departamenta politsii (materialy k obzory deiatel'nosti MVD s 1802 po 1902 g.)," GARF, Departamenta politsii, 302/707, sheet 153.

45 The figures are cited by Leikina-Svirskaia in *Intelligentsiia v Rossii vo vtoroi polovine XIX veka*, 314. They are from a secret internal document printed first in French by the Ministry of the Interior under the editorship of N.I Shebeko and then translated into Russian and published in 1906 as *Khronika sotsialisticheskogo dvizheniia v Rossii 1878–1887 gg. Ofitsial'nyi otchet.*

46 As quoted in Al'tman, "Sledstvennaia dokumentatsiia kak istochnik po istorii revoliutsionnogo dvizheniia v Rossii v kontse XIX veka," 41–2.

47 Lukashevich, "The Holy Brotherhood," 491–505.

48 Ibid., 505.

49 N.P. Ignatiev, "Polozhenie o neglasnom politseiskom nadzore," TSGIA Moskvy, 16/70/454, 1 March 1882, sheet 23.

50 "Ob ustroistve i deiatel'nosti Sekretnoi Politsii," GARF, 3 deloproizvodstvo, 1882, 977, sheets 9–12.

CHAPTER FOUR

1 Spiridovich, *Zapiski Zhandarma*, 52.

2 "Perepiska otnosiashchaia k deiatel'nosti E.P. Mednikova," GARF, 111/5/678 1905 sheets 1–10. Part of this discussion is drawn from this archival document, a Department of Police summary of the record of Mednikov.

3 Zhilinsky, "Organizatsiia v zhizni okhrannogo otdeleniia vo vremena tsarskoi vlasti," 262.

4 Ibid., 252.

5 Ibid., 267.

6 Polovtsov, *Dnevnik gosudarstvennogo sekretaria A. A. Polovtsova*, 157.

7 A method Dostoevsky describes as the main one of the court investigator in *Crime and Punishment.*

8 Zagorsky, "V 1881–1882 gg.," 155–78.

9 Ibid., 173.

10 Pribylovaia-Korba, "Sergei Petrovich Degaev," 1–17.

11 Kantor, "Provakator Stepan Belov," 141–52.

12 Statkovsky's career is described in an introduction to his reports on the Okhranka in the 1990s. See Statkovsky, "S-Peterburgskoe okhrannoe otdelenie v 1895–1901 gg.," [108]-136.

13 "Psikhologiia predatel'stva (Iz vospominanii 'sotrudnika')," 225–37.

14 Steffens's most complete treatment of this theme came as a result of his muckraking investigation of municipal corruption in Minneapolis. See Steffens, *The Shame of the Cities*, 63–100.

15 Ellis Tennant [Edward Ellis Smith], "The Department of Police, 1911–1913," Hoover Institution Archive, Smith Collection, box 1, 10.

16 Zhilinsky, "Organizatsiia v zhizni," 267.

17 "Delo Departamenta Politsii," TSGIA Moskvy, D3–635–1893, 15 March, 1895, sheets 66, 67, 74, 76.

18 Police Director Zuev to the heads of local O.O.s and Gendarmes, Secret Circular of 12 August 1909, Hoover Institution Archive, XIIId(i), folio 10.

19 Director Vissiaronov to the Regional O.O.s, Secret Circular of 5 July 1909, ibid.

20 GARF, 1467/1/1000, sheet 97 ob.

21 Durnovo to the emperor, 5 May 1895, GARF, 1467/1/1000, sheet 12.

22 Iablochkov's testimony to the Moscow Circuit Court is in GARF, 1467/1/1002, sheet 4.

23 Bakai, "Iz vospominanii M.E. Bakaia. O chernykh kabinetakh v Rossii," 123.

24 Zavarzin, *Zhandarmy i revoliutsionery*, 160.

25 Kurlov to Fomin, November 1910, GARF, 1467/1/1001, sheet 26 ob.

26 Lopukhin, *Otryvki iz vospominanii*, 13.

27 Komissarov's testimony was in 1917 to the Extraordinary Investigative Commission of the Provisional Government and is to be found in Shchegolev, ed., *Padenie tsarskogo rezhima*, 3:142.

28 Vissarionov to Kurlov, 3 April 1910, GARF, 1467/1/1001, sheet 19.

29 From a Department of Police information sheet about Krivosh. 1 February 1912, GARF, 1467/1/1001, sheet 89 ob.

CHAPTER FIVE

1 The figure of 19,000 rubles for 1878 is in the Financial Estimates of the Third Section (GARF, 109/3/570, sheet 7). Expenditures for foreign agents, therefore, remained a relatively small part of the budget through 1880. The breakdown for internal expenditures of secret funds for 1880

was as follows: St Petersburg Chief of Police, 29,00 rubles; Moscow Chief of Police, 7,500 rubles; Kiev Gendarme Administration, 7,080 rubles; and for the internal agency, 65,000 rubles. These figures are in Zaionchkovsky, *Krizis samoderzhaviia na rubezhe 1870–1880 godov*, 172.

2 Lukashevich, "The Holy Brotherhood," 491–509.

3 S.G. Svatikov, "Sozdanie 'Sionskikh Protokolov' po dannym ofitsial'nogo sledstviia 1917 goda," Hoover Institution Archives, Nicolaevsky Collection, box 20, folder 1, 63.

4 A factual summary of Rachkovsky's career can be found in Shchegolov, ed., *Padenie tsarskogo rezhima*, 7: 403–0. There is also an outline of his career in "Kar'er P.I. Rachkovskogo," 78–87.

5 That Rachkovsky became an agent in 1879 is asserted by the later head of the Okhranka in St Petersburg, Gerasimov, in *Na lezvii s terroristami*, 30. Interestingly, Gerasimov, who later worked with Rachkovsky, found that he had "neither investigative talents nor political flair." If so, Rachkovsky made up for these deficiencies in other ways.

6 Agafonov, *Zagranichnaia okhranka*, 21.

7 Rachkovsky's activities in France are described in Nikolaevsky, *Istoriia odnogo predatelia*, 126–8.

8 Agafonov, *Zagranichnaia okhranka*, 28.

9 The document is in GARF, 5802/2/267, sheet 4.

10 Chernavskaia-Bokhanovskaia, "Iz istorii bor'by russkogo samoderzhaviia s 'Narodnoi Volei' za granitsei," 97.

11 Agafonov, *Zagranichnaia okhranka*, 26.

12 Quoted by Svatikov, "Sozdanie 'Sionskikh Protokolov'," 18.

13 Quoted from a letter from Rachkovsky to Fragnon in 1887 by Zuckerman, "The Russian Political Police at Home and Abroad," 224–6.

14 Rachkovsky to St Petersburg, GARF, 5802/2/267, sheet 5.

15 Ibid., sheet 6.

16 Longe, *Terroristy i okhranka*, 190.

17 For several years, the Foreign Agency had tried to find a way to remove Tikhomirov from Paris. The agency saw him as a powerful influence on the revolutionary movement. In 1884 Rachkovsky, according to the editor of Tikhomirov's memoirs, was hatching plans to seize Tikhomirov and hustle him down to the railway station bound to a stretcher as a madman. He would be transported to Berlin, and from there to Russia. Russian diplomats would not agree to this scheme. See Tikhomirov, *Vospominaniia L'va Tikhomirova*, 481.

18 Landezen was also said to have had a role in the conversion of Tikhomirov. See *Russkoe Slovo*, 21 July 1908. Their relations appear to have been fairly close. Tikhomirov recorded on 1 January 1887 that he

had received 150 francs from Landezen to help with pressing expenses (*Vospominaniia L'va Tikhomirova*, 194).

19 Tikhomirov noted in his diary for 8 September 1888 a meeting the day before with Rachkovsky (whom he identifies as Leonov) for over two hours at the Russian consulate in Paris. Tikhomirov left his petition in Rachkovsky's hands. He then returned on 9 September for another meeting. These negotiations led to a final version of Tikhomirov's petition which he submitted 12 September. Additional negotiations went on into the next year and only on 12 October 1889 did Tikhomirov report that he had met with high Russian officials and received permission to return to his homeland. Rachkovsky, according to Tikhomirov's brief notations, was the key negotiator on the Russian side. Tikhomirov described him as "a very interesting and even sympathetic person." See *Vospominaniia L'va Tikhomirova*, 240, 259, 370.

20 Agafonov, *Zagranichnaia okhranka*, 35.

21 GARF, 5802/2/267, sheet 4.

22 Durnovo Memorandum, 15 November 1889, GARF, 5802/1/207, sheet 5.

23 Additional documentation that Landezen was "Miller" is to be found in the A.I. Spiridovich Collection, Manuscripts and Archives, Yale University. Spiridovich made extensive notes on this operation, including extracts from correspondence between Durnovo and Rachkovsky and Rachkovsky and Landezen. As the operation wound down in early 1890, Durnovo said that he now wished to attract Burtsev back to St Petersburg. In this he was unsuccessful. See Spiridovich Collection, box 25.

24 Durnovo Memorandum, 29 November 1889, GARF, 5802/1/207, sheet 13.

25 Ibid., 17 December 1889, GARF, 5802/1/207, sheet 23.

26 Ibid., sheet 26.

27 Ibid., 17 January 1890, GARF, 5802/1/207, sheet 30.

28 Burtsev, *Bor'ba za svobodnyiu Rossiiu*, 94.

29 Stepanov, "Iz zagranichanykh vospominanii starogo narodovol'tsa," 130–1.

30 Tiutchev, "Sud'ba Ivana Okladskogo," 226.

31 "Perepiska otnosiashchaia k deiatel'nosti E.P. Mednikova ...," GARF, 111/5/678, sheet 4.

32 Stepanov, "Iz zagranichanykh vospominanii starogo narodovol'tsa," 125, 128.

33 The Russian ambassador, Baron von Mohrenheim, had been pressing Constant for some time to make the arrests. See "Franko-russkoe shpionstvo i franko-russkii soiuz," 60.

34 In Bulgaria, reading the details of the arrests in Paris in the French press, Burtsev concluded: "For me, it had become clear, although nothing was

said about it in the papers, that we had been betrayed by none other than Landezen, that he was an agent of the Russian secret police." See Burtsev, *Za svobodnyiu Rossiiu*, 99–100.

35 For additional biographical details on Landezen-Harting, see *Padenie tsarskogo rezhima*, 7:322.

36 Rachkovsky's management of the affair of the "Paris bombers" and the strengthening of Russo-French relations is credited in a later Okhranka report to his work as head of the Foreign Agency. "Zapiska o deiatel'nosti Rachkovskogo," in Svatikov, *Zagranichnaia agentura Departamenta politsii*, 102–3.

37 Kennan, *The Fateful Alliance: France, Russia and the Coming of the First World War*, 112–15.

38 Witte, *The Memoirs of Count Witte*, 291–2.

39 Quoted in Shchegolev, *Okhranniki i avantiuristy*, 83.

40 Ibid., 86.

41 Bertram Wolfe describes the famous Tiflis "expropriation" on 26 June 1907 and the coordinated police operation covering several countries leading to the arrest of a number of Bolshevik party figures who were designated to exchange rubles for European currencies at banks. Zhitomirksy had been appointed by Lenin as the organizer of the exchange and so he was able to supply serial numbers of the notes and descriptions of Lenin's agents. See Wolfe, *Three Who Made a Revolution*, 391–5.

42 "G.V. Plekhanov i shpionskii sabavy," 261–4.

43 Pauli to the director, Department of Police, Paris, n.d., GARF, 5802/2/205, sheet 55.

44 Rataev to Peter Ivanovich [Rachkovsky], GARF, 5802/2/205, sheet 55. Svatikov mentions that Rachkovsky at one point paid Pauli 600 francs for two months' work as an agent. See Svatikov, *Zagranichnaia agentura Departamenta politsii*, 23.

45 Rachkovsky to Zvoliansky, 19 July 1901, GARF, 5802/2/205, sheet 58.

46 Lopukhin says he learned of this incident while procurator of the St Petersburg Circuit Court in 1900–2 from Gredinger, the procurator of the Court of Appeals. Lopukhin was told that a Rachkovsky agent by the name of Iagolkovsky carried out the bombing at some loss of life. Lopukhin, "Pokazaniia, dannye Chrezvychainoi Sledstvennoi Komissii dlia rassledovaniia protivozakonnykh po dolzhnosti deistvii byvshikh ministrov i proch.," 6 November 1917, Hoover Institution Archives, Nicolaevsky Collection, box 12, folder 12, 1.

47 Svatikov, *Zagranichnaia agentura Departamenta politsii*, 102–4. According to Svatikov, this memorandum was found among the papers of Plehve, who was assassinated in 1904. Durnovo showed it to Nicholas II on 24 January 1905. The tsar wrote on it, "I want you to take serious measures to cut Rachkovsky's connections with the French police."

48 Rataev, "Kratkii obzor deiatel'nosti zagranichnoi agentury s 13-sentia-bria 1902 goda po iiul' 1905 goda," Hoover Institution Archives, Nico-laevsky Collection, box 203, folder 22.

49 The budget estimates were signed by Lopukhin, GARF, 1723/2/13, sheet 87.

50 "Departament politsii v 1892–1908 gg.," 20.

51 Burtsev to Rataev, 1909, GARF, 5802/2/497, sheet 7.

52 These allegations were widely publicized. See, for instance, the report in the *London Daily News*, 7 July 1909.

53 Zuckerman, "The Russian Political Police at Home and Abroad," 286–347.

54 Andreev to the director, 9/16 August 1909, GARF, 1723/2/34, sheet 231.

55 Agafonov, *Zagranichnaia okhranka*, 102.

56 Andreev to the director, 4/17 July 1909, GARF, 1723/2/34, sheet 231.

57 Agafonov, *Zagranichnaia agentura*, 102.

58 Krasil'nikov to Zuev, 24 December 1909, GARF, 1723/2/34 sheets 331–2.

59 Ibid., 26 December–8 January 1909–1910, GARF, 1723/2/34, sheets 332–4.

60 Krasil'nikov to the Department of Police, 11/12 June 1910, in Svatikov, *Russkii politicheskii sysk za granitsei*, 35.

61 Krasil'nikov to the Special Section, 5/18 June 1912, GARF, 5802/2/205, sheet 167.

62 Ibid., sheets 165–6.

63 Krasil'nikov to sirector, Department of Police, June 1912, GARF, 5802/2/205, sheet 169.

64 This account is based on Svatikov, *Russkii politicheskii sysk za granitsei*, 64–6.

65 "Report on the Organization of Surveillance on the Basis of New Princi-ples," GARF, 1723/2/34, sheets 266–73.

66 Filenas to the Special Section, 13 September 1913, GARF, 5802/2/205, sheets 125–6.

67 Svatikov, *Russkii politicheskii sysk za granitsei*, 33.

68 Thorpe to Krasil'nikov, 10 November 1913, GARF, 5802/2/205, sheets 128–9.

69 Krasil'nikov to Brune de St Hyppolite, May 1915, in Svatikov, *Russkii politicheskii sysk za granitsei*, 61–3.

CHAPTER SIX

1 According to a police report on monarchist parties in the second half of 1909, members of the Union of Russian People, concealing that affilia-tion, had penetrated other political parties on the left in service to the monarchist cause. "Obzor dvizheniia monarkhicheskikh organizatsii s iiu-niia po dekabr' 1909 goda," GARF, 847, sheet 77.

2 Extreme fanaticism is suggested about Black Hundred adherents in Gomel, Poland, who allegedly had to write a signed confession of suicide which, should they betray a comrade, would be placed in their pocket when they were exterminated for their treachery. New members in St Petersburg, in contrast, had only to sign an oath of allegiance emblazoned with a death's head.

3 The head of the St Petersburg Okhranka in 1905, A.V. Gerasimov, writes that he had asked Rachkovsky in this period "why no efforts were being made [by the government] to found legal organizations to oppose the revolutionaries' harmful influence on the popular masses?" Rachkovsky replied that such efforts were being made and "he promised to introduce me to Dr. Dubrovin, who had undertaken to create a monarchist organization." Gerasimov, *Na lezvii s terroristami*, 149.

4 Union founder B.V. Nikolsky would describe Poltoratsky as a lower-middle-class Muscovite endowed with the "natural gifts of a modest titan." Nikol'sky, "Dnevnik Borisa Nikol'skogo," 86.

5 Meshchersky, "Dnevnik V.P. Meshcherskogo," 67.

6 "Protokol doprosa A.V. Polovneva v ChSK 26 maia 1917," GARF, 1467/1/862, sheet 14 ob.

7 This was the Mukhin case, concerning a Bolshevik worker murdered by members of a right-wing squad in 1906.

8 From the context it is possible to deduce that Kraskovsky was speaking about Easter 1906. Snesarev's house was burned down on 3 April 1906 and Snesarev was killed on 26 April.

9 Timofeev, "Rabochie i politiki," x.

10 "Zapiska zaveduiushchego politsei na Kavkaze o Tiflisskom russkom patrioticheskom obshchestve 21 aprelia 1906," GARF, 102,00, 1905(2)/1255, pt. 27, sheet 8.

11 RGIA, 520/1/296, zakaz no. 34, sheet 21.

12 "Zapiska I.V. Toropova," GARF, 102,00/1916/538, sheet 33 ob.

13 Ibid.

14 "Pokazaniia V.N. Stepanova 13 avgusta 1906 g. Delo Departamenta Politsii," GARF, 102,00, 1906 (1)/905, sheet 3.

15 Stepanova's information was sent in written form on the evening of the 9th to the chief of police. Stepanova also asked one of the members of the Society of Active Struggle, N.P. Boborykin, to take advantage of her acquaintanceship with Stolypin (they had been students together in the gymnasium) to warn him personally. Boborykin tried, but was denied access to the minister and handed a report to a chancellery official who did not pass the information on. After the bombing of the dacha, an inquiry looked into this matter but reached no conclusion (GARF, 102,00 1906/905, sheet 37).

16 Report of the head of the Gendarme Gatchina division of the St Peters-burg–Warsaw Railway, 2 September 1906, GARF, 102, 4 d-vo, 1905/999, ch. 101, sheet 5.

17 "Nariad po sekretnoi perepiske," GARF, 102,00, 1906(2)/828, pt. 1–22; 4 del-vo, 1907/164(1); "Svedeniia o politicheskikh partiiakh i soiuzakh," RGIA, 1284/187/157. Because the usual source for a local count was a local member naturally inclined to exaggerate, the totals filed by the department, as officials recognized, are somewhat inflated.

18 This information on the Odessa White Guard can be found in a staff officer's report to the Odessa chief of police (GARF, 102,00 1905/999).

19 From a report of Senator Tregubov about monarchial organizations oper-ating in Odessa, 8 August 1917, GARF, 1467/71/847, sheet 12.

20 Doneseniia pomoshchnika nachal'nika Mogilevskogo gubernskogo zhan-darmskogo upravleniia v Departament politsii 13 avgusta 1906," GARF, 102,00, 1906/999, pt. 39, vol. I., sheet 164 ob.

21 The Okhranka compiled a report in 1907 on political circumstances in the city of Aleksandrovsk in Ekaterinoslav province that related to the pogrom in December 1906 and subsequent preparations for others. That report quotes the local vice-governor as saying that officials in Aleksan-drovsk gave protection to various "drunken and unrestrained" persons who engaged in anti-Semitic activities and described them as having initi-ated the local – and altogether legal – Union of the Russian People. He also described the Gendarme chief, one Budagovsky, as a "fanatically dedicated nationalist and patriotic idealist" but with "extremist" views on the land question (GARF, 1467/1/851, sheet 2). When Budagovsky was summoned to the capital to explain his role in the events, an inter-nal investigation cleared him of any wrongdoing (ibid., sheet 38).

22 Witte's account of the discovery of the bombs is in *The Memoirs of Count Witte*, 639–43.

23 Gerasimov, *Na lezvii s terroristami*, 152.

24 *Russkoe znamia*, 31 January 1907.

25 "Shifrovannaia telegramma ministra Vnytrennikh del komanduiush-chemu voiskami generalu ot kavalerii A.V. Kaul'barsu 28 apreliia 1907 g.," GARF, 102,00, 1905/999, pt. 39, lit. A, sheet 125.

26 "Doklad zaveduiushchego sysknym otdeleniem Ratsishevskogo odesskomu politsmeisteru," RGIA, 268/1/12, sheet 23 ob.

27 P.N. Miliukov, *Vospominaniia, 1859–1917*, 2 vols. (New York, 1955), 2:433.

28 "Protocol doprosa A.S. Stepanova v ChSK 16 iiunia 1917," GARF, 1467/1/862, sheet 87.

29 "Protocol doprosa A.I. Prussakova v ChSK 9 iiunia 1917 g.," GARF, 1467/1/862, sheet 63.

30 Witte, *Vospominaniia*, 3:420; see also *The Memoirs of Count Witte*, 636–7.
31 "Kopiia zaiavleniia V.D. Fedorovu prokuroru Peterburgskogo okruzhnogo suda 24 sentiabria 1907 g.," GARF, 124/65/30, sheet 17.
32 *Rus'*, 14 July 1907.
33 *Rech'*, 20, 28 June 1907.
34 *Iuzhnye vedomosti*, 10 July 1907.
35 "Perliustrirovannoe pis'mo iz Odessy za podpis'iu "Sasha" k Zavadskomu v Dobrovelichkovu Khersonskoi gub. ot 30 iiulia 1907 g.," GARF, 102,00 1907/219, sheet 79.
36 "Spravka Departamenta politsii o vydache denezhnykh summ V.M. Purishkevichu," GARF, 102,00, no. 1976/307, lit. A, vol. 1, sheet 179.
37 Letter of N.N. Rodzevich to B.V. Nikol'sky, 19 December 1907, GARF, 588/2/122.
38 I.N. Tolmachev to director, Department of Police, 2 September 1908, GARF, 1467/1/849, sheet 5 ob.
39 "Pokazaniia V.L. Burtseva v chSK 1 aprelia 1917 g.," *Padenie tsarskogo rezhima*, 1:320.
40 "Protokol doprosa A.V. Polovneva v chSK maia 1917. Dopolnitel'nye pokazaniia," GARF, 1467/1/862, sheet 15 ob.
41 "Protokol doprosa V.P. Roznatovskogo v chSK, GARF, 1467/1/852, sheet 15.
42 His confession is in "Protokol doprosa obviniaemago," 11 March 1911, GARF, 520/1/296, sheet 21.
43 Letter of E.A. Poluboiarinova to A.I. Dubrovin, 2 July 1909, GARF, 124/57/110, Supplement, sheet 10.
44 Frederik's telegram to P.A. Stolypin, n.d., GARF, 601/1/953, sheet 4.
45 "Vsepoddanneishii doklad ministra iustitsii I.G. Shcheglovitova 27 dekabria 1909, GARF, 124/65/27, sheet 149.
46 "Kopiia pokazanii T.A. Zapol'skogo v Kivineppskom sude 8 avgusta 1907 g.," GARF, 124/65/26, sheet 57.

CHAPTER SEVEN

1 Most young Jews in the late nineteenth century held radical views. They provided a fertile recruiting ground, for instance, for the Bund (Assembly of Jewish Workmen), a Marxist union.
2 Head of the Don Gendarmes to the director, Department of Police, 9 May 1893, GARF, 102,00/420, sheet 8 ob.
3 *Russkoe Slovo*, 7 May 1909.
4 Azeff to the Department of Police, 28 December 1897, GARF, 102,00, 420, sheet 173.
5 Azeff to Rataev, 17 March 1900, GARF, 102,00, 1898, 2, pt. 8, sheets 7–8.

6 Spiridovich, *Zapiski zhandarma*, 70.

7 Azeff to Rataev, 15 January 1901, GARF, 102,00, 1898, 2, pt. 8, sheet 26 ob.

8 Azeff to Rataev, 23 September 1904, "Doneseniia Evno Azefa (Perepiska Azefa s Rataevym v 1903–1905 gg.)," 212.

9 "Interv'iu s byvshim kollegoi sosluzhivuem Azefa," *Birzhevye vedomosti*, 25 January 1909.

10 Spiridovich, *Zapiski zhandarma*, 78.

11 Azeff to Rataev, 9 November 1901, GARF, 102,00, 1898, 2, pt. 8, sheet 34 ob.

12 Azeff to Rataev, 26 December 1901, GARF, 102,00, 1898, 2, pt. 8, lit. A, sheet 2.

13 Ibid.

14 Gerasimov, *Na lezvii s terroristami*, 70–1.

15 Ibid., 144.

16 Testimony of M.S. Komissarov to the ChSk, in Shchegolev, ed. *Padenie tsarskogo rezhima*, 3:144.

17 Lunacharsky, *Velikii provakator Evno Azef*, 78–9.

18 Azeff to Rataev, 23 September 1904, in "Doneseniia Evno Azefa (perepiska Azefa s Rataevym v 1903–1905 gg.)," 212.

19 *Delo A.A. Lopukhina v Osobom prisutstvii Pravitelstvuiushchego Senata*, 40–61.

20 *Zakliuchenie sudebno-sledstvennoi komissii po delu Azefa*, 23.

21 Gershuni was sentenced to death, but his sentence was commuted to exile for life. He escaped in 1906, but an investigating commission of the party concluded that Azeff had nothing to do with Gershuni's arrest. V.L. Burtsev asserted that Azeff had confessed to him in 1912 that he had planned the betrayal of Gershuni.

22 Savinkov, *Vospominaniia terrorista*, 44.

23 *Zakluchenie sudebno-sledstvennoi komissii po delu Azefa*, 38.

24 Savinkov, *Vospominaniia terrorista*, 44.

25 Rataev, "Evno Azef. Istoriia ego predatel'stva. Delo Pleve," 207.

26 Gerasimov contends that Azeff had given his superiors adequate warning of the plot against Plehve, and it was not the fault of the agent that the Okhranka failed to use the information. See Gerasimov, *Na lezvii s terroristami*, 137–8.

27 Shchegolev, ed., *Provokator. Vospominaniia i dokumenty o razoblachenii Azefa*, 152–3.

28 Agafonov, *Zagranichnaia okhranka. Ocherk Evno Azef*, 261.

29 Ibid.

30 Burtsev attributes these words to Azeff (*Padenie tsarskogo rezhima*, 1:304).

31 Gerasimov, *Na lezvii s terroristami*, 85.

32 Savinkov, *Vospominaniia terrorista*, 254–60.

33 The "Petersburg letter" was first published in *Zakliuchenie sudebno-sledstvennoi komissii po delu Azefa*, 55. It appeared again in Men'shchikov, *Zagranichnaia okhrana. Ocherk E. Azef*, 266.

34 Rutenberg, *Ubiistvo Gapona*, 46.

35 Ibid.

36 Ibid.

37 Gerasimov, *Na lezvii s terroristami*, 71.

38 "Delo S. Ryssa," 239.

39 *Zakliuchenie sudebno-sledstvennoi komissii po delu Azefa*, 60.

40 Ibid., 61.

41 Burtsev, *V pogone za provokatorami*, 68 (reprint from the 1928 edition).

42 Ibid., 103.

43 Ibid., 96.

44 Azeff to Savinkov, 10 October 1908, 213.

45 Savinkov, *Vospominaniia terrorista*, 271.

46 Azeff to Savinkov, 10 October 1908, 213.

47 An account of Burtsev's meeting with Lopukhin appears in chapter 8.

48 *Delo A.A. Lopukhina v Osobom prisutstvii Pravitel'stvuiushchego Senata*, 51–2.

49 Savinkov, *Vospominaniia terrorista*, 287–8.

50 Argunov, "Azef – sotsialist-revoliutsioner," in Shchegolev, ed., *Provokator. Vospominaniia i dokumenty o razoblachenii Azefa*, 129.

51 *Zapros o Azefe v III Gosudarstvennoi dume po stenograficheskomu otchetu*, 55.

52 *Golos Moskvy*, 14 February 1909.

53 *Russkii narod*, 25 February 1909.

54 *Stolichnaia zhizn'*, 18 May 1909.

55 Copy of Azeff's letter to L.G. Azef (Menkina), 13 April 1909, GARF, 5802/2/271, sheet 42. About the time Azeff wrote this letter, Leonid Andreev published his "The Story of the Seven Hanged Men" which made heroes of one of the terrorist groups denounced by Azeff.

56 Copy of a letter from Azeff to L.G. Azeff (Menkina), 14 June 1909, GARF, 5802/2/271, sheet 47.

57 Agafonov, *Zagranichnaia okhranka*, 251.

58 A. Geifman, "Tri legendy vokryg 'Dela Azefa'," Supplement to Nikolaevsky, *Istoriia odnogo predateliia*, 330–61. The author utilizes unlikely information about the reason for the action of Lopukhin, whose daughter was said to have been kidnapped by the SRs in a blackmail scheme.

59 Rataev, "Evno Azef. Istoriia ego predatel'stva. Delo Pleve," 194.

60 Lur'e, "Asef i Lopukhin," 167.

61 "Iz zapisok M.E. Bakaia. Azef, Stolypin i provokatsiia," 205.

62 R. Gul', *Azef* (Moscow: 1991), 64–5. This is a reworking of a novel first published in Berlin in 1929 with the title *General of the Battle Organization*. Among the most recent works in this genre is V. Zhukhrai, *Tainy tsarskoi okhranki: avantiuristy i provokatory*, Moscow, 1991, pp. 57–58.

63 Nikolaevsky, *Konets Azefa*, Leningrad, 1926, and *Istoriia odnogo predatelia. Terroristy i politicheskaia politsiia*, Moscow, 1991.

CHAPTER EIGHT

1 Lopukhin, "Pokazaniia, dannye Chrezvychainoi Sledstvennoi Komissii ...," 6 November 1917, Hoover Institution Archives, Nicolaevsky Collection, box 12, folio 12, 1.

2 S.D. Urusov, "Zapiski," RO GBL, 550/2/3, sheet 42. Citing the many liberals who believed that Plehve had genuinely converted to reformism, Urusov says that Lopukhin accepted the directorship as "an opportunity to advance legality in the Department of Police."

3 Spiridovich, *Zapiska Zhandarma*, 110.

4 As quoted in Judge, *Plehve: Repression and Reform in Imperial Russia*, 218.

5 Urusov, "Zapiski," RO GBL, 550/2/3, sheet 3.

6 Lopukhin to P. A. Stolypin, 14/27 June 1906, Hoover Institution Archives, Nicolaevsky Collection, box 112, folio 10, 5.

7 Many assert, with scant documentation, that Plehve convinced the tsar to fire Rachkovsky because he had exposed a favourite of the tsarina (one Monsieur Philippe, who claimed his counsel would enable her to conceive a male heir to the throne) as fraudulent. Evidence also shows that others subsequently held Lopukhin responsible for the dismissal.

8 Lopukhin, "Vremennoe polozhenie ob Okrannykh Otedeleniiakh," 30 June 1902, Hoover Institution Archives, Okhrana Collection, box 158, xiiid (1), folio 9. Security investigators were required to justify all searches and seizures in advance and to report all their actions to the procuracy so that that their findings would be admissable to judicial inquiry.

9 P., "Departament politsii v 1892–1908 gg.," 22.

10 Zubatov also had plans, never as far advanced as his police unions, to apply the same principles of control to the radical student movement. He sought to break up the student movement into groups under selected student and professorial leadership that could be isolated from radical influence. See Ovchenko, "Iz istorii bor'by tsarskoi okhranki s revoliutsionnym studencheskim dvizheniem," 66–9.

11 *Delo A. A. Lopukhina v osobom prisutstvii pravitel'stvuiushego senata*, 113, 114.

12 Ibid., 113.

13 "Evno Azef. Istoriia ego predatel'stva," 200–1.

14 Lopukhin, "Zapiska ... o stachkakh," 382–95.

15 Ibid., 386.

16 Lopukhin's brother-in-law, Prince S.D. Urusov, who later became governor of Bessarabia, also believed that local police had clandestinely abetted the pogrom in defiance of standing orders.

17 Lopukhin, *Otryvki iz vospominanii (Po povodu 'Vospominanii' gr. S.Iu. Witte)*, 15.

18 Lopukhin to Zubatov, 25 September 1903, in Koz'min, ed., *S.V. Zubatov i ego korrespondenty*, 39.

19 Judge, *Plehve*, 214.

20 This was clear from Lopukhin's position on the Obolensky Commission in 1904.

21 P., "Departament Politisii v 1892–1908 gg.," 21.

22 Lopukhin, *Otryvki iz vospominanii*, 77. Count Witte heard that there had been a denunciation of Lopukhin in St Petersburg by the commander of the military in Reval. The charge was that Lopukhin "because of cowardice played the liberal in extreme fashion and surrendered power to the revolutionaries." See Witte, *Vospominaniia*, 3:85.

23 Lopukhin, *Otryvki iz vospominanii*, 79.

24 Ibid., 81.

25 "Protokol no. 6," 18–22 January 1909, Hoover Institution Archives, Nicolaevsky Collection, box 205, folio 9, 11.

26 Lopukhin describes his meeting with Witte in *Otryvki iz vospominanii*, 81–9.

27 Ibid., 88.

28 Ibid., 89.

29 *Gosudarstvennaia Duma. Stenograficheskie otchety. 1906 god*, col. 1129.

30 Lopukhin to Stolypin, 14/27 June 1906, Hoover Institution Archives, Nicolaevsky Collection, box 112, folio 10, 1. In May Lopukhin had sent a letter to the daily newspaper of the Constitutional Democratic party, *Speech* (*Rech'*), giving facts about police incitement of anti-Semitism. Although a pending court case caused Lopukhin to withdraw the letter, it was printed elsewhere. He was also writing articles for other papers on the issue of the police.

31 Lopukhin said that the press in use in January, for example, printed one thousand copies an hour and that the January pamphlets stressed a single theme: that most revolutionaries were Jews.

32 Lopukhin to Stolypin, 14/27 June 1906, 4.

33 Ibid., 5.

34 Lopukhin, "Pokazaniia, dannye Chrezvychainoi Sledstvennoi Komissii," 1.

35 Lopukhin, *Nastoiashchee i budushchee russkoi politsii*.

36 A full account of Burtsev's activities can be found in Zuckerman, "Vladimir Burtsev and the Tsarist Police in Conflict, 1907–1914," 193–219.

37 Burtsev, *Bor'ba za svoboduiu Rossiiu. Moi vospominaniia,* 1:244–5.

38 Ibid., 1:247, 248–54.

39 S.D. Urusov, "Zapiski," sheet 44. His former colleague Rataev interpreted Lopukhin's moral dilemmas somewhat differently; the conflict within Lopukhin was because he felt compelled to repudiate his beliefs as a police official by conveying inside information to the enemy. "I know and completely understand," he wrote to the police official Zuev, "that Lopukhin suffered not because he believed in the guilt of Azeff, but because of the incompatibilites between his former position and the methods he employed for Azeff's exposure." Rataev to Zuev, 20 October 1910, Paris, "Evno Azef. Istoriia ego predatel'stva," 188.

40 Svatikov, *Zagranichnaia agentura Departamenta politsii,* 30. Harting's telegram was dated 7 November 1908, and his gloom over the revelations emanating from Bakai surely deepened when L.P Men'shchikov defected, especially because he himself became a victim of Men'shchikov's revelations and was forced to flee Paris.

41 Bakai, "Iz vospominanii M.E. Bakaia," 163.

42 "Protokol no. 6 o doprose obvinaemogo," 17–18. Lopukhin's alarm caused him to write a letter describing his meetings with Azeff and Gerasimov and to send it to Stolypin, with copies to his assistant Makarov, and Trusevich, the director of police. He also gave copies to two trusted persons. Lopukhin asked Stolypin to protect his personal security.

43 Gerasimov, *Na lezvii s terroristami,* 133–4.

44 Lopukhin, "Protokol no. 6 o doprose obviniaemogo," 21. The revolutionaries were Savinkov, Chernov, and Argunov. Lopukhin says they could have easily found out about his trip to London and where he was staying while in the city. Okhranka agents in London reported on the meeting to Gerasimov, who concluded that Lopukhin was consorting with terrorists: "The former director of the Department of Police and a personal friend of Plehve had met with the terrorist Savinkov, the organizer of the murder of Plehve." See Gerasimov, *Na lezvii s terroristami,* 134.

45 Schleifman documents the collapse of the party in Russia following the revelation of Azeff's role as a police agent, in *Undercover Agents in the Russian Revolutionary Movement.*

46 Svatikov, *Russkii politicheskii sysk za granitsei,* 27. Harting's report in full can be found in "Otchet o sostoiavshemsia 1/14 ianvaria 1909 v Parizhe zasedanii … 'Pravoi' gruppy partii sotsialistov-revoliutsionerov po delu Azeva," GARF, 1732/2/34, sheet 202.

47 "Pokazaniia, dannye Chrezvychainoi Sledstvennoi Komissii," 2–3. Prince Urusov, evidently relying on hearsay evidence, says that on Stolypin's written report to the tsar on the forthcoming Lopukhin trial, Nicholas II wrote, "I hope that it will be hard labour" (Urusov, "Zapiski," sheet 44).

48 "Rech' o dele Azeva," in Stolypin, *Nam nuzhna Velikaia Rossia*, 201–4.

49 This is the position of Nicolaevsky in *Aseff: The Spy*, Russian Terrorist and Police Stool, 20. In recounting Lopukhin's admission to Burtsev that Azeff was an Okhranka agent, Nicolaevsky ascribes these thoughts to Lopukhin: "The exposure would bring him moral satisfaction; it would balance the account of his long struggle with Rachkovsky." Schleifman is inclined towards this interpretation of Lopukhin's motive. See *Undercover Agents*, 93.

50 Vassilyev, *The Ochrana*, 75.

51 Gessen, *V dvukh vekakh: Zhiznennyi otchet'*, 149–51.

52 "Protocol no. 6 o doprose obviniaemogo," 9.

53 This highly specialized court was established in 1872 as one of the subdivisions of the state's highest judicial institution, the Senate. It was a court of first instance and used only in exceptional cases for the trial of public officials. Both judges and prosecutors of this court usually had behind them long and stable careers in the judicial system and were inclined to be conservatives. See Levin-Stankevich, "Cassation, Judicial Interpretation and the Development of Civil and Criminal Law in Russia," 177–9, 189–96.

54 *Novoe Vremia*, 29 April 1901, 1 May 1909.

55 *Vechernaia Vremia*, 15 October 1912.

56 "Leonid Men'shchikov o samom sebe," *Russkoe Slovo*, 3 September 1910, in GARF, 5802/2/1104, sheet 1322.

57 M.P. Gots, "S.V. Zubatov," *Byloe* 9 (September 1906): 66.

58 This "absolutely secret" internal Okhranka document is located at the Hoover Institution, Nicolaevsky Collection, box 179, folio 1.

59 Svatikov, *Zagranichnaia agentura Departamenta politsii*, 27.

60 Hoover Institution Archives, Nicolaevsky Collection, box 179, folio 1.

61 Ia.V., "Leonid Men'shchikov po lichnym vospominaniiam," *Russkoe Slovo*, 5 October 1910, in GARF, 5802/2/1104, sheet 1335.

62 Gorev, "Leonid Men'shchikov," 134.

63 So reported *Paris Newssheet (Parizhskii Listok)* on 15 October 1910, in GARF, 5802/2/1104, sheet 1358.

64 *New Times*, a conservative newspaper, reported Men'shchikov motives as less pure than the defector himself would have his readers think. According to the paper's account, when M.E. Trusevich became director of police in 1906 he wished to remove from influential positions all important "Zubatovites." This was the reason for Men'shchikov's reassignment

to Finland. Men'shchikov, continues the account, asked to retire instead, but was offered a lower pension than he wanted. For this reason he defected, says the paper. See *Novoe Vremia*, 21 September 1910, in GARF, 5802/2/1104, sheet 1329.

65 "Leonid Men'shchikov o samom sebe," sheet 1325.

66 The quotations are from a series of letters written by Zhuchenko in August and September 1909 to her former superiors in Moscow. The letters are in Pavlov, *Agenty, zhandarmy, palachi*, 32–45.

67 Gorev, "Leonid Men'shchikov," 135.

68 This summary is based on Wolfe's account in *Three Who Made a Revolution*, 393–4.

CHAPTER NINE

1 Testimony of D.G. Bogrov in court, 11 September 1911, GARF, 271/1/1, sheet 51.

2 Kuliabko had served prior to his appointment as assistant to the head of the Kiev Okhranka. Before that, his career had largely been spent in the military. He had been educated in the Nizhnii Novgorod Cadet Corps, then the First Pavlovsk Military Academy from which he was graduated in 1893. For the next three years he was a lieutenant in the Troitsky regiment and moved into the civil service in 1897. During the Russo-Japanese War of 1904–5 Kuliabko was again back in the military but not in combat.

3 Testimony of N.N. Kuliabko in court, 5 September 1911, GARF, 271/1/1, sheet 44. Bogrov's apologists maintain that he contrived the gambling story as a pretext for joining the Okhranka on behalf of the revolutionary cause (see, for example, Mushin, *Dmitrii Bogrov i ubiistvo Stolypina*, 183). But whatever Bogrov claimed seems beside the point in that the Okhranka took on informers whatever their pretext and then judged their usefulness by the apparent validity and relevance of what they reported. Logically, police officials were also not blind to the possibility that a volunteer informer might be attempting to infiltrate the political police on behalf of revolutionaries.

4 Mushin, *Dmitry Bogrov i ubiistvo Stolypina*, 183; Bogrov, *Dmitry Bogrov i ubiistvo Stolypina*, 77.

5 Kuliabko had only one defence for his limitless confidence in Bogrov: that Bogrov had proved beyond any doubts his competence and loyalty in the four and a half years between the time he began working for the Okhranka and the assassination. Kuliabko had to refute the kind of claims of Vladimir Bogrov that his brother provided information to the police only to gain their confidence in order to carry out a terroristic act.

6 This information was gathered by the agent "Alensky" from 1 November 1908 and shown in two documents prepared by the police following assassination of Stolypin. Clearly, the purpose was to show that Bogrov had been an effective agent. The first was written in St Petersburg, the second in Kiev. See GARF, 102,00, 1911/124, lit. A, sheets 106–13; and "Spravka Kievskogo GZHU," 18 August 1912, GARF, 271/1/26, without numeration. These numbers do not include the participants of the Kiev group of anarchist-communists under Naum Tysh and German Sandomirsky, who were sentenced to different periods of hard labour and prison. The numbers of persons arrested cannot be precisely attributed to Bogrov's information because another agent, code name "Moskovskii" (whose identity remains unknown) also provided information at the same time. On the other hand, Bogrov may have provided information leading to arrests in cities other than Kiev.

7 As quoted in Serebrennikov, ed., *Ubiistvo Stolypina. Svidetel'stva i dokumenty*, 103. The selection by Sandomirsky appeared in "K voprosu o Dmitrii Bogrove," 11–34.

8 Sandomirsky, "K voprosu o Dmitrii Bogrove," 16.

9 Kuliabko to the director, Department of Police, 25 July 1908, GARF, 271/1/6, sheet 225.

10 "Kopiia pokazannii D. Bogrova na doprose ot 6 sentiabria 1911," GARF, 271/1/1, sheet 50.

11 I. Grossman-Roshchin, "Dmitrii Bogrov, ubiistvo Stolypina. Iz zapisnoi knizhki," *Byloe* 26 (1924): 156.

12 Testimony of Bogrov, 2 September 1911, in Strumillo, "Materialy o Dmitrii Bogrove," 232.

13 Lazarev, "Dmitrii Bogrov i ubiistvo Stolypina," 43, 45.

14 Bogrov, *Dmitrii Bogrov i ubiistvo Stolypina*, 76.

15 Kuliabko to N.P. Zuev, 16 September 1909, GARF, 271/1/5, sheet 20.

16 For a summary of Gerasimov's criticisms of the Kiev Okhranka, see pages 181–2 below.

17 "Pokazaniia podpolkovnika Belevtseva," 13 August 1912, GARF, 271/1/25, sheet 264.

18 Sandomirsky writes about the rumours, but says that he did not believe them.

19 "Kopiia pokazanii D. Bogrova na doprose 2 sentiabria 1911, GARF, 271/1/1, sheet 31.

20 Little is known about this episode and it is not possible to date it precisely. See Liatkovsky, "Nechto o Bogrove," 37.

21 As quoted in Serebrennikov, ed., *Ubiistvo Stolypina*, 99.

22 "Kopiia pokazanii D. Bogrova na doprose 2 sentiabria 1911, GARF, 271/1/1, sheet 32.

23 Quoted in Prilezhaeva-Barskaia, "Dmitrii Bogrov," 84.

24 Solzhenitsyn, *August, 1914: The Red Wheel*, 476.
25 "Protocol no. 10" based on the interrogation of Bogrov, 2 September 1911," GARF, 271/1/2, sheet 296. If he did not wish to do anything that would incite mobs against the Jews, Bogrov exercised poor judgment in selecting Stolypin as his target. Immediately after the assassination, an exodus of the Jews from Kiev began.
26 Bogrov to his father, 18 August 1911, in Serebrennikov, ed., *Ubiistvo Stolypina*, 101.
27 "Otchet A.V. Gerasimova," GARF, 271/1/4, sheet 28.
28 Testimony of M.Ia. Belevtseva, 1 October 1911, GARF, 271/1/2, sheet 1 ob.
29 "Spravka Departamenta politsii o deiatel'nosti kievskogo okhrannogo otdeleniia," 16 December 1910, GARF, 271/1/5, sheets 96–8. Here was a breakdown in Okhranka communication: officials in Petersburg knew more about the Social Democrats in Kiev than the local Okhranka chief. It is unclear where headquarters had acquired the information or why it had not sent the information in its possession earlier to Kiev, but the compartmentalization of the Okhranka's information-gathering system from time to time produced such confusion.
30 "Kopia perepiski A.I. Spiridovicha s dvortsovym komendatom V.A. Dediulinym," GARF, 271/1/2, sheet 61.
31 Letter of Kiev chief of police A.A. Skalon to the prosecutor of the St Petersburg Court of Appeals V.E. Korsak, 14 October 1911, GARF, 271/1/10 sheet 37.
32 Gerasimov, *Na lezvii s terroristami*, 153–4.
33 Kurlov, *Konets russkogo tsarizma*, 140.
34 Spiridovich was appointed head of the Kiev Okhranka in January 1903 and served until 1905, when he was wounded by a terrorist. He describes his service there in Spiridovich, *Zapiski zhandarma*, 114–204.
35 "Pokazaniia polkovnika Kievskogo politsmeistera A.K. Voronchuka," 7 October 1911, GARF, 271/1/7, sheet 65.
36 Testimony by I.D. Grigoriev in "Proizvodstvo senatora M.I. Trusevicha po rassledovaniiu deistvii dolzhnostnyhk lits, prinimavshikh uchastie v osushchestvlenii mer okhrany vo vremia vysochaishego prebyvaniia v Kieve v 1911 g.," GARF, 271/1/15, sheet 64.
37 Testimony of M.N. Verigin, GARF, 271/1/1, sheet 35.
38 Testimony of A.I. Spiridovich, GARF, 271/1/1, sheet 39.
39 Serebrennikov, ed., *Ubiistvo Stolypina*, 143.
40 Testimony of N.N. Kuliabko, GARF, 271/1/16, sheet 45.
41 Bogrov's "Zapiska" is in GARF, 271/l/1, sheet 79.
42 Quoted in Gan, "Ubiistvo Stolypina," 205.
43 Ibid., 205–6.
44 Serebrennikov, *Ubiistvo Stolypina*, 202.

45 Testimony of A.F. Giers, GARF, 271/1/1, sheet 81.

46 Pankratov, "Pervoe sentiabria 1911 goda," 613.

47 Serebrennikov, *Ubiistva Stolypina*, 200.

48 Testimony of N.N. Kuliabko, GARF, 271/1/16, sheet 45.

49 "Vsepoddanneishii doklad senatora M.I. Trusevicha," GARF, 271/1/24, sheet 31.

50 Testimony of Kuliabko, GARF, 271/1/16, sheet 45.

51 Testimony of Spiridovich, GARF, 271/1/25, sheet 442.

52 A.F. Giers, "Smert' Stolypina. Iz vospominanii byvshego kievskogo gubernatora," in Stolypin, *P.A. Stolypin, 1862–1911*, 95.

53 Testimony of P. Samokhvalov, 21 September 1991, GARF, 271/1/1, sheet 91.

54 Testimony of G.G. Chaplinsky, GARF, 271/1/3, sheet 26.

55 Testimony of A.A. Ivanov, GARF, 271/1/1, sheet 69.

56 *Novoe vremia*, 4 September 1911.

57 Ibid.

58 Testimony of I.I. Kostenko, GARF, 271/1/1, sheet 185 ob.

59 Liatkovsky, "Nechto o Bogrov," 44. Liatkovsky was in the same cell as Bogrov at the time.

60 Maisky, "Stolypinshchina i konets Stolypina," 137.

61 *Groza*, 20 September 1911.

62 Zenkovsky, *Pravda o Stolypine*, 237.

63 Trotsky, *Moia zhizn'. Opyt avtobiografii*, 248.

64 "Delo Departamenta politsii o pokushenii na zhizn' stats-sekretaria Stolypina," GARF, 102,00 1911/124, lit. A, sheet 21.

65 *Novoe vremia*, 9 September 1911.

66 "Delo o prestupnom soobshestve...odnim iz uchastnikov kotorogo M. Bogrovym bylo sovershenno ubiistvo ... Stolypina," Tsentral'nyi gosu-darstvennyi voenno-istoricheskii arkhiv, 1769/13/18, sheets 20–1.

67 Testimony of Bogrov before the court, 9 September 1911, GARF, 271/1/1, sheet 51 ob.

68 Ibid., sheet 52.

69 Liatkovsky, "Nechto o Bogrov," 39–40.

70 The Trusevich report can be found as "Vsepoddanneishii doklad sena-tora Trusevicha," GARF, 271/1/24.

71 Tolkmakoff, "Stolypin's Assassin," 314; Izgoev, *P.A. Stolypin*, 104.

72 *Gosudarstvennaia duma. 3 sozyv. Stenograficheskii otchet. Sessia* 5, ch. 1, St Petersburg, 1911, cols, 32–3; Guchkov, "Iz vospominaniia A.I. Guchkov," 185–6.

73 Avrekh, *Stolypin i tret'ia Duma*, 408.

74 Bazilev, "Zagadka 1 sentiabria 1911 g." 127; Zyrianov, "Petr Arkadi-evich Stolypin," 75.

75 P., "Departament politsii v 1892–1908," 23.

76 Shchegolev, ed., *Padenie tsarskogo rezhima*, 3:232.
77 Trusevich, *Vsepoddanneishii doklad senatora Trusevicha*, 36.

CHAPTER TEN

1 Boris I. Nicolaevsky (1889–1966), of Russian background, became a well-known American writer on the Russian revolutionary movement. He compiled an extensive archive, and many of the materials relate to the operations of the Okhranka. The collection is in the Hoover Institution Archives. Nicolaevsky describes the different Russian editions of the Protocols and the differences among them in "O proiskhozhdenii 'Protokolov sionskikh mudretsov'," Hoover Institution Archives, Nicolaevsky Collection, box 20, folio 5.
2 Although Nicolaevsky refers to this text as "lithographed," he must mean "hectographed" – that is, the transfer of text onto a gelatinous material and then onto paper. This was the only way to transfer hand-written text at the turn of the century.
3 Nicolaevsky, "O proiskhozhdenii," 10.
4 From the report of the censor, Sokolov, in "Vypiska iz zhurnala zasedaniia Moskovskogo Tsenzurnogo Komiteta ot 28 sentiabria 1905 goda," Hoover Institution Archives, Nicolaevsky Collection, box 20, folio 7, 10.
5 Appendix to "Vypiska," 1. As part of a larger book, it was reasoned, the Protocols would not be read by a popular audience and thereby influence the lower classes of the population, who were ill-equipped to deal with the controversial writings. This principle had been enshrined in censorship law and practice in Russia for decades.
6 [A.S. Spiridovich], "S.A. Nilus i ego antisemitskaia rabota," typescript in Manuscripts and Archives, Yale University Library, Spiridovich Collection, box 26.
7 Provisions of the tsar's Manifesto of October 1905 would end most state controls on periodicals on 24 November 1905 and on books on 26 April 1906.
8 Nicolaevsky, "O proiskhozhdenii," 13, and Spiridovich, "S.A. Nilus i ego antisemitskaia rabota," 3, quote the same words about how Nilus received the manuscript.
9 Nicolaevsky, "O proiskhozhdenie," 4–5.
10 Ibid., 10–11.
11 Translations of the Protocols had proliferated in the West by 1920, most of them arguing that the Bolsheviks' seizure of power proved the authenticity of the Protocols. That is, the Bolsheviks, many of them Jewish, had used the very means and methods prescribed in the Protocols to foment revolution. On 8 May 1920 a review in *The Times* of a 1920 printing in London of the Protocols agreed that recent history had given the tract

"an uncanny note of prophecy" and argued that "unless one wants to strengthen the hand of the typical anti-Semite ... an impartial investigation of these would-be documents and of their history is most desirable."

12 V. Burtsev, in his account of the Protocols, generally follows Radziwill, and uses the surname Orzhevsky. The reference is to Lieutenant-General P.V. Orzhevsky, the assistant minister of the interior and head of the Corps of Gendarmes, 1882–7.

13 We have found no such memoirs by General Cherevin.

14 "'Protocols Forged in Paris' Says Princess Radziwill," *American Hebrew* 15 (25 February 1921): 422.

15 The writer of the article has Mrs Hurlbut first speaking of the writer of the manuscript as "Orgewsky" and later in the article as "Golowinsky." This seems an error on the part of the writer, but it may also suggest uncertainty on the part of Mrs Hurlbut. "Evidence of Protocol Forgery Substantiated," *American Hebrew* 16 (4 March 1921): 452.

16 A copy of a typed document at the Hoover Institution is an attestation by F.P. Stepanov in April 1921. Stepanov is identified as a former procurator of the Moscow Patriarchal Office who asserts that he received from the owner of a neighbouring estate in Tula province, A.N. Sukhotin, a copy of the Protocols brought from Paris by an unnamed woman. Stepanov said he attempted to print the Protocols and that one of his copies was passed on to S.A. Nilus in 1897 who eventually reprinted it. See Hoover Institution Archives, Nicolaevsky Collection, box 20, folio 2.

17 A. du Chayla, "Vospominaniia o S.A. Nilus i Sionskikh Protokolakh (1909–1920)," *Evreiskaia Tribuna* 72 (14 May 1921): 3–6. An English translation appeared as "Nilus, Perpetrator of the Protocols, Exposed," in *American Hebrew* (17 June 1921). This translation was reprinted at the time of the Berne trial on the Protocols in two parts on 23 and 30 November 1934.

18 Sergei Svatikov, "Podlogi Rachkovskogo (K voprosu o Sionskikh Protokolakh," *Evreiskaia Tribuna* 87 (26 August 1921): 1–2.

19 S.G. Svatikov "Sozdanie 'Sionskikh protokolov' po dannym ofitsial'nogo sledstviia 1917 goda," Hoover Institution Archives, Nicolaevsky Collection, box 20, folio 1.

20 *The Times*, 16, 17, and 18 August 1921. Graves reported that the plagiarism was clumsy. He stated, without factual evidence, that Rachkovsky had a hand in it. Graves says he was tipped off on the origins of the Protocols by a former Russian official, whom he does not name, in Constantinople in 1921.

21 A copy of the typescript is in Manuscripts and Archives, Yale University, Spiridovich Collection, box 26, folder 3. The letter was notarized by a Polish notary in Poznan and dated by him 26 March 1936.

22 Young Nilus announces himself to Rosenberg as "the son of the discoverer of the *Protocols of the Elders of Zion*." The quotation is in Cohn, *Warrant for Genocide* 98.

23 Sergei Sergievich Nilus to the editors of the *American Hebrew* (in French), 5, Manuscripts and Archives, Yale University, Spiridovich Collection, box 26, folder 3.

24 Ibid.

25 Ibid.

26 Ibid., folder 5.

27 Burtsev, *Protokoly zionskikh mudretsov*. The typescript is [V.L. Burtsev], "K voprosu o fal'sifikatsii 'Protokolov,'" Hoover Institution Archives, Nicolaevsky Collection, box 20, folder 2.

28 [V.L. Burtsev], "K voprosu o fal'sifikatsii 'Protokolov'," Hoover Institution Archives, Nicolaevsky Collection, box 20, folio 2.

29 Ibid., folder 7.

30 Burtsev here injects, as testimony of his own, that A.A. Lopukhin, former director of the police, was pressing Stolypin to investigate the printing of anti-Semitic publications in the Department of Police headquarters at this same time.

31 These responses are alluded to in the manuscript, but Burtsev omits them from his printed version.

32 Burtsev, "K voprosu," 13.

33 Manuscripts and Archives, Yale University, Spiridovich Collection, box 25, folder 3.

34 Durnovo to Lamsdorff, 3 January 1905, as quoted in Avrekh, *Masony i revoliutsiia*, 245–6.

35 Elkin, "Attempts to Revive Freemasonry in Russia," 462.

36 Avrekh, *Masony i revoliutsiia*, 246–7.

37 Ibid., 274–5.

38 Rataev, "Zapiska dlia Pamiati," GARF, 11 February 1902, 102/oo/835, sheets 1–7.

39 Rataev, "O legal'noi oppozitsii," GARF, 102/oo, 835, 18 May 1902, sheets 1–8.

40 The regulations governing these new posts, the "Polozhenie o nachal'nykh rozynskikh otdelenii," are in GARF, 102/2-do/825, 1902; and in the Hoover Institution Archives, Okhrana Collection, box 158, folder xiiid (1), no. 8. Lopukhin explained his reasoning in a circular letter to the heads of all provincial Gendarme administrations on 13 August 1902. On 21 October 1902 Lopukhin issued thirty-seven rules to govern the operations of the observation points. See the document cited above in the Hoover Institution Archives.

41 These and other budget estimates for 1903 are found in GARF, 102/2/825, sheets 167–71. Altogether, Lopukhin approved a budget of 299,270 rubles for secret operations within the Empire.

42 N.V. Veselago, an official in the Department of Police from 1911 to 1913, gives the number of seventy-five. See Ellis Tennant [Edward Ellis Smith], "The Department of Police, 1911–13: From the Recollections of Nicholas Vladimirovich Veselago," typescript in the Hoover Institution Archives, Smith Collection, box 1, p. 9.

43 "Vremennoe polozhenie ob okhrannykh otdeleniiakh," 30 June [1903], Hoover Institution Archives, Okhrana Collection, box 158, xiiid (1), folder 9.

44 G.M. Trutkov [untitled memorandum], GARF, 102/2/825, 13 September 1903, sheets 202–9.

45 Komissarov's comments came in testimony before the Extraordinary Investigating Commission of the Provisional Government. See *Padenie tsarskogo rezhima*, ed. Shchegolev, 3:145.

46 Report of the Moscow Okhrannoe Otdelenie, 14 December 1904, GARF, 102/oo/1250, vol. 2, sheet 37.

47 Miliukov, *Political Memoirs*, 13.

48 "O soiuze soiuzov," GARF, 102/oo/999, vols. 1 and 2, 1905, sheets 7 and 76.

49 Rachkovsky to the heads of the Provincial and Oblast Gendarme Administrations and the Security Divisions, 2 July 1905, GARF, 1723/2/23, sheet 20.

50 "Soiuz soiuzov," GARF, 102/oo/999, vol. 2, sheet 14.

51 GARF, 102/oo, 1250, vol. 2, sheets 303–4.

52 "Brozhenie sredi chinov Politsii," GARF, 102,5/oo, 1974, sheets 65–73.

53 "Tsirkuliary o professional'nykh soiuzov," GARF, 102/260/277, 10 May 1907, sheets 2, 9.

54 Avrekh, *Masony i revoliutsiia*, 256–7.

55 Shchegolev, *Okhranniki i avantiuristy*, 53–8.

56 Ibid., 70.

57 Quoted in Russian in Avrekh, *Masony i revoliutsiia*, 283.

58 Kerensky says he knew about a group of Masons called the Barbara Ovchinnikova Organization who were Rosicrucians, a branch of Masonry of a more mystical type. This organization, founded under the auspices of Grand Duke Alexander Mikhailovich, enrolled courtiers and aristocrats (Kerensky, *Russia and History's Turning Point*, 89).

59 Shchegolev, *Okhranniki i avantiuristy*, 75.

60 Schchegolev, ed., *Padenie tsarskogo rezhima*, 3:334.

61 V.A. Brune de St Hippolyte circular of 24 May 1914, Hoover Institution Archives, Okhrana Collection, xiiid (1), folder 11.

62 Participants in Russian political neo-Masonry give various dates for the beginning of the movement. Prince V.A. Obolensky, a leader in the Constitutional Democratic party says he joined in the winter of 1910–11 (Smith, "The Role of Russian Freemasonry in the February Revolution,"

604–8). Kerensky says he joined in 1912, just after his election to the Fourth Duma (Kerensky, *Russia and History's Turning Point*, 88–9). Mel'gunov, a leading liberal politician, dates the beginning of the movement to the fall of 1915 (Mel'gunov, *Na putiakh k dvortsovomu perevorotu*, 185–6).

63 Avrekh, *Masony i revoliutsiia*, 146.

64 Smith, "Political Freemasonry in Russia," 167. Avrekh, quoting Nekrasov, cites the figure (*Masony i revoliutsiia*, 184).

65 Avrekh, *Masony i revoliutsiia*, 199.

66 Schchegolev, ed., *Padenie tsarskogo rezhima*, 2:74–5.

67 The future prime minister of the Provisional Government Prince G. L'vov, and cabinet members A.I. Konovalov and A.I. Guchkov were not Masons, although many have asserted that they were. Mel'gunov did not join because he did not feel that a Masonic-type secret organization could be effective in Russian political conditions. He favoured the regular political parties.

68 Kerensky, *Russia and History's Turning Point*, 88–9. In later years, while working at the Hoover Institution Archives in the Okhrana Collection, Kerensky says he found no evidence that the police knew of this organization or his connections with it.

69 Smith, "The Role of Russian Freemasonry in the February Revolution," 604–8.

70 Avrekh, "Dokumenty Departamenta Politsii kak istochnik po izucheniiu liberal'no-oppozitsionogo dvizheniia v gody pervoi mirovoi voiny," 35.

CHAPTER ELEVEN

1 Altstadt-Mirhadi, "Baku: Transformation of a Muslim Town," 311. One Meshadi Azizbekov, a Social Democratic leader in Baku, is quoted as having said that the riots could not have taken place without the approval of the police.

2 The Pale of Settlement consisted of fifteen provinces of western and southwestern Russia and included such major cities as Vilnius and Kiev.

3 S. Dubnow, "Antievreiskoe dvizhenie v Rossii v 1881–1882 gg.," 93.

4 Novitsky, *Iz vospominanii zhandarma*, 155–61.

5 "Pis'mo i.d. chernigovskogo gubernatora kn. Shakhovskogo ministru vnutrennikh del grafu N.P. Ignat'evu 17 sent. 1881," GARF, 102/3 d-vo/ 52, 1881, sheet 30 ob.

6 Dubnow, "Iz istorii 80-kh gg. (1882)," 12.

7 Sonin, "Vospominaniia o iuzhnorusskikh pogromakh 1881," 209.

8 Novitsky, the head of Kiev Gendarmes, says that he pointed these facts out to a street mob of pogromists in Kiev and that the information had some effect in quieting the crowd. See *Iz vospominanii zhandarma*, 158.

9 Gessen, *Istoriia evreiskogo naroda v Rossii*, 218.

10 Ignatiev's order is in the spirit of the Statute on Measures for the Protection of State Security and Public Tranquillity which he issued several months later on 14 August 1881. See chapter 3 for a discussion of this legislation and its relationship to the issue of pogroms.

11 D.P. "Pogromy," *Evreiskaia entsiklopediia* 12 (1912): 615–16.

12 Rogger, *Jewish Policies and Right-Wing Politics in Imperial Russia*, 28–30.

13 Aronson, "Geographical and socioeconomic factors in the 1881 anti-Jewish pogroms in Russia," 31. Also see his fuller treatment of the same subject, *Troubled Waters: The Origins of the 1881 Anti-Jewish Pogroms in Russia*.

14 Bliokh, *Sravnenie material'nogo byta i nravstvennogo sostoiania naseleniia v cherte osedlosti evreev i vne ee. Tsifrovye dannye i issledovaniia po otnosheniiu k evreiskomu voprosu*, 2:138, 163; 3:142, 216, 266.

15 Brafman, *Evreiskie bratstva mestnye i vsemirnye*, 82–3.

16 Quoted in Gessen, *Istoriia evreiskogo naroda v Rossii*, 2:221.

17 Bikerman, *Cherta evreiskoi osedlosti*, 43.

18 *Evreiskaia entsiklopediia* 13: 221.

19 Troitsky, *Narodnaia volia pered tsarskim sudom*, 164–99. Information for 1892–1902 has been generously provided by Professor N.I. Erofeev.

20 The *Banner* also published the *Protocols of the Elders of Zion*. See chapter 10.

21 Lopukhin, Plehve's director of police, criticizes Count Witte for repeating in his memoirs without proof the allegation that Plehve was responsible for the Kishinev pogroms. See Lopukhin, *Otryvki iz vospominanii (Po povodu 'Vospominanii' gr. S.Iu. Witte)*, 14–15.

22 "Doklad ministra vnutrennikh del V.K. Plehve imperatoru Nikolaiu II, 8 aprelia 1903," GARF, 601/1/1046, sheet 2. Here was another instance where the statute of 14 August 1881 was invoked to deal with pogroms.

23 See Lopukhin's comments on Plehve's anti-Semitism and Plehve's politics in chapter 8.

24 "Doklad ministra vnutrennikh del V.K. Plehve imperatoru Nikolaiu II," GARF, 102,00, 1903/555, vol. 2, sheets 84–5 ob.

25 Urusov, *Zapiski gubernatora*, 62. Edward Judge explains that the case against the Russian government "is based largely on impression, conjecture, and circumstantial evidence, and it fails to take into account the limits of state power and the overriding official interest in maintaining internal order." See his *Easter in Kishinev*, 125–6.

26 Shumatsky, *Revoliutsionnaia provintsiia (zapiska proletariia)*, 28.

27 "Doklad general-maiora barona Medema tovarishchu ministra vnutrennikh del fon-Valiu," 11 September 1903, GARF, 102,00, 1903/555, lit. A, sheet 65.

28 "Shifrovannaia telegramma nachal'nika Mogilevskogo GZHU polkovnika Poliakova tovarishchu vnutrennikh del fon-Valiu 4 sentiabria 1903," GARF, 102,00, 1903/555, lit. A, sheet 40.

29 *Gomel'skii protsess*, 52.

30 Ibid., 999.

31 "Doklad Mogilevskogo gubernatora ministru vnutrennikh del V.K. Pleve," 12 September 1903, GARF, 102,00, 1903/555, lit. A, sheet 86.

32 *Evreiskaia entsiklopedia* 12: 620; V.I. Lenin, "Doklad o revolutsii 1905 g.," PSS 30:324. Lenin took his statistical information from the German edition of L.D. Trotsky, *Rossiia i revoliutsiia*, 1909.

33 Subbotin to the commander, Corps of Gendarmes, 22 October 1905, GARF, 102,00 1905(2)/2000, pt. 16, sheet 34.

34 *Iuzhnaia Rossia*, 26 October 1905.

35 The story is from V.F. von-der-Launits, "Zapiski S.D. Urusova. Tri goda gosudarstvennoi sluzhby," OR RNB, 55/3/2, sheet 115.

36 Sergei Alexandrovich to D.F. Trepov, January 1905, GARF, 595/1/51, sheet 5.

37 Mosolov, *Pri dvore imperatora. Vospominaniia nachal'nika kantseliarii ministerstva imperatorskogo dvora*, 125.

38 *Byloe* 14 (1919): 110.

39 Trepov's long-time opponent and the author of the October Manifesto, Count Witte, was one who accused Trepov of influencing Nicholas II by means of his proximity to the tsar. These charges are exaggerations.

40 V.F. Dzhunkovsky, who was governor of Moscow province at the time, recalled a Trepov who was suffering from the assaults on him: "Late in his life he was extremely nervous, anxious and it seemed to him that he was being pursued and that the very house where he lived was surrounded by revolutionaries; he had begun to suffer from hallucinations." See Dzhunkosvksy, "Vospominaniia," GARF, 826/1/47, sheets 247–8.

41 GARF, 102,00, 1905(2)/2000, pt. 6, sheet 45.

42 *Kazanskii telegraf*, 8 November 1905.

43 *Delo o pogrome v Tomske v 1905 g.*, 6.

44 *Tomskie gubernskie vedomosti. Chast' neofitsial'naia*, November 1905, 23.

45 *Volyn'*, 25 October 1905.

46 *Vostochnoe obozrenie* , 30 October 1905.

47 *Delo o oktiabr'skom pogrome v Simferopole*, 18.

48 Rafal'ski to Trepov, 21 October 1905, GARF, 102,00, 1905(2), 2000, pt. 2, sheet 33 ob.

49 *Kievskii i odesskii pogromy v otchetakh senatorov Turau i Kuzmin-skogo*, 68.

50 Weinberg, "Workers, Pogroms and the 1905 Revolution in Odessa," 72.

51 "Reviziia g. Odessy senatorom A.M. Kuzminskim," RGIA, 1536/1/2, sheet 64 ob.
52 "Reviziia...sen. Kuzminskim," sheet 39.
53 *Kievskii i odesskii pogromy v otchetakh senatorov Turau i Kuzminskogo*, 160 and *passim*.
54 *Kurskaia zhizn'*, 13 June 1906.
55 GARF, 102,00, 1905(2), 2000, pt. 1, sheet 11.

CHAPTER TWELVE

1 Quoted in Samuel, *Blood Accusation*, 180–1.
2 *Russkoe Slovo* 250 (13 October 1913).
3 Tager, *Tsarskaia Rossiia i delo Beilisa*. In his introduction to the 1934 edition, A. V. Lunacharsky, the former Soviet minister of public enlightenment, without citing evidence, claimed that the Beilis case was a deliberate ploy by the imperial government in the class struggle, used by rulers desperate to keep the working classes under control by directing their discontent against Jews. Tager largely blames Shcheglovitov for the Beilis trial but makes key mistakes in his narrative and downplays evidence that points away from his thesis.
4 Tager, *The Decay of Czarism*, xiv.
5 Samuel, *Blood Accusation*, 6–7.
6 Rogger, *Jewish Policies and Right Wing Politics in Imperial Russia*, 51–5.
7 For the government crackdown following the Kishinev pogrom, see chapter 11.
8 See George Kennan, "The 'Ritual Murder' Case in Kiev," *The Outlook* (8 November 1913): 531.
9 Coded telegram, A.F. Giers to P.G. Kurlov, 13 April 1911, GARF, 102, 4 deloproizvodstvo, 1911/148, sheet 12.
10 Coded telegram, Kurlov to Giers, 13 April 1911, GARF, 102, 4 deloproizvodstvo, 1911/148, sheet 14.
11 Tager, *The Decay of Czarism*, 34. Tager cites no document. He writes: "Finally, also on the same day [April 18], Stsheglovitoff himself prepared a telegram to the chief district attorney Chaplinsky asking him to undertake the direction of the investigation personally." Tager claims that the minister of justice learned on 18 April of the upcoming rightist interpellation and that he at once asked Stolypin to "recommend the Yustchinsky case to the special attention of the Minister of the Interior." (Stolypin was, of course, the minister of the interior.) The evidence cited in the text, however, shows that Stolypin was already taking measures in the Beilis case at least five days earlier. The case came to his attention several days before 18 April and he brought the matter before the justice minister, who put Chaplinsky in charge.

12 The Russian phrase, "usilennaia okhrana" is more usually, and less precisely, translated as "Reinforced Protection" in English-language discussions of the highly important statute of 14 August 1881. See the discussion of this statute in chapter 4.

13 "Testimony of Liadov to the Extraordinary Investigating Commission of the Provisional Government (hereafter chSK)," GARF, 1457/1/494, sheet 224. Liadov also says that he conveyed during his Kiev visit that he and the justice minister suspected that Jews had killed Iushchinsky. Liadov was an experienced official. He had served in the Ministry of Justice since 1888 and since 1910 had been vice-director of the ministry and assistant minister.

14 Shchegolev, ed., *Padenie tsarskogo rezhima*, 7:265.

15 Ibid., 7:277.

16 *Gosudarstvennaia duma, 3–1 sozyv. Stenograficheskie otchety*, Session 4, vol. 3, St Petersburg, 1911, col. 3116.

17 Shchegolev, ed., *Padenie tsarskogo rezhima*, 3:353.

18 "Testimony of V.S. Golubev to V.I. Fenenko," 5 May 1911, Gosudarstvennyi Arkhiv Kievskoi Oblasti (hereafter GAKO), 864/6/65, sheet 129 ob.

19 Chaplinsky to Shcheglovitov, 11 May 1911, GARF, 124/65/222, sheet 66.

20 Deposition of K.S. Shakhovsky to V.I. Fenenko, 20 July 1911, GAKO, 864/6/65, sheet 129 ob.

21 "Raport G.G. Chaplinskogo ministru iustitsii I.G. Shcheglovitovu, 21 July 1911, GARF, 124/65/222, sheet 235. Chaplinsky must have been filing reports on a regular basis to the minister of justice with respect to the Iushchinsky case and, almost certainly, these reports were passed on to the minister of the interior.

22 Tager, *Tsarskaia Rossiia i delo Beilisa*, 1934 ed., fn 105. Tager relegated Chaplinsky's important statement, which provides a key to the entire Beilis affair, to a footnote. He may have buried this testimony because it undercuts his general thesis assigning blame to Shcheglovitov and Chaplinsky. The English edition was not footnoted.

23 This testimony was given by Fenenko in Kiev in 1917 to the chSK, but was not published. It is in GARF, 1467/1/494 (3), sheet 229 ob.

24 Tager, *The Decay of Czarism*, 75. Tager claims to have read the actual telegrams in an official archive, but this information is not included in the English edition. See Tager, *Tsarskaia Rossia i delo Beilisa*, 106.

25 Beiliss, *The History of My Suffering*, 47.

26 Koshko, "O dele Beilisa," 169.

27 There was no turning back for Chaplinsky after the fall of 1911. His mindset became fixed on the purpose that he eventually revealed to the journalist Trifonov: that it was all the same to him whether Beilis was convicted or acquitted; most important to him was the "recognition by

the court of the central fact of the killing of Iushchinsky for ritualistic purposes." See GARF, 1467/1/474 (3), sheet 219; 1467/1/494 (3), sheet 157.

28 Deposition of Krasovsky to Fenenko, 29 July 1911, GAKO, 864665, sheet 156.

29 The doctor in attendance, L.S. Tyrnavsky, testified that the boy had grown progressively weaker, "and I saw that there was almost no hope of saving him," GAKO, 864/6/65, sheet 273.

30 GARF, 1467/1/494 (3), sheet 157. E.F. Mishchuk, the head of the Kiev criminal police, believed that Beilis was not guilty. On 25 August, he reported that the victim's personal belongings and the tools of the crime had been found and concluded that the items pointed in the direction of the gang of thieves.

But closer examination of the items showed the evidence was fake. Chaplinsky wrote to Shcheglovitov that "Mishchuk either was badly cheated by somebody or failed to discover the cheating because of his low intelligence or, which is more likely, had set it all up hoping to mislead the judicial authorities and set the investigation along a false track." Chaplinsky to Shcheglovitov, 27 August 1911, GARF, 124/65/222, sheet 318. Mishchuk was tried and convicted of forgery, although he claimed he had been trapped into participating in the crime by a subordinate who was helping his rival N.A. Krasovsky. With removal of Mishchuk, Krasovsky assumed control over the investigation.

After changing his mind several times, Krasovsky concluded that the murderer was among the gang of thieves. To Chaplinsky, the detective had responded to outside pressures: he wrote Beletsky that "Krasovsky has changed his course of action under the influence of a bribe from the Jewish colony." (See testimony of Beletsky before the CHSK, GARF, 1467/1/494, sheet 128.) Krasovsky's superiors dismissed him in September 1911.

31 For a full discussion of Bogrov and his motives, see chapter 9.

32 Kuliabko to director, Department of Police, 6 September 1911. A photostat and translation appears in Tager, *The Decay of Czarism*, 253.

33 Deposition of Cheberiak to N.A. Mashkevich, 11 July 1912, GAKO, 864/10/6, sheet 12 ob.

34 Report of the director of the Special Section to S.P. Beletsky, 5 August 1912, GARF, 102,00/1911/157, vol. 1, sheet 41. Karaev was sent for a period of punitive exile by Beletsky and could not appear as a witness for Beilis. His deposition was read at the trial. It seems unconvincing to argue, therefore, as has been done, that the exile was another device used by Beletsky to assist the prosecution.

35 Shredel' to N.P. Kharlamov, 28 January 1912, A.S. Tager, ed., "Tsarskoe pravitel'stvo i protsess Beilisa," *Krasnyi Arkhiv* 54–55 (1932): 156–66.

Kharlamov was another former prosecutor who had moved into police work.

36 Shredel' to Kharlamov, 14 February 1912, ibid., 166–7.

37 Ibid., 166–8.

38 Shredel' to Kharlamov, 14 March 1911, ibid., 166.

39 Giers to Assistant Minister of the Interior Kharuzin, 19 April 1912, ibid., 170–1.

40 Margolin, *The Jews of Eastern Europe*, 200.

41 Ivanov to Beletsky, 5 August 1912, GARF, 102,00/1911/57, vol. 1, sheet 41.

42 Chaplinsky to Liadov, 28 May 1912, "Tsarskoe pravitel'stvo i protsess Beilisa," 173.

43 Ibid., 172.

44 Koshko, "O dele Beilisa," 173.

45 Tager, *Tsarskaia Rossiia i delo Beilisa*, 11.

46 Makarov to Shcheglovitov, 3 May 1912, "Tsarskoe pravitel'stvo i protsess Beilisa," 171.

47 Shcheglovitov to Chief Justice, Kiev Circuit Court, GARF, 124/65/223, sheet 146.

48 Koshko, "O dele Beilisa," 171.

49 *Vestnik soiuza russkogo naroda*, 30 January 1914.

50 Shchegolev, ed., *Padenie tsarskogo rezhima*, 3:355. This matter had been much discussed, prompted by a petition from 166 members of the Duma early in 1911, before Stolypin's assassination, calling on the government to abolish the Pale of Settlement and permit Jews free movement throughout the Empire. As for Maklakov, he believed, said Beletsky, that Jewish capitalists had used their money to cause the revolution of 1905.

51 Koshko, "O dele Beilisa," 167–77. Koshko says that Beletsky told him he did not know the reason for the detective's summons to the capital, but this is unlikely.

52 *Delo Beilisa. Stenograficheskie otchety* 1: 35.

53 Testimony of G.G. Chaplinsky to the ChSK, GARF, 1467/1/494, sheet 249a.

54 Testimony of V.G. Tal'berg to the ChSK, GARF, 1467/1/494, sheet 207a.

55 Trifonov, in testimony to the ChSK, GARF, 1467/1/494 (3), sheet 218 ob. Trifonov's recollections were given in 1917 to the Extraordinary Investigating Commission of the Provisional Government and may well have been influenced by the passage of time and the changed political circumstances of Russia.

56 GARF, 1467/1/494 (3), sheet 218 ob.

57 Sukovkin to N.A. Maklakov, 9 October 1913, GARF, 102,00/1913/157, vol. 2, sheet 186. Shul'gin would receive a sentence of three months under arrest, but Nicholas II pardoned him.

58 Kashkarov (vice-governor) to Department of Police, 2 September 1913, "Tsarskoe pravitel'stvo i protsess Beilisa," 173–5.

59 N. Sukovkin to Maklakov, 9 October 1913, ibid., 176–7.

60 Coded telegram from Beletsky to Shredel', 17 September 1913, ibid., 178.

61 Sukovkin to Maklakov, 9 October 1913, ibid., 176–7.

62 Sukovkin to Maklakov, 9 October 1913, GARF, 102,00/1913/157, vol. 2, sheet 186.

63 Telegraph circular, minister of the interior, 10 October 1913, GARF, 102,00/1913/157, vol. 2, sheet 167.

64 Shredel' to Sukovkin, 10 October 1913, GARF, 102,00/1913/157, vol. 3, sheet 86 ob.

65 Korolenko, "Delo Beilisa," 9:651.

66 Liubimov to Beletsky, 25 September 1913, in A.S. Tager, ed., "Protsess Beilisa v otsenke Departamenta politsii," *Krasnyi arkhiv* 1, no. 44 (1931): 93.

67 Black Hundred activists considered Shmakov an expert on the Jewish question. He had authored a six-hundred-page book titled *Jewish Speeches*, and had published what he viewed as a learned paper, "International Secret Government," which he devoted to the subject of the world-wide Jewish-Masonic conspiracy. He had also taken part as defence counsel in a number of trials of alleged pogromists. Both were ardent anti-Semites.

68 Liubimov to Beletsky, 28 September 1913, in Tager, ed., "Protsess Beilisa v otsenke departamenta politsii," 96–7.

69 From the deposition Grigorovich-Barsky (a defence attorney) to the chSK, GARF, 1467/1/494, sheet 162 ob.

70 Zamyslovsky was also paid from secret funds for his participation in the trial. In addition, the Department of Police paid for the book search in Europe and the searching of the country for expert witnesses. Evidence of the payments to individuals can be found in notes from Zamyslovsky and Kosorotov, in "Tsarskoe pravitel'stvo i protsess Beilisa," 179, 183.

71 *Taina krovi. Ekspertiza I.E. Pranaitisa.*

72 *Delo Beilisa. Stenograficheskie otchety*, vol. 3, 63.

73 D'iachenko to Beletsky, 19 October 1913, in Tager, ed., "Protsess Beilisa v otsenke Departamenta politsii," 170–1.

74 D'iachenko to Beletsky, 24 October 1913, ibid., 114.

75 The summation is by Kucherov in *Courts, Lawyers, and Trials under the Last Three Tsars*, 264.

76 Beiliss, *The History of My Suffering*, 194–5.

77 Shcheglovitov to Dzhunkovsky, 17 December 1913, GARF, 102,00, 1911/157, vol. 5, sheet 234.

CHAPTER THIRTEEN

1 M.S. Trusevich, the director of the Department of Police, issued the first circular and N.P. Zuev, his successor, the second. The circulars also placed political investigation exclusively in the hands of Gendarmes. A copy of Iodlovsky's report is in GARF, 5802/2/239. The discussion of the circulars is on sheets 1–4.

2 Vassilyev, *The Ochrana*, 256.

3 Cited in Geifman, *Thou Shalt Kill: Revolutionary Terrorism in Russia*, 21.

4 Quoted by Iodlovsky in GARF, 5802/2/239, sheet 21.

5 Circulars of 2 and 20 March 1908, as cited by Iodlovsky, GARF, 5802/2/239, sheet 10.

6 Vissarionov circular letter of 10 March 1911 to the heads, Regional Security Divisions, Hoover Institution Archives, Okhrana Collection, xiiid (1), folder 10.

7 Zuev circulars of 15 May 1910; 25 June 1910, 30 October 1910, and 18 and 20 December 1910, as cited by Iodlovsky, GARF, 5802/2/239, sheets 12 and 13.

8 Zuev to the Provincial and Regional Gendarme Administrations and the Security Divisions, 24 June 1911, Hoover Institution Archives, Okhrana Collection, xiii d (1) folder 10.

9 Vissarionov to the heads, Regional Okhranka Divisions, 10 March 1911, Hoover Institution Archives, Okhrana Collection, xiiid (1), folder 10.

10 The Beletsky circulars were those of 19 May, 16 June, 12 and 21 September, and 3 October, all 1912, as quoted in Iodlovsky, GARF, 5802/2/239, sheet 14.

11 Ibid., sheet 16.

12 Klimovich circular, 31 July 1916, Hoover Institution Archives, Okhrana Collection, xiiid (1), folder 12.

13 Vassilyev circular of 12 October 1916, as quoted by Iodlovsky, GARF, 5802/2/239, sheet 18.

14 Beletsky in testimony to the Supreme Investigating Commission, Shchegolev, ed., *Padenie tsarskogo rezhima*, 3:377.

15 By an irony of fate, numerous "wooden engravings" distributed later by the security organs of the USSR were introduced to Russia in the form of several listening devices that Beletsky acquired abroad and installed on the premises of the Bolshevik faction of the Duma.

16 Zavarzin, "Iz vospominanii," *Delo provakatora Malinovskogo*, 254–5.

17 Elwood, *Roman Malinovsky: A Life Without a Cause*, 23.

18 Shchegolev, ed., *Padenie tsarskogo rezhima*, 3:381–2.

19 Vassilyev, *The Ochrana*, 256–7.

20 Shchegolev, ed., *Padenie tsarskogo rezhima*, 3:280.

21 Ibid., 3:282.

22 Ibid., 5:84.

23 Ibid., 5:219.

24 Dzhunkovsky, "Vospominaniia za 1913," sheets 13, 91–2.

25 Ibid., sheets 93–6.

26 Dzhunkovsky, "Vospominaniia za 1914," GARF, 826/1/54, sheets 89–91.

27 Dzhunkovsky set a demanding physical pace. On one tour of inspection around Moscow province as governor he was delayed along the road, had his last official meeting of the day at 3 a.m., and arrived at his destination an hour later (see Robbins, *The Tsar's Viceroys*, 55). Dzhunkovsky as assistant minister exercised this same determination to see for himself his own subordinates in action and he made many trips for this purpose.

28 Dzhunkovsky explained how he had arranged matters for Krasil'nikov in a letter of 2 October 1913 to S.D. Sazonov, the Russian minister of foreign affairs, in GARF, 1732/2/34, sheets 296–97.

29 A.V. Brune de St. Hippolite, secret circular, 2 September 1914, GARF, DO,oo/27, 1915, sheets 87–8. Brune was of French origin and a former procurator in the judicial system.

30 Brune, 2 September 1914, ibid., sheet 92.

31 There appear to be two circulars making the same point from Brune. The first, 6 September 1914, is cited in Kerensky, *The Crucifixion of Liberty*, 247. The second, 16 September 1914, is in Iodlovsky, GARF, 5802/2/239. The similarity of the wording and similarity of the dates could mean that they were one and the same.

32 Dzhunkovsky, "Vospominaniia za 1912," sheet 313.

33 Rodzianko testified before the Extraordinary Investigating Commission of the Provisional Government. See Shchegolev, ed., *Padenie tsarskogo rezhima*, 7:167.

34 Elwood offers this and other speculations as other possible reasons for Dzhunkovsky's ending the operation. See *Roman Malinovsky*, 42–3. Dzhunkovsky might also have wished to discredit his predecessor, Beletsky. However, Dzhunkovsky had already taken a year to prepare his case against Beletsky and had fired him in January, several months before Malinovsky's resignation. As for the theory that Dzhunkovsky intended to end the Okhranka policy of splitting Mensheviks and Bolsheviks and therefore had to get rid of its principal agent, Beletsky, the policy actually continued after Malinovsky's departure.

35 Dzhunkovsky, "Vospominaniia za 1912," sheet 316.

36 Shchegolev, ed., *Padenie tsarskogo rezhima*, 5:84.

37 Dzhunkovsky, "Vospominaniia za 1913," sheets 181–2, 184.

38 These figures were compiled directly from archival sources by A.A. Miroliubov and were published in "Dokumenty po istorii Departamenta politsii perioda pervoi mirovoi voiny," 80–4. Miroliubov shows the staff of the Department of Police rising from 387 in 1914 to 405 in 1915.

39 Svatikov, *Russkii politicheskii sysk za granitsei*, 7.

CHAPTER FOURTEEN

1 That the tsarina had a special predilection for persons who claimed special powers was shown earlier in chapter 5 in the episode of the fradulent French physician, Philippe. In that instance, too, a leading police official, Rachkovsky, engaged in an intrigue in order to force Philippe from the court.

2 In order to avoid the unpleasant associations with the name, the family by special ukaz changed its name to Novykh in later years.

3 "Poslednii vremenshchik poslednogo tsaria," 120. This article reviews the documents collected about Rasputin that were prepared in 1917 by B.N. Smitt, assistant chairman of the Extraordinary Investigative Commission of the Provisional Government.

4 The *khlysty* believed that only castration could solve the problem of sexual passions.

5 *Dnevnik imperatora Nikolaia II*, 229.

6 It could well have been at some other time that Rasputin first seemed to demonstrate his ability to moderate episodes of hemophilia. There is conflicting evidence on this point, summarized by Fuhrmann in *Rasputin: A Life*, 25–6.

7 Dzhanumova, *Moi vstrechi s Rasputinym*, 29.

8 "Poslednii vremenshchik poslednogo tsaria," 99.

9 Gerasimov, *Na lezvii s terroristami*, 161–2.

10 Ibid., 162.

11 Kurlov, *Konets russkogo tsarizma*, 179.

12 Stolypin's daughter so recounted in her memoirs about her father. See Bok, *P.A. Stolypin. Vospominaniia o moem otse*, 331. There is an English translation: *Reminiscences of My Father, Peter A. Stolypin*, 269.

13 A.V. Krivoshein recounted this to A.I. Guchkov. "Iz vospominanii Guchkova," 185.

14 "Iz vospominanii A.N. Khvostova," 162. See also Khvostov's testimony to the CHSK in March 1917. He said he simply could not take Rasputin seriously as an emissary from the tsar, with whom he felt he had good relations. He said he saw Rasputin as "one of the spiritual diversions" at Tsarskoe Selo. See Shchegolev, ed. *Padenie tsarskogo rezhima*, 1:3.

15 Stolypin's actions in the March 1911 political struggle over the "Western Zemstvo Bill" in the State Council alienated the tsar from his prime

minister. Stolypin had advised the tsar to suspend the legislative bodies and to promulgate the controversial bill by means of his emergency powers. Even legislators who tended to support the government could not accept a measure which so blatantly violated the constitutional order.

16 Tolkmakoff, "Stolypin's Assassin," 314.

17 Witte, *The Memoirs of Count Witte*, 738–9.

18 Iliodor, *Sviatoi chert*, 135. Hermogen sharply regretted that he had helped Rasputin become acquainted with the tsarist family. Mitia Kozelsky saw him as a rival who had weakened his position at court.

19 Kokovtsov, *Iz moego proshlago: vospominaniia 1903–1919 gg.*, 2:26–8.

20 This assessment came from the head of the Moscow Okhranka on 20 January 1912. See GARF, 102, 4 del., 1912/119, vol. 2, pt. 1, sheet 25.

21 Gerasimov, *Na lezvii s terroristami*, 182.

22 Iliodor, *Sviatoi chert*, 31.

23 Makarov to V.N. Kokovtsov, in Kokovtsov, *Iz moego proshlogo: vospominaniia*, 2:44. The genuineness of the letters was also confirmed by A.A. Vyrubova.

24 Dzhunkovsky, "Vospominaniia za 1914," sheets 130–1.

25 Shchegolev, ed., *Padenie tsarskogo rezhima*, 5:102.

26 "Poslednii vremenshchik poslednego tsaria," 125.

27 The records of the surveillance over Rasputin have been preserved in GARF. A compendium was prepared for publication by M.S. Komissarov, the chief of the Moscow Okhranka, and later published in *Red Archive (Krasnyi Arkhiv)* 5 (1924): 270–87. Minister of the Interior A.N. Khvostov used these materials for his reports to the tsar. Authors of apologetic accounts of Rasputin's career have claimed that the compendia showed signs of fabrication.

28 Dzhunkovsky, "Vospominaniia za 1914," sheet 135.

29 Dzhunkovsky's description of the events at the Yar restaurant, based on police reports, is in ibid., sheets 124–36.

30 The origins of the Progressive Bloc began in a meeting of the Constitutional Democratic party on 6 June 1915 against a background of a series of military disasters for Russia. The party demanded a government of "public confidence" – that is, a government to be formed with the agreement of the Duma. Nicholas also replaced in the summer of 1915 two other unpopular ministers, V.K. Sabler, the procurator of the Holy Synod, and I.G. Shcheglovitov, the minister of justice, and he dismissed the minister of war, General V.A. Sukhomlinov.

31 Beletsky says Rasputin told him he had never seen the tsar so angry as following the Dzhunkovsky report. Beletsky summarizes what Rasputin did then. "He, in his own justification, said that he, like other people, was a sinner, not a saint." Beletsky says that henceforth, "Rasputin

could not to the end of his life hear or speak calmly about General Dzhunkovsky." Rasputin told Beletsky, confirming Dzhunkovsky's report, that the tsar refused to see him for a long time. See Beletsky, "Vospominaniia," *Arkhiv russkoi revoliutsii,* 12:9.

32 Zavarzin, *Zhandarmy i revoliutsionery,* 231.

33 Beletsky so testified to the CHSK in 1917. See Shchegolev, ed., *Padenie tsarskogo rezhima,* 4:152.

34 For a discussion of Beletsky as head of the Department of Police, see chapter 13.

35 Spiridovich, *Velikaia voina i fevral'skaia revoliutsiia, 1914–1917 gg.,* 1:221.

36 Ibid., 1:225.

37 Beletsky, "Vospominaniia," *Arkhiv russkoi revoliutsii,* 12:10.

38 Kryzhanovsky, *Vospominaniia,* 148.

39 Gessen, "Beseda s A.N. Khvostovym v fevrale 1916 g.," *Arkhiv russkoi revoliutsii,* 12:81.

40 Lopukhin, "Liudi i politiki," 115.

41 "Rasputin v osveshchenii 'okranki'," 278.

42 Ibid., 279.

43 The affair connected with the Yar supper and the firing of Dzhunkovsky is to be found in his memoirs for 1914, GARF, sheets 124–36. Although the matter reached a climax with Dzhunkovsky's dismissal in 1915, it had commenced with the assassination attempt by Guseva in the spring of the previous year.

44 Dzhunkovsky, "Vospominaniia za 1915," GARF, 826/1/55, sheet 301, 322. He wrote, "I am convinced, that the Sovereign, in dismissing me, did not for a minute doubt my correctness ... but against the Empress of course I could not stand my ground."

45 Departing two months after Shcherbatov was his director of the Department of Police, R.G. Mollov, a former prosecutor from Odessa, who was of Bulgarian origin. The entrance of Bulgaria into the First World War on the side of the Central Powers brought an end to Mollov's tenure.

46 Beletsky's deposition to the Extraordinary Investigating Commission, 24 June 1917, in Shchegolev, ed., *Padenie tsarskogo rezhima,* 4:162.

47 Kafafov's testimony in April 1917 to the Extraordinary Investigating Commission, ibid., 2:135–40.

48 See Beletsky's testimony in ibid., 4:240–2. Beletsky gave very detailed testimony, and no other highly placed official could match him in his appearances before the Extradordinary Investigative Commission. There are different views about Beletsky's performance, some coming from the investigators themselves. Some consider that by his frankness Beletsky

was hoping to save himself, others that he wished to make a name for himself through the boulevard press by sensational exposures.

49 Beletsky's deposition in 1917 to the Extraordinary Investigating Commission, ibid., *Padenie tsarskogo rezhima*, 4:360.

50 This information comes from Beletsky's written testimony to the Supreme Investigating Commission on 24 June 1917, ibid., 4:242.

51 "Iz vospominanii A.N. Khvostova," *Golos minuvshego*, 167.

52 Khvostov cited his own words to Komissarov to the CHSK on 18 March 1917. They are in Shchegolev, ed., *Padenie tsarskogo rezhima*, 1:43. Beletsky was a witness to Khvostov's conclusion, as he explains in his own testimony before the commission, 24 June 1917. See ibid., 4:367.

53 See Beletsky's written deposition to the commission given on 24 June 1917, ibid., 4:364. See also Beletsky's memoirs published in *Arkhiv russkoi revoliutsii*, 12:8.

54 Beletsky's 1917 testimony in Shchegolev, ed., *Padenie tsarskogo rezhima*, 3:391. Beletsky explained that Maklakov, the minister of the interior, would not approve the venture.

55 Beletsky's testimony in 1917, in ibid., 4:404–07.

56 Beletsky in ibid., 4:362–3; Beletsky, "Vospominaniia," 64. He dispatched Komissarov to the provinces, who returned with several vials of "poison" – actually harmless powder obtained at a drug store owned by his wife. Komissarov then lectured Khvostov in detail about the effects of the toxins, repeating to him information that he had lifted a half hour earlier from a textbook on pharmacology. To lend greater verisimilitude to the project, Komissarov told Khvostov that he had tried out the poison on his cat. Khvostov called one of the detectives (earlier briefed by Komissarov) to ask him whether the cat had suffered for a long period.

57 Beletsky's 1917 testimony, in ibid., 4:387.

58 An investigator for the Extraordinary Investigating Commission, V.M. Rudnev, noted that the Iliodor telegram contained incorrect information. See Rudnev, "Pravda o tsarskoi sem'e," 46.

59 Some contemporaries (for example, Maurice Paleologue and A.I. Spiridovich) concluded that Beletsky had ordered the Gendarmes to the border station to provoke an incident so that Rzhevsky's name would wind up in the police protocol, revealing his incognito.

60 Manasevich-Manuilov appears earlier in this account of the Okhranka, in particular in chapter 5 as a foreign agent. In 1915 he was positioning himself to take advantage of changes in the government and, as a loyal Rasputinite, emerged as a secretary to Sturmer when he became prime minister.

61 As quoted in Gessen, "Beseda s A.N. Khvostovym v fevrale 1916," 78.

62 Khvostov's 1917 testimony is in Shchegolev, ed., *Padenie tsarskogo rezhima*, 40–2.

63 Testimony by F.F. Manasevich-Manuilov on 8 April 1917 before the Extraordinary Investigative Commission, in ibid., 2:37.

64 Simanovich, *Rasputin i evrei*, 87. This book is a partly fictionalized version of the oral memoirs of Simanovich, who was involved in the affair of Rzhevsky. Beletsky also came to the conclusion that Khvostov was attempting to shift responsibility for the Rzhevsky affair on to him and Komissarov. See Beletsky, "Vospominaniia," 73.

65 *Birzhevye vedomosti*, "Utrennii vypusk," 7 March 1916.

66 Beletsky's 1917 testimony in Shchegolev, ed., *Padenie tsarskogo rezhima*, 4:418.

67 Sturmer became chairman of the Council of Ministers on 20 January 1916 and held the position until 10 November. From 3 March to 7 July, he was simultaneously minister of the interior and chief of the Corps of Gendarmes.

68 See chapter 5 for an earlier discussion of Manasevich-Manuilov.

69 Klimovich's testimony in March 1917 to the Extraordinary Investigating Commission, in Shchegolev, ed., *Padenie tsarskogo rezhima*, 1:60–1.

70 Klimovich so stated in his deposition to the commission in March 1917, in ibid., 1:89.

71 As quoted in Rodzianko, *Krushenie imperii*, 173.

72 From Manuilov's testimony before the commission, April 1917, in Shchegolev, ed., *Padenie tsarskogo rezhima*, 2:65.

73 Robert Massie explains that Badmaev had been treating Protopopov for an advanced case of syphilis. Partly because of the persuasiveness of Badmaev, Tibetan medicine had achieved wide acceptability in aristocratic circles in the capital and many high government officials had enormous confidence in Badmaev. See Massie, *Nicholas and Alexandra*.

74 Protopopov so testified to the commission in March 1917. He also stated that he was convinced that the tsar alone was responsible for his appointment, that he saw Rasputin a number of times at Badmaev's, but that he went to Badmaev only to be cured. See Shchegolev, ed., *Padenie tsarskogo rezhima*, 1:114–16.

75 Protopopov's written deposition to the commission, 4 June 1917, in ibid., 4:14.

76 Paleologue, *Rasputin: Vospominaniia*, 92.

77 The ukaz indicting Kurlov was never presented for official confirmation before the Senate, evidently as a result of intervention by Protopopov. Kurlov retained his office as assistant minister of the interior for only about four months until January 1917.

78 Kurlov, *Konets russkogo tsarizma*, 169.

79 Spiridovich, *Velikaia voina i Fevral'skoi revoliutsii*, 2:126.

80 *Perepiska Nikolaia i Aleksandry Romanovykh, 1916–1917*, 5:204.
81 Quoted by Avrekh, *Tsarizm nakanune sverzhenia*, 64–5.
82 S.V. Zavadsky, "Na velikom izlome," *Arkhiv russkoi revoliutsii*, 8:37.
83 Iusupov, *Konets Rasputina: Vospominaniia*, 117.

CHAPTER FIFTEEN

1 "V kontse 1916 g.," 153. The report, dated 5 December 1916 from an Okhranka agent assigned to the State Duma, stated that Princess S.N. Vasil'chikova had broached the idea to the tsarina and, as a result, had been ordered from the capital. The agent wrote that "almost with one voice the deputies of all parties" were saying, "the approaching catastrophe is inevitable if this irresponsible interference in the foreign and internal affairs of the country continues."

2 Such an assessment came in an Okhranka review of the political situation in Russia six months before the February revolution. See "Politicheskoe polozhenie Rossii nakanune fevral'skoi revoliutsii v zhandarmskom osveshchenii," 3–35. All political parties were in agreement, it was reported, that the country was hurtling toward revolution.

3 The Okhranka's belief after 1905 that the Westernized liberals were the main enemy of the tsarist regime was strengthened during the years of the First World War because of liberal political activities. Avrekh argues that the Okhranka poorly understood Russian liberalism because it could not penetrate liberal leadership circles and relied for information about the liberals on its Moscow agent I.I. Drilikh ("Blondinka") who worked as a political reporter for the daily newspaper, *Russian Word*. Drilikh was skilled at telling the Okhranka what it wanted to hear. See Avrekh, "Dokumenty Departamenta politsii kak istochnik po izucheniiu liberal'no-oppozitsionnogo dvizheniia v gody pervoi mirovoi voiny," 32–49.

4 Additional information on the setting up of the commission can be found in Avrekh, "Chrezvychainaia sledstvennaia komissiia vremennogo pravitel'stva: zamysel i ispolnenie," 72–101.

5 Beletsky argued that any government faced with secret revolutionary organizations would have to penetrate them by means of secret agents in order to learn their intentions.

6 In tandem with the work of the commission, investigators poured through the remaining archives of the Department of Police. The commission despatched experts abroad to investigate the archives of the Foreign Agency, especially in Paris. These archives were later to wind up at the Hoover Institution.

Bibliography

A.P. "Departament politsii v 1892–1908 gg. (Iz vospominanii chinovnika)." *Byloe* 5–6(27–8), (1917): [17]-24.

Agafonov, V.K. *Zagranichnaia okhranka: sostavleno po sekretnym dokumentam zagranichnoi agentury i Departamenta politsii* Petrograd, 1918.

Alekseev, I.V. *Provokator Anna Serebriakova.* Moscow, 1932.

Alstadt-Mirhadi, Audrey. "Baku: The Transformation of a Muslim Town," in Michael Hamm, ed., *The City in Late Imperial Russia*, Bloomington, 1986: 283–318.

Al'tman, I.S. "Sledstvennaia dokumentatsiia kak istochnik po istorii revoliutsionnogo dvizheniia v Rosss v kontse XIX veka." Dissertation for the *kandidat* degree, Leningrad, 1983.

Antonovich, M.A. "Arest N. G. Chernyshevskogo," *N.G. Chernyshevsky v vospominaniiakh sovremennikov*, ed. N.K. Gei, Moscow, 1982: 274–9.

Aronson, I.M. "Geographical and socioeconomic factors in the 1881 anti-Jewish pogroms in Russia," *The Russian Review* 39(1) (1980): 18–31.

– *Troubled Waters: The Origins of the 1881 Anti-Jewish Pogroms in Russia*, Pittsburgh, 1990.

Ascher, Abraham. *The Revolution of 1905: Russia in Disarray*, 2 vols., Stanford, 1988.

Avrekh, A.Ia. "Chrezvychainaia sledstvennaia komissiia vremennogo pravitel'stva: zamysel i ispolnenie," *Istoricheskie zapiski* 118, (1990): 72–101.

– "Dokumenty Departamenta politsii kak istochnik po izucheniiu liberal'no-oppozitsionnogo dvizheniia v gody pervoi mirovoi voiny," *Istoriia SSSR*, no. 6 (1987): 32–49.

– *Masony i revoliutsiia*, Moscow, 1990.

– *Stolypin i tret'ia Duma*, Moscow, 1968.

– *Tsarizm nakanune sverzheniia*, Moscow, 1989.

Azeff, Evno. "Doneseniia Evno Azefa (Perepiska Azefa s Rataevym v 1903–1905 gg." *Byloe* 1 (1917): 196–228.

- "Azeff to Savinkov." *Byloe* 9–10 (1909): 212–17.
- *Pis'ma Azefa E.F., 1893–1917,* ed. and comp. D.B. Pavlov and Z.I. Peregudova, Moscow 1994.
Babkin, D.S. *Protsess A. N. Radishcheva,* Moscow, 1952.
Bailey, S. "Police Socialism in Tsarist Russia," *Review of Politics* 19 (1957): 462–71.
Bakai, M.E. "Iz zapisok M.E. Bakaia: Azef, Stolypin i provokatsiia," *Byloe* 9–10 (1909): [191]-211.
- "Iz vospominanii M.E. Bakaia: o chernykh kabinetakh v Rossii," *Byloe* 7 (1908): 119–33.
- "Iz vospominanii M.E. Bakaia. Provokatory i provokatsiia," *Byloe* 8 (1908): [99]-136; 11/12 (1909): [162]-67.
Bazilevsky, V., ed. *Gosudarstvennye prestupleniia v Rossii v XIX veke.* 3 vols., St Petersburg, 1905–6.
Bazilev, L. "Zagadka 1 sentiabria 1911 g." *Voprosy istorii* 7 (1975): 115–129.
Beiliss, Mendel. *The History of My Suffering,* n.p., 1925.
Beletsky, S.P. *Grigory Rasputin,* Petrograd, 1923.
- "Vospominaniia." *Arkhiv russkoi revoliutsii,* ed. I.V. Gessen, (1927), 12:5–75 (reprint, 1970).
Belostokskii pogrom. Krovovaia politika i Belostokskii pogrom, Moscow, 1961.
Benkendorff, A.Kh. "Graf Benkendorff o Rossii v 1827–1832 gg." ed. A. Sergeev, *Krasnyi Arkhiv* 38 (1930): 109–32.
Bikerman, I.M. *Cherta evreiskoi osedlosti.* St Petersburg, 1911.
Bil'basov, V.A. *Istoriia Ekateriny II.* 2 vols., 1891.
Bliokh, I.S. *Sravnenie material'nogo byta i nravstvennogo sostoianiia naseleniia v cherte osedlosti evreev i vne ee. Tsifrovye dannye i issledovaniia po otnosheniiu k evreiskomu voprosu* 3 vols., St Petersburg, 1891.
Bogoliubov, V. *N.N. Novikov i ego vremiia,* Moscow, 1916.
Bogrov, V. *Dmitrii Bogrov i ubiistvo Stolypina. Razoblachenie "deistvitel'nykh i mnimykh tain."* Berlin, 1931.
Bogucharsky, V. "Tret'e otdelenie Sobstevennoi E.I.V kantseliarii o sebe samom." *Vestnik Evropy* (March 1917): 94–117.
- "V 1878 g. Vsepoddanneishee donesenie shefa zhandarmov." *Golos minuvshego* 7–8 (1917): 124–68.
Bok, M.P. *P.A. Stolypin. Vospominaniia o moem otse.* Moscow, 1992. In English, Maria Petrovna von Bock. *Reminiscences of My Father, Peter A. Stolypin,* tr. and ed. Margaret Patoski. Metuchen, NJ, 1970.
Bolotov, A.T. *Zhizn' i prikliucheniia Andreiia Bolotova, opisannye samim im dlia svoikh potomkov.* 2 vols., St Petersburg, 1871–73.
Brafman, Ia. *Evreiskie bratstva mestnye i vsemirnye.* Vilno, 1869.
Bukhbinder, N.A. "Zubatovshchina v Moskve: Neizdannye materialy." *Katorga i ssylka* 1 (1925): 96–133.

Burtsev, V.L. *Bor'ba za svobodnyiu Rossiiu. Moi vospominaniia (1882–1922 gg.).* 2 vols., Berlin, 1922.

– "Police Provocation in Russia: Azef, the Tsarist Spy." *Slavonic Review* 6 (1927): 247–60.

– *Protokoly zionskikh mudretsov.* Paris, 1938.

– *V pogone za provokatorami.* Moscow, 1928; [reprint, 1989].

Chernavskaia-Bokhanovskaia, "Iz istorii bor'by russkogo samoderzhaviia s 'Narodnoi Volei' za granitsei." *Katorga i ssylka* (4)65 (1930): 95–8.

Cherniavsky, Michael. "The Old Believers and the New Religion," in *The Structure of Russian History: Interpretive Essays,* ed. Michael Cherniavsky. New York, 1970: 140–88.

Chernyshevskaia, N.M. *Letopis' zhizni i deiatel'nosti N. G. Chernyshevskogo,* ed. S.S. Borshchevsky. Moscow, 1953.

Chernyshevsky, N.G. "O novykh usloviiakh sel'skogo byta," pt. 1, *Polnoe Sobranie Sochinenii,* ed. V. I. Kirpotin et al. 16 vols., Moscow, 1939–50: 5:65–107.

Chukarev, A.G. "Metody i sredstva politicheskogo rozyska v tsarskoi Rossii," *Voprosy istorii filosofii, geografii i ekonomiki Dal'nego Vostoka.* Vladivostok, 1968: 193–201.

– "Organizatsiia politicheskogo rozyska v tsarskoi Rossii v XIX–XX v.," *Trudy instituta istorii, arkheologii i etnografii narodov Dal'nego Vostoka* 9. Vladivostok, 1973: 160–9.

Cohn, Norman. *Warrant for Genocide: The Myth of the Jewish World Conspiracy and the Protocols of the Elders of Zion.* London, 1967.

Conroy, M. *Peter Arkad'evich Stolypin: Practical Politics in Late Tsarist Russia.* Boulder, 1976.

Curtiss, J.S. *An Appraisal of the Protocols of Zion.* New York, 1942.

D.P. "Pogromy." *Evreiskaia entsiklopediia* 12 (1912): 611–22 (reprint, 1991).

Daly, Jonathan W. "Emergency Legislation in Late Imperial Russia." *Slavic Review* 54(3) (1995): 602–29.

– "The Watchful State: Police and Politics in Late Imperial Russia, 1896–1917." Ph.D. dissertation, Harvard University, 1992.

"Degaevshchina: Materialy i dokumenty." *Byloe* 4 (1906): 18–39.

Deich, Lev G. [Sonin]. *Provokatory i terror. Po lichnym vospominaniiam.* Tula, 1926.

Delo A.A. Lopukhina v Osobom prisutstvii Pravitelstvuiushchego Senata. St Petersburg, 1910.

Delo o oktiabr'skom pogrome v Simferopole. Simferopol, 1907.

Delo o pogrome v Belostoke 1–3 maia 1906 g. Obvinitel'nyi akt. 2nd ed. St Petersburg, 1906.

Delo o pogrome v Orshe. St Petersburg, 1909.

Delo o pogrome v Tomske v 1905 g. Tomsk, 1909.

Delo provokatora Manilovskogo: Materialy, dokumenty, vospominaniia sovremennikov, comp. B.I. Kaptelov, I.S. Rozental', V.V. Shelokhaev. Moscow, 1992.

"Delo S. Ryssa." *Byloe* 9–10 (1909): 237–44.

Dewey, H. "Defamation and False Accusation (Iabednichestvo) in old Muscovite Society." *Etudes Slaves et Est-Européennes*, 11(3–4) (1966–67): 109–20.

– and A. Kleimola. "Suretyship and Collective Responsibility in pre-Petrine Russia." *Jahrbucher fur Geschichte Osteuropas* 3 (1970): 337–54.

"Doklady gen. adj. A.R. Drentel'na Aleksandru II (aprel'-noiabr' 1879 g.)," ed. P.E. Shchegolev. *Krasnyi arkhiv* 3(40) (1930): 125–75.

"Doklady gen.-leit. Selivestrova i gen.-ad. Drentel'na – Aleksandru II (avgust-dekabr' 1878 g.)," ed. P.E. Shchegolev. *Krasnyi arkhiv* 6(49) (1931): 112–43.

Dolgorukov, P. *Peterburgskie ocherki*. Moscow, 1992.

"Donesenie P.N. Liubimova S.P. Beletskomu 25 sentiabria 1913. Protsess Beilisa v otsenke Departamenta politsii." *Krasnyi arkhiv* 1(44): 85–123.

Dostoevsky, F. "Dostoevsky's Statement on the Petrashevsky Affair," *Dostoevsky As Reformer: The Petrashevsky Case*, ed. and tr. Liza Knapp. Ann Arbor, 1987: 29–43.

Dubnov, S.M. "Zapiski o antievreiskikh besporiadkakh 1881 g." *Golos minuvshego* 3 (1916): 243–53.

– "Antievreiskoe dvizhenie v Rossii v 1881–1882 gg." *Evreiskaia Starina* 1(1) (1909): 88–109; (3) (1909): 265–76.

– "Iz istorii 80-kh gg. (1882)." *Evreiskaia Starina* 9(1) (1916): 1–30; (3) (1916): 357–79.

Dzhanumova, E.F. *Moi vstrechi s Rasputinym*. Moscow, 1923 (reprint, 1990).

Efremova, N.N. *Ministerstvo iustitsii rossiiskoi imperii 1802–1917 gg.* Moscow, 1983.

Eidel'man, N.Ia. *Tainye korrespondenty 'Poliarnoi Zvezdy'.* " Moscow, 1966.

Elkin, Boris. "Attempts to Revive Freemasonry in Russia." *The Slavonic and East European Review* 104 (July 1966): 454–72.

Elwood, Ralph Carter. *Roman Malinovsky: A Life Without a Cause*. Newtonville, MA, 1977.

Erenfel'd, B.K. "Delo Malinovskogo (Iz istorii politicheskikh provokatsii tsarskoi tainoi politsii)." *Voprosy istorii* 7 (1965): 106–16.

– *Tiazhelyi front: iz istorii bor'by bol'shevikov s tsarskoi tainoi politsiei.* Moscow, 1983.

– *Istoriia gosudarstvennykh uchrezhdenii dorevoliutsionnoi Rossii*, 3d ed. Moscow, 1983.

Esipov, G. *Raskol'nich'i dela XVII stoletiia. Iz del Preobrazhenskogo prikaza i Tainoi rozysknykh del kantseliarii.* St Petersburg, 1861.

Evans, John L. *The Petrasevskij Circle, 1845–1849*. The Hague, 1974.

"Evno Azef. Istoriia ego predatel'stva." *Byloe* 2(24) (1917): 200–1.

Feoktistov, E.M. *Vospominaniia: Za kulisami politiki i literatury, 1848–1896*, ed. Iu.G. Oksman. Leningrad, 1929; Moscow, 1991.

"Franko-russkoe shpionstvo i franko-russkii soiuz." *Byloe* 8 (1908): 58–64.

Fuhrmann, Joseph T. *Rasputin: A Life*. New York, 1990.

Fuller, William C., Jr. "Civilians in Russian Military Courts, 1881–1904." *Russian Review* 41(3) (1982): 288–305.

– *Civil-Military Conflict in Imperial Russia, 1881–1914*. Princeton, NJ, 1985.

"G.V. Plekhanov i shpionskii sabavy," ed. S.N. Volk. *Krasnyi Arkhiv* 5 (1924): 261–4.

Gan, L. "Ubiistvo Stolypina." *Istoricheskii vestnik* 135(4) (1914): 960–97; 136(4) (1914): 129–215.

Gapon, G. *The Story of My Life*. New York, 1906.

"Gazeta Departamenta politsii." *Byloe* 8 (1908): 45–54.

Geifman, Anna. *Thou Shalt Not Kill: Revolutionary Terrorism in Russia, 1894–1917*, Princeton, NJ, 1993.

Gel'big, George von. "Russkie izbrannye i sluchainye liudi." *Russkaia Starina* 56(10) (1887): 1–30.

Gerasimov, A.V. *Na lezvii s terroristami*. Moscow, 1991.

Gessen, I.V. "Beseda s A.N. Khvostovym v fevrale 1916 g." *Arkhiv russkoi revoliutsii*. 12 vols. (1923): 12:76–82.

– *V dvukh vekakh: Zhiznennyi otchet'*, Berlin, 1937.

Gessen, Iu.I. *Istoriia evreiskogo naroda v Rossii*. Leningrad, 1927.

Golikov, G. and S. Burin. *Kantseliariia nepronitsaemoi t'my (Politicheskii sysk i revoliutsionery)*. Moscow, 1994.

Golikova, N.B. "Organy politicheskogo syska i ikh razvitie v XVII-XVIII vv.," in *Absoliutizm v Rossii, XVII-XVIII vv.*, ed. N.M. Druzhinin. Moscow, 1964: 243–80.

Gol'tsev, V.A. *Zakonodatel'stvo i nravy v Rossii XVIII v.*, 2nd ed. St Petersburg, 1896.

Gomel'skii protsess (podrobnyi otchet), comp. B.A. Krever. St Petersburg, 1907.

Gorev, B.I. "Leonid Men'shchikov. Iz istorii politicheskoi politsii i provokatsii (Po lichnym vospominaniam)." *Katorga i ssylka* 3(10) (1924): [130]-140.

Gosudarstvennaia Duma. Stenograficheskie otchety. 1906 god. Sessia pervaia, vol. 2. St Petersburg, 1906.

Guchkov, A.I. "Iz vospominaniia A.I. Guchkov," *Novyi Zhurnal* 161 (1985): 185–86; 162 (1986): 184–221.

Gurevich, P. "Nezabvennyia mysli nezabvennykh liudei (K istorii reaktsii 60-kh godov." *Byloe* 1–4 (1907): 236–46.

Gurliand, I.Ia. *Prikaz velikogo gosudariia tainykh del*. Iaroslavl', 1904.

Hamm, Michael F., ed. *The City in Late Imperial Russia*. Bloomington, 1986.

Hellie, Richard, tr. and ed. *The Muscovite Law Code (Ulozhenie) of 1649*, pt. 1. Irvine, Calif., 1988.

Herzen, Alexander. *My Past and Thoughts: The Memoirs of Alexander Herzen*, tr. Constance Garnett. Berkeley and Los Angeles, 1982.

Hingley, Ronald. *The Russian Secret Police: Muscovite, Imperial, Russian and Soviet Political Security Operations, 1565–1970*. London, 1970.

Horsey, Sir Jerome. "The Travels of Sir Jerome Horsey," in *Russia at the Close of the Sixteenth Century*. New York, n.d.

Iarmysh, A.N. "Politicheskaia politsiia Rossiiskoi imperii, 1880–1904." Dissertation for the *kandidat* degree, Khar'kov, 1978.

Iliodor. *Sviatoi chert*. Moscow, 1917.

"Instruktsiia grafa Benkendorfa chinovniku Tret'ego otdeleniia." *Russkii Arkhiv* 7, book 2 (1889): 396–7.

Instruktsiia nachal'nikam okhrannykh otdelenii po organizatsii naruzhnykh nabliudenii. St Petersburg, 1908. See also *Byloe* 9–10 (1909): 165–76.

"Istoricheskie razskazy i anekdoty, zapisannye so slov imenitykh liudei P.F. Karabanovym. Tsarstvovanie Ekateriny II." *Russkaia Starina* 5(1) (1872): 129–47.

"Istoricheskie zapiski o khode tainogo pechataniia v Rossii, 1861–1881 gg." *Byloe* 11–12 (1909): 173–9.

Iusupov, F.F. *Konets Rasputina: Vospominaniia*. Moscow, 1990.

Ivianski, Zeev. "Provocation at the Center: A Study in the History of Counter-Terror." *Terrorism: An International Journal* 4 (1980): 53–88.

"Iz zapisnoi knizhki arkhivista (posle pervogo marta 1881 g.)." *Krasnyi arkhiv* 2(45) (1931): 147–64.

"Iz obzora sostavlennogo departamentom politsii za 1882 god." *Byloe* 11 (1906): 244–61.

"Iz otcheta o perliustratsii departamenta politsii za 1908 g." *Krasnyi arkhiv* 2(27) (1928): 139–59; 3(28) (1928): 205–24.

"Iz zapisok politseiskogo ofitsera." *Na chuzhoi storone* 9–10 (1925): 143–52.

Izgoev, A. *P.A. Stolypin: Ocherk zhizni i deiatel'nosti*, Moscow, 1912.

Johnson, Richard J. "Zagranichnaia Agentura: the Tsarist Political Police in Europe," in George L. Mosse, ed., *Police Forces in History*. London, 1975: 221–42.

Judge, Edward H. *Easter in Kishinev*. New York and London, 1992.

– *Plehve: Repression and Reform in Imperial Russia, 1902–1904*. Syracuse, 1983.

Kaczynska, Elzbieta and Dariusz Drewniak. *Ochrana: Carska Policja Polityczna*. Warsaw, 1993.

Kantor, R. "Pokushenie na N.V. Murav'eva (Epizod iz istorii N.V.)." *Katorga i ssylka* 23 (1926): 123–39.

– "Provokator Stepan Belov." *Katorga i ssylka* 3(10) (1924): 141–52.

Kaptelov, B.I. and Z.I. Peregudova. "Byl li Stalin agentom okhranki?" *Voprosy istorii KPSS* 4 (1989): 90–8.

"Kar'era P.I. Rachkovskogo. Dokumenty." *Byloe* 8(30) (1918): 78–87.

Keep, J.L.H. "The Regime of Filaret." *Slavonic and East European Review* 38 (1959): 343–44.

Keep, John. "The Sugarov Affair, 1831: A Curious Conspiracy," in Ezra Mendelsohn and Marshall S. Schatz, eds., *Imperial Russia, 1700–1917: State, Society, Opposition. Essays in Honor of Marc Raeff.* DeKalb, Ill., 1988: 177–97.

Kennan, George. "The 'Ritual Murder' Case in Kiev," *The Outlook* (8 November 1913): 529–35.

Kennan, George K. *The Fateful Alliance: France, Russia and the Coming of the First World War.* New York, 1984.

Kerensky, A. *Russia and History's Turning Point.* New York, 1965.

– *The Crucifixion of Liberty.* New York, 1934.

Khitrovo, N.P. "Moi otnosheniia k shtabu otdel'nogo korpusa zhandarmov v 1871, shefu zhandarmov grafu Shuvalovu i izvestnomu publitsistu slavianofilu g. Aksakovu. *Russkaia Starina* 158(5) (1914): 383–91.

Khronika sotsialisticheskogo dvizheniia v Rossii 1878–1887 gg. Ofitsial'nyi otchet, ed. N.I. Shebeko. Moscow, 1906.

Khvostov, A.N. "Iz vospominanii A.N. Khvostova." *Golos minuvshego* 2 (1923): 160–8.

Kievskii i odesskii pogromy v otchetakh senatorov Turau i Kuzminskogo. St Petersburg, 1907.

Kimball, Alan. "The Harassment of Russian Revolutionaries Abroad: The London Trial of Vladimir Burtsev in 1898." *Oxford Slavonic Papers,* new series 6 (1973): 48–65.

Kleimola, A.M. "The Duty to Denounce in Muscovite Russia." *Slavic Review* 31(4) (1972): 759–9.

Kletochnikov, N.V. "Iz zapisok N.V. Kletochnikova," *Byloe* 7 (1908): 146–52.

Klier, John and Shlomo Lambroza, eds. *Pogroms: Anti-Jewish Violence in Modern Russian History.* Cambridge, 1992.

Kobrin, V. *Ivan Groznyi.* Moscow, 1989.

Kokovtsov, V.N. *Iz moego proshlogo: vospominaniia 1903–1919 g.g.* 2 vols., Paris, 1933. The English edition is V.P. Kokovtsov, *Out of My Past.* Stanford, 1935.

Korolenko, V.G. "Delo Beilisa," *Sobranie Sochinenii.* 10 vols., Moscow, 1955, 9: 638–56.

Korsakov, A. "Stepan Ivanovich Sheshkovsky (1727–1794). Biograficheskii ocherk," *Istoricheskii vestnik* 12 (1885).

– *Iz zhizni russkikh deiatelei XVIII v.* Kazan', 1981.

Koshelev, Alexander I. *Zapiski, 1812–1833*. Berlin, 1884.

Koshko, A. "O dele Beilisa." *Novyi zhurnal* 91 (1968): 162–83.

Kostromskoe okhrannoe otdelenie (Zapiski zhandarmskogo ofitsera. Kostroma, 1917.

Kotoshikhin, G. "O Moskovskom gosudarstve v seredine XVII stoletiia." *Russkoe istoricheskoe povestvovanie XVI-XVII vv.* Moscow, 1984.

Koz'min, B.P., ed. *Nechaev i nechaevtsy*. Moscow, 1931.

– ed. *S.V. Zubatov i ego korrespondenty*. Moscow, Leningrad, 1928.

Kratkii sistematicheskii svod deistvuiushchikh zakonopolozhenii i tsirkuliarnykh rasporiazhenii, otnosiashchikhsia do obiazannostei chinov Gubernskikh, zhandarmskikh upravlenii po nabliudeniiu za mestnym naseleniiam i po proizvodstvu doznanii, comp. V.I. Dobriakov. St Petersburg, 1895; supp. 1897 and 1903.

Krovavoe poboitse v Tule. Tula, 1925.

Kryzhanovsky, S.E. *Vospominaniia*. [Berlin, 1938], n.d.

Kucherov, Samuel. *Courts, Lawyers, and Trials under the Last Three Tsars*. New York, 1953.

Kulakov, A.A. "O trekh predateliakh (El'ko, Ostroumov, Geier)." *Katorga i ssylka* 6(67) (1930): [79]-88.

Kurlov, P.G. *Konets russkogo tsarizma: Vospominaniia byvshego komandira Otdel'nogo korpusa zhandarma*. Petrograd, Moscow, 1928 (reprint, 1991).

Lapman, Mark Charles, "Political Denunciations in Muscovy, 1600–1649: The Sovereign's Word and Deed." Ph.D. Dissertation, Harvard University, 1982.

Laquer, Walter. *Black Hundred: The Rise of the Extreme Right in Russia*. New York, 1993.

Lazarev, E. "Dmitrii Bogrov i ubiistvo Stolypina." *Volia Rossii* 6–7 (1926): 53–98; 8–9 (1926): 28–65.

Leikina-Svirskaia, V.R. *Intelligentsiia v Rossii vo vtoroi polovine XIX veka*. Moscow, 1971.

Lemke, M. *Nikolaevskie zhandarmy i literatura, 1826–1865*. n.p., 1908.

"Leonty Vasil'evich Dubel't. Biograficheskii ocherk i ego pis'ma." *Russkaia Starina* 60(11) (1888): 491–514.

Levin-Stankevich, Brian L. "Cassation, Judicial Interpretation and the Development of Civil and Criminal Law in Russia, 1864–1917: The Institutional Consequences of the 1864 Court Reform in Russia." Ph.D. dissertation, State University of New York at Buffalo, 1984.

Liatkovsky, P. "Nechto o Bogrove." *Katorga i ssylka* 2(23) [1926]: 35–49.

Lieven, Dominic, "The Security Police, Civil Rights, and the Fate of the Russian Empire," in *Civil Rights in Imperial Russia*, eds. O. Crisp and L. Edmondson. Oxford, 1988: 235–62.

Longe, Zhak. *Terroristy i okhranka*. Moscow, 1924.

Lopukhin, A.A. *Nastoiashchee i budushchee russkoi politsii*. Moscow, 1907.

- *Otryvki iz vospominanii (Po povodu 'Vospominanii' gr. S.Iu. Witte).* Moscow, 1923.
- "Zapiski A.A. Lopukhina o razvitii revoliutsionnogo dvizheniia." *Byloe* 9–10 (1909): 74–8.
- "Zapiska direktora depart. pol. Lopukhina o stachkakh v iiule 1903 g. v Odesse, Kieve, Nikolaeve." *Krasnaia letopis'* 4 (1922): 382–95.

Lopukhin, I.V. *Zapiski senatora I.V. Lopukhina.* Moscow, 1963 (reprinted from the 1859 edition).

Lopukhin, V.B. "Liudi i politiki, (konets xix v – nachalo xx v.)" *Voprosy istorii SSSR* 9, 10, 11 (1966): 120–36, 110–22, 116–28.

Luchinskaia, A.V. *Velikii provokator.* Petrograd, 1923.

Lukashevich, Stephen. "The Holy Brotherhood, 1881–1883." *American Slavic and East European Review* 184 (1959): 491–505.

Lunacharsky, A.V. *Velikii provakator Evno Azef.* Petrograd, Moscow, 1923.

Lur'e, F. "Asef i Lopukhin." *Neva* 9 (1990): 165–76.

- "Provokatory i politseiskie." *Neva* 11 (1989): 157–70.

Maisky, B.Iu. "Stolypinshchina i konets Stolypina." *Vopros istorii* 1, 2 (1966): 134–44, 123–40.

Makletsova, N.P. [Degaeva]. "Sudeikin i Degaev." *Byloe* 8 (1906): 265–72.

Margolin, A.D. *The Jews of Eastern Europe.* New York, 1926.

Martynov, A.P. *Moia sluzhba v Otdel'nom korpuse zhandarmov: Vospominaniia,* ed. Richard Wraga. Stanford, 1972.

Materialy k istorii russkoi kontrrevoliutsii: vol. 1, *Pogromy po ofitsial'nym dokumentam.* St Petersburg, 1908.

Massie, Robert. *Nicholas and Alexandra.* London, 1968.

Mazour, Anatole G. *The First Russian Revolution, 1825: The Decembrist Movement, Its Origins, Development, and Significance.* Stanford, Calif., 1937.

Mel'gunov, S.P. *Na putiakh k dvortsovomu perevorotu (Zagovory pered revolitsiei 1917 goda).* Paris [1979].

Men'shchikov, L.P. *Okhrana i revoliutsiia: k istorii tainykh politicheskikh organizatsii sushchestvovavshikh vo vremena samoderzhaviia.* 3 vols., Moscow, 1925.

- *Russkii politicheskii ssysk za granitsei,* pt. 1. Paris, 1914.

- *Zagranichnaia okhrana. Ocherk E. Azef.* St Petersburg, 1918.

Meshchersky, V.P. "Dnevnik V.P. Meshcherskogo." *Grazhdanin* 6 (1906).

Miliukov, Paul. *Political Memoirs, 1905–1917,* ed. Arthur Mendel, tr. Carl Goldberg. Ann Arbor, 1967.

Miliutin, D.M. *Dnevnik.* 4 vols., Moscow, 1947–50.

"Ministerstvo vnutrennikh del." *Istoricheskii ocherk.* St Petersburg, 1901.

Miroliubov, A.A. "Dokumenty po istorii Departamenta politsii perioda pervoi mirovoi voiny." *Sovetskie arkhivy* 3 (1988): 80–4.

Monas, Sidney. *The Third Section: Police and Society Under Nicholas I.* Cambridge, Mass., 1961.

Mosolov, A.A. *Pri dvore imperatora. Vospominaniia nachal'nika kantseliarii ministerstva imperatorskogo dvora.* Riga, 1936. The English edition is A.A. Mosolov, *At the Court of the Last Tsar.* London, 1935.

Muller, Alexander V., tr. and ed. *The Spiritual Regulation of Peter the Great.* Seattle and London, 1972.

Mushin, A. *Dmitry Bogrov i ubiistvo Stolypina.* Paris, 1914.

"N.G. Chernyshevsky v doneseniiakh agentov III otdeleniia (1861–62)," *Krasnyi Arkhiv* 1(14) (1926): 87–127.

Nicholas II. *Dnevnik imperatora Nikolaia II.* Berlin, 1923.

Nikitenko, A.V. *Dnevnik.* 3 vols., Moscow, 1955.

Nikolaevsky, Boris. *Istoriia odnogo predatelia: Terroristy i politicheskaia politsiia,* comm. V.M. Shevyrin. Moscow, 1991 (reprint of the 1980 edition). See also earlier editions, Boris Nicolaevsky, *Aseff: The Spy, Russian Terrorist and Police Stool,* 1934 (reprint, 1969).

– *Konets Azefa.* Leningrad, 1926.

"Nikolai II i samoderzhavie v 1903 g.: Iz itogov perliustratsii." *Byloe* 8(30) (1918): 190–222.

"Nikolai II po departamentu politsii." *Katorga i ssylka* 23 (1926): 139–42.

Nikolsky, Boris. "Dnevnik Borisa Nikol'skogo (1905–1907)." *Krasnyi Arkhiv* 2(63) (1934): 55–97.

N-skogo, B. [Boris Nikolsky]. "L.N. Tolstoi v departamente politsii." *Byloe* 3(31) (1918): 204–14.

Norton, Barbara. "Russian Political Masonry and the February Revolution of 1917." *International Review of Social History* 28, pt. 2 (1983): 240–55.

Noskov, N.D. *Okhranitel'nye i reaktsionnye partii v Rossii.* St Petersburg, 1906.

Novitsky, V.D. *Iz vospominanii zhandarma,* ed. P.E. Shchegolev. Moscow, 1929 (reprint, 1991).

– "Vospominaniia tiazhelykh dnei moei sluzhby v korpuse zhandarmov." *Byloe* 5–6(27–8) (1917): [91]-124.

– "Zapiska gen. Novitskogo podannaia na vysochaishee imia cherez kn. Sviatopolk-Mirskogo." *Sotsialist-Revoliutsioner* 2 (1910): 51–113.

"Novoe o Zubatovshchine." *Krasnyi arkhiv* 1 (1922): 289–328.

Novombergsky, N. *Slovo i delo gosudarevo. Materialy.* 2 vols., Tomsk, 1909, and Moscow, 1911. See also N. Novombergsky, "Slovo i delo gosudarevo. Protsessy do izdaniia Ulozheniia Alekseiia Mikhailovicha 1649 g., vol. 1. *Zapiski Moskovskogo arkheologicheskogo instituta* 14 (1911): 1–593.

"O pytkakh v Ryzhskom Sysknom otdelenie." *Byloe* 13 (1910): 138–48.

Obzor vazhneishikh doznanii, proizvodivshikhsia v zhandarmskikh upravleniiakh imperii, po gosudarstvennym prestypleniiam za 1892–1902. 26 vols., St Petersburg, 1892–1905.

"Okhranka i chernye kabinety." *Revoliutsionnaia mysl'* 1 (1908): 10–11.

Okhrannye otdeleniia v poslednie gody tsarstvovaniia Nikolaiia II. Moscow, 1917.

Oktiabr'skie dni v Tomske. Opisanie krovavykh sobytii 20–23 oktiabria. Tomsk, 1905.

Orzhekhovsky, I.V. "Reorganizatsiia zhandarmskogo upravleniia v sviazi s pravitel'stvennoi reaktsiei 60-kh–70-kh xix veka," in *Voprosy istorii obshchestvenno-politicheskoi mysli vnutrennei politiki Rossii v XIX veke.* Gor'ky, 1971: 42–88.

– *Samoderzhavie protiv revoliutsionnoi Rossii,* Moscow, 1982.

Osipovich, N. "Odin iz svoikh: Iz 'Rasskazov o sekretnykh sotrudnikakh'." *Katorga i ssylka* 2(9) (1924): 61–98.

Osorgin, M.A. "Dekabr'skoe vozstanie 1905 g. v opisanii zhandarma." *Golos minuvshego* 7–8 (1917): 351–60.

– *Okhrannoe otdelenie i ego sekrety.* Moscow, 1917.

Ovchenko, Iu.F. "Iz istorii bor'by tsarskoi okhranki s revoliutsionnym studencheskim dvizheniem." *Sovetskie arkhivy* 3 (1989): 66–9.

– "Moskovskoe okhrannoe otdelenie v bor'be s revoliutsionnym dvizheniem v 1880–1890 gg." Dissertation for the kandidat degree, Moscow, 1989.

P. "Departament politsii v 1892–1908 gg. (Iz vospominanii chinovnika)." *Byloe* 5–6 (1917): 17–24.

Pahlen, K.I. "Zapiska ministra iustitsii grafa Palena." *Byloe* 9 (1907): 268–77.

Paleologue, M. *Rasputin: Vospominaniia.* Moscow, 1923 (reprint, 1990).

Pankratov, A.S. "Pervoe sentiabria 1911 goda (Vpechatleniia ochevidtsa ubiistva P.A. Stolypina)." *Istoricheskii vestnik* 126(11) (1911): 613–39.

Papmehl, K.V. "The Empress and 'Un Fanatique': A Review of the Circumstances Leading to the Government Action Against Novikov in 1792." *Slavonic and East European Review* 68(4) (1990): 674–83.

Pavlov, P. *Agenty, zhandarmy, palachi; po dokumentam.* Petrograd, 1922.

– *Tainy okhranki (Iz uzhasov sekretnykh zastenkov).* Moscow, 1917.

Pavlova, T.F. and L.I. Tiutiunik. "TSGAOR SSSR: Krug istochnikov rasshiriaetsia." *Voprosy istorii SSSR* 4 (1989): 99–108.

Peregudova, Z.I. "Departament politsii v bor'be s revoliutsionnym dvizheniem v gody reaktsii i novogo revoliutsionnogo podema." Dissertation for the *kandidat* degree, Moscow, 1988.

– "Istochnik izucheniia sotsial-demokraticheskogo dvizheniia v Rossii (materialy fonda departamenta politsii)." *Voprosy istorii KPSS* 9 (1988): 88–100.

– "Vazhnyi istochnik po istorii revoliutsionnogo dvizheniia (Kollektsiia perliustratsii TSGAOR SSSR)," *K 90-letiiu akademika I.M. Mintsa,* ed. S.L. Tikhvinsky. Moscow, 1986: 376–90.

Perepiska Nikolaia i Aleksandry Romanovykh, 1916–1917. 5 vols., Moscow, 1927. In English, see *The Letters of the Tsaritsa to the Tsar, 1914–1917,* ed. B. Pares, London, 1923; and *The Letters of the Tsar to the Tsaritsa, 1914–1917*, tr. A.L. Hynes. Stanford, 1973.

Perets, E.A. *Dnevnik E.A. Peretsa, gosudarstvennogo sekretaria (1880–1883)*. Moscow, 1927.

"Peterburgskoe obshchestvo pri vosshestvii na prestol imperatora Nikolaia. Po doneseniiam M.Ia. Foka – A.Kh. Benkendorfu." *Russkaia Starina* 132(10, 11) (1881): 303–36, 519–60.

"Pokazaniia V.A. Kiraulova, dannyia 7 avg. 1884 v Kiev polk. Novitskomu." *Byloe* 15 (1913): 30–5.

"Politicheskoe polozhenie nakanune fevral'skoi revoliutsii v zhandarmskom osveshchenii." *Krasnyi arkhiv* 4(17) (1926): 34–5.

Polovtsov, A.A. *Dnevnik gosudarstvennogo sekretaria A.A. Polovtsova, 1883–1886*. Moscow, 1966.

"Poslaniia Ioganna Taube i Eperta Kruze." *Russkii istoricheskii zhurnal* book 8 (1922): 39.

"Poslednii vremenshchik poslednogo tsaria." *Voprosy istorii* 10 (1964): 120.

Pribylovaia-Korba, A. "Sergei Petrovich Degaev." *Byloe* 4 (1906): 1–17.

Prilezhaeva-Barskaia, B.M. "Dmitrii Bogrov." *Minuvshie dni* 4 (1928): 80–6.

"Proekt g. A. Benkendorfa ob ustroistve vyshei politsii." *Russkaia Starina* 104(12) (1900): 615–16.

"Protsess Beilisa v otsenke departamenta politsii," intro. A.S. Tager. *Krasnyi arkhiv* 44 (1931): 85–125.

Protsess 20-i narodovol'tsev v 1882 godu. Rostov-on-Don, 1906.

"Psikhologiia predatel'stva (Iz vospominanii 'sotrudnika')." *Byloe* n.s. 27/28 (1924): 225–37.

Raeff, Marc. *The Decembrist Movement*. Englewood Cliffs, NJ, 1966.

"Rasputin v osveshchenii 'Okhranki'." *Krasnyi arkhiv* 5 (1924): 270–88.

Rasputina, Maria. *Rasputin: the Man Behind the Myth (A personal memoir by Maria Rasputina*. London, 1977.

Rataev, L.A. "Evno Azef. Istoriia ego predatel'stva. Delo Pleve." *Byloe* 2(23) (1917): 191–207.

– "Evno Azef. Razoblachennyi Azev." *Byloe* 2(24) (1917): 192–215.

– "Pis'ma L.A. Rataeva – S.V. Zubatova [1900–1903], ed. S.P. Mel'gunov. *Golos minuvshego* 1 (1922): [51]-59.

Rechi po pogromnym delam. 2 vols., Kiev, 1908.

"Revoliutsionnoe i studentcheskoe dvizhenie 1869 g. v otsenke Tret'ego Otdelenia," ed. V.P. Alekseev. *Katorga i ssylka* 3(10) (1929): 106–21.

Robbins, Richard. *The Tsar's Viceroys: Russian Provincial Governors in the Last Years of the Empire*. Ithaca and London, 1987.

Rodzianko, M.V. *Krushenie imperii*. Khar'kov, 1990.

Rogger, Hans. *Jewish Policies and Right-Wing Politics in Imperial Russia*. Berkeley and Los Angeles, 1986.

– "The Beilis Case: Anti-Semitism and Politics in the Reign of Nicholas II." *Slavic Review* 25(4) (1966): 613–29.

Rozenbliut, N.G. "G.G. Perets – agent III otdelenia." *Literaturnoe nasledstvo* 67 (1959): 685–97.

Rozental', I.S. "Eshche raz o dele provokatora Malinovskogo." *Voprosy Istorii KPSS* 5 (1989): 103–17.

Rudnev, V.N. "Pravda o tsarskoi sem'e." *Russkaia letopis'*, book 2 (1922): 39–58.

"Russkoe politicheskoe masonstvo, 1906–1918 (Dokumenty iz arkhiva Guverovskogo instituta voiny. revolitsii i mira)," *Istoriia SSSR*, comm. V.I. Startsev, 6 (1989): 119–34.

Rutenberg, P.M. *Ubiistvo Gapona.* Moscow, 1990 (reprint of the 1925 edition).

Ruud, C.A., and S.A. Stepanov. *Fontanka 16: Politicheskii ssysk pri tsariakh.* Moscow, 1993.

S.G. *Okhrannyia otdeleniia v poslednie gody tsarstvovania Nikolaia II.* Moscow, 1917.

"SPB. Sovet Rabochikh Deputatov po dannym okhrannago otdeleniia. Sekretno." *Byloe* 8 (1908): 40–4.

"S.V. Zubatov i A.I. Spiridovich." *Krasnyi arkhiv* 2 (1922): 281–3.

Samoilov, V. "Vozniknovenie tainoi ekspeditsii pri Senate." *Voprosy istorii* 6 (1948): 79–81.

Samuel, Maurice. *Blood Accusation: The Strange History of the Beilis Case.* London, 1967.

Sandomirsky, G. "K voprosu o Dmitrii Bogrove." *Katorga i ssylka* 2(23) (1926): 11–34.

Savinkov, B. *Vospominaniia terrorista.* Moscow, 1990 (reprint of 1928 edition).

Sbornik sekretnykh tsirkuliarov obrashchennykh k Nachal'nikam gubernskikh zhandarmskikh upravlenii, gubernatoram i pr. v techenie 1902–1907 gg. [New York, 1929].

Schleifman, Nurit. *Undercover Agents in the Russian Revolutionary Movement: The SR Party, 1902–1914.* New York, 1987.

Schneidermann, Jerome. *Sergei Zubatov and Revolutionary Marxism. The Struggle for the Working Class in Tsarist Russia.* Ithaca, NY, 1976.

– ed. and tr. "From the Files of the Moscow Gendarmes Corps: A Lecture on Combatting Revolution." *Canadian Slavonic Papers* 2(1) (1968): 87–99.

Semevsky, M.I. *Slovo i delo, 1700–1725.* Moscow, 1884 (reprint, 1991).

Serebrennikov, A., ed. *Ubiistvo Stolypina. Svidetel'stva i dokumenty,* Riga, 1990.

Sergeev, A.A. "Zhandarmy-istoriki." *Golos minuvshego* 9–10 (1917): 364–80.

Sergeevsky, N.D. *Nakazanie v russkom prave XVII v.* St Petersburg, 1887.

Shchegolev, P.E. "Iz letopisei Shlissel'burgskoi kreposti." *Byloe*, new series 16 (1921): [187]-200.

– *Okhranniki i avanturisty*. Moscow, 1930.

– ed. *Padenie tsarskogo rezhima*. 7 vols, Moscow-Leningrad, 1927.

– ed. *Provokator: Vospominaniia i dokumenty o razoblachenii Azefa*. [Leningrad], 1929.

Shil'der, N.K. *Imperator Aleksandr I*. 2 vols., St Petersburg, 1897.

"Shkola filerov." *Byloe*, n.s., 3(25) (1917): 40–67.

Shumatsky, Ia. *Revoliutsionnaia provintsiia (zapiska proletariia)*. Moscow, 1926.

Shvetsov, S.P. *Provocator Okladsky*. Moscow, 1925.

Sidorov, N.A. and L.I. Tiutiunik. "V.L. Burtsev i rossiiskoe osvoboditel'skoe dvizhenie (po materialam TSGAOR SSSR)." *Sovetskie arkhivy* 2 (1989): 56–62.

Sidorov, N.I. "Statisticheskie svedeniia o propagandistakh 70-kh godov v obrabotke III otdeleniia." *Katorga i ssylka* 1(38) (1928): 26–56.

Simanovich, A. *Rasputin i evrei*. Moscow, 1991 (first published in Paris, 1930).

Sistematicheskii sbornik tsirkuliarov Departamenta politsii i Shtaba Otdel'nago Korpusa Zhandarmov, otnosiashchikhsia k obiazannostiam chinov Korpusa po proizvodstvu doznanii, ed. S.V. Savitsky et al. St Petersburg, 1908.

Skrynnikov, R.G. *Ivan Groznyi*. Moscow, 1983.

– "Oprichnyi terror." *Uchenye zapiska Leningradskogo gosudarstvennogo pedagogicheskogo instituta im. A.I. Gertsena* 374 (1969): 38–9.

Slikhting, Al'bert. *Novoe izvestie o Rossii vremen Ivan Groznogo. Skazanie Al'berta Shlikhtinga*. 2nd ed., Leningrad, 1934.

Smith, Edward Ellis. *The Okhrana*. Stanford, Calif., 1967.

Smith, Nathan. "Political Freemasonry in Russia, 1906–1918: A Discussion of the Sources." *Russian Review* (April 1985): 157–71.

– "The Role of Russian Freemasonry in the February Revolution: Another Scrap of Evidence." *Slavic Review* 27(4) (1964): 604–8.

Squire, P.S. *The Third Department: The Establishment and Practices of the Political Police in the Russia of Nicholas I*. London, 1968.

Sobornoe Ulozhenie 1649 goda. Tekst. Kommentarii. Leningrad, 1987.

Sofronenko, K.A. "Zakonodatel'nye akty Petra I." *Pamiatniki russkogo prava*. 8 vols., Moscow, 1961.

Soiuz russkogo naroda. Po materialam Chrezvychainoi sledstvennoi komissii Vremennogo pravitel'stva. Moscow, Leningrad, 1929.

Solov'ev, M.E. "Tsarskie provokatory i delo sotsial-demokraticheskoi fraktsii II Gosudarstvennoi dumy." *Voprosy istorii* 8 (1966): 124–9.

Solzhenitsyn, A. *August, 1914: The Red Wheel. A Narrative in Discrete Periods of Time*, tr. H.T. Willetts. London, 1989.

Sonin, P. "Vospominaniia o iuzhnorusskikh pogromakh 1881." *Evreiskaia Starina* 2(2) (1909): 207–18.

"Spiridovich i ego istoriia revoliutsionnogo dvizheniia v Rossii." *Krasnyi arkhiv* 26 (1928): 213–20.

Spiridovich, A.I. *Partiia sotsialistov-revoliutsionerov i ee predshchestvenniki, 1886–1916*. Petrograd, 1918.

– *Pri tsarskom rezhime: Zapiski nachal'nika okhrannogo otdeleniia*. Moscow, 1926.

– *Rasputin*. Parizh, 1935.

– *Revoliutsionnoe dvizhenie v Rossii*. 2 vols., St Petersburg, 1914–16.

– *Velikaia voina i fevral'skaia revoliutsiia, 1914–1917 gg.* 3 vols., New York, 1960.

– *Zapiski zhandarma*, Moscow, 1929 (reprint, 1991).

Startsev, A. *Radishchev. Gody ispytanii. Ocherki*. 2nd ed., Moscow, 1990.

Statkovsky, P. "S-Peterburgskoe okhrannoe otdelenie v 1895–1901 gg. ('Trud' chinovnika Otdeleniia P. Statkovskogo)." *Byloe*, n.s., 16 (1921): [108]-136.

Steffens, Lincoln. *The Shame of the Cities*. New York, 1948.

Stepanov, E. "Iz zagranichnykh vospominanii starogo narodovol'tsa." *Katorga i ssylka* 24 (1926): 130–1.

Stepanov, S.A. *Chernaia sotnia v Rossii, 1905–1914*. Moscow, 1992.

– *Zagadki ubiistva Stolypina*. Moscow, 1995.

– "Delo Beilisa," in *Delo Beilisa: Issledovaniia i materialy*. Moscow-Jerusalem, 1995.

Stolypin, A. *P.A. Stolypin, 1862–1911*. Paris, 1927.

Stolypin, Petr Arkad'evich. *Nam nuzhna Velikaia Rossia*. Moscow, 1991.

Stroev, V.N. *Stoletie sobstvennoi ego imperatorskogo velichestva kantseliarii*. St Petersburg, 1912.

Strumillo, B. "Materialy o Dmitrii Bogrove." *Krasnaia Letopis'* 9,10 (1923, 1924): 177–89, 226–46.

Svatikov, S.G. "Iz proshlogo russkoi politicheskoi politsii za granitsei." *Golos minuvshego. Na chuzoi storone* 10 (1925): 180–5.

– *Russkii politicheskii ssysk za granitsei: Po dokumentam Parizhskogo arkhiva zagranichnoi agentury Departamenta politsii*. Rostov-on-Don, 1918.

– *Zagranichnaia agentura Departamenta politsii: Zapiska S. Svatikova i dokumenty zagranichnoi agentury*, eds. I. Nikitinsky and S. Markov. Moscow, 1941.

"Svod pravil, vyrabotannykh v razvitie utverzhdennogo g. ministrom vnutrennikh del 12 avgusta tekushchego goda [1902]. Polozheniia o nachal'nikh rozysknykh otdelenii." *Byloe* 8 (1908): 54–67.

Szeftel, Marc, "Personal Inviolability in the Legislation of the Russian Absolute Monarchy." *American Slavic and East European Review* 17 (1958): 2.

– *The Russian Constitution of April 23, 1906: Political Institutions of the Duma Monarchy*. Bruxelles, 1976.

Tager, Alexander S. *The Decay of Czarism*. Philadelphia, Jewish Publication Society of America, 1935.

– *Tsarskaia Rossiia i delo Beilisa: K istorii antisemitisma. Issledovanie po neopublikovannym dokumentam*. Moscow, 1933, 1934.

Taina krovi. Ekspertiza I.E. Pranaitisa. St Petersburg, 1913.

Tel'berg, G.G. *Ocherki politicheskogo suda i politicheskikh prestuplenii v Moskovskom gosudarstve XVII v.* Moscow, 1912.

Tikhomirov, L. *Vospominaniia L'va Tikhomirova*, intro. N.V. Nevsky. Moscow, 1927.

– *Zagovorshchiki i politsiia*. Moscow, 1927.

Timofeev, P. "Rabochie i politiki." *Russkoe Bogatstvo* 8 (1906): 165–82.

Tiutchev, N. "Sud'ba Ivana Okladskogo." *Byloe* 10–11 (1918): 221–9.

Tiutiunik, L.I. "Departament politsii v bor'be s revoliutsionnym dvizheniem v Rossii na rubezhe XIX-XX vv., 1880–1904." Dissertation for the *kandidat* degree, Moscow, 1986.

– "Sostoianie politicheskogo ssyska v Rossii v 60–70 gg. XIX v. (Krizis III otdeleniia). *Gosudarstvennye uchrezhdeniia i obshchestvennye organizatsii SSSR. Istoriia i sovremennost'*. Moscow, 1985: 101–7.

Tokmakoff, G. "Stolypin's Assassin." *Slavic Review* (June 1965): 314–21.

Troitsky, I.M. *Tret'e otdelenie pri Nikolae I*. Moscow, 1930.

Troitsky, N.A. "Degaevshchina." *Voprosy istorii* 3 (1976): 125–33.

– *Narodnaia volia pered tsarskim sudom, 1880–1891*. Saratov, 1971.

Trotsky, L. *Moia zhizn'. Opyt avtobiografii*. Moscow, 1990.

"Tsarskaia okhranka o politicheskom polozhenii v strane v kontse 1916 g." *Istoricheskii arkhiv* 1 (1960): 203–9.

"Tsarskoe pravitel'stvo i protsess Beilisa," ed. A.S. Tager. *Krasnyi Arkhiv* 54–5 (1932): 156–66.

"Tsenzura v tsarstvovanie Imp. Nikolaia I," comp. V.V. Stasov. *Russkaia Starina* 107(7) (1901): 151–67.

Tsiavlovsky, M.A., ed. *Bol'sheviki: dokumenty po istorii bol'shevizma s 1903 po 1916 god byvsh. Moskovskogo okhrannago otdeleniia*. Moscow, 1918.

– "Sekretnye sotrudniki Moskovskoi Okhranki 1880-kh godov (Iz arkhiva byvshago Otdeleniia po okhraneniiu obshechestvennoi bezopastnosti i poriadka v Moskve)." *Golos minuvshego* 7–8 (1917): [180]-183.

Trusevich, M.I. *Vsepoddanneishii doklad senatora Trusevicha o proizvedennom im po vysochaishhemu poveleniiu rassledovaniiu deiatel'nosti dolzhnostnykh lits, prinimavshikh uchastie v osushestvlenii okhrany vo vremia prebyvaniia ego imperatorskogo velichestva v Kieve*. St Petersburg, 1912, in S.A. Stepanov, *Zagadki ubiistva Stolypina*. Moscow, 1995: 244–304. Although printed in 1912, this document appeared only in a handful of copies for internal government use. Its appearance in Stepanov's book in 1995 is the first publication.

"Ubiistvo Rasputina. Ofitsial'noe doznanie." *Byloe* 1 (1917): 64–83.

"Uchet departamenta politsii opyta 1905 goda," intro. M. Korbut. *Krasnyi arkhiv* 18 (1926): 219–27.

Urusov, S.D. *Zapiski gubernatora*. Moscow, 1907.

Ustrialov, N. *Istoriia tsarstvovaniia Petra Velikogo: Tsarevich Aleksei Petrovich*. St Petersburg, 1859.

"V kontse 1916 g." *Byloe*, n.s. (2)(30) (1918): 148–56.

Valishevsky, K. *Petr Velikii*. book 3, Moscow, 1990 (reprint of the 1911 ed.).

Valuev, P.A. *Dnevnik*, ed. P.A. Zaionchkovsky. 2 vols., Moscow, 1961.

Vassilyev, A.T. *The Ochrana: The Russian Secret Police*, ed. R. Fülop-Miller. Philadelphia, 1930.

Veretennikov, B.I. *Istoriia Tainoi kantseliarii petrovskogo vremeni*. Kharkov, 1910.

Verner, Andrew W. *The Crisis of Russian Autocracy: Nicholas II and the 1905 Revolution*. Princeton, NJ, 1990.

Vilensky, B.V. *Sudebnaia reforma i kontrreforma v Rossii*. Saratov, 1969.

Voznyi, A.F. *Petrashevsky i tsarskaia tainaia politisiia*. Kiev, 1985.

Weinberg, R. "Workers, Pogroms and the 1905 Revolution in Odessa." *Russian Review* 46(1) (1987): 53–76.

Witte, S.Iu. *The Memoirs of Count Witte*, tr. and ed. Sidney Harcave. London, 1990 (earlier editions in 1921 and 1967).

– *Vospominaniia*. 3 vols., Moscow, 1960.

Wolfe, Bertram D. *Three Who Made a Revolution*. New York, 1964.

Za kulisami okhrannogo otdeleniia sostavil A.B. S dnevnikom provokatora pis'mami okhrannikov, tainymi instrukstiiami. Berlin, 1910.

Zagorsky, K.Ia. "V 1881–1882 gg. (Vospominaniia)." *Katorga i ssylka* 3(76) (1931): 155–78.

Zaionchkovsky, P.A. *Krizis samoderzhavia na rubezhe 1870–1880 godov*. Moscow, 1964.

Zaionchkovsky, Peter A. *The Russian Autocracy in Crisis, 1878–1882*, ed. and tr. Gary M. Hamburg. Gulf Breeze, Fla., 1979.

Zakliuchenie sudebno-sledstvennoi komissii po delu Azefa. n.p., 1911.

Zapiski inostrantsev o vosstanii Stepana Razina. Leningrad, 1968.

Zapiski senatora I.V. Lopukhina. Moscow, 1859.

Zapros o Azefe v III Gosudarstvennoi dume po stenograficheskomu otchetu. St Petersburg, 1909.

Zavarzin, P.P. *Rabota tainoi politsii*. Paris, 1924.

– *Zhandarmy i revoliutsionery: Vospominaniia*. Paris, 1930.

Zenkovsky, A.V. *Pravda o Stolypine*. New York, 1956. In English as A.V. Zenkovsky, *Russia's Last Great Reformer*. Princeton, NJ, 1986.

Zenzinov, V. *Razoblachenie provokatsii Azefa*. New York, 1924.

Zhilinsky, V.B. "Organizatsiia i zhizn' Okhrannago Otdeleniia v vremia tsarskoi vlasti." *Golos minuvshego* 9–10 (1917): 247–306.

Zhurnal mezhduvedomstvennoi komissii po preobrazovaniia politsii v Imperii. 6 vols., St Petersburg, 1911.

Zubarev, I.D. "Tret'e otdelenie. Otryvok iz vospominanii." *Istoricheskii vestnik* 148(5–6) (1917): 428–46.

Zuckerman, F.S. "The Russian Political Police at Home and Abroad: Its Structure, Functions, and Methods, and Its Struggle with the Organized Opposition." Ph.D. dissertation, Columbia University, 1973.

– "Vladimir Burtsev and the Tsarist Secret Police in Conflict, 1907–1914." *Journal of Contemporary History* 12(1) (1977): 193–219.

– *The Tsarist Secret Police in Russian Society, 1880–1917.* New York, 1996.

Zyrianov, P.N. "Petr Arkadievich Stolypin." *Voprosy istorii* 6 (1990): 54–75.

Index